Bonfire of the Liberties

Bonfire of the Liberties

NEW LABOUR, HUMAN RIGHTS, AND THE RULE OF LAW

K D EWING

OXFORD
UNIVERSITY PRESS

OXFORD
UNIVERSITY PRESS

Great Clarendon Street, Oxford ox2 6DP

Oxford University Press is a department of the University of Oxford.
It furthers the University's objective of excellence in research, scholarship,
and education by publishing worldwide in

Oxford New York

Auckland Cape Town Dar es Salaam Hong Kong Karachi
Kuala Lumpur Madrid Melbourne Mexico City Nairobi
New Delhi Shanghai Taipei Toronto

With offices in

Argentina Austria Brazil Chile Czech Republic France Greece
Guatemala Hungary Italy Japan Poland Portugal Singapore
South Korea Switzerland Thailand Turkey Ukraine Vietnam

Oxford is a registered trade mark of Oxford University Press
in the UK and in certain other countries

Published in the United States
by Oxford University Press Inc., New York

© K D Ewing, 2010

The moral rights of the authors have been asserted
Database right Oxford University Press (maker)

First published 2010

British Library Cataloguing in Publication Data
Data available

Library of Congress Cataloging in Publication Data
Data available

Typeset by MPS Limited, A Macmillan Company
Printed in Great Britain
on acid free paper by the
MPG Books Group, Bodmin and King's Lynn

ISBN 978–0–19–958477–2 (Hbk)
ISBN 978–0–19–958478–9 (Pbk)

1 3 5 7 9 10 8 6 4 2

For Gail

Preface

This is a book about the erosion of civil liberties in Great Britain since 1997, a feature of modern life about which we are reminded on a daily basis. We live in a society where the police have more power, where we are watched and monitored more closely and more often, and in which our ability to speak out and protest is subject to more and more restraints.

The symptoms of this erosion are everywhere, from high-profile events to mundane day-to-day activities. But it is the latter that really bring home the growing authority of the State, in a country where freedom was once highly prized. In my case it was a non-league football match, which I attended with a friend in September 2009. Cambridge United were playing Luton Town in the Blue Square Premier League.

It was close to kick off and my son had not yet arrived to meet us outside the ground. So I phoned to ask his whereabouts, and happily he was on Newmarket Road, only a few minutes away. On completing the call, I turned round to find that I was being videotaped by a police officer standing only a few yards away. For what purpose? With what legal authority was the police officer acting? What would happen to the images which the officer had recorded? Can I have them back?

It was not to end there. This Blue Square Premier League football match on a Saturday afternoon in a fairly small English city attracted a modest crowd of less than 5,000 hardy souls. But it also attracted a most remarkable and highly visible police presence, which for the first time in my experience (and I have been going there regularly since 1989) included very intimidating police officers with riot shields and 'UN style' helmets, as well as the dogs which are now standard issue.

What exactly is going on? Random surveillance by the State? Militarization of the police? An intimidating police presence at a non-league football match? It was not supposed to be like this. New Labour promised a new 'culture of liberty', and introduced a flagship Human Rights Act, which would not only 'bring rights home', but would also ensure that the culture would be embedded, and that the rule of law would be strengthened.

As will be shown in the pages that follow, there is thus a contradiction at the heart of the New Labour project—more rights but less liberty; more iconography but less good practice. Trapped by this contradiction, the Human Rights Act has been hopeless, failing to stop the rising tide of restraint, with the heavy lifting continuing to be done by the European

Court of Human Rights (as on the DNA database, the use of secret evidence, and the police powers of stop and search).

I must confess at this stage that I have always been sceptical about the ability of legal instruments like Bills of Rights or Human Rights Acts to create a meaningful 'culture of liberty'. The historical evidence simply did not justify the claims made about rights and litigation by supporters of the Human Rights Act before its enactment. However, that scepticism is greatly reinforced by the experience of the Act in operation: another chapter in a sorry story of an ineffective judicial response to the exercise of real State power.

It is of course the case that the Human Rights Act was born just before the 'War on Terror'. It is equally true that something had to be done following the events of 9/11 and 7/7. But it is also the case that the Act was designed to ensure that the State did not over-react in times of crisis; that the Act's operation was not supposed to be suspended at the first sign of stress; and that it was never anticipated that while the Act was in force we would have internment without trial in peacetime, or house arrest for lengthy periods.

In the pages that follow, my concern is to track the growing power of the police and the erosion of the right to liberty (Chapter 2); the growing surveillance practices of a wide range of agencies, and with it the erosion of the right to privacy (Chapter 3); and the growth of a wide and varied range of formal and informal restraints on protestors, and with it the erosion of the right to freedom of assembly (Chapter 4). It is difficult to find the positive contribution of the Human Rights Act in any of these areas.

Attention is also directed to a number of restraints on freedom of expression (though there are others not addressed in this volume) (Chapter 5), as well as the implications for human rights of the permanent emergency caused by the Anglo-American 'War on Terror' (Chapters 6 and 7). The final chapter is concerned with alternative strategies for protecting human rights. Here the message is that there is no quick fix to be found in rights' instruments, by whichever political party they are produced.

This is an area in which I have been working for a number of years. In that time, I have had the great fortune to have known and to have worked with a number of outstanding lawyers and activists. I know that most of these people do not share my views: at best they may share the concerns, but not the criticisms or the conclusions. Although I have no desire to embarrass anyone by association, it would nevertheless be remiss of me not to acknowledge my debt to colleagues and friends.

In particular, I would like to thank Jim Allan, Anthony Barnett, Tony Bradley, Tom Campbell, Sionaidh Douglas-Scott, Janet Hiebert, Aileen McColgan, Joan Mahoney, Alastair Mowbray, George Newlands,

Joo Cheong Tham (to whom I am also grateful for permission to reproduce in Chapter 7 some work that we did together), Adam Tomkins, and Stuart Weir. At OUP, my thanks to Alex Flach, John Louth and Benjamin Roberts, and at King's to Grace Alleyne in particular.

Finally, I wish to record my debt to Gail, Kate and Kartik, Lucy and Leo, and Alexander; and to welcome Lila.

KDE
15 January 2010

Contents

PREFACE   vii

TABLE OF CASES   xiii

TABLE OF STATUTES   xix

STATUTORY INSTRUMENTS, RULES, AND ORDERS   xxii

1. Introduction   1

2. The Growth of Police Powers   17

3. Surveillance and the Right to Privacy   53

4. Freedom of Assembly and the Right of Public Protest   96

5. Free Speech and the National Security State   138

6. A Permanent Emergency and the Eclipse
   of Human Rights Law   180

7. From Detention—to Control Orders—to Rendition   223

8. Conclusion: Power not Rights   265

BIBLIOGRAPHY   287

INDEX   295

Table of Cases

A v HM Treasury [2008] EWHC 869 (Admin); [2008] EWCA
   Civ 1187 .... 199–200, 205, 280
A v Home Secretary [2002] EWCA Civ 1502....................234–236, 237, 241, 247, 262
A v Home Secretary [2004] UKHL 56 ....272, 282, 283
A v Home Secretary (No 2) [2002] EWCA Civ 1502... 231, 263
A v The Scottish Ministers, 2002 SC (PC) 63 271
A v United Kingdom [2009] ECHR 301.. 236, 251, 252, 265
Adams v The Scottish Ministers, 2004 SC 665 279
AF (No 2) see Home Secretary v AF
Agee v Lord Advocate, 1977 SLT (Notes) 54 223
Alconbury see R v Environment Secretary, ex p Alconbury Developments Ltd
Alexander v Smith, 1984 SLT 176 113
Animal Defenders International case see R v Secretary of State for Culture,
   Media and Sport, ex p Animal Defenders International
AS and DD (Libya) v Home Secretary [2008] EWCA Civ 289 257
Associated Provincial Picture Houses Ltd v Wednesbury Corporation [1948] KB 223...........189
Attorney General v Guardian Newspapers Ltd [1987] 3 All ER 316; 1 WLR 1248 .... 143, 179
Attorney General v Guardian Newspapers Ltd (No 2) [1990] 1 AC 109 ....69, 143, 179
Attorney General v Leveller Magazine Ltd [1979] AC 440 .... 140, 160
Attorney General v Punch Ltd [2002] UKHL 50.. 174–176, 178
Attorney General v Times Newspapers Ltd [1992] 1 AC 191...143
Attorney General's Reference (No 3 of 1999) [2000] UKHL 63 .... 43–45, 51
Attorney General's Reference (No 3 of 2003) [2004] EWCA Crim 868...............................165
Attorney General's Reference (No 4 of 2002) [2004] UKHL 43 184
Austin v Metropolitan Police Commissioner [2009] UKHL 5 ....9, 10, 105, 136

BB (and 6 others) v Home Secretary [2008] EWCA Civ 844 259
Blum and Others v Director of Public Prosecutions [2006] EWHC 3209 (Admin) 120
Bradlaugh v Gossett (1884) LR 12 QBD 271 171
British Railways Board v Pickin [1974] AC 765 3
Brown v Stott [2003] 1 AC 681 281

C v The Police IPT/03/32/H 63
Campbell v Mirror Group Newspapers Ltd [2004] UKHL 22 .... 94, 282, 283, 284
Carltona Ltd v Minister of Works [1943] 2 All ER 560 70
Chahal v United Kingdom (1996) 23 EHRR 413 ....224, 225, 226, 231, 253, 254, 256, 261
Colhoun v Friel, 1996 SCCR 497 113
Connor v HM Advocate, 2002 JC 255 61
Council of Civil Service Unions v Minister of State for Civil Service [1985] AC 374 283
Countryside Alliance see R v Attorney General, ex p Countryside Alliance
Cullen case see R v RUC Chief Constable, ex p Cullen

Daiichi Pharmaceuticals UK Ltd v SHAC [2003] EWHC 2337 (QB);
   [2004] 1 WLR 1503 121
Derbyshire County Council v Times Newspapers Ltd [1993] AC 534 153
Director of Public Prosecutions v Haw [2007] EWHC 1931 (Admin) see also R v Home
   Secretary, ex p Haw 119

Director of Public Prosecutions v Jones [1999] 2 All ER 257 .... 112, 136
Donnelly v Jackman (1970) 54 Cr App R 229...19
Douglas v *Hello!* [2001] 2 WLR 992... 83, 94
Duncan v Jones [1936] 1 KB 218.. 103, 283
Durant v Financial Services Authority [2003] EWCA Civ 1746..57

Eichman v United States, 496 US 310 (1990) 110
Entick v Carrington (1765) 19 St Tr 1030 .... 70, 237
ex parte Kebeline *see* R v Director of Public Prosecutions, ex p Kebeline

Factortame case *see* R v Transport Secretary, ex p Factortame Ltd
Ferguson v Carnochan (1889) 16 R(J) 93 112

Goodwin v United Kingdom (1996) 22 EHRR 123 150
Guzzardi v Italy (1980) 3 EHRR 533 248

Halford v United Kingdom (1997 24 EHRR 523 74
Hector v Attorney General of Antigua [1990] 2 AC 312 153
Hewitt and Harman v United Kingdom (1992) 14 EHRR 657 69
Hirst v Chief Constable of West Yorkshire (1987) 85 Cr App R 143 111
HM Advocate v Cumming (1848) J Shaw 17 182
Hoekstra v HM Advocate 2001 SLT 28 12
Home Secretary v AF [2009] UKHL 28..251, 252, 271
Home Secretary v E [2007] UKHL 47; [2007] WLR 1 ....247, 249–251, 271
Home Secretary v GG [2009] EWCA Civ 786 263
Home Secretary v JJ [2006] EWCA Civ 1141; [2007] UKHL 45 .... 243, 247–251, 262, 271
Home Secretary v Rehman [2001] UKHL 47 238
Huntingdon Life Sciences Ltd v Curtin, The Times, 11 December 1997 121–124

Jackson v Attorney General [2005] UKHL 56 .... 280, 281
Jackson v Stevenson (1879) 2 Adam 255 19
Joined Cases C-402/05 and C-415/05 P Yassin Abdullah Kadi and Ali Barakaat International
    Foundation v Council of the European Union *see* Yassim Abdullah Kadi and Ali Barakaat
    International Foundation v Council of the European Union
Jones case *see* Director of Public Prosecutions v Jones
Jones v Procurator Fiscal, Dunbarton XJ264/03 .... 114, 115

Kebeline *see* R v Director of Public Prosecutions, ex p Kebeline 80
Kenlin v Gardner [1967] 2 QB 510...19
Khan v United Kingdom (2001) 31 EHRR 1016..44

Lawless v Ireland (1961) 1 EHRR 15 235
Liversedge v Anderson [1942] AC 206 283
Longley case *see* Attorney General's Reference (No 3 of 1999)
Lord Alton of Liverpool v Home Secretary, PC/02/06 (30 November 2007) 187–190

Malone v Metropolitan Police Commissioner [1979] 2 All ER 620 3
Malone v United Kingdom (1985) 4 EHRR 14.. 3, 74, 82
Mapp v Ohio, 367 US 643 (1961) 51
Marper v United Kingdom [2008] ECHR 1581 *see also* R v Chief Constable of
    South Yorkshire, ex p Marper..83–88, 94, 265
Martin v McGuiness, 2003 SLT 1424..63

MB and AF v Home Secretary [2007] UKHL 46 *see also* Home
   Secretary v AF 247, 249–252, 271, 286
McAvoy v Jessop, 1989 SCCR 301 113
McCann case *see* R v Manchester Crown Court, ex p McCann
McCartan Turkington Breen v Times Newspapers Ltd [2001] 2 AC 277 179
McEldowney v Forde [1971] AC 632 183
Moss v McLachlan [1985] IRLR 76 .... 104, 283
MT (Algeria) v Home Secretary [2007] EWCA Civ 808 257

New York Times v Sullivan, 376 US 254 (1964) 153

Observer v United Kingdom (1992) 14 EHRR 153 ....69, 143, 162
O'Kelly v Harvey (1883) 14 LR 105 105
Osman v Southwark Crown Court [1999] EWHC Admin 622 .... 25, 52
Othman (Jordan) v Home Secretary [2008] EWCA Civ 290 .... 257, 260–261
Oxford University v Broughton [2004] EWHC 2543 (QB); [2006]
   EWCA Civ 1305 .... 124, 284

Paul v Butler Sloss [2007] EWHC (Admin) 408 74
Peck v United Kingdom (2003) 36 EHRR 719 57
Poole case 65–66

R v ACPO, ex p Saunders [2008] EWHC 2372 (Admin) 47
R v Attorney General, ex p Countryside Alliance [2007] UKHL 52 281
R v Attorney General, ex p Jackson [2005] UKHL 56 3
R v Chalkley [1998] QB 848 43
R v Chief Constable of South Yorkshire, ex p Marper [2002] EWCA Civ 1275
   see also Marper v United Kingdom 80, 83, 95, 282
R v Director of Public Prosecutions, ex p Kebeline [2000] 2 AC 326 281
R v El-Faisal [2004] EWCA Crim 456 216
R v Environment Secretary, ex p Alconbury Developments Ltd [2001] UKHL 23 281
R v Foreign Secretary, ex p Abbasi [2002] EWCA Civ 1598, [2003] UKHRR 76 264
R v Foreign Secretary, ex p al Rawi [2006] EWHC 972 (Admin) 264
R v Foreign Secretary, ex p Binyam Mohamed [2009] EWHC 152 (Admin) 264
R v G [2009] UKHL 13 213–214
R v Gloucestershire Chief Constable, ex p Laporte [2006] UKHL 55 .... 19, 102–106, 135
R v Graham-Campbell, ex p Herbert [1935] 1 KB 594 170
R v H [2004] UKHL 3 232
R v Halliday [1917] AC 260 283
R v Home Secretary, ex p Amin [2002] EWCA Civ 390; [2002] 3 WLR 505 47
R v Home Secretary, ex p Baiai [2006] EWHC 823 (Admin); [2006]
   EWHC 1454 (Admin) 271
R v Home Secretary, ex p Cheblak [1991] 2 All ER 319; [1991] 1 WLR 890 .... 223, 224, 283
R v Home Secretary, ex p Haw [2005] EWHC 2061 (Admin); [2006] EWCA
   Civ 532 *see also* Director of Public Prosecutions v Haw 119–120
R v Home Secretary, ex p Hosenball [1977] 3 All ER 452; 1 WLR 766 .... 223, 224, 283
R v Home Secretary, ex p Kurdistan Workers' Party [2002] EWHC 644 (Admin) 185, 187
R v Home Secretary, ex p O'Driscoll [2002] EWHC 2477 (Admin) 192–194
R v Home Secretary, ex p Simms [2000] 2 AC 115 179
R v Horsham JJ, ex p Farquharson [1982] 1 QB 762 160
R v Inner North London Coroner, ex p Sharman [2005] EWHC 857 (Admin) 47, 49
R v Inner North London Coroner, ex p Stanley [2003] EWHC 1180 (Admin) 47–50

R v K [2008] EWCA Crim 185 212
R v Khan [1997] AC 558 44
R v Lemsatef [1977] 2 All ER 835 19
R v Lord Saville of Newdigate, ex p A [1999] 4 All ER 860 74
R v Malik [2008] EWCA Crim 1450 211–213
R v Manchester Crown Court, ex p McCann [2002] UKHL 39 30–31
R v Metropolitan Police Commissioner, ex p Gillan [2006]
    UKHL 12 ....19, 27, 136, 205–210, 221, 282
R v Metropolitan Police Commissioner, ex p Gillan; Quinton [2004]
    EWCA Civ 1067 ....206, 210
R v Metropolitan Police Commissioner, ex p W [2006] EWCA Civ 458 33
R v Ponting [1985] Crim L Rev 318 ....10, 141–142
R v RC [2005] 3 SCR 99 84
R v RUC Chief Constable, ex p Cullen [2003] UKHL 39 ....45–46, 51
R v Sang [1980] AC 402 43
R v Secretary of State for Culture, Media and Sport, ex p Animal Defenders
    International [2008] UKHL 18 ....271, 283
R v Shayler [2002] UKHL 11 ....173–174, 176–179, 283
R v South Yorkshire Chief Constable, ex p S [2004] UKHL 30 80–81
R v Transport Secretary, ex p Factortame Ltd (No 1) [1990] 2 AC 95; Case C-213/89 13
R v Transport Secretary, ex p Factortame Ltd (No 2) [1991] AC 603 13
R v West Midlands Chief Constable, ex p Singh [2005] EWHC 2840 (Admin) 34–35
R v (West Somerset Coroner and another) Home Secretary, ex p Middleton [2004]
    UKHL 10; [2004] 2 AC 182 49–50
R v Z [2005] UKHL 35 ....183, 221
R v Zafar [2008] EWCA Crim 184 211–213
RAF Fairford case see R v Gloucestershire Chief Constable, ex p Laporte
Raffaelli v Heatly, 1949 JC 101 ....112, 113
RB and OO v Home Secretary [2009] UKHL 10 ....259, 261, 263
Redknapp v City of London Police [2008] EWCA (Admin) 1177 41–42
Redmond-Bate v Director of Public Prosecutions (1999) 163 JP 789 97
Reynolds v Times Newspapers Ltd [2001] 2 AC 1 152–153
Rice v Connelly [1966] 2 QB 414 ....19, 20
Richmond case see R v Metropolitan Police Commissioner, ex p W
Robertson v Keith, 1936 SC 29 ....60–61, 63

Secretary of State for Defence v Guardian Newspapers Ltd [1985] AC 359 ....10, 141
Shayler case see R v Shayler
Sinclair v Annan, 1980 SLT (Notes) 55 113
Smith v Donnelly, 2001 SLT 1007 ....113, 114, 115
Southern Cross Nursing Homes case see YL v Birmingham City Council
Spycatcher case see Wright v United Kingdom
Sunday Times v United Kingdom (1979–80) 2 EHRR 245 3

Teixeira de Castro v Portugal (1998) 28 EHRR 101 43
Texas v Johnson, 491 US 397 (1989) 110
Times Newspapers Ltd v R [2007] EWCA Crim 1925 ....158, 160–162
Tucker v Director of Public Prosecutions [2007] EWHC 3019 (Admin) 120

Wednesbury see Associated Provincial Picture Houses Ltd v Wednesbury Corporation
Whaley v The Scottish Ministers, 2004 SLT 424; 2006 SC; [2007] UKHL 280
Willcock v Muckle [1951] 2 KB 844 89

Wilson v Brown, 1982 SCCR 49 113
Wood v Metropolitan Police Commissioner [2009] EWCA Civ 414 126–127
Wright v United Kingdom (1987) 8 NSWLR 351; (1987) 75 ALR 353;
    (1988) 87 ALR 449 142–143

XC v Home Secretary, Appeal No SC/77/81/82/83/2009, 21 May 2009 11

Y v Home Secretary, SIAC Appeal No SC/36/2005 258–259
YL v Birmingham City Council [2007] UKHL 27..286
Young v Heatly, 1959 JC 66 ....113, 114
Yassim Abdullah Kadi and Al Barakaat International Foundation,
    Joined Cases C-402/05 P and C-45/05 P, 3 September 2008 200

Ziliberberg v Moldova, Application No 61821/00 of 4 May 2004...120

Table of Statutes

Administration of Justice Act 1960
  s 12(1)(c)..161
Anti-social Behaviour Act 2003............ 28, 30
  s 30 32–35
  s 32 32
Anti-terrorism, Crime and Security Act
  2001 (ATCSA 2001) 10, 181, 191,
                    196–198, 200, 226,
                    228, 237, 257, 272
  Part 2 196–198
  s 23 .... 226, 227, 234, 238
Asylum and Immigration Bill 73

Badgers Act 1992...24
Bill of Rights 1688
  Art 9 167–168

Civil Authorities (Special Powers) Act
  (Northern Ireland) 1922 182
Civil Contingencies Act 2004.....................269
  ss 22, 23, 27 270
Communications Bill 2003 271
Communications Data Bill 54
Constitutional Reform Act 2005 .... 1, 70
  s 1 3
Contempt of Court Act 1981............. 138, 179
  s 4(2)..158–161
  s 6(c) 161
  s 10 141
  s 11 .... 158, 160–162
Coroners Act 1988.......................................47
Counter-Terrorism Act 2008 181
  Part 6 200
Crime and Disorder Act 1998............... 30–31
  s 1 .... 28, 31
Criminal Justice Act 1988...........................24
Criminal Justice Act 2003.........................182
Criminal Justice and Police Act 2001
  ss 80-82...80
Criminal Justice and Public Order
  Act 1994 .... 56, 107
  s 60 .... 24, 25, 26, 103
  s 68 .... 101, 102
  s 163...56
Criminal Law Act 1977 135
  s 3 49

Criminal Law and Procedure (Ireland)
  Act 1887 182

Data Protection Act 1998 (DPA)......... 57–59,
                             79, 82, 129
  s 1 57
  s 7 58
  s 17 57
  s 18 57
  s 29 .... 58, 82
  Sch 1 58
  Sch 2 82
  Sch 3 82
Defamation Act 1996
  s 9 151
Defence of the Realm Bills 1914–15.........268

Emergency Laws (Re-enactments and
  Repeals) Act 1964...............................196
Emergency Powers Act 1920 268

Freedom of Information Act 2000 14

Health and Safety at Work Act 1974
  s 3 17
Highways Act 1980
  s 137.. 107, 117
Human Rights Act 1998 (HRA) 1, 6,
        12–15, 16, 27, 44, 54, 86, 94, 97,
    103–112, 116, 121, 124, 135, 138, 139,
      173–179, 181, 193, 194, 198, 205,
   208–210, 222, 225, 227, 234, 261, 262,
      265, 269, 270, 280, 281, 284–286
  s 3 .... 251, 284
  s 4 .... 234, 284
  s 19 271

Identity Cards Act 2006 .... 9, 88–93
  s 1(3)..89
  s 2 .... 89, 91
  s 3 91
  s 4 89
  ss 5, 6, 7..91
  s 10 92
  s 13(2)..92
  s 16 54

s 17 92
s 22 92
ss 24, 25 92
ss 27, 28 92
ss 32, 33 93
s 34 92
s 35 90
Sch 1 91
Immigration Act 1971 223
Incitement to Disaffection Act 1934 268
Intelligence Services Act 1994
    (ISA) 69–70, 71, 72, 74
    s 1 70
    s 5 71
    ss 8, 9 73
    Sch 1 73
Interception of Communications
    Act 1985 .... 16, 74, 75

Justice and Security (Northern Ireland)
    Act 2007
    s 21 21

Magna Carta 1215 266
Misuse of Drugs Act 1971 .... 24, 61

National Registration Act 1915
    s 4(1) 89
National Registration Act 1939 89
Northern Ireland (Sentences) Act 1998
    s 3(8) 190

Obscene Publications Acts 1959–64 138
Offences against the Person Act 1861
    s 4 216
Official Secrets Act 1911 ... 154, 164, 167, 267
    s 1 130
    s 2 .... 139–144, 165, 269
Official Secrets Act 1989 .... 38, 138, 144, 146,
                            147, 154, 164, 165,
                            176–179, 269, 283
    s 3 156
    s 5 .... 156, 157

Police Act 1997 .... 62, 70, 71
    s 91 73
    s 97 .... 62, 63, 69
Police and Criminal Evidence Act 1984
    (PACE) 16, 24, 26, 80,
                            129, 171, 214
    s 1 27
    s 2 25

s 8 169–170
s 8(3) 42
ss 9–14 172
s 17 39
s 18 .... 107, 108
s 22 193
ss 24–25 35
s 32 .... 39, 107
s 41 39
s 63 79
s 78 43–44
Prevention of Terrorism Act 1974 268
Prevention of Terrorism Act 1989 45–46
Prevention of Terrorism
    Act 2005 .... 181, 238, 239, 254,
                            256, 271, 272–273
    s 1(1) 239
    s 1(2)(b) 239
    s 1(4) 241
    s 1(5) 241
    ss 2, 3 242
    s 2(1)(a) 239
    s 2(4) 241
    s 3(10),(11) 242
    s 4(1)(a) 239
    Sch, para 2(b) 242
Prevention of Terrorism Act 2006 10–11
Prevention of Terrorism (Temporary
    Provisions) Act 1974 .... 181, 227
Protection from Harassment
    Act 1997 121–124
Protection of Wild Mammals (Scotland)
    Act 2002 279
Public Order Act 1936 268
Public Order Act 1986 .... 35, 116,
                            124, 217
    ss 4, 4A 107
    s 5 .... 107, 109, 110, 116
    s 11 .... 12, 102, 123
    s 12 .... 102, 123
    s 13 123
    s 14 .... 123, 130–133

Race Relations Act 1976 27
Regulation of Investigatory Powers Act 2000
    (RIPA) 53, 63, 66, 68, 70–76, 98
    Part II 61
    s 1 74
    s 5 75
    s 7 76
    s 8 75
    s 17 78

s 22 76
s 26(3)(b) 71
ss 28, 29 62
s 30 .... 62, 71
s 32 62
s 42 71
s 46 71
s 57 75
s 57(2)..77
s 65 75
s 67(8).. 73, 75
s 91 63
Regulation of Investigatory Powers
    (Scotland) Act 2000 61

Security Service Act 1989 ....16, 69, 74
Serious Organised Crime and Police
    Act 2005 .... 18, 35–39, 41, 284
ss 113, 114...40
Serious Organised Crime and Public Order
    Act 2005 (SOCPA) 120
s 132..118
s 134..118
Special Immigration Appeals Commission
    Act 1997 .... 224, 231–232
s 6(4)..232
Sporting Events (Control of Alcohol)
    Act 1985 24
'sus' laws 1839 24

Terrorism Act 2000....... 10, 24, 181–189, 196,
                        210, 215, 218, 219,
                        220, 222, 258, 284

s 1 195
s 4(2)(b) 188
s 5(3)..188
s 11 .... 184, 186
ss 12, 13 184
s 15 191
s 16 191–195
ss 17, 18 191
s 40 .... 192, 214
s 41 ....182, 192, 214
s 44 .... 24, 201–210
s 44(1)(2) 207
s 45(1)..201
ss 57, 58 210–213
s 121..191
s 126..207
Sch 7...193
Sch 8...182
Terrorism Act 2006..........................181, 184,
                        218–219
s 1 218
s 1(5)(b) 219
s 2 219
ss 3, 4 219
s 24 182
Trade Disputes Act 1906 267
Trade Union and Labour Relations
    (Consolidation) Act 1992 35

United Nations Act 1946..........................198

Vagrancy Act 1824
s 4 30

Statutory Instruments, Rules, and Orders

al Qaeda and Taliban (United Nations
  Measures) Order 2006 (SI 2006
  No 2952) (Order 2)................... 198, 200

Civil Procedure (Amendment No 2) Rules
  2005 (SI 2005 No 656) (L 16)... 242, 252
  r 76.22(1)...242
  r 76.22(2)...242
  r 76.25..242
  r 76.26(4)...242
  r 76.32(1)...243

Defence of the Realm Regulations.............182

Investigatory Powers Tribunal Rules 2000
  (SI 2000 No. 2665)...............................73

National Registration Regulations 1939
  (SR&O 1939 No. 1248)
  reg 8...89

Special Immigration Appeals Commission
  (Procedure) Rules 2003 (SI 2003 No 1034)
  r 36...233
  r 36(2)(4) 233

Terrorism Act 2000 (Proscribed
  Organisations) (Amendment) Order
  2001 (SI 2001 No 1261)............ 184, 186
Terrorism Act 2000 (Proscribed
  Organisations) (Amendment) Order
  2002 (SI 2002 No 2724)....................184
Terrorism Act 2000 (Proscribed
  Organisations) (Amendment) Order
  2005 (SI 2005 No 2892)....................184
Terrorism Act 2000 (Proscribed
  Organisations) (Amendment) Order
  2006 (SI 2006 No 2016)....................184
Terrorism Act 2000 (Proscribed
  Organisations) (Amendment) Order
  2007 (SI 2007 No 2184)....................184
Terrorism (United Nations Measures)
  Order 2006 (SI 2006 No 2657)
  (Order 1)................................... 198, 200
  Art 4(2)... 199

1967 Regulations 183

CODES OF PRACTICE

Civil Service Code 166
Code of Practice on Stop and Search 21, 24

Home Office, Police and Criminal
  Evidence Act, Code of Practice
  A (2005) 18, 21–23
Home Office, Police and Criminal Evidence
  Act, Code of Practice G (2005)
  para 2.9 37

Information Commissioner's Code of
  Practice on CCTV Cameras 57–60

INTERNATIONAL TREATIES, CONVENTIONS, AND CHARTERS

Council of Europe's Social Charter 1961 6

EC Treaty...13
European Convention on Human Rights 1950
  (ECHR)........... 3, 6, 11–15, 86, 113, 138,
                    206, 208, 217, 226, 255,
                    268, 277, 279, 283, 284, 285
  Art 2 .... 47–49, 254
  Art 3 ....228, 254, 257, 258, 259
  Art 5 ......104–106, 115, 209, 227, 234, 239,
                    247–250, 253, 254, 272–273
  Art 5(1)..253
  Art 5(1)(a) 227
  Art 5(1)(c) 38
  Art 5(1)(f) 228, 254
  Art 5(4)....................................... 224, 252
  Art 6 .... 135, 242, 247, 250,
                    251, 257, 259, 260, 273
  Art 7 113
  Art 8 .... 44–45, 61, 80–81,
                    84–85, 198, 208, 209, 279
  Art 8(2)..30
  Art 10 ....109, 110, 115, 120, 143,
                    168, 193, 209, 217, 219, 271
  Art 10(2)................ 176–177, 193, 194, 209
  Art 11 .... 97, 110, 115, 120, 135, 209
  Art 11(2)..209
  Art 14 .... 27, 233, 234, 279
  Art 15 .... 228, 234–236

European Convention on Human Rights,
   First Protocol
   Art 1 .... 193, 197–198
European Social Charter 1961 .... 6, 284, 285

International Covenant on Civil and
   Political Rights 1966 (ICCPR) 6, 234
   Art 17 198
International Convention on Economic, Social
   and Cultural Rights 1966 (ICESCR) 6
International Labour Organisation (ILO)
   Convention on Child Labour
   (Convention No. 182) 1999 6

International Labour Organisation (ILO)
   Convention on Collective Bargaining
   (Convention No. 98) 1949 87 284
International Labour Organisation (ILO)
   Convention on Freedom of Association
   (Convention No. 87)
   1948 .... 6, 284

United Nations Charter 1945
   Art 41 198
United Nations Convention against
   Torture 1984
   Art 3 257

Chapter 1

Introduction

Introduction

ON a bright Saturday in February 2009, over 1,000 people gathered at the Institute of Education in central London under the banner of the Convention on Modern Liberty. This extraordinary event—which had parallel events in other major British cities—brought together people from all political parties and none, and from a bewildering range of pressure groups, from the TUC to Amnesty International to Red Pepper. Taunted subsequently as a 'Convention of Cant' by the New Labour establishment,[1] this was an assembly of the dismayed, expressing measured anger and deep disquiet about the continuing corrosion of civil liberties and political freedom in the United Kingdom under the Blair and Brown governments. It was also an assembly of the betrayed, people who had believed that New Labour would presage a radical shift in the role of the State and the protection of the individual, in the wake of the erosion of liberty under Conservative governments, now well documented but overshadowed in the light of what has happened since. For despite the vain protestations of ministers and those who would defend them, the New Labour record on civil liberties has been one of contradiction and paradox, with high profile measures such as the Constitutional Reform Act 2005 (designed to improve the independence and autonomy of the judiciary) and the Human Rights Act 1998 (designed to strengthen the rights of the subject) being contradicted by the conduct of central government, local authorities, the security and intelligence services, and the police, to say nothing of the paradoxical ineffectiveness of the courts and other supervisory bodies charged with the responsibility of defending our liberties. This book is concerned mainly to document this contempt for liberty and the principal means by which that contempt has been expressed.

---

[1] *The New Statesman*, 19 March 2009.

But it is also concerned to reveal the failure of constitutional principle in terms of the rule of law, and the futility of rights as a defence against State power in the modern British constitution. Sadly, it cannot be exhaustive, nor is it likely that matters will change under Cameron's New Tories.

The corrosion of liberty is a highly visible symptom of the failings of constitutional government and democratic politics in the United Kingdom. It is true that the New Labour administration embarked on a major programme of constitutional reform, to address some long-standing underlying problems. In addition to the measures already referred to, the programme included legislative devolution to Scotland, Wales, and Northern Ireland, freedom of information, the regulation of political parties, and the removal of the bulk of hereditary peers from the House of Lords (Bogdanor, 2009). But while these various measures are extremely important in their different ways, they are hardly revolutionary, and do not begin to address the core problem of British government, which Thatcher and Blair turned into an art form. This is the problem of centralised power and executive dominance, and the ability of governments with the support of the House of Commons to do pretty much what they want. It is also true that at the time of writing a Constitutional Reform and Governance Bill is swilling around, albeit with an uncertain chance of being passed before the general election in 2010. That Bill proposes to remove the remaining hereditary peers from the House of Lords, to allow for the resignation of life peers from the burden of a lifetime of service, to put the civil service on a statutory basis, and to require treaties to be laid before Parliament before being ratified. But while again these are admirable initiatives, they hardly strike at the core problem of British government, and the publication of the Bill was greeted with raspberries rather than applause, as a less than adequate response to the constitutional malaise that has gripped the nation. None of this will stop fresh restraints on liberty, a constant and evolving process that will be reversed—if at all—only by the introduction of meaningful political constraints on the power of government, of whichever 'New' variety. So while important skirmishes continue to be fought at the margins of the constitution (geographically and politically), as matters now stand it is chronic incapacities rather than constitutional niceties that impede the progress of State power.

Constitutional Principle and Civil Liberties

The first theme to be explored in the pages that follow is the context of constitutional principle within which the *Bonfire of the Liberties* ignited. As always, the starting point for any such discussion is the rule of law, one of the three foundation principles of the British constitution.[2] The link between the rule of law on the one hand, and personal and political freedom on the other, is both clear and compelling, as those familiar with the work of Kafka and Orwell will be only too well aware.[3] The principle is, however, impossible to define in a way that commands universal agreement, with 'thin' and 'thick' versions (Goldsworthy, 2001), and many varieties in between. There is no thinner a version of the rule of law than that expressed by Vice Chancellor Sir Robert Megarry in *Malone v Metropolitan Police Commissioner*,[4] where he said that England (sic) is not a country where everything done by government is prohibited unless expressly permitted; rather England is a country where everything done by government is permitted unless formally prohibited. So it was held in that case that as a matter of common law the government was perfectly entitled to tap people's telephones, because in doing so it was not doing anything unlawful. But the position is now at least modified as a result of the European Convention on Human Rights (ECHR) which requires the government to act in a manner 'prescribed by law' before it violates some of the human rights protected by the Convention (and then only if the law meets certain standards of accessibility and precision).[5] This, however, is not so much a thin as a skeletal version of the principle, in the sense that the requirements of the rule of law would be met by a government that could point to legal authority under laws that had been properly made (Craig, 2005), regardless of their content or manner of operation. But even the qualification that law must be properly made would be of little significance in a constitutional system (such as that of the United Kingdom) where the rule of law states that the courts are not permitted to question the procedure for the making of an Act of Parliament, but are required only to give effect to an Act, whatever procedural impropriety may have occurred in the process of its enactment.[6]

It is true that there are as many theories or definitions or penumbra of the rule of law as there are people who write about it. Nevertheless, rule of law authors usually now require something more than the existence of legal authority alone. While important, a requirement that government should

---

[2] Indeed, according to Lord Hope, 'the rule of law enforced by the courts is the controlling principle upon which our constitution is based', observing also that 'it is no longer right to say that [Parliament's] freedom to legislate admits of no qualification': *R (Jackson) v Attorney General* [2005] UKHL 56, para [105]. See also Constitutional Reform Act 2005, s 1.

[3] See pp 53–54, 93 below.

[4] [1979] 2 All ER 620, and subsequently *Malone v United Kingdom* (1985) 4 EHRR 14.

[5] *Sunday Times v United Kingdom* (1979–80) 2 EHRR 245; *Malone v Metropolitan Police Commissioner*, above.

[6] *British Railways Board v Pickin* [1974] AC 765.

have legal authority for its actions is to express no more than a duty to rule *by* law. The rule *of* law is a step further, with some of the minimum requirements being most famously identified by Professor Raz (1977), as follows:

- all laws should be prospective, open and clear;
- laws should be relatively stable;
- the making of particular laws ... should be guided by open, stable, clear and general rules;
- the independence of the judiciary must be guaranteed;
- the principles of natural justice must be observed;
- courts should have review powers over the implementation of the other principles;
- courts should be easily accessible;
- the discretion of crime prevention agencies should not be allowed to pervert the law.

But while thicker in content than the negative legality conception of the (now largely redundant) rule of law identified by Sir Robert Megarry, even this definition of the rule of law is 'not concerned with the actual content of the law, in the sense of whether the law is just or unjust, provided that the formal precepts of the rule of law are themselves met' (Craig, 2005). According to Professor Raz, the rule of law is only one of many virtues of a legal system, though it is nevertheless about something quite fundamental. Apart from the need for legal authority for government action, it imposes requirements about the nature and form of the law; the nature and manner of the exercise of legally grounded power by public officials; and the nature and form of the accountability of those who exercise that power. To require the rule of law to bear a heavier load (in terms of the substance of the law, rather than in terms of (a) its nature and form, and (b) the manner of its exercise) would be to rob the principle of what has been referred to as its 'independent function' (Craig, 2005), while its impact and significance would be diminished if 'in breach of the rule of law' were simply to become a slogan used by anyone who disagreed with a particular law.

A refinement of Professor Raz's position on the rule of law is to be found in Lord Bingham's well known lecture delivered some 30 years later at Cambridge University (Bingham, 2007), where he said that the rule of law contains a general overarching principle, which was no more than a requirement that

all persons and authorities within the state, whether public or private, should be bound by and entitled to the benefit of laws publicly and prospectively promulgated and publicly administered in the courts (ibid: 69).

4

From this, however, Lord Bingham deduced a number of sub-rules, as follows:

- the law must be accessible and so far as possible intelligible, clear, and predictable;
- questions of legal right and liability should ordinarily be resolved by application of the law and not the exercise of discretion;
- the law must afford adequate protection of fundamental human rights;
- the laws of the land should apply equally to all, save to the extent that objective differences justify differentiation;
- means must be provided for resolving, without prohibitive cost or inordinate delay, bona fide civil disputes which the parties themselves are unable to resolve;
- ministers and public officers at all levels must exercise the powers conferred on them reasonably, in good faith, for the purpose for which the powers were conferred and without exceeding the limits of such powers;
- adjudicative procedures provided by the State should be fair;
- compliance by the State with its obligations in international law, the law which whether deriving from treaty or international custom and practice governs the conduct of nations.

Much of this is incontestable and very close to Professor Raz, with the exception of the third and eighth sub-rules, whereby Lord Bingham appears to put his weight behind those who wish to give the rule of law a thicker or more substantive meaning. The former is a repudiation of Raz, inspired by a belief that a 'state which savagely repressed or persecuted sections of its people could not in [his] view be regarded as observing the rule of law' (ibid: 76), while the latter was said simply not to be 'contentious' (ibid: 82), perhaps surprising given that no apparent limits were placed on the international obligations to which it referred, while it would be hugely contentious constitutionally if this conception of the rule of law were to have domestic legal effects.[7]

For present purposes, however, it is not necessary (and in any event it is not possible) to resolve whether the rule of law should contain a commitment to human rights, or require compliance with international treaty obligations.[8]

---

[7] On the constitutional position of international treaties not yet incorporated into domestic law by statute, see Bradley and Ewing, 2007.

[8] However, Lord Bingham's sub-rules are controversial simply because it is unclear just what they mean, and also because they are contradictory. Lord Bingham takes the view in relation to his third sub-rule that it would not be contrary to the rule of law to violate all human rights, but only some, conceding that this is 'a difficult area' (Bingham, 2007: 76), that there is not 'a standard of human rights universally agreed even among civilised nations' (ibid), and that there is 'an element of

Nor is it necessary to conflate the principle beyond recognition, or devalue its currency beyond utility. As defined by Professor Raz and modified by Lord Bingham (without sub-principles 3 and 8) the rule of law applied to the question of civil liberties would have the following implications:

- the need for prior legal authority means in the context of personal liberty that State officials do not by virtue of their position alone have the right to stop, search, question, or detain people without their consent, while people should only be penalised for wrongs committed and not for suspicion that they might do something wrong. It also means that State officials do not by virtue of their position alone have the right to enter people's homes or businesses, place them under surveillance, or store information about them. They ought to be able to point to laws that are 'prospective, open and clear' (Raz, 1977); as well as 'intelligible, clear and predictable' (Bingham, 2007);

- the need for public power based on legal authority to be exercised lawfully means that State officials (uniformed or otherwise) should not use their powers arbitrarily, unnecessarily, or irrationally. Nor should power be used in a discriminatory way or to target particular political groups or individuals, if the 'discretion of crime prevention agencies [is] not to be allowed to pervert the law' (Raz, 1977); and if questions of 'legal rights and liability [are] ordinarily [to] be resolved by the application of the law and not the exercise of discretion', and if public officials are to 'exercise the powers conferred on them reasonably' (Bingham, 2007); while

- the need for accountability in the exercise of public power (with or without ostensible legal authority) means that public officials should obey the law, should have prior judicial authority before interfering with the rights of citizens, and should be answerable when they exceed the limits of their power. It also means that those whose rights have been violated by the

---

vagueness about the content of this sub-rule, since the outer edges of fundamental human rights are not clear-cut' (ibid: 76–77). So it is far from certain which human rights are necessary for the rule of law, beyond those which are 'seen as fundamental' within a particular society (ibid: 77), that is to say those that fall within the 'measure of agreement on where the lines are to be drawn' (ibid), the idea of human rights thus being disarmingly relative (and majoritarian) rather than absolute. If, however, only fundamental human rights are included by the third sub-rule, are not all human rights included by virtue of the eighth? Human rights instruments give rise to obligations under international law, and these transcend 'the full range of freedoms protected by bills of rights in other countries or in international instruments of human rights, or those now protected by our recently enacted Human Rights Act 1998 (Jowell, 2004: 23). Beyond the ECHR, they include the Council of Europe's Social Charter of 1961 (ratified by the UK), as well as the UN Conventions on Civil and Political Rights, and Economic, Social and Cultural Rights respectively, together with ILO conventions dealing with child labour, and freedom of association, which in the latter case are routinely violated by British law (Ewing and Hendy, 2004).

police, the security services, or other agencies of the State, should have a right of redress before an 'independent' judiciary, sitting in courts which are 'easily accessible' (Raz, 1977); or in accordance with 'adjudicative procedures provided by the State [which] should be fair' (Bingham, 2007).

As already suggested, compliance with these principles on a consistent basis is a necessary precondition for the protection of personal and political liberty against the arbitrariness of the State. Although respect for the rule of law (as an instrument of formal legality) is not a guarantee that civil liberties will be fully protected, disrespect for the rule of law (as an instrument of formal legality) will almost certainly help to ensure that they are fatally undermined. While it cannot be said that there is no respect for the rule of law under New Labour, it can be said that there is a lack of sufficient respect, contributing to the type of corrosion of liberty that we encounter in Chapters 2 and 3 in particular (to say nothing of the allegations of complicity in torture in relation to the security and intelligence services).

The Culture of Liberty under New Labour

This brings us to the second—and major—theme pursued in this book, which is simply to document the extent to which governments under New Labour have used the full extent of public power to continue the attack on liberty that had been associated with the Thatcher and Major regimes. Although—as already suggested—the election of a New Labour government had been expected to lead to a substantial improvement in the condition of liberty, if anything the situation is now worse, much worse, and it is thus New Labour's singular achievement to make us pine for the halcyon days of Freedom under Thatcher. Critics of those concerned by the corrosion of liberty under New Labour are right to remind us, however, that 'in recent years the power of the police and of the state generally has been regulated by statute in ways that simply did not exist in years gone by' (Gearty, 2009), the suggestion being that things have only got better as a result. But the fact that police powers are now in the legislation we encounter in Chapter 2 may be of little consequence if the same legislation has gradually but inexorably extended the already wide powers of the police.[9] And it may be of even less consequence if these extended powers are accompanied by the continuing militarisation, aggression, and lack of self control of police officers who now turn up in 'NATO helmets, [while] wearing ... protective equipment and carrying

[9] See pp 35–42 below.

shields' (HMIC, 2009: 60), with others at the same time appearing to use vicious dogs as weapons. The death of news vendor Ian Tomlinson on 1 April 2009 as he made his way home after work around a demonstration in the City of London against the G20 meeting is only the latest in a long line of incidents under New Labour (as under previous governments) that scream 'danger', in the face of real police power.[10] Mr Tomlinson died following a violent confrontation with a police officer,[11] an incident which is being investigated at the time of writing, but which the police are said to have gone to some lengths unsuccessfully to cover up,[12] also allegedly covering themselves up so that the personal numbers and faces of officers were concealed behind military-style clothing.

But it is not only the police, with concerns also about the rise in the Surveillance Society, which perhaps more than anything else had been responsible for the Convention on Modern Liberty in the first place. Here under the supervision of the Home Office, we have a surveillance regime that would have caused Erich Honecker to glow with pride. As discussed in Chapter 3, it begins with the saturation coverage of CCTV cameras for the purpose of general surveillance,[13] it is followed by the targeting and watching of individuals by local authorities and others,[14] and it is extended by the growth of the DNA database, which the government boasts is now the largest in the world.[15] Alongside all of this, there is continuing reliance on the old staples, even if 'oddly' the exercise of State power has led to a more benign regime, with 'the rules regulating the interception of communications, brought in to replace an entirely unaccountable executive scheme which had operated for years in total secrecy' (Gearty, 2009). Under this more benign exercise of State power, however, the annual incidence of phone tapping has increased by 400 per cent since 1988, no doubt explained innocently by the increase in the number of phones now in use. And under this more benign exercise of State power, warrants continue to be issued by the Home Office (as they were under the entirely unaccountable executive scheme), with the statutory regime subject to scrutiny by a judicial commissioner (just like the entirely unaccountable executive scheme), who is not only appointed by the Prime Minister but who also reports to the Prime Minister (partially in secret).[16] On top of all of which

---

[10] For details, see *The Observer*, 5 April 2009, *The Guardian*, 6–11 April 2009, *The Observer*, 12 April 2009, *The Guardian*, 18 April 2009, *The Observer*, 19 April , *Sunday Times*, 19 April 2009, *The Guardian*, 20–22 April 2009.

[11] See <http://www.youtube.com/watch?v=HECMVdl-9SQ> for video footage of the incident.

[12] *The Guardian*, 9 April 2009, criticising also the slow response of the Independent Police Complaints Commission.

[13] See pp 55–60 below.   [14] See pp 60–68 below.

[15] See pp 79–83 below.   [16] See pp 74–79 below.

we must now add the anticipated National Identity Register, though concerns here have been overshadowed by the concerns about ID cards, despite both being the nasty offspring of the same piece of legislation (the Identity Cards Act 2006), to be phased in gradually to diminish what will be an inevitable public backlash as its full horrors become known.[17] In particular, the register will require a bewildering amount of personal information to be recorded by a State authority (for what purpose?), and will require individuals to update the register in the event of any change of circumstances, failure to do so giving rise to the risk of substantial financial penalties.

But it is not only surveillance. There is also the question of those people—some of whom we encounter in Chapters 4 and 5 below—who would confront the power of the State, with different forms of political protest, all encountering the intolerance of dissent.[18] We have the botched attempt to infiltrate the protest group Plane Stupid, with tax-free financial inducements to activist Matilda Gifford if she would betray her colleagues;[19] we have brutal policing directed at climate camp protesters Val Swain and Emily Apple who had the audacity to seek to hold the police to account by asking officers to reveal their numbers;[20] and we have examples made in the criminal courts of those who dare to protest peacefully in the wrong place or in the wrong manner.[21] It is said, however, that there has been progress in the form of 'a recent House of Lords' decision on public protest which 'overruled police use of the common law on the basis that the police should now work within the statutory framework that parliament had enacted for them' (ibid).[22] But that 'progress'ive decision appeared on the contrary to accept the existence of the common law powers of the police, which more recently has provided the legal authority for the controversial practice of kettling,[23] justified paradoxically by one member of the House of Lords as necessary to prevent a fatality.[24]

[17] See pp 88–93 below.

[18] Though there is also the surveillance of protesters, with reports of the attempted infiltration of protesters (*The Guardian*, 25 April 2009), and a 'police databank on thousands of protestors' (*The Guardian*, 7 March 2009). See Ch 4 below.

[19] *The Guardian*, 25 April 2009. See Ch 4 below.

[20] *The Guardian*, 21 June 2009. See <http://www.guardian.co.uk/environment/2009/jun/21/kingsnorth-protester-arrests-video-complaint> for a video recording. See Ch 4 below.

[21] Including Milan Rai (Whitehall), Lindis Percy (US bases), and Jane Tallents (Faslane). See Ch 4 below.

[22] See *Austin v Metropolitan Police Commissioner* [2009] UKHL 5.

[23] Said to have been used to describe the activities of the Nazi government in Warsaw: Professor John Veit-Wilson, Letter to the Editor, *The Guardian*, 8 April 2009; the same day's *Guardian* editorial said that the practice 'recall[ed] the Red Army's tactics at the Battle of Stalingrad'.

[24] *Austin*, above, para [47], per Lord Walker, referring specifically to Red Lion Square on 15 June 1974, when Kevin Gately, a Warwick university student was killed.

And evoking still more memories of Freedom under Thatcher when the Official Secrets Acts were deployed against people like Sarah Tisdall,[25] Clive Ponting,[26] and Duncan Campbell (Ewing and Gearty, 1990), we have witnessed the persecution, prosecution, and conviction of public servants who in the public interest put into the public domain information that the government wanted to keep secret. The roll-call includes Kathryn Gun, for leaking details of a dirty tricks operation against UN Security Council members in advance of a vote on the invasion of Iraq;[27] David Keogh and Leo O'Connor for leaking details of a meeting between Tony Blair and George Bush, in which the latter is alleged to have discussed plans to bomb *al Jazeera*;[28] and Dr David Kelly who had spoken to a BBC journalist about the conduct of the government in its preparation for the invasion of Iraq.[29]

And then there was the aftermath of 9/11, the carpet-bombing of Afghanistan, and the invasion of Iraq, which together served as an emetic for all manner of unpleasant discharges, most of them related in some way to what was then regarded as a 'global war on terror' (a term now regarded by those who coined it as being foolish and as counterproductive as the restraints on liberty it has produced), though the softening of the rhetoric has not led to a relaxation of controls. New Labour had already placed its Terrorism Act 2000 on the statute book, giving wide powers to the police to deal with terrorism, a term widely defined to include all forms of protest involving the use of criminal damage, the definition being so wide that it would have caught the suffragettes and striking miners had it been in force in earlier times, but applicable now to catch those who advocate the violent overthrow of the most vile regimes overseas. In the panic engendered post 9/11, these powers were not enough and new powers were introduced, powers which we encounter in Chapters 6 and 7 below. Prominent among the growing list of repressive measures unprecedented in peacetime Britain were the Anti-terrorism, Crime and Security Act 2001 (introducing executive detention of unlimited duration), the Prevention of Terrorism Act 2005 (introducing powers to impose control orders on terrorist suspects not convicted of any offence), and the Terrorism Act 2006 (introducing new restraints on free speech in an awkwardly drafted offence of 'glorifying terrorism').[30] Prominent among the growing list of casualties in the war on terror were 12 men (of whom 11 were Pakistani nationals) arrested (in some

[25] See *Secretary of State for Defence v Guardian Newspapers Ltd* [1985] AC 359.
[26] *R v Ponting* [1985] Crim L Rev 318.
[27] See p 154 below.   [28] See pp 154–158 below.   [29] See pp 145–149 below.
[30] See Chapters 6 and 7 below.

cases in the presence of gun carrying police officers) on 8 April 2009 at various locations in the North West, including the campus of Liverpool Hope University.[31] The men (mainly students) were seized for suspected terrorist offences, in a high profile operation that was said to have foiled a major terrorist attack. By 22 April, however, all had been released, the police stating that there was insufficient evidence to pursue charges and that 'these people are innocent'.[32] Nevertheless (and despite condemnation from the Muslim Council of Britain),[33] nine of the men were handed over to the UK Borders Agency for immediate deportation on grounds of national security, their appeal against a refusal of bail being denied by the Special Immigration Appeal Commission.[34]

The Futility of Human Rights

This is quite a record, and these are only the introductory highlights. But they bring us to the third theme of this book, namely the evident futility of human rights as a defence against executive power, and the failure of the judiciary to make more use of the powers that they sought. In retrospect the most prominent of the judges making claims for such new powers was Sir Thomas Bingham (as he then was). In another powerfully argued lecture delivered in 1992 while he was Master of the Rolls, Sir Thomas said:

I would suggest that the ability of English judges to protect human rights in the courts and to reconcile conflicting rights in the manner indicated is inhibited by the failure of successive governments over many years to incorporate into United Kingdom law the European Convention on Human Rights (Bingham, 1993: 390).

Later in the same lecture, Sir Thomas said that incorporation would:

restore this country to its former place as an international standard bearer of liberty and justice. It would help to reinvigorate the faith, which our 18th and 19th century forebears would not for one instant have doubted, that these were fields in which Britain was the world's teacher, not its pupil. And it would enable the judges more effectively to do right to all manner of people after the laws and usages of this realm, without fear or favour (ibid: 400).

Lord Bingham (who was to become the Senior Law Lord) was not the only judge to have made the case for incorporation so openly, though not

---

[31] *The Guardian*, 9 April 2009.
[32] *The Guardian*, 22 April 2009.   [33] Ibid.
[34] *XC v Home Secretary*, Appeal No SC/77/81/82/83/2009, 21 May 2009.

all judges were in support (McCluskey, 1987). Others were drawn in, with a number making public statements, apparently concerned about the inadequate nature of the legal system which meant that it was unable properly to protect the vulnerable individual (Browne-Wilkinson, 1992; Laws, 1995). Such advocacy was not thought to compromise the political neutrality of the judges, and indeed the only judge who appears to have encountered difficulty professionally since the ECHR was incorporated is Lord McCluskey, who spoke out strongly against it.[35] The judges did not—of course—campaign alone; but their voice was an important and influential one, which was ultimately to secure a great prize.

With the Human Rights Act 1998, the Blair government would thus build on the legacy of the Attlee government (which had played a crucial part in drafting the ECHR) and the Wilson government (which had allowed the right of individual petition to the Strasbourg Court) by going a step further in allowing Convention rights to be enforced in British law. In taking this step, the government denounced those who questioned whether so much power should be given to the courts, with the finely considered response that they were 'ageing Marxist[s] decrying the establishment's conspiracy against the proletariat'.[36] Moreover, having been for so long the scourge of Labour governments, Lord Denning was now wheeled out as a hero by Mr Mike O'Brien, referring to him for the proposition that 'we have to trust someone, so why not trust the judges'.[37] The judges it seems were happy with the idea that they should be trusted, with the great bulk of the speeches in the Second Reading debate of the Human Rights Bill being given by serving or retired Law Lords, in what seems a curious twist of constitutional principle. Sometime opponents of incorporation like Lord Donaldson of Lymington joined the queue to pledge allegiance at the feet of an instrument that would extend their power, to enable them to do things for which in the past they had shown little inclination.[38] Some serving Law Lords were, however, so happy to be trusted that they took an active part in the Committee proceedings of the Bill as well,[39] with Lord Browne-Wilkinson speaking out strongly against an Opposition amendment that would have required the British courts to be bound by the jurisprudence of the European Court of Human Rights (rather as they are bound in another context by the

[35] See *Hoekstra v H M Advocate* 2001 SLT 28; and *Scotland on Sunday*, 6 February 2000 where Lord McCluskey criticises the Act in strong terms. See subsequently, McCluskey, 2007.

[36] HC Debs, 16 February 1998, col 858 (Mr Michael O'Brien).

[37] Ibid, col 857, citing Lord Denning (1982): 'Someone must be trusted. Let it be the judges' (p 330). The obvious question '*Why?*' was not asked.

[38] On the judicial record on civil liberties, see Ewing and Gearty, 1990, 2000; and Ewing, 2004.

[39] For a full account, see Ewing, 1999.

jurisprudence of the European Court of Justice). Although this has much to commend it on rule of law grounds, Lord Browne-Wilkinson rather disarmingly informed the House that as the only person present who would have responsibility for the interpretation of the Act , he saw no reason why the British judges should be constrained in this way.[40]

Unlike other countries (notably Canada and the United States) where rights are constitutionally entrenched, the Human Rights Act 1998 does not give the courts the power to strike down legislation. And unlike the EC Treaty (as construed by the European Court of Justice in the famous *Factortame* case),[41] the Act does not require the courts to refuse to apply legislation which is inconsistent with Convention rights. This does not mean, however, that the courts have no power over legislation, whether that legislation is passed before or after the Human Rights Act came into force on 2 October 2000. Nor does it mean that the power the courts wield is ineffective or of no consequence. In the first place, section 3 provides that 'so far as possible to do so', both primary and delegated legislation is to be read and given effect in a way that is compatible with these rights. There may, of course, be cases where it is not possible to construe a statute consistently with Convention rights, if an intention to violate these rights is clear on the face of the statute. In these cases, section 4 empowers a court to make a declaration of incompatibility, a power that applies to both primary and secondary legislation, though in the latter case only where the primary legislation authorising the making of the subordinate instrument 'prevents removal of the incompatibility'. The power to make such a declaration is limited to the higher courts (though the section 3 duty to interpret legislation consistently with Convention rights applies to all courts). If granted, a declaration of incompatibility has 'no operative or coercive effect', and 'does not prevent either party relying on, or the courts enforcing, the law in question':[42] it does not affect the validity, continuing operation, or enforcement of the legislation in question; nor is it binding on the parties in the proceedings in which it is made. Nevertheless, the current position seems to have satiated the judicial appetite, as the following exchange between the Chairman of the Joint Committee on Human Rights and Baroness Hale tends to indicate:

Q193 *Chairman:* Do you think there is any judicial appetite for more extensive powers than those in the Human Rights Act, the certificate of incompatibility and so forth?

---

[40] HL Debs, 19 January 1998, col 1260.

[41] *R v Transport Secretary, ex p Factortame Ltd (No 1)* [1990] 2 AC 95; *Case C-213/89, R v Transport Secretary, ex p Factortame Ltd (No 2)* [1991] AC 603.

[42] HL Debs, 18 November 1997, col 546.

Baroness Hale of Richmond: I have not detected any in the cases we have heard so far. Perhaps that is partly because of the approach we have taken to declarations of the incompatibility and because of the approach that the government and parliament have then taken to what to do about declarations of incompatibility.[43]

During the same exchange, Baroness Hale also pointed out that the declaration of incompatibility power was not 'in practice' all that different from the position in Canada, where the judicial power is formally much greater.[44] This is a revealing indication of what has been referred to as the inflationary effect of Bills of Rights (Allan, 2006; Allan and Huscroft, 2006; 2007), in the sense that they end up creating a greater de facto judicial power than might otherwise formally appear.[45] In the United Kingdom, this inflationary pressure is encouraged by the fact that an application to Strasbourg hangs over ministers like a sword of Damocles, which means that it is difficult to see how the government could do anything other than give effect to a declaration of incompatibility. In any event, it is a striking feature of the complaints that have been made to Strasbourg that most of them were not about the requirements of legislation alleged to breach the Convention, but about the use of statutory powers or the exercise of common law powers by the government or government agencies. Although there is growing concern about legislative restrictions on freedom as well as the manner of their exercise, the real engine of the Human Rights Act is nevertheless to be found in section 6 rather than section 4. This provides that it is unlawful for a public authority to act in a way that is incompatible with Convention rights, with a 'public authority' being widely defined to include a court or tribunal which exercises functions in relation to legal proceedings. The definition of a public authority was left deliberately open-ended, the government taking a policy decision to avoid a list,[46] and declining an invitation to specify precisely to which bodies the Convention rights should apply. This contrasts with the approach adopted in the case of the Freedom of Information Act 2000, which sets out in a Schedule the bodies to which it applies. Nevertheless, the intention of the government was clearly that the Human Rights Act should apply to central government (including executive agencies), local government, the police, immigration officers, the prison service, as well as to others. Ultimately, however, it is for the courts to decide the scope of application of the Human Rights Act, both in terms of the substance of the rights (guided but not bound by Strasbourg jurisprudence) and to whom

---

[43] Joint Committee on Human Rights, *A British Bill of Rights?*, Minutes of Evidence, 4 March 2008, HL 165-ii/HC 150-ii (2007–08), Q 192.

[44] Ibid, Q 195.   [45] See also, pp 279–284 below.   [46] HL Debs, 18 November 1997, col 796.

they apply. That is real power. But as should be clear from the previous section, and as will be developed in the pages that follow, it is a power with which the courts have not yet fully engaged.

Conclusion

What then is the case for the defence? Returning to the Convention on Modern Liberty, the event was sufficiently important to exercise the mind of the Lord Chancellor who felt obliged to pen a piece for a newspaper, published on the day before the Convention opened its doors.[47] In a rather tired and stale attempt at pre-emption, Jack Straw wrote that occasionally he asks the asylum seekers at his constituency surgeries 'why they made the very long journey to the United Kingdom rather than a much shorter one somewhere else'. 'The answer', he said, 'is almost always the same: it is better here. People have more rights and greater protection'. More to the point, 'despite the claims of a systematic erosion of liberty by those organising [the] Convention on Modern Liberty, my very good constituency office files show no recent correspondence relating to fears about the creation in Britain of a "police state" or a "surveillance society"'. And although accept-ing that 'Labour since 1997 has not achieved a state of grace in terms of the crucial balance between security and liberty', 'on any objective basis, this government has done more to reinforce and strengthen liberty than any since the war'. According to Mr Straw (like others after him):

Part of the problem for those who question this is that their analysis assumes the loss of a golden age of liberty. No such age existed. The 60s, 70s and 80s were the decades of the informal 'judges' rules', the absence of statutory protections for suspects, 'fitting up', egregious abuses of power, miscarriages of justice, arbitrary actions by police, security and intelligence agencies, phone tapping without any basis in statute law or any legal protection for the citizen whatsoever, gaping holes where there should have been parliamentary scrutiny.

No one has, however, suggested that there is such a 'golden age'. Indeed, any such suggestion would reflect 'a serious lack of historical perspective', about something that 'has never existed' (Gearty, 2009).[48] On the contrary, what is being asserted is that there is a continuing corrosion of liberty, which is singularly more striking for the fact that it is happening on the watch of

---

[47] *The Guardian*, 27 February 2009. See also David Miliband, 'Free Society', <http://blogs.fco.gov. uk/roller/miliband/entry/free_society>.

[48] See also Gearty, 2007; and Bonner, 2009: 'More questionable is any implication that that we can hark back to some "golden age" of liberty'.

a Labour administration, which on this issue—as on others—appears too often to be in government but not in power.

As for the examples given in the preceding passage, it is also striking that the steps taken to deal with the abuses identified by the Lord Chancellor were initiatives of the Thatcher government—the Police and Criminal Evidence Act 1984, the Interception of Communications Act 1985, and the Security Service Act 1989, all attacked by Real Labour at the time for not doing enough to protect the individual, yet all still on the statute book in their original form, except where they have been toughened up subsequently. The Lord Chancellor's killer punch, however, is the Human Rights Act, by means of which New Labour provided an 'overriding and systematic protection for people's rights and liberties', Mr Straw promising that so long as New Labour remains in office it won't be 'watered down'. But as already suggested and as will be demonstrated at greater length in the chapters that follow, the Lord Chancellor's killer punch is a feather duster. The Human Rights Act more often than not fires blanks, and had it been wholly effective it would not have been necessary or possible to write this book to document the corrosion of civil liberties since 1997. More significantly perhaps (and despite claims that the Act won't be watered down so long as New Labour is in office), rather than provide a robust defence of liberty, the Human Rights Act has itself provided a political vehicle for further restraints, the government having decided that we cannot have (paper) rights without (more) responsibilities:

The fundamental universal rights enshrined in the Act are not contingent on behaviour, but nor do they come without responsibility. Implicit in the [Human Rights Act] is the notion that we all owe one another obligations in the way we exercise our rights. The forthcoming green paper on a bill of rights and responsibilities is designed to generate public debate about how we can articulate these implicit duties more explicitly.[49]

The Green Paper has been duly published (Ministry of Justice, 2009), and although we may not be any more enlightened about the substance of our duties, we are much better informed about the continuing direction of travel on the issue of civil liberties. The route does not entail a strengthening of liberty, any more than it entails a commitment to equality, with inequality having increased under New Labour in the 2000s to a level unknown since the Old Tories in the 1960s.[50]

---

[49] For a critique, see G Aitchison, 'End Game Reaches the Bill of Rights Debate', <http://www.opendemocracy.net/ourkingdom/front?page=4>.

[50] The Guardian, 8 May 2009: 'Britain under Gordon Brown is a more unequal country than at any time since modern records began in the early 1960s, after the incomes of the poor fell and those of the rich rose in the three years after the 2005 general election'.

C H A P T E R 2

The Growth of Police Powers

Introduction

O N the morning of 22 July 2005 Jean Charles de Menezes was shot dead on a tube train at Stockwell station in south London; he was killed by armed police officers who mistakenly believed him to be a terrorist. Three Specialist Firearms Officers from a special police unit (SO 19) are said to have followed five surveillance officers onto the train, and to have discharged up to what were said to have been nine bullets at close range, of which seven entered the 27 year old Brazilian electrician, with one mis-firing and the other missing his body.[1] Mr de Menezes was unarmed, he was not carrying a bomb, and he had no terrorist connections. These events set in motion a number of developments that led to the prosecution of the Metropolitan Police Force, not for causing the death of Mr de Menezes, but for breaching the Health and Safety at Work Act 1974.[2] In what is perhaps the most incongruous use ever of this latter measure, the police force was convicted for failing to comply with a provision which states that it is an offence for any employer 'to conduct his undertaking in such a way as to ensure, so far as is reasonably practicable, that persons not in his employment who may be affected thereby are not thereby exposed to risks to their health or safety'.[3] Although the police force faced a record £175,000 fine, none of the individual officers involved was found guilty of any wrongdoing, and the jury made a point of making clear that in its view no blame could be attached to those who had led the operation on the day. And despite the conviction, the Metropolitan Police Commissioner obviously did not feel that the circumstances were such as to merit his resignation, a view which appears to have been shared by the Home Secretary. The incident was notable also for revealing a 'shoot to kill' policy—'a vernacular term that the

---

[1] *BBC News*, 1 November 2007.   [2] Ibid.
[3] Health and Safety at Work Act 1974, s 3.

police prefer not to use'[4]—as part of what was known as Operation Kratos, a national policy adopted by the Association of Chief Police Officers in 2003.[5] This was the first time the existence of such a policy was acknowledged to exist in relation to Great Britain.[6]

There is perhaps no other single event that in recent years has done more to shatter the illusion of the police officer as being simply a 'citizen in uniform'. The transformation of the police as State agents some distance apart from the communities they serve is highlighted in other ways than by the power to discharge lethal firearms (containing 'dum dum' bullets)[7] with the intention of causing death. At airports and railway stations we see very public displays of the armed copper, many of whose colleagues have now been tooled up in other ways, by equipment such as tasers and pepper spray. However, it is not just the equipment that sets the police apart from the rest of us, for alongside the new tools they are authorised to use are new powers with major implications for the individual's right to liberty, albeit in circumstances much less highly charged and with consequences much less dramatic than in the de Menezes affair, or the incidents such as those discussed in Chapter 7 below. What is significant about these recent initiatives is that they do not involve simply an extension of existing powers—such as arrest on the one hand and search on the other—though that has happened, notably in the Serious Organised Crime and Police Act 2005. They also involve the granting of new powers to restrain the individual who—for example—may be prevented by an ASBO from engaging in certain kinds of anti-social behaviour (widely defined), or required by a dispersal order to leave a particular location to which he or she should not return. And in addition to the formal extension of existing powers of arrest and search, and the granting of new powers of restraint, we also see the emergence informally of police practices for which there is no legal authority, including the practice of 'stop and account' which has been given a seal of official approval,[8] at a time of rather slack and equivocal lines of judicial accountability. The main concern of this chapter is to highlight this contradiction of

[4] See Metropolitan Police Authority, Memorandum from Catherine Crawford, Chief Executive and Clerk to the Authority, 8 August 2005, reproduced at <http://www.mpa.gov.uk/downloads/foi/log/kratos-attach.pdf>.

[5] Ibid.

[6] Under the terms of the policy, 'it was necessary for suspected suicide bombers to be shot in the head rather than the torso, which is the accepted firearms practice, because of the risk of detonating explosives': ibid.

[7] BBC News, 1 November 2007; also BBC News, 15 October 2007.

[8] Home Office, Police and Criminal Evidence Act, Code of Practice A (2005), paras 4.12–4.13. See also Kent Police, M17 Searching of Persons, Vehicles and Road Checks, para 6.1 (<http://www.kent.police.uk/About%20Kent%20Police/policies/m/m017.html>).

growing accountability of the citizen to the police on the one hand, and the declining accountability of the police to the citizen on the other.

Questions of Legality

It is a well-established principle of the common law that the police have no power to stop and search and no power to stop and question,[9] a principle so deeply ingrained that it has been said on more than one occasion to be a 'constitutional principle'.[10] Any such power needs clear statutory authority, and any such statutory authority should be reluctantly granted by Parliament and closely scrutinised by the courts. The reason for such a principle in a liberal society is obvious: people should be free from interference by the State unless they are suspected on reasonable grounds of having done something wrong, in which case they should be arrested. Once arrested they will be entitled to a panoply of protection which is not available to the individual casually stopped by the police, likely unwittingly to incriminate himself or herself without the benefit of legal representation or the other safeguards to which the arrested person is entitled and which ought to constrain the conduct of the police. That legal principle has not only been recognised as one of the greatest importance, but it is one that has been applied time after time,[11] with the only significant contradiction in modern times being *Donnelly v Jackman*,[12] where the accused responded to a tap on the shoulder from a police officer requesting him to stop, by assaulting him 'with some force'. Convicted for assaulting a police officer in the execution of his duty, the accused's appeal was dismissed by Mr Justice Talbot according to whom 'it is not every trivial interference with a citizen's liberty that amounts to a course of conduct sufficient to take the officer out of the course of his duty'. In a short judgment that did not deal with the significance of the points raised, Mr Justice Talbot added that 'the facts do not justify the view that the officer was not acting in the execution of his duty when he went up to the appellant and wanted to speak to him'. But even here there is nothing to challenge the established view that 'although a police officer acting in the execution of his duty was entitled to ask a citizen questions, including

[9] *Jackson v Stevenson* (1879) 2 Adam 255; *Rice v Connelly* [1966] 2 QB 414; *Kenlin v Gardner* [1967] 2 QB 510; *R v Lemsatef* [1977] 2 All ER 835. Also *R(Laporte) v Gloucestershire Chief Constable* [2006] UKHL 55: 'her refusal to give her name, which however irritating to the police was entirely lawful', at para [55].

[10] *Jackson v Stevenson*, above (Lord Robertson). See also *R (Gillan) v Metropolitan Police Commissioner* [2006] UKHL 12, para [1], p 204 below.

[11] Note 9 above.   [12] (1970) 54 Cr App R 229.

questions as to his name and address, there was no legal duty upon the citizen, in the absence of some obligation imposed by statute'.[13]

Power without Legality?

Notwithstanding the clear legal position, however, there has come to public attention a practice which has been given the benign and sanitised epithet of 'stop and account', a practice described by Sir Ronnie Flanagan in his *Independent Review of Policing* for the Home Office as the 'stopping and checking of people [by the police] in public places', applying where the people in question 'are asked to account for such things as their presence, for what is in their possession or for their movements etc' (Flanagan, 2008: 5.56). Despite its benign epithet, and despite the fact that it is 'not governed by any specific legislation',[14] it is far from clear that stop and account is an entirely non-coercive process. According to various police forces:

- Stop and account can be a valuable tool in the detection and prevention of crime;[15]
- 'A police officer has a right to stop and speak to you at any time' (from a website directed at young people);[16]
- 'Asking someone to account for themselves means asking questions which are more than just general conversation';[17]
- 'A failure to provide a satisfactory account [may lead] the officer to suspect offences for which he/she has dedicated powers';[18] and
- 'Officers can stop and talk to you at any time—to ask whether you have witnessed an incident, for example. This is not a stop and account'.[19]

Although used for a variety of purposes, stop and account is thus likely to be directed in some cases against specific suspects, and it is likely to be the first step for some on a journey through the criminal justice system, even if the overall arrest rate following stop and account is extremely low.

---

[13] *Rice v Connelly*, above, at p 417. In the same case, the Lord Chief Justice said that 'the whole basis of the common law is the right of the individual to refuse to answer questions put to him by persons in authority, and to refuse to accompany those in authority to any particular place, short, of course, of arrest' (at p 419).

[14] Kent Police, M17 Searching of Persons, Vehicles and Road Checks, para 6.1 (<http://www.kent. police.uk/About%20Kent%20Police/policies/m/m017.html>).

[15] <http://www.met.police.uk/foi/pdfs/policies/search_account_rec_61_mpsps_version.pdf>.

[16] <http://www.norfolkbeatwise.org.uk/wiseup/youlaw2.php>.

[17] <http://www.hampshire.police.uk/Internet/rightinfo/foi/informationclasses/stopsearch.htm>.

[18] <http://www.thamesvalley.police.uk/aboutus/aboutus-sop/aboutus-sop-stsea.htm>.

[19] Ibid.

At '1.9%, very similar to the figure for 2006/07 (2.0%)', Greater Manchester Police explain the low arrest rate as being 'due to the nature of the encounter', with the power being used where the officer has no 'specific suspicion giving grounds to search, which would be anticipated to lead to an arrest'.[20] Nevertheless, stop and account is widely used, rising to a recorded 1.87 million stops nationally in 2006–07 (compared to 1.4 million in the previous year).[21]

The existence of this practice had previously been acknowledged and considered by Sir William Macpherson's Report on the murder of Stephen Lawrence (Macpherson, 1999), where concerns of a different kind were expressed, that stop and account was being used in an overtly racist way, deployed disproportionately against black youths. In order to help address this problem, Sir William recommended that these so-called 'voluntary stops' should be formalised, in the sense that police officers should give a written record to anyone who is stopped to account (ibid: R 61), and that a record should be kept for the purposes of ethnic monitoring. A disappointing feature of these recommendations, however, is that they were made without a full assessment of the legal basis for the practice in the first place, and without any consideration of whether it needs to be regulated by statute. By requiring better administrative regulation of the way stop and account is used, Sir William effectively gave a judicial blessing to activity for which there is precious little legal authority. In contrast to the position in Northern Ireland,[22] the only formal recognition of the practice in English law is to be found in the Code of Practice on Stop and Search where it occupies a twilight zone, somewhere between 'general conversations such as when giving directions to a place, or when seeking witnesses' on the one hand,[23] and the more formal exercise of legal powers of stop and search and arrest on the other.[24] Between these two clear positions of voluntary engagement and legal power, thus lies a procedure which applies where 'an officer requests a person in a public place to account for themselves, i.e. their actions, behaviour, presence in an area or possession of anything'.[25] The inclusion of this power in the Code of Practice—under the heading 'Recording of Encounters not Governed by Statutory Powers'—does not, however, give

---

[20] <http://www.gmp.police.uk/mainsite/pages/stopaccount.htm>.

[21] *Guardian*, 8 July 2008.

[22] Justice and Security (Northern Ireland) Act 2007, s 21, which formally empowers the police (and the army in some cases) to stop and question someone about their identity and their movements, though also provides that it is an offence not to stop or to answer questions, not something that we would want to adopt in Great Britain.

[23] Home Office, Police and Criminal Evidence Act, Code of Practice A (2005), para 4.13.

[24] Ibid.   [25] Ibid, para 4.12.

it legal authority, even though the Code of Practice has been approved by Parliament, which may in the eyes of some tend to give the power a spurious form of official legitimacy.

Power without Safeguards

That 'legitimacy' raises questions about the nature of the safeguards that should accompany the use of this de facto power, to ensure that the subject is being encountered in a purely voluntary and consensual manner. For not everyone stopped by the police in this way—not even the most assiduous follower of ITV's *The Bill*—will be aware that they are being asked to succumb to an entirely voluntary activity. Nevertheless, there is no requirement in the Code of Practice for the police to inform anyone subject to stop and account that while the police are entitled to put questions to the subject, the subject has no corresponding duty to answer these questions, and indeed has a fundamental common law right neither to be detained by the police, nor to respond to the police against their will. Although the Code makes clear that people are not required to provide personal details, *there is no duty on the part of the police to inform them of this right*, though the Metropolitan Police advises its officers that there is no 'power to detain if the person is unwilling to provide'.[26] All of which raises questions about the safeguards which are supposed to be in place to regulate this heavily used power, and to prevent abuse. Here we find that having won official approval and recognition of the practice from Sir William Macpherson, there has now been a quick back-pedalling by the Home Office and the police on the Macpherson recommendations. As already pointed out, Sir William had recommended that police officers should give a written record to anyone who is subject to the exercise of stop and account. This did not appear unduly to trouble the Kent police:

The record will include an explanation of why that particular individual was required to account for him/herself (as opposed to anyone else). This reason does not require to be complex or backed in legal requirement, but merely a written record outlining why the officer invested additional time with that person. In addition, the record will highlight 'the outcome of the interaction' which in many situations is expected to be no further action.[27]

In his *Independent Review of Policing*, however, Sir Ronnie Flanagan discovered that the procedures relating to stop and account were 'an example of where the police have gone further bureaucratically than was intended'

[26] Note 15 above.
[27] See <http://www.kent.police.uk/About%20Kent%20Police/policies/m/m017.html>.

by Sir William Macpherson's 'eminently sensible recommendation to protect the police, the public and the relationship between them' (Flanagan, 2008: 5.56).

Although made in 1999, that recommendation had only been implemented in November 2004, after having been piloted for more than a year.[28] It was complained that 'What has evolved is a manually recorded system of stop and account which takes on average 7 minutes per individual encounter and which ... however careful an officer is in explaining the purpose of the process, usually leads to suspicion on the part of the member of the public involved' (ibid: 5.57). According to Sir Ronnie, in London alone 'it has been estimated that stop and account consumes over 48,000 hours annually of officers' time', a calculation that did not 'include the time taken to log each form once it is returned to the station, or the time supervisors spend checking and counter-signing each form' (ibid). Rather than question the extent of the practice, these figures led Sir Ronnie to question the self-imposed restraints on the manner of its use, which were said to be too bureaucratic and to be in need of an 'overhaul' (ibid: 5.58). With this in mind (and after consulting Sir William Macpherson), Sir Ronnie recommended that the existing 'comprehensive form for Stop and Account should be removed', and replaced with a procedure whereby any officer who asks individuals to account for themselves should be required to 'provide that individual with a 'receipt' of the encounter in the form of a business card or similar', and 'use airwave to record the encounter, including the ethnicity of the person subject to the encounter to enable disproportionality monitoring' (ibid: R 24).[29] Perhaps predictably, these proposals were seized upon with alacrity by a grateful Home Office and welcomed by the Conservatives and Liberal Democrats.[30] The Code of Practice has thus been changed, following a Home Office circular announcing that:

From 1 January 2009, a police officer or member of police staff conducting an encounter under paragraphs 4.11–4.20 of Code A will be required to record only the ethnicity of the person. Whilst the change removes the form filling process, it maintains the important requirement to record the ethnic classification of the person and to provide the person with a receipt of the encounter.[31]

---

[28] *BBC News*, 17 November 2004.
[29] Supervisory officers would then 'dip sample' these recordings, adding to the massive savings which these changes were said to promise, which were said to be somewhere in the region of an extraordinary five to seven million hours, or the equivalent to 2,500–3,500 officers.
[30] HC Debs, 7 February 2008, col 1144.
[31] Home Office Circular, 032/2008, para 2.

Power and Legality

In contrast to stop and account, there is an abundance of power to stop and search, which has a pedigree stretching back at least to the notorious 'sus' laws in 1839 (Scarman, 1981). But although these powers have been controversial and although there have been serious concerns for decades about the manner of their exercise, the trend in recent years has been gradually to extend them, while beginning to dilute the statutory safeguards which must accompany their use.[32] These safeguards are important because at this stage there is insufficient evidence to arrest someone on suspicion of having committed a crime. Apart from the Misuse of Drugs Act 1971, a key statutory power authorising stop and search is the Police and Criminal Evidence Act 1984. When first introduced, the latter applied only where the police had reasonable grounds to suspect that an individual was carrying stolen goods or prohibited articles, defined to mean offensive weapons or items to be used for purposes of burglary or theft. Since 1984, however, the definition of prohibited articles has been extended to include items that can be used for the purposes of fraud or for the purpose of destroying or causing damage to property.[33] At the same time, a growing list of statutes authorise stop and search for other specific purposes, with a list of no fewer than 19 of these statutes being contained in the Code of Practice on Stop and Search. Apart from the Terrorism Act 2000 (which is considered more fully in Chapter 6 below), such powers are to be found also in measures as diverse as the Sporting Events (Control of Alcohol) Act 1985, the Criminal Justice Act 1988, the Badgers Act 1992, and the Criminal Justice and Public Order Act 1994. The last allows a police superintendent to authorise the use of stop and search powers for periods of up to 24 hours where there are reasonable grounds to believe that acts of violence will take place in a particular locality, in which case the power may be used to stop and search for offensive weapons or dangerous instruments. Unlike the power under the 1984 Act this particular provision may be used by a police officer 'whether or not he has any grounds for suspecting that the person or vehicle is carrying weapons or articles of that kind'.[34]

The problem then is not a want of power, but too much power. The other problem concerns the way these powers are used with the erosion of safeguards relating to the non statutory practice of stop and account being

---

[32] See, for example, Terrorism Act 2000, s 44; below, pp 201–203.

[33] The Act has also been extended to allow the police to stop and search for prohibited fireworks.

[34] Criminal Justice and Public Order Act 1994, s 60.

mimicked in the case of the statutory powers of stop and search.[35] An example of the rather informal way in which 'section 60' is used can be seen in *Osman v Southwark Crown Court*,[36] where the appellant was convicted of assaulting a police officer following an incident in which he was subject to a stop and search for knives, the police using the powers provided by the 1994 Act. The appellant was one of a number of youths stopped by the police as they tried to enter a park where there had been 'continuous trouble throughout the previous week from groups of youths carrying weapons'. The appellant was told that he was going to be searched, and when he resisted, he was held down by two police officers worried that he might be carrying a knife. In the course of the incident, one officer was assaulted, for which the appellant was convicted by the Crown Court, despite the fact that the police officers had not complied with section 2 of the 1984 Act, not having provided the appellant with their names, or the station to which they were attached. The Crown Court had taken the view, however, that because 'the officers were clearly local officers policing a local event in broad daylight as expeditiously as possible and because numbers could readily be obtained from the officers' lapels, the breach was not so serious as to render the search unlawful on that account'. This finding was reversed by the Divisional Court, which quashed the conviction on the ground that 'the failure of the officers to supply details of their names and station rendered the search unlawful'. While noting an 'excessive use of time in having to recite the constable's name and station to every person searched', Lord Justice Sedley nevertheless acknowledged 'Parliament's view that such formality is of great importance in relation to civil liberties'. He also suggested, however, that there was nothing:

to prevent uniformed officers, who are sent out to make searches of this kind from carrying in their pocket slips of paper giving their name and station, so that the person searched not only is told what these are but can carry the information away with him or her, and the officer is saved the trouble of going through an oral rigmarole.[37]

Power and Discrimination

Apart from questions of informality in the application of the law, the other issue here relates to the problem of the discriminatory use of the powers, a problem shared with stop and account. Stop and search powers were described in 2007 as a 'central historical flashpoint in relations between black

---

[35] See *BBC News*, 16 September 2009.
[36] [1999] EWHC Admin 622.
[37] Ibid, para [12].

people and the police', and as 'a major trigger for the riots which broke out in Bristol in 1980 and in London, Liverpool, Manchester, Birmingham and elsewhere in 1981, leading Lord Scarman to call for a new approach to policing black communities' (HAC, 2007: paragraph 167). Nevertheless, it remains the case that these powers continue to be used disproportionately against young black youths. This is a matter identified by the Macpherson inquiry into the murder of Stephen Lawrence, it being acknowledged in the report that:

In the 1998 statistics on race and the criminal justice system, commended both by the Home Secretary and Lord Justice Rose, the figures for 1997/98 show that *'black people were, on average, five times more likely to be stopped and searched by the police than white people. The use of these powers for Asians and other ethnic groups varied widely.'* Black people are also *'more likely to be arrested than white or other ethnic groups'*. There is no doubt that for the minority communities the formal statistics are the tip of an iceberg. If all the other stops under additional legislation were recorded it is clearly felt that discrimination would be even more evident. (Macpherson, 1999: 45.9; emphasis in original)

Indeed, the Macpherson Report went so far as to claim that it was 'pointless for the police service to try to justify the disparity in these figures purely or mainly in terms of the other factors which are identified', with a 'majority of police officers' who testified before the inquiry accepting that 'an element of the disparity was the result of discrimination' (ibid: 45.10). It was said in the same report that:

Nobody in the minority ethnic communities believes that the complex arguments which are sometimes used to explain the figures as to stop and search are valid. In addition their experience goes beyond the formal stop and search figures recorded under the provisions of the Police and Criminal Evidence Act, and is conditioned by their experiences of being stopped under traffic legislation, drugs legislation and so called 'voluntary' stops. It is not within our terms of reference to resolve the whole complex argument on this topic. Whilst there are other factors at play we are clear that the perception and experience of the minority communities that discrimination is a major element in the stop and search problem is correct. (ibid: 45.8)[38]

The Macpherson Report recommended that when exercising the power of stop and search, the police should record the ethnicity of any individual who has been stopped and searched (ibid: R 61). This would help to improve ethnic monitoring and help deal with discrimination in the use of the powers. Although accepted at the time, the disproportionate use of these powers against black youths continues to be a matter of acute concern, and has been identified

---

[38] The problems with the 1984 Act apply also to the 1994 Act (the so-called section 60), with black people again more likely than white people to be affected, thereby increasing further the 'disproportionate impact of searches on innocent black people' (HAC, 2007: para 179).

as such by the Metropolitan Police Authority. Even as recently as 2007, the House of Commons Home Affairs Committee reported that 'black people are nearly twice as likely to enter the criminal justice system as a result of stop and search (11.3%) in comparison with their white counterparts (6.2%)' (HAC, 2007: paragraph 166). More specifically, the Committee pointed out that:

Black people of all ages are 6 times as likely to be stopped and searched and Asian people twice as likely as their white counterparts. Overall, there has been a decline in the numbers of white people stopped and searched since 1997–98, whereas for black and Asian people the numbers are broadly similar to levels recorded in 1997–98. These national figures reflect particularly high numbers of [Police and Criminal Evidence Act 1984,] section 1 searches of black people in three of the 43 police forces—Greater Manchester, West Midlands and the Metropolitan Police. Over 80% of all section 1 searches on black people take place in these three forces (ibid: para 169).

The Home Affairs Committee pointed out further that in London, 'young black people represent 37% of those stopped and searched overall but only 15% of the youth population', with the disproportionate impact of the use of the power being felt even more sharply in some London boroughs with a relatively small black population. The example was given of Kingston-upon-Thames where 'black people are 14.4 times more likely than whites to be stopped and searched relative to their proportion of the population', and of Richmond-upon-Thames where black people were '13.1 times more likely' (ibid: paragraph 172).[39] These remarkable statistics have given rise to claims that police conduct could be unlawful under the Race Relations Act 1976, as well as to doubts about whether a significant proportion of stops and searches comply with the statutory standard of reasonable suspicion (Lustgarten, 2002). But whatever may be the position under race relations legislation, as will be seen in Chapter 6 it is unlikely that any claim could be brought under the Human Rights Act (HRA), despite the inclusion of a protection against discrimination in article 14 of the European Convention on Human Rights (ECHR).[40]

Restriction without Conviction

So far we have thus encountered police powers which (a) operate without formal legal authority; (b) operate in breach of legal authority; and (c) operate in both cases in a way that is openly discriminatory on racial grounds.

---

[39] More recently still, the Home Affairs Committee has reported that 'In 1999, a black person was six times more likely to be stopped and searched under the Police and Criminal Evidence Act 1984, s 1; in 2006/07 it was seven times' (HAC, 2009b: para 6).

[40] *R (Gillan) v Metropolitan Police Commissioner* [2006] UKHL 12; pp 205–210 below.

A second major development so far as liberty is concerned is the introduction of anti-social behaviour orders (ASBOs) by the Crime and Disorder Act 1998, and dispersal orders by the Anti-social Behaviour Act 2003. These orders are controversial for a number of reasons, but not least because they impose restrictions on the liberty of individuals who have not been prosecuted of any offence, thereby violating one of the first principles of English law that people should be penalised for what they have done, not for what they may do (Goodhart, 1936). So far as ASBOs are concerned, an application may be made by the police, a local authority, or a housing trust to a local magistrates' court, where it is alleged that the person to whom the order is directed has acted in an anti-social manner.[41] This is defined to mean 'a manner that caused or was likely to cause harassment, alarm or distress to one or more persons', provided that the alleged victims of the anti-social behaviour are 'not of the same household as himself'.[42] It is not enough, however, that there should be a pattern of anti-social behaviour in the past, for the ASBO is not designed to punish but to prevent. So a second condition for the granting of an ASBO is that there is a threat of continuing anti-social behaviour from which third parties need to be protected.[43] If these conditions are met, the ASBO will prohibit the defendant from doing anything described in the order, which—depending on the conduct complained of—could be far-reaching and wide-ranging. Once made, the ASBO lasts for at least two years, and can only be discharged before the two years expire with the consent of both parties.[44] Any breach of the terms of an ASBO is a criminal offence, carrying a penalty of up to six months' imprisonment on summary conviction or five years on indictment.[45]

The Use and Abuse of ASBOs

Concerns about ASBOs were raised by the National Association of Probation Officers (NAPO), in its evidence to the House of Commons Home Affairs Committee in 2005. According to NAPO, the system was now being abused, with ASBOs being used for purposes for which they had not been intended, pointing out that they were being imposed in relation to conduct such as prostitution and begging which 'may be anti-social but not necessarily threatening', and which may constitute a nuisance that could be dealt with in other ways (NAPO, 2005). NAPO also noted the escalation in the number of ASBOs, from 104 in 1999 to 2,600 from November 2003

[41] Crime and Disorder Act 1998, s 1(1).
[42] Ibid, s 1 (1)(a).   [43] Ibid, s 1(1)(b).
[44] Ibid, s 1(9).   [45] Ibid, s 1(10).

to January 2005. Moreover, out of 322 ASBOs issued in 2001, 114 persons were jailed for breach, with the numbers rising to 212 jailed out of 403 issued in 2002. According to NAPO, '[t]hese figures would suggest that around 50% of those who are the subject of an ASBO eventually end up in jail' (ibid). This is a matter for particular concern because in 'many incidents, individuals are receiving a custodial sentence where the original offence was not itself imprisonable', with the result that the 'ASBO is clearly, therefore, moving offenders up tariff and resulting in the inappropriate use of custody' (ibid). The other concern expressed by NAPO was the apparent 'postcode lottery' in the issuing of ASBOs. Thus, it was pointed out that '[a]n individual is far more likely to be the subject of an ASBO in Greater Manchester than in Merseyside, with 155 persons the subject of an ASBO in Greater Manchester in the first six months of 2004 compared with just 27 in Merseyside. Moreover, 'the number of individuals subject to an ASBO in West Yorkshire during the same period was 128, compared with just 22 in South Yorkshire'. Similarly, 38 ASBOs were issued in Lancashire compared with just four in Leicestershire (ibid).

There is no question that some of these orders were issued against people who were doing some very unpleasant things on a regular basis. Some of the bizarre features of this jurisdiction were nevertheless identified by NAPO (2005) highlighting examples of the way in which ASBOs had been used, giving the following examples, among many:

- 'An 18-year-old youth was ... made the subject of an ASBO in [Manchester] with a condition not to congregate with three or more other youths. He was subsequently arrested for breach of his order when he was entering a local youth club on the grounds that there were more than three youths in the premises. This was a successful club with a good reputation providing a valuable service to young people locally, and on the particular evening the session scheduled for the youths was how to deal with anti-social behaviour.'

- '... in Manchester, the Council used its powers to obtain an ASBO to stop mobile soup vans operating in the city centre. These vans provide food and assistance regularly each evening to about 100 homeless people. The Council however argued that after the vans had left there was a mess all over the place and people had complained. Probation staff argued that the same could be said about every kebab shop, pub, chip shop and off-licence in the city ...'

- 'A drug addict faced jail if he was caught sleeping in the street or begging in "an earnest or humble way". Greater Manchester police obtained an ASBO against Peter Broadbent aged 36 after he pleaded guilty to rough sleeping. . . . He was found under the Mancunian Way surrounded by needles and now faces up to five years jail . . . Broadbent's ASBO prevents him from sleeping rough contrary to Section 4 of the Vagrancy Act 1824 and asking "earnestly or humbly" for money in a place to which the public have access.'

Other bizarre uses of this procedure include the case of Anthony Delaney, a 43-year-old unemployed chef who was jailed for breaching an ASBO that banned him from Gatwick airport. Mr Delaney—who was homeless and did not suffer from mental illness, did not have any problems with drink or drugs, and did not cause any trouble—lived on the site and only left to collect his Jobseeker's Allowance. According to his barrister, he stayed there because it was 'clean, dry and warm'.[46]

ASBOs, the Courts and Human Rights

Yet despite these concerns, ASBOs have been given the green light from both the Joint Committee on Human Rights (JCHR) and the courts. It is true that the Crime and Disorder Act 1998 was passed before the JCHR was established, so that it was not possible for that Committee to comment on the human rights implications of introducing ASBOs. This is perhaps just as well, given that the Committee was persuaded that the extension of the power to grant ASBOs in the Anti-social Behaviour Act 2003 'would be justifiable under ECHR Article 8(2) as a proportionate response to a pressing social need' (JCHR, 2003: paragraph 45). If the extension of the procedure could be presumed not to breach human rights commitments, it seems likely that in the view of the Committee the principal legislation (that is to say the 1998 Act) would be clean as well. So far as the courts are concerned, an opportunity to confront human rights issues arose in the *McCann* case which made it all the way to the House of Lords. ASBOs were issued in that case against two brothers who were alleged to have been engaged in anti-social and other behaviour in Manchester.[47] The effect of the orders—which had been issued in part on the basis of hearsay evidence—was to prevent them from entering a particular part of the city. The case had been through four different courts before reaching the House of Lords, where the issue related to the nature of the proceedings, that is to say whether they were to be regarded as civil or criminal, an important issue that would affect the admissibility of evidence and the standard of proof. All the lower courts were unanimous in concluding that

---

[46] *BBC News*, 19 February 2008.
[47] *R (McCann) v Manchester Crown Court* [2002] UKHL 39.

the procedure was civil rather than criminal and that hearsay evidence was admissible. In agreeing with this view, Lord Steyn laid bare his own position on anti-social behaviour, making it clear that his starting point was 'an initial scepticism of an outcome which would deprive communities of *their* fundamental rights'. He was thus in 'no doubt' that Parliament had 'intended to adopt the model of a civil remedy of an injunction, backed up by criminal penalties', when it enacted the 1998 Act.[48]

According to Lord Steyn, 'the view was taken that the proceedings for an anti-social behaviour order ... would not attract the rigour of the inflexible and sometimes absurdly technical hearsay rule which applies in criminal cases'.[49] It was thus held that the proceedings were civil, that they did not involve a criminal charge, and that there was no 'conviction or condemnation that the person is guilty of an offence'. No penalty is imposed, an ASBO cannot be entered on a defendant's record as a conviction, and it is 'not a recordable offence for the purpose of taking fingerprints'. As a result, it followed that hearsay evidence could be admitted, and although the 'weight of such evidence might be limited', nevertheless 'in its cumulative effect it could be cogent'. It also followed that 'the standard of proof ordinarily applicable in civil proceedings, namely the balance of probabilities, should apply'. Given the seriousness of matters involved, however, it was held that the magistrates must apply the more demanding criminal standard of proof when issuing ASBOs, in order *'to be sure* that the defendant has acted in an anti-social manner', and for this purpose it was accepted that 'hearsay evidence depending on its logical probativeness is quite capable of satisfying the requirements of section 1'.[50] In so holding, the House of Lords thus provided valuable ammunition for the House of Commons Home Affairs Committee's subsequent defence of the ASBO regime from a number of criticisms. Made by children's charities, think tanks, and civil liberties organisations, the main criticisms were: (a) ASBOs blurred the boundaries between civil and criminal law; (b) their use against young people 'runs the risk of net-widening, that is to say bringing more young people into contact with the criminal justice system'; (c) they have been used inappropriately, with several having included unrealistic conditions that have invited breach; (d) they are 'ineffective in reducing [anti-social behaviour], because they are negative and do not address young people's support needs'; and (e) the 'practice of enforcement by publicity, or "naming and shaming" is inappropriate and puts child safety at risk' (HAC, 2005). But like the JCHR and the House of Lords before it, the HAC was unmoved in what was a curious report.

[48] Ibid, para [18].   [49] Ibid.
[50] Ibid, para [37].

The Use and Abuse of Dispersal Orders

ASBOs are, however, only the half of it, with additional powers of restraint being introduced by the Anti-social Behaviour Act 2003, this time in the form of dispersal orders. Section 30(1) of the Act applies where a senior police officer is concerned that (a) 'members of the public have been intimidated, harassed, alarmed or distressed' by people in the police area, and (b) 'anti-social behaviour is a significant and persistent problem in the relevant locality'. In these circumstances (and with the consent of the local authority for the relevant area), uniformed police officers—as well as community support officers (CSOs)—may be given an authorisation to disperse groups of two or more people where the police officer or CSO in question has reasonable grounds for believing that 'the presence or behaviour' of a group of two or more people 'in any public place in the relevant locality' has resulted, 'or is likely to result', in any members of the public being intimidated, harassed, alarmed, or distressed.[51] Where this power of dispersal has been activated, the constable or the CSO may give a direction requiring the members of the group to (a) disperse (either immediately or within a specified time); (b) leave the locality in the case of those members of the group who do not live there; and (c) refrain from returning to the locality for up to 24 hours (in the case of those who do not live there).[52] Moreover, in the case of people who are believed to be under the age of 16 and not in the company of a parent or other responsible adult, a police officer or a CSO may 'remove' the child in question to his or her 'place of residence'.[53] Where this latter power is exercised, the local authority must be informed; it is a criminal offence to fail to comply with a dispersal order, with the possibility of a fine or imprisonment on conviction.[54] Unlike ASBOs, these dispersal orders are general powers which are not targeted at named individuals requiring them to behave or not to behave in a particular way; rather they authorise restraints on the freedom of unidentified groups of people to congregate in particular places.

A study by the Joseph Rowntree Trust on the way these dispersal powers are used reported Home Office estimates 'that between January 2004 and April 2006 over 1,000 areas were designated dispersal zones in England and Wales, as compared to six areas across Scotland'. It was also reported that there had been 'considerable local variation in the take-up and use of dispersal order powers' (Crawford and Lister, 2007), while even the most cursory glance at the use of the powers reveal that they (a) have sometimes

---

[51] Anti-social Behaviour Act 2003, s 30(3).
[52] Ibid, s 30(4).   [53] Ibid, s 30(6).
[54] Ibid, s 32.

been invoked for up to the full six months permitted by the Act, and sometimes for shorter periods of three months; (b) are used sometimes to operate for periods of 24 hours each day, and sometimes for shorter periods (such as between 12 noon and 4 am); and (c) are used in different ways in relation to children under 16, the power being used in one case where the child was unaccompanied after 11 pm and in others where the child was unaccompanied between 9 pm and 6 am. One particularly notorious case which ended up in the Court of Appeal relates to Richmond-upon-Thames,[55] where at the request of the police, the Council had made two dispersal orders, the first (for a period of five months or so) to deal with alcohol-fuelled anti-social behaviour as a result of thousands of people congregating at various points in the borough in the summer months. Problems arose when a 15-year-old boy thought he was being followed by a CSO in the dispersal zone one evening. On confronting the officer, the boy was told about the dispersal order, and also that the officer thought he had been acting suspiciously. Although no action was taken against him, the boy remained concerned that he could not now go out on his own after 9 pm, and 'could not even meet his friends or go to the cinema because he might be picked up by a policeman or a CSO, and he did not want the ignominy of being taken home by the police'. According to the Court of Appeal, however, the Act 'does not confer an arbitrary power to remove children who are not involved in, nor at risk from exposure to, actual or imminently anticipated anti-social behaviour'. Moreover, said the court, the Act 'does not confer a power to remove children simply because they are in a designated dispersal area at night'.[56]

Dispersal Orders, the Courts and Human Rights

According to the Court of Appeal in the *Richmond* case, there was also an additional requirement from administrative law that the power to remove had to be exercised reasonably, even when there was authority to use it. But despite this clarification, it remains uncertain how far the penny has dropped the length and breadth of English local authorities and police forces. Press releases are still being issued in which it is confidently stated that 'after 11pm [the police] are authorised to escort home any child they believe is under 16 and not with a responsible adult (Salford)', and that between the hours of 9 pm and 6 am, the police are empowered to 'remove any person 16 years or under who is not under the effective control of a parent or a responsible

---

[55] *R (W) v Metropolitan Police Commissioner* [2006] EWCA Civ 458.
[56] Ibid, para [35] (May LJ).

person aged 18 years or over, to the people's place of residence' (sic) (North Wales). But not only do the courts appear to have failed to prevent the existence of apparently de facto if not de jure curfews for the under 16s, they have also managed to extend the power to impose dispersal orders well beyond the anti-social behaviour for which they were intended, to include what only be described as restraints on freedom of expression and assembly. The decision in *R (Singh) v West Midlands Chief Constable*[57] is thus a potentially worrying harbinger of 'function creep' into an area where—as discussed in Chapter 4—it may be thought that the police already have adequate powers without the need to create a new one. In this case the police had already obtained a dispersal order for an area in the centre of Birmingham to deal with the anti-social behaviour of seasonal revellers. During the period when the order was in operation, a controversial play was staged in a theatre which was within the dispersal zone. The play was controversial in the sense that it was offensive to Sikhs, and led to vigorous demonstrations outside the theatre by a group of people who unsuccessfully tried to stop the play being performed. These demonstrations led in turn to a dispersal direction being made by the police, requiring those present to leave and not to return for 24 hours.

The claimant was one of those issued with such a direction which he refused to comply with and was arrested under the 2003 Act. In subsequent legal proceedings, the claimant challenged the legality of the direction on a number of grounds, but not least because it was being used for a purpose for which the original dispersal order had not been anticipated, and also because it was being used for a purpose that violated his Convention rights. Both arguments were given short shrift by the court, even if they were carefully considered. So far as the first is concerned, it was held simply that:

If public disorder is a continuing problem in a town centre or a part of one, it would be absurd if the police were to have to procure a separate authorisation to deal with each successive manifestation or source of disorder, perhaps giving rise to numerous authorisations with temporal overlaps. I find that to be unnecessary and undesirable. It is an important safeguard that there can be no authorisation at all unless the demanding requirements of section 30(1) are met. Once they are, there is no reason why an authorisation should not be used in relation to a previously unforeseen group, subject to the further important safeguards that a dispersal direction can only be given if section 30(3) is satisfied and its use is proportionate and otherwise in conformity with public law criteria.[58]

---

[57] [2005] EWHC 2840 (Admin).
[58] Ibid, para [33] (Maurice Kay LJ).

So far as the second argument is concerned, the court rejected the claim that the 2003 Act was not designed to apply to public protests on the ground that an express exemption was made in section 30 itself for peaceful picketing under the Trade Union and Labour Relations (Consolidation) Act 1992 and for processions under the Public Order Act 1986.[59] The express exclusion of these forms of conduct from the scheme of the Act provided a 'very clear indication' that Parliament did not intend to exclude protests which led to members of the public being intimidated, harassed, alarmed or distressed. If Parliament had intended to exclude protests, it would have made express provision, as in the case of processions.[60] There was no consideration of the question whether this was an appropriate or proportionate restraint on Convention rights.

New Police Powers of Arrest and Search

The days are long gone when the subject could be arrested without a warrant only for treason, felony, wounding, or breach of the peace. The power of arrest without a warrant was expanded dramatically by the Police and Criminal Evidence Act 1984, which extended the power of summary arrest to a long list of arrestable offences, but bizarrely also conferred a right of summary arrest for what were called non-arrestable offences.[61] Yet this was found by the Home Office under New Labour to be unacceptable because—apart from a long list of specified offences—an arrestable offence included all crimes which carried a penalty of five years in jail for a first offence, a provision which it was thought to be quite hard to apply in practice. According to the Home Secretary, there was 'a very odd situation', whereby 'certain people had to be facing a sentence of at least five years for the constable to be able to work out—through the police and criminal evidence code—whether they could engage in an arrest'.[62] So, because the already wide powers of arrest in the 1984 Act were difficult for the police to understand and remember, these powers have been extended so that there is now a power to arrest without a warrant for any offence, serious or trivial. Under the new law introduced by the Serious Organised Crime and Police Act 2005, there is thus no restriction on the nature of the offences for which the power can be used, the only requirement being that the exercise

---

[59] Anti-social Behaviour Act 2003, s 30(5).
[60] [2005] EWHC 2840 (Admin), para [24] (Maurice Kay LJ).
[61] Police and Criminal Evidence Act 1984, ss 24, 25.
[62] H C Debs, 7 December 2004, col 1050 (David Blunkett).

of the power is necessary for one of a number of reasons listed in the Act. But although the 2005 Act contains 'significant extensions to the powers of police officers to arrest people for criminal offences' (JCHR, 2005, para 1.59), concern was expressed by the JCHR that in the debates about the Bill, the Government had failed to offer Parliament 'an explanation of or justification for' measures which were said to 'significantly' shift 'the balance between [individual] rights and police powers', reducing in the process the protection for the former (ibid: paragraph 1.75).

The New Powers of Arrest

The extension of the powers of arrest in these ways gave rise to strong criticism that they would allow the police to arrest for the most trivial reasons. According to Dominic Grieve for the Conservatives, 'the powers will extend to everything—not only road traffic matters but, potentially, the amazing plethora of minor regulatory offences that usually lead to no action at all or to a summons through the post'.[63] In his view, 'the power is onerous, unnecessary and a step too far',[64] complaining also that it was likely that some police officers would make ready use of these powers, leading to a challenge to the principle of policing by consent. Some attempt to address these concerns was made in Standing Committee by the Minister for Crime Reduction, Policing and Community Safety (Hazel Blears) who argued that:

[r]ather than lowering the threshold for accountability, we are almost raising it; we are saying that the constable must think carefully, exercising his or her professional discretion, training and skills to reach a decision in the particular circumstances. They will not simply have the automatic power of arrest and be able to arrest someone without thinking about it; they will have to go through the necessity test because it will be looked at in court and perhaps by the Independent Police Complaints Commission, which will have judicial oversight. Having to go through that process places quite a rigorous burden on the constable, given that he or she does not have to go through it at the moment.[65]

This, of course, is nonsense, which contrives to contradict the reasons given by the minister's boss when he introduced the legislation at Second Reading. It appears to suggest that the lot of the police officer will be made more rather than less difficult, on the ground that complex questions of judgment are to replace or complement knowledge on the part of the officer. Whether or not this is the case will depend to a very large extent on whether there is in fact real scope for independent judgment,

---

[63] Official Report, Standing Committee D, 18 January 2005, col 228.
[64] Ibid.   [65] Ibid, col 239.

or whether on the contrary that burden is in fact constrained by guidance that an arrest will almost always be necessary.

Questions were raised in Standing Committee about whether the police would not be able to arrest in cases involving serious crimes, if the necessity of the arrest is the crucial factor in determining whether there is power to make an arrest. This gives rise to the possibility that arrest may not be possible in a murder case, if the accused could be summonsed to appear and otherwise cooperates with the police. We are now in the realms of fantasy, simply because the Act makes clear what kind of conduct would justify an arrest on the ground that it was necessary, giving rise to the likelihood that anything that was an arrestable offence before the law was changed will continue to provide a basis for arrest on the ground of necessity in the future. Thus, under the Act an arrest will be necessary where it is made to (a) 'enable the name [or address] of the person in question to be ascertained', assuming it is unknown to the police officer; (b) prevent injury to a possible witness; (c) allow the prompt and effective investigation of the offence or of the conduct of the person in question; or (d) prevent the suspect from absconding. The third of these has been widely construed in the Code of Practice issued to accompany the new legislation, where an arrest to allow prompt and effective investigation has been defined to include the situation where there are reasonable grounds to believe that the suspect has made false statements; has made statements which cannot readily be verified; has presented false evidence; may steal or destroy evidence; may make contact with co-suspects or conspirators; may intimidate or threaten or make contact with witnesses; or where it is necessary to obtain evidence by questioning. Moreover, in the case of an indictable offence an arrest will be necessary for the prompt investigation of the offence if there is a need to (a) enter and search any premises occupied or controlled by a person; (b) search the suspect; prevent the suspect contacting others; or take finger-prints, footwear impressions, samples, or photographs of the suspect; and (c) ensure compliance with statutory drug testing requirements.[66]

The Power of Arrest in Practice

Despite the minister's claims about the police having to think carefully before making an arrest, it is clear that the purpose of these measures was to tilt the balance in the direction of the police at the expense of the citizen. This was revealed by the minister's response to a line of questioning in Standing Committee when she said that the changes would enable the police 'to do their job more effectively' and that 'the purpose of the provisions' was

---

[66] Home Office, Police and Criminal Evidence Act, Code of Practice G (2005), para 2.9.

'to ensure that the police have sufficient powers'.[67] This alone confirms that the focus on necessity would not impair effectiveness (but indeed would enhance it), while the focus on 'the victim and the conduct of the offence' suggests that the serious nature of the offence is never likely to be an irrelevant factor in the decision to make an arrest. The real concern with these changes is thus not that they will affect or undermine the capacity to arrest for what were previously arrestable offences, but that they will enhance the capacity to arrest 'those who have committed minor offences or who are alleged to have done so—this will be an allegation, not a proven fact—will end up being arrested unnecessarily under [the government's] proposals'.[68] Nor is there any question that this further expansion of police powers is perfectly consistent with the requirements of the ECHR, with the right to liberty is article 5 of the Convention being qualified (by article 5(1)(c)) to allow for 'the lawful arrest or detention of a person effected for the purpose of bringing him before the competent legal authority on reasonable suspicion of having committed an offence ...' It is a striking feature of this provision that it makes no reference to a warrant: reasonable suspicion would seem to be enough as a basis for an arrest, whatever the nature of the offence. To this extent the 2005 amendments may be said to be a dilution of standards to meet the human rights minimum, rather than a raising of standards to meet the minimum, as might normally be expected.

The fragile nature of necessity as a safeguard against the misuse of the power of summary arrest was seen in the high profile arrest of Tory MP and Shadow Cabinet member Damien Green in November 2008, in the course of an investigation into leaks from the Home Office, which were then used by Mr Green to embarrass the government. As discussed more fully in Chapter 5 below, Mr Green was arrested on suspicion of 'conspiring to commit misconduct in a public office' and 'aiding and abetting, counselling or procuring misconduct in a public office',[69] and was detained and questioned by the police for nine hours before being released. This affair proved to be hugely controversial, not least because it led to a search of Mr Green's parliamentary office (as well as his home and his constituency office). So far as the arrest is concerned, however, it has not yet been satisfactorily explained why it was necessary for the purposes of the police inquiry, even if embarrassing leaks were taking place, nor why it was appropriate to arrest an MP, under a common law offence the use of which was calculated to undermine the reforms to the official secrets legislation made in 1989. Nevertheless,

---

[67] Official Report, Standing Committee D, 18 January 2005, col 247.
[68] Ibid, col 246 (Dominic Grieve).
[69] BBC News, 8 December 2008.

a review into the arrest by the Chief Constable of the British Transport Police is said to have found the arrest to have been 'lawful',[70] though the report was not published. This is not to suggest that we should be concerned that an MP has been arrested, or that MPs should have some kind of immunity from the consequences of criminal liability. But it is to suggest that we should question the minister's claim that the extended powers of arrest without a warrant introduced in 2005 'impose a rigorous burden on the constable'.[71] If high profile Tory MPs can be arrested in this way without a warrant (when there is no evidence to suggest that they would not voluntarily assist the police with their inquiries in circumstances where it is inconceivable that the MP in question would ever be charged), just how likely is it that any of the rest of us will be able to challenge the necessity of police conduct?

The New Powers of Search

One of the consequences of extending the power of arrest is that it also automatically extends the circumstances in which other police powers may be used, such as the power of entry under PACE, section 17; the power to search a suspect or his or her property under PACE, section 32; and the power to detain for the purposes of questioning under PACE, section 41. This is because these powers of the police may be exercised at the point of a lawful arrest without the need for any additional formality, though in the case of some of these powers the 2005 Act has introduced the additional requirement that the offence for which the individual has been arrested is an indictable offence, thereby apparently contradicting the government's need for simplicity. But apart from these consequential erosions of the right to privacy, a number of formal steps were also taken, particularly in relation to search warrants, where here too 'modernisation' became a synonym for extension and the dilution of safeguards. In the case of search warrants, the law was very clear in the sense that in the event of a serious arrestable offence, the police could make an application to a justice of the peace, who if satisfied that a warrant should be issued would grant it in respect of premises specified in the warrant, with the warrant to authorise only one entry and to be executed within one month of being issued.[72] These procedures served a number of useful purposes, not the least being that they stopped people from being troubled by the police engaged in fishing expeditions of all their properties, ensured that they would not be constantly harassed by officers waiving

[70] *BBC News*, 16 December 2008.
[71] Official Report, Standing Committee D, 18 January 2005, col 239.
[72] Police and Criminal Evidence Act 1984, ss 8–16.

a warrant, and ensured that any invasion of privacy would take place within a reasonable time of the warrant being issued. Under the 2005 Act, however, each of these principles (specified premises, no multiple entry, and tight time limits) has been dispensed with.[73]

The new law relating to search warrants was challenged in Parliament on a number of grounds, not least for enabling warrants to be issued for indictable offences rather than serious arrestable offences as was previously the case: not all indictable offences are grave enough to be serious arrestable offences (JCHR, 2005). But it is not only the extension of the power to issue search warrants that is a concern. So too is the extended power which a search will confer in what is now a wider range of circumstances, with two kinds of warrants now being possible: these are 'specific premises' warrants (which may specify more than one set of premises) and (more controversially) 'all premises warrants'. In its valuable critique of these provisions, the Joint Committee on Human Rights, highlighted in particular the 'power to issue a warrant covering all premises occupied or controlled by a person [which] raises significant human rights concerns' (ibid: paragraph 1.89):

- 'the premises to be entered and searched need not be specified in the warrant, making it difficult for an occupier of premises to know whether police are acting lawfully when they seek entry, and severely limiting the quality of judicial oversight of the process';
- 'the power would apply to all kinds of premises, including domestic dwellings, intimately affecting people's privacy';
- 'as the warrant could cover premises controlled by the named person, and not only those occupied by him or her, other people might be living in the premises, who could be unconnected with the named person (except by virtue of having taken a lease of the premises, or a licence to occupy them …)'.

Concern was also expressed that 'a single application to a justice of the peace could produce authorisation to search a large number of premises on an unlimited number of occasions without a subsequent judicial assessment of the continuing need for or proportionality of individual entries and searches'. It was pointed out further that the entries to and searches of the same or multiple premises could continue for up to three months, which was three times as long as the law then in force authorised an entry and search of single premises on a single occasion (ibid: paragraph 1.90). In a stinging critique, the provisions were seen to authorise the issuing of general

---

[73] Serious Organised Crime and Police Act 2005, ss 113, 114.

warrants 'of a kind that has been anathema to the common law for centuries on account of the very wide discretion it confers on public officials, and the lack of effective prior judicial control over the decision to enter (if need be, by force) private premises including dwellings' (ibid: paragraph 1.91).

The Magistrate as a Safeguard?

Far reaching though these initiatives are, the government appears to have had second thoughts about yet another proposal that appeared in the consultation paper *Modernising Police Powers* which preceded the 2005 amendments. This was the suggestion that it would be possible 'to introduce scope for applications for warrants to be dealt with by telephone or using other electronic links such as email'. Moreover, '[i]t might also be feasible for warrant documents to be transmitted between the authoriser and the applicant by fax' (Home Office, 2004: paragraph 3.11). Responses to the White Paper revealed, however, that 'some groups were concerned that this could reduce the process of applying to a court to an administrative exercise', while others 'felt that the appearance in person of the applicant before a magistrate was an important and vital safeguard in order to be able to respond in person to any queries that may arise in considering the application' (Home Office, 2005: 6). Even the police were said to have 'recognised the need to retain the judicial oversight of warrants both in terms of applying for warrants and returning the endorsed warrant when it expires' (ibid). Despite being saved by the police from itself, the government's response to these proposals nevertheless provokes questions about whether the search warrant procedure is anything more than the administrative formality that the Home Office appeared unwittingly to reveal. This is an issue about which there is little research and little insight in terms of how the police choose which justice of the peace to approach for a warrant; the procedure which is adopted before warrants are granted; and the frequency with which requests for a warrant are refused, all of which go to the nature of the independent scrutiny which justices of the peace are supposed to bring to this role. There are, however, some concerns recently expressed from the Bench about 'wholly unacceptable' procedures adopted in some cases where warrants have been granted, with judges complaining about the 'slipshod completion of application forms'.[74]

One such case was the case of Harry Redknapp, then the manager of Portsmouth Football Club, caught up in a police investigation about the making of disguised payments to a player, using an agent to receive these payments offshore. On 11 July 2007, a warrant was granted by an Old Bailey judge

---

[74] *Redknapp v City of London Police* [2008] EWHC (Admin) 1177, para [13].

to search the business premises of a number of people in connection with the inquiry; and on the back of this warrant an application was made to a magistrate four months later for a warrant to search Mr Redknapp's home, in the exclusive Sandbanks area of Poole, Dorset. As an insight into current practice, the *Redknapp* case reveals that the warrant was 'so far ranging as to justify the seizure of any document or means of communication'; that it failed to specify which of the grounds under section 8(3) of PACE it was being sought; and that the same warrant included both 'specific premises' and 'all premises'. Yet although emphasising that the 'obtaining of a search warrant is never to be treated lightly', in this case the Administrative Court accepted that 'the police were justified in drawing the description of the material widely in the circumstances of the case', and that although Parliament distinguished 'descriptively' between 'specific premises' and 'all premises' warrants, there was no indication in the 2005 amendments that one warrant could not include both kinds of authorisation. The Court did, however, draw the line at the failure to identify on which of the grounds in PACE the warrant was being sought, being unprepared to infer that the magistrate must have been told: 'it is wholly unsatisfactory, where the validity of such a warrant is in issue, to be asked to rely on anything other then the application itself, and if necessary, a proper note or record of any further information given orally to the magistrate'.[75] The Court did not, however, uphold a complaint that the 'search took place in the presence of journalists from *The Sun* newspaper', there being no evidence that the 'police had in some way procured the presence of the journalist', who was coincidentally passing by at 6.06 am as the raid took place in one of the most exclusive parts of the country. Nor did the Court cavil at the fact that the search was conducted at such an hour, despite the statutory requirement that search warrants be executed at a 'reasonable hour'.

Questions of Accountability

The concern of this chapter so far has been principally with the formal extension of police powers through legislation. But we have also seen how the informal powers of the police have been extended (in the context of stop and account) to engage in activity for which there is no express legal authority, even if there are now in place (diluted) procedures to regulate the exercise of this power. There are, however, other ways by which the considerable informal powers of the police can be stretched or extended, this time not by the gradual emergence or recognition of a new administrative practice, but by

[75] Ibid, para [16].

judicial indulgence, in the sense of a willingness on the part of the courts to tolerate unlawful conduct on the part of the police. Such tolerance can occur in one of a number of ways, but first by admitting evidence that has been illegally obtained, that is to say obtained in circumstances which exceed the formal powers of the police. The common law has typically set its face against any suggestion that the courts should exclude evidence obtained as a result of illegal police conduct, and thereby act as one of the first lines of the citizen's defence against police conduct violating the rights of the individual. In declining such a role, Lord Diplock was heard to say in one famous case that the judge 'has no discretion to refuse to admit relevant admissible evidence on the ground that it was obtained by improper or unfair means', adding that 'the court is not concerned with how [the evidence] was obtained'.[76] Since 1984 the position in England and Wales has changed slightly to the extent that the courts have a statutory power to exclude evidence if

it appears to the court that, having regard to all the circumstances, including the circumstances in which the evidence was obtained, the admission of the evidence would have such an adverse effect on the fairness of the proceedings that the court ought not to admit it.[77]

The courts have made clear, however, that this is not to be used as a vehicle to regulate the unlawful conduct of the police, it being pointed out in one leading case that illegality on the part of the police is not the same as unfairness to the accused.[78]

Admissibility of Evidence and Convention Rights

The position has not been affected by the HRA, partly because this is an issue on which the European Court of Human Rights has abdicated all responsibility to the national courts.[79] The first indication that little had changed is provided by the 'horrendous' *Longley* case in which the appellant had been convicted of the burglary and rape of an elderly woman.[80] The accused was charged initially only with the burglary as a result of which a non-intimate sample was taken for DNA analysis. Longley was, however, acquitted on the burglary charge and as the law stood at the time, it was expressly provided that the DNA sample should be destroyed, and should not be used for the purposes of any investigation. In an apparent breach of that

---

[76] *R v Sang* [1980] AC 402.
[77] Police and Criminal Evidence Act 1984, s 78, on which see Choo and Nash, 1999.
[78] *R v Chalkley* [1998] QB 848.
[79] *Teixeira de Castro v Portugal* (1998) 28 EHRR 101.
[80] *Attorney General's Reference (No 3 of 1999)* [2000] UKHL 63.

requirement, the police in this case nevertheless used the sample to compare it with samples taken from the rape victim, and a positive match was found. At this stage the accused was re-arrested and a fresh sample was taken to be used as evidence in the prosecution, in the course of which the key question was whether the evidence obtained during the investigation was admissible. The lower courts (including the Court of Appeal) held that it was not and the accused was acquitted, a conclusion which clearly appalled the House of Lords, prepared to perform some fairly sophisticated forensic gymnastics to hold the evidence admissible. Thus it had been argued that the conduct of the police in using the first sample constituted a breach of article 8 of the ECHR, which could be justified only if it was in accordance with law and done for one of a number of reasons permitted by article 8(2). As counsel logically argued, how could it 'ever be "in accordance with the law" to admit in evidence the results of a prohibited investigation'?[81] According to Lord Steyn, however, the 'critical point' for this purpose was that 'admissibility is governed by judicial discretion under section 78'. The requirement that the interference be in accordance with law thus met, there was no difficulty with the rest, it being 'plainly necessary in a democratic society to ensure the investigation and prosecution of serious crime'.[82]

In a desire to do justice, the House of Lords may have done so at the expense of legality, for the approach was far from convincing: it was the admissibility of illegally obtained evidence, not the violation of rights that was in accordance with law: it does not follow from an indulgence to evidence secured in breach of a clear statutory prohibition that the evidence was obtained lawfully. The point appears, however, to be unimportant, for as Lord Steyn pointed out, there is 'no principle of Convention law that unlawfully obtained evidence is not admissible',[83] a line of authority to which the British courts had contributed. Shortly before the HRA was passed, the House of Lords had rejected a claim that evidence obtained in breach of what were then unincorporated Convention rights was inadmissible.[84] This is a view shared by the Strasbourg court in the same case,[85] which was concerned with the placing of a bugging device on the outside of the Sheffield home of a suspected heroin dealer. The evidence recorded on the device was then used in proceedings against a number of people for drugs related offences. It was claimed, however, that the placing of the device was unlawful: not only was it a trespass, but the placing of the device involved the commission of an offence (criminal damage). Moreover, the use of such instruments was wholly

---

[81] Ibid, p 119.   [82] Ibid.
[83] Ibid.   [84] *R v Khan* [1997] AC 558.
[85] *Khan v United Kingdom* (2001) 31 EHRR 1016.

unregulated by statute at the time (though not now), giving rise to claims that the police conduct also violated the Convention rights of the accused (the right to private life as provided in article 8(1) of the ECHR), in circumstances where the violation had not been prescribed by law, quite apart from any question of its being justified on one of the grounds provided for in article 8(2). Despite hearing an argument that 'it is contrary to the rule of law to permit a criminal conviction to be based solely on evidence obtained by illegal acts of law-enforcement agents', the European Court of Human Rights held that the Convention right to a fair trial was not breached by the admission of evidence obtained in breach of the Convention right to privacy.

Violating Convention Rights with Impunity

A second way in which the informal powers of the police have been extended by judicial indulgence is by denying citizens remedies when their rights are violated. In the absence of any exclusion of evidence, the principal remedy available to the victim of police misconduct is damages. There are, of course, many cases in the law reports where individuals have successfully sued the police for searching their property without a warrant, or for arresting them without lawful authority. In recent years, however, we see a desire on the part of the courts to reduce the amount of damages recoverable, and in other cases to deny that damages are recoverable at all. A good example of the latter is the case from Northern Ireland decided by the House of Lords in 2003, in which the applicant had been arrested under the Prevention of Terrorism Act 1989 following the murder of a police officer.[86] Accused of withholding information, James Cullen was held by the police for six days, charged and convicted after pleading guilty, before being sentenced to 160 days' community service. During his period in custody, Cullen asked to see a lawyer, but this was denied on four occasions, the applicant being permitted only one unsupervised and two supervised consultations with his solicitor. Although the police were entitled—under the Prevention of Terrorism Act 1989—to deny access by a suspect to a solicitor provided certain statutory criteria were met, in this case the police conduct was challenged on two grounds: first, the decisions to deny access were made before Cullen had even made a request; and second, no reasons were given for denying access. In an action by the applicant after his conviction, the question for the House of Lords was whether the denial of a right of access to a solicitor by someone in police custody gives rise to a claim in damages for breach of statutory duty, a crucially important question with implications

---

[86] *R (Cullen) v RUC Chief Constable* [2003] UKHL 39.

extending well beyond the detention of suspects under the Prevention of Terrorism Act 1989, to include also the detention of suspects under PACE and other legislation.

The court split 3:2 to deny liability, though the majority were fully aware of the importance of the issues at stake. Opening his speech, Lord Millett expressly recognised that:

Access to legal advice and the independence and integrity of the legal profession are cornerstones of a free society under the rule of law. They are guarantees against the practice of holding undesirables incommunicado, which is a hallmark of a totalitarian regime.[87]

Later in the same speech, Lord Millett was heard to say that:

The right of access to a solicitor affords a vital protection for persons in custody, but I do not think that such persons constitute a limited class of the public in the sense in which that expression is used in the present context. It is a quasi-constitutional right of fundamental importance in a free society—indeed its existence may be said to be one of the tests of a free society—and like *habeas corpus* and the right to a fair trial it is available to everyone. It is for the benefit of the public at large. We can all of us, the innocent as well as the guilty, sleep more securely in our beds for the knowledge that we cannot be detained at any moment at the hands of the state and denied access to a lawyer.[88]

But not vital enough a protection, it seems. According to the majority, there was no remedy in damages in cases such as this, partly because—in the words of Lord Hutton—the applicant 'suffer[ed] no personal injury, injury to property or economic loss' (with there being no evidence of him having suffered any harm), while 'judicial review would have afforded an effective and speedy remedy'.[89] These reasons drew a very testy response from Lords Bingham and Steyn in the minority who complained that 'there are plainly formidable practical problems in a detainee applying for judicial review when he has been denied access to a solicitor'. They added with unchallengeable logic that 'in any event, it is not easy to know whether one has an arguable case for judicial review unless reasons have been given'.[90]

Challenging the Coroner . . .

The charge against the courts is not just that they are failing properly to hold the police to account, but that they have stood in the way of others also well placed to do so. A good example of this relates to the role of coroners' courts

---

[87] Ibid, para [50]. [88] Ibid, para [67].
[89] Ibid, para [42]. [90] Ibid, para [20].

in the context of the use by the police of lethal force. The de Menezes case referred to above is easy to discount or to explain away as being concerned with terrorism in the context of a very grave terrorist threat to the people of London. Notwithstanding these threats, at a subsequent inquest the jury in that case returned an open verdict, having been denied the opportunity by the coroner to return a verdict of unlawful killing.[91] More to the point for present purposes, however, is that the de Menezes case is not an isolated example, with other notable cases involving the use of lethal force by the Metropolitan Police in recent years including the tragic cases of Harry Stanley in 1999 and Mark Saunders in 2008.[92] Harry Stanley was shot by two members of the Metropolitan Police's Firearms Unit SO 19 outside a pub in East London, where he had stopped off to buy some lemonade. He had been to his brother's home to collect a table leg, which his brother had repaired and which was tightly wrapped in a blue plastic bag. As he left the pub, a member of the public phoned 999 to report the presence of a man with an Irish accent carrying a sawn-off shot gun, mistaking Mr Stanley's Scottish accent for an Irish one. Mr Stanley was dead within 11 minutes of that phone call being made, having been challenged by two armed officers, who 'because of their perception of his reaction' each discharged their firearms. One of the bullets entered above Mr Stanley's left ear and killed him. As was pointed out by Mr Justice Leveson in one of the two High Court cases to which this incident gave rise, Mr Stanley:

was lawfully going about his business walking home having collected a coffee table leg which had been repaired. He appears to have been slightly the worse for wear having consumed an amount of alcohol that afternoon. Whether that caused him to react to the police challenge in the way that he did does not matter: he was entitled to be where he was and was doing absolutely nothing wrong.[93]

Under the Coroners Act 1988, where a violent or unnatural death takes place, the coroner must hold an inquest as soon as practicable, and that inquest must take place with a jury where there is reason to suspect that the death occurred as a result of an injury caused by a police officer in the purported execution of his duty. An inquest was duly held and it too recorded an open verdict, from which Mr Stanley's widow sought judicial review on the ground that the Coroner had withheld from the jury the option of holding that her husband had been unlawfully killed. This ruling by the Coroner was said to contravene

---

[91] *BBC News*, 12 December 2008.

[92] See *R (Stanley) v Inner North London Coroner* [2003] EWHC 1180 (Admin); *R (Sharman) v Inner North London Coroner* [2005] EWHC 857 (Admin); and *R (Saunders) v ACPO* [2008] EWHC 2372 (Admin).

[93] *R (Sharman) v Inner North London Coroner*, above, para [2].

Convention rights and in particular the right to life in article 2 of the ECHR. Article 2 imposes an obligation on States 'to procure an effective and official investigation' where 'fatal force' has been used 'by agents of the State'. For these purposes 'a coroner's inquest shall or may be the appropriate forum for complying with the State's obligation to procure an effective and official investigation'.[94] According to Lord Chief Justice Woolf in an earlier case, the purpose of the inquest in the context of article 2 is to 'minimise the risk of future like deaths; to give the beginnings of justice to the bereaved; [and] to assuage the anxieties of the public'.[95] Mr Stanley's widow raised a number of concerns about the conduct of the proceedings by the Coroner, and there was little resistance to his decision being quashed. In the first place, he improperly allowed evidence to be admitted of Mr Stanley's previous convictions, said to be irrelevant because they were not known to the police officers at the time they discharged their firearms. Secondly, the Coroner improperly admitted evidence that the CPS did not intend to bring charges against the officers. According to Mr Justice Silber, 'the jury was bound to have been greatly influenced' by this information.[96] Thirdly, the Coroner had failed to give reasons as to why certain verdicts were being withheld from the jury;[97] while finally, concern was expressed about the Coroner's failure to call expert firearms witnesses, apart from one Inspector Glover who was a commanding officer of the two police officers who shot Mr Stanley:

Two of the fundamental issues raised at the inquest related to, first, whether Mr Stanley was facing or turned away from the officers and, second, whether Mr Stanley was holding the chair leg in such a manner that it could have looked as if he was about to fire a shotgun at the officers. Another crucial issue was to consider how the officers conducted the operation and whether the actual shooting was justified.[98]

... Challenging the Jury

According to Mr Justice Silber, two of the experts the Coroner could have called but failed to do so dealt with the latter issue in their written reports, with one concluding that the actions of the officers 'fell far below those that one would expect from well-trained and properly commanded police officers', while the other thought that 'the actions of the officers

---

[94] R (Stanley) v Inner North London Coroner, above, para [13].
[95] R (Amin) v Home Secretary [2002] 3 WLR 505, para [62].
[96] Ibid, para [30].   [97] Ibid, para [38].
[98] Ibid, para [44].

were "negligent", but he stated that the term grossly negligent "should be considered by legally trained professionals due to its significance in the law".[99] As Mr Justice Silber also pointed out, the evidence of these witnesses would have had the virtue of being 'independent of the police force' unlike the evidence the Coroner actually called.[100] A second inquest over two years later returned a verdict of unlawful killing, though on this occasion this verdict was successfully challenged by the police officer who fired the fatal shot on the ground that the verdict of unlawful killing should never have been left to the jury to consider in the first place.[101] According to Mr Justice Leveson who heard this application by the police officer, at the heart of the case was section 3 of the Criminal Law Act 1977 which allows for the use of reasonable force in self defence. Here Mr Justice Leveson was not persuaded by the argument for Mrs Stanley that:

a reasonable jury could conclude that the officers' account was a carefully fabricated justification for the use of deadly force and that "to suggest that there is some other (unexpressed and unexplained) justification for the use of force is fanciful and calculated to distract the jury from the central thrust of the evidence they have heard".[102]

He also pointed out that:

although the forensic evidence may serve to undermine the precise description which the officers gave of what happened, that evidence says nothing about the configuration of Mr Stanley and the officers to allow the inference to be drawn that the officers could not, however mistakenly, have honestly believed that they were under imminent threat of attack.[103]

One of the difficulties with the unlawful killing verdict was the ruling that for the purposes of section 3 of the Criminal Law Act 1977, 'an honest belief of imminent danger such that it was necessary to use force does not have to be reasonable; the test is subjective not objective'. This was given much more prominence in the judgment of Mr Justice Leveson than it had been in the judgment of Mr Justice Silber, while the provisions of article 2 of the ECHR were given correspondingly much less prominence by the former than the latter. It is true that Mr Justice Leveson referred to the House of Lords decision in *R v Home Secretary, ex parte Middleton*, where Lord Bingham said that:

It seems safe to infer that the state's procedural obligation to investigate is unlikely to be met if it is plausibly alleged that agents of the state have used lethal force without justification, if an effectively unchallengeable decision has been taken not

---

[99] Ibid, para [45].   [100] Ibid.

[101] *R (Sharman) v Inner North London Coroner*, above.

[102] Ibid, para [33].   [103] Ibid, para [38].

to prosecute and if the fact-finding body cannot express its conclusion on whether unjustifiable force has been used or not, so as to prompt reconsideration of the decision not to prosecute.[104]

In the light of the foregoing, it is perhaps easy to understand why the Stanley family were disappointed by the Leveson judgment, especially in the light of the broader purpose of the inquest which seemed to move Mr Justice Silber two years earlier. Having battled for the inquest jury to consider the full range of verdicts and having secured a verdict of unlawful killing, they were to be denied by the quashing of the latter verdict, basically taking them back to where they started in a deadly game of snakes and ladders. What is particularly important about the Leveson judgment, however, is the example it sets of the courts protecting the police from the most vivid accountability of all, namely accountability to the citizens on behalf of whom they act.

Conclusion

The ineffectiveness of constitutional principle and Convention rights in this area is particularly disappointing. Indeed the unwillingness of both the Strasbourg court and the House of Lords to ensure such rights are properly respected is a matter of even greater concern in view of the growing centralisation of the police and with it the continuing absence of any meaningful form of political accountability. So far as constitutional principle is concerned:

- the police have acquired wide powers of stop and account without any formal legal authority, powers with a fragile legal base, and receding safeguards as to their use;
- the police have extensive statutory powers of stop and search which it is claimed are used in a racially discriminatory way and in breach of the requirements designed to trigger their use;
- the police and others have the right to apply for ASBOs to restrain the liberty of individuals, not because they have committed an offence but because they may behave in an anti-social way;
- the police and others have the right to apply for an order authorising the dispersal of groups of people, again not because they have committed an offence;

---

[104] [2004] 2 AC 182.

- the police have acquired greater powers of arrest without a warrant, powers which ostensibly are constrained by a requirement that the arrest must be 'necessary', a requirement which in turn is widely defined;
- the extended powers of arrest expand the circumstances in which the police may violate other rights, with arrest in some cases activating police powers of entry, search, and seizure of private property;
- the police have acquired new powers of search of premises, with search warrants to authorise the multiple entry of premises and to be active for an extended period of time; and for 'general warrants' to be issued; and
- although the police have acquired and have been given more powers, there is evidence that police officers still act illegally in their treatment of suspects, holding people without lawful authority and denying access to lawyers.

It is not suggested that the courts are excluded from or that they are wholly inactive in this field, with damages being recoverable on traditional grounds where there has been an unauthorised arrest, an unauthorised search, or a use of excessive force.[105] As already indicated, however, even here there is evidence of the courts retreating, both in terms of the quantum of damages that may be recovered by those whose common law rights have been violated,[106] and in terms of the reluctance to extend common law principles by developing new areas of liability where there have been alleged failures of police practice.[107] But it is in the area of Convention and statutory rights that the inactivity of the courts is perhaps most keenly felt, raising questions about the point of having such rights if they are as fragile as they appear to be in *Longley* and *Cullen*. It is true that in both of these cases, the police were investigating brutal offences committed by people for whom no right-thinking person will have any sympathy (though there is absolutely no reason to believe that Cullen was in any way involved in the principal offence in that case). But the principles established in these cases apply to everyone, the deserving as well as the undeserving suspect. In any event, what is at stake here is a wider principle identified by the US Supreme Court in *Mapp v Ohio*,[108] namely that 'Nothing can destroy a government more quickly than its failure to observe its own laws'.[109] It is also true that there is

---

[105] But see *Brooks v Metropolitan Police Commissioner* [2005] UKHL 24, and *Van Colle v Chief Constable of Hertfordshire Police* [2008] UKHL 50.

[106] *Thompson v Metropolitan Police Commissioner* [1998] QB 498.

[107] *Brooks v Metropolitan Police Commissioner* [2005] UKHL 24; *Van Colle v Chief Constable of Hertfordshire Police* [2008] UKHL 50.

[108] 367 US 643 (1961).

[109] Ibid, p 659 (Mr Justice Clark).

a countervailing rule of law argument, namely that people should be secure in their homes and on the street, and should be protected from crime, while the victims of crime are entitled to see the perpetrators of the crimes against them being pursued and prosecuted under the law. The last three words are, however, the point: people should be pursued and prosecuted under the law. If the courts are benignly to tolerate police malpractice or to be indulgent about a breach of the law by police officers, how do we stop the police from taking shortcuts in all cases? Sometimes the courts will pounce—as in *Osman* above;[110] but the judicial response is sufficiently unpredictable as to make the cavalier disregard of suspects' rights a lottery, which for the police is a lottery worth playing with at the very least a reasonable prospect of success.

[110] See pp 24–25.

CHAPTER 3

Surveillance and the Right to Privacy

Introduction

READERS familiar with Orwell's *Nineteen Eighty-Four* will recall the opening pages in which Winston Smith—the central character— returns home to Victory Mansions one lunch time, furtively to begin work on his diary. As he opened the door to his dingy flat, we are introduced to a world of surveillance in London, now the capital city of Airstrip One, the third biggest province of Oceania. We encounter a world in which every sound made by party members is overheard and every movement scrutinised, a world of telescreens pumping out messages while also watching people in their homes, telescreens being a cross between a single channel flat screen television (which can never be turned off) and a personalised CCTV camera. We also encounter a world of police helicopter patrols 'snooping into people's windows', of a practice 'not even secret' whereby 'all letters were opened in transit' (with few people now writing letters), of public places (such as Victory Square—known to us as Trafalgar Square—in central London) being 'full of telescreens', of patrols at railway stations to check on the movements of people and examine their papers (it being necessary to have one's passport endorsed for journeys of more than 100 kilometres), of people being followed and of microphones hidden in urban and rural areas to keep tabs on the populace. It is also a world of spies, informers, and agents provocateur, who were ultimately to entrap Winston Smith and his lover Julia, guilty not only of an unauthorised liaison but also of seditious tendencies in favour of the 'Brotherhood' and the mythical 'Goldstein'. In other words, we are introduced to a world of the Regulation of Investigatory Powers Act 2000 (RIPA): random surveillance, 'directed surveillance', 'intrusive surveillance', 'covert human intelligence sources', as well as the interception of communications. But paradoxically in this world of Big Brother, Newspeak, and Thought Crime, it was also a world of personal privacy, albeit only in the sense that citizens were protected from having their personal details revealed to each other. Thus, 'except by direct enquiry it was never possible to discover where anyone lived', there being 'no directories of any kind'. As human rights lawyers might say, horizontal but (definitely) not vertical protection of privacy.

Today, this is not the condition of London, or any other part of Airstrip One (a propitious appellation, though for different reasons). But there are many who are concerned (party and non-party members alike) that Great Britain is sleepwalking into a surveillance society, a fear easy to understand (HL, 2009). CCTV cameras mean that we are under constant surveillance, the use of bugging devices and informers is not confined to the police looking for terrorists or serious criminals, and telephone tapping and email interceptions grow at an alarming rate. The DNA database includes details of the innocent along with the guilty, the National Identity Register is about to record an extraordinary amount of personal information about British citizens, while only a fool would believe that ID cards will not become eventually a convenient tool for the police,[1] as well as the citizen for whom they are designed disingenuously in *doublethink* as a passport to public services. In the meantime, the Prime Minister has launched an Interception Modernisation Programme 'to update our capability' to ensure that 'our national interests will continue to be protected',[2] while the Draft Communications Data Bill will require internet service providers to store emails for up to a year, for the prevention and detection of crime and protection of national security.[3] Yet despite growing concerns about the erosion of personal privacy, it is a remarkable feature of these developments that they have taken place since the implementation of the Human Rights Act in 2000, the culture of liberty clearly not being the midwife of a culture of privacy. It is true that the seeds of many of these developments were planted long before the Human Rights Act was passed in 1998, and indeed that the culture of liberty has helped to overturn a number of stones and cast some light on the dark practices operating underneath. It remains the case, nevertheless, that under the shadow of the Human Rights Act and the culture of liberty it was designed to cultivate, these different powers have been developed, extended and in some cases re-enacted, while other major restrictions on personal privacy have been introduced for the first time.

---

[1] There would be nothing to stop the police asking to see such a card, from a person who is subject to 'stop and account', or who has been stopped and searched, or arrested under general police powers. Although there may be no formal requirement to produce an identity card (Identity Cards Act 2006, s 16), it is likely that their production will in time become a feature of the exercise of such powers by the police.

[2] <http://www.number10.gov.uk/Page14490>.

[3] The NHS patient database is also proving to be controversial, providing as it does for the inclusion of the medical records of all NHS patients, even if it is for their own good.

Random Surveillance: CCTV Cameras

A good example of first principle being traduced by the Surveillance State is provided by the huge expansion in the use of CCTV cameras, especially in city centres. There is no law on CCTV cameras, authorising their installation, determining the circumstances by which they might be used, and subjecting those who use this technology to any form of supervision.[4] This is a problem identified by a House of Lords Committee in 1998, which looked at the civil liberties implications of CCTV cameras (at a time when their use was still developing) (HL, 1998). The Committee expressed concern that 'there are no statutory, or other, controls on the use of public space CCTV systems' (ibid, paragraph 4.9), and recommended that 'the Government give urgent consideration to introducing tighter control over any system, either publicly or privately owned, covering sites to which the public has free access' (ibid, paragraph 4.14). According to the Committee, any control system ought to include

'the need for some form of licensing; for statutory or other enforceable codes of practice; and for powers to inspect and audit the use and handling of surveillance systems, including the images, their storage and disposal' (ibid).

These recommendations do not appear to have been acted upon, and in 2009 the BBC claimed that there are now as many as 3.2 million such cameras operating in Great Britain, with this country using CCTV cameras 'much more than other countries'.[5] Like various other forms of surveillance, these cameras are said to play a crucial role in detecting criminals, though there are those who question their utility in some cases. But even though they may be useful—nay indispensable—the constitutional lawyer must always ask two questions; the first is whether the use of these cameras is authorised by law, and the second is whether the law is being complied with by those who operate them.

CCTV: The Regulatory Framework

Although there is thus an absence of any systematic and coherent regulation of the installation and use of CCTV cameras, this is not to say that they are wholly unregulated. Thus, local authorities were empowered by legislation introduced in 1994 to install and use cameras on land in their area, for

---

[4] See also Liberty, 2007: there is no regulation of 'the need to justify location for cameras, details on notification of location, . . . and so on' (para 7); and the House of Lords Constitution Committee: 'there are few restrictions on the use of public area CCTV cameras in the UK' (HL, 2009: para 213).

[5] *BBC News*, 20 July 2009. Transport for London alone uses 10,000 in its rail networks, stations, roads, and buses (HL, 2009: para 77).

the limited purposes of 'promot[ing] the prevention of crime or the welfare of the victims of crime'.[6] The only apparent restriction is that the local authority must consult the police (but not local citizens) before exercising their power.[7] The legislation is enabling, apparently concerned with the fear that the use of cameras could violate the ultra vires rule relating to local authorities, rather than a need to overcome the privacy concerns of the citizens in the local authority's area. There is thus a blanket approval for the use of cameras, but no need for prior authorisation by an independent figure, and no need to show that the use of CCTV cameras is necessary and proportionate. As it is, however, a number of local authorities make it clear that they use CCTV cameras for purposes other than those referred to in the 1994 Act. Under Cambridge City Council's Code of Practice on CCTV Cameras, the use of cameras in Cambridge is designed not only to prevent and deter crime, but for several other purposes as well, some related, some not. These other purposes include 'reducing anti-social behaviour and aggressive begging'; 'reducing fear of crime'; 'encouraging better use of city facilities and attractions'; and 'maintaining and enhancing the commercial viability of the city and encouraging continued investment'.[8] Exeter City Council is even more extravagant, with its Code of Practice making clear that the purpose of the CCTV system is not only to 'help reduce the fear of crime' and to 'help deter and detect crime and provide evidential material for court proceedings', but also:

- to assist in the overall management of Exeter City Centre;
- to help deter and detect acts of anti-social behaviour;
- to enhance community safety, assist in developing the economic well-being of the Exeter area and encourage greater use of the City Centre;
- to assist the Local Authorities in their enforcement and regulatory functions within the Exeter area;
- to assist in Traffic Management, and encourage safer and more sustainable use of all modes of transport and provide travel information to the media and public;
- to assist in supporting civil proceedings; and
- to monitor all modes of travel to enable improvement and better management of the public highway.[9]

---

[6] Criminal Justice and Public Order Act 1994, s 163.
[7] Ibid.
[8] See <http://www1.eaststaffsbc.gov.uk/CMISWebPublic/Binary.ashx?Document=935>.
[9] See <http://www.exeter.gov.uk/media/pdf/g/k/code_of_practice_2006_revision_3.pdf>.

But although used extensively by local authorities, CCTV cameras are not used only by local authorities, and are to be found in other public places such as railway and underground stations, airports and ports, housing estates, and shopping centres, as well as football grounds and other sporting arenas. In these cases, it appears that there is no need for any formal authority to use CCTV cameras, despite the fact that they entail a breach of the privacy of everyone who is being monitored, and despite the fact that the tapes may be requested by the police for use in criminal proceedings.[10] It is true that these other users of CCTV systems may be subject to the Data Protection Act 1998 (DPA), as the use of this technology constitutes the processing of data for the purposes of the Act, though there are doubts about the extent to which the legislation does apply (Liberty, 2007), following a Court of Appeal decision restricting its scope.[11] But even if the Information Commissioner is right that 'most uses of CCTV by organisations or businesses will be covered' (Information Commissioner, 2008: 8), neither the Data Protection Act nor the Information Commissioner's Code of Practice on CCTV Cameras impose unduly onerous obligations on the users of cameras. Those who use a CCTV system may fall within the definition of a data controller, and be obliged to register with the Information Commissioner:[12] but there is no need for approval from the Commissioner to make use of a CCTV system. In making the application for registration, the data controller is required only to describe the data to be processed, the purposes for which the data are to be processed, and the persons to whom any data are to be disclosed. The application should also indicate the steps to be taken to prevent the unlawful or unauthorised processing of personal data.[13] Once registered, those operating CCTV systems should comply with the fairly straightforward data protection principles in the Act, such as the requirement that personal data shall be fairly and lawfully processed, that the data shall be obtained only for a specified and lawful purpose, that the data shall not be kept any longer than necessary, and so on.[14] One final obligation on data controllers is that they should

---

[10] The European Court of Human Rights has held that the 'the monitoring of the actions of an individual in a public place by the use of photographic equipment which does not record the visual data does not, as such, give rise to an interference with the individual's private life' but that 'the recording of the data and the systematic or permanent nature of the record may give rise to such considerations': *Peck v United Kingdom* (2003) 36 EHRR 719.

[11] *Durant v Financial Services Authority* [2003] EWCA Civ 1746.

[12] Data Protection Act 1998, ss 1 and 17 respectively.

[13] Ibid, s 18.

[14] Ibid, Schedule 1.

inform people (on request) that their data are being processed, and supply copies of the information being processed.[15] Although potentially alarming for the CCTV operators, this last obligation is so shot through with holes as to make it wholly benign.

CCTV and the Rule of Law

Yet despite the remarkably lax legal obligations applying to CCTV operators, it has been claimed that as many as 90 per cent of the cameras do not properly comply with the Data Protection Act 1998 and the Information Commissioner's Code of Practice on CCTV cameras, and that 'many installations are operated illegally'.[16] A host of reasons were suggested for failure to comply with existing standards:[17]

- it is claimed that a(n unspecified) number of CCTV systems are not registered with the Information Commissioner, as required by the Act;
- it is claimed that viewing monitors are often poorly sited in public spaces, so that members of the public—as well as those employed to watch the monitors—can see who is being filmed, despite the Information Commissioner's Code of Practice stating that '[a]ccess to the recorded images should be restricted to a manager or designated member of staff';
- it is claimed that the problem most frequently encountered is the failure to keep camera tapes secure, despite the advice in the Information Commissioner's Code of Practice that 'access to, and disclosure of, the images recorded by CCTV and similar surveillance equipment [must be] restricted and carefully controlled';
- it is claimed that the cameras are frequently used for purposes other than those for which they are 'registered', which would be a clear breach of the Data Protection Act 1998, which—by section 20—makes it an offence to process personal data for a non-registered purpose, a point reinforced by the Information Commissioner's Code of Practice; and
- finally, it is claimed that 'the necessary clear signage is regularly missing', in breach of the clear terms of the Information Commissioner's Code of Practice which—based on the first data protection principle—states

---

[15] Ibid, s 7(1), (2).
[16] *The Times*, 31 May 2007. The claims were made by CameraWatch, reported to be a national advisory body and to have the backing of the police and the Information Commissioner's office (ibid).
[17] Ibid.

that 'signs should be placed so that the public are aware that they are entering a zone which is covered by surveillance equipment'.[18]

These concerns about possible non-compliance with existing standards were said to have caused some anxiety among senior police officers, worried that the improper use of cameras might lead to evidence being ruled inadmissible in a criminal trial. There is, however, no precedent as yet, though at least one Scottish QC was sceptical, unable to 'imagine any judge saying such evidence was not admissible when there is the argument that it is in the greater public good'.[19] This is because—as we saw in Chapter 2—under both English and Scots law, the courts may admit evidence that has been unlawfully obtained (even in breach of Convention rights).[20] Although this may help to re-assure the police, it is hardly a satisfactory state of affairs.

There are thus three questions of legality relating to the use of CCTV cameras: the first is the absence of a need for specific authority to install cameras, the second is the alleged failure to comply with the modest standards currently in force under the Data Protection Act 1998, and the third is the power of the courts to turn a blind eye to any impropriety involved in the use of the cameras. There are also potentially serious issues of privacy, which make these issues of legality all the more pressing. Privacy issues are highlighted by the local authority codes of practice, some of which are proudly posted on the internet. For many people it is alarming enough that they are being watched while in a public place, though most are no doubt willing to compromise an element of their privacy in the interests of public safety, in a context where they are largely anonymous. More alarming, however, is that the cameras can be trained on intimate private places, something anticipated by both the Information Commissioner's Code of Practice and users of CCTV systems themselves. Preston City Council attempts to provide reassurance by stating in terms that the system is 'not to be used to invade the privacy of any individual, in residential, business or other private premises, buildings or land', finding it necessary also expressly to prohibit the use of cameras for the purposes of 'voyeurism'.[21] Cambridge City Council permits Control Centre Operators to use the cameras only 'to view public areas and not to look into the interior of any private premises or any other area where an infringement of privacy of individuals

---

[18] These assessments were made on the basis of the first edition of the Information Commissioner's Code of Practice. This was replaced by a second edition in 2008, which although differently expressed contains in essence the same provisions as those referred to above.

[19] *The Times*, 31 May 2007.

[20] See pp 43–45 above.

[21] Preston City Council, *Code of Practice for the Operation of Closed Circuit Television* (2005), para 3.6.

may occur'. There are, however, several exceptions to this prohibition, one of which applies where 'an Operator, whilst operating the cameras in accordance with this Code of Practice, nevertheless *happens* to observe something which s/he believes indicates that a serious crime is being, or is about to be committed in a non-public area.' Just as worrying is Exeter City Council, which also provides that 'cameras will not be used to look into private residential property, unless pursuing a suspect and this is considered to be in the interests of the private residents'. In order to ensure that 'the interior of any private residential property within range of the System is not surveyed by the cameras', 'Privacy zones' will be 'programmed into the System', but only where the equipment permits this to be done. If this is not permitted by the system, there is no question of the use of CCTV being restricted to prevent any possible gratuitous invasion of privacy, with sufficient safeguard being provided by an undertaking that 'operators will be specifically trained in privacy issues'.[22]

Covert Surveillance: Watching, Infiltrating, and Informing

Until very recently various forms of targeted surveillance by the police and other law enforcement agencies operated without the need for any legal authorisation in advance. Here we are concerned principally with tactics such as watching people and their homes, and infiltrating their organisations or communities in various ways, whether by recruiting informers from inside or placing undercover officers from the outside. This is conduct which did not violate any legally recognised rights of the individuals or organisations who were the subject of surveillance, and consequently was not unlawful. The issue was raised as long ago as 1936 in the Scottish courts, when Mrs Margaret Robertson brought an action against the Chief Constable of Lanarkshire claiming damages for loss suffered as a result of a continuous watch of her house by police officers.[23] The latter were looking for a colleague who had gone missing, and Mrs Robertson claimed that their conduct had given rise to alarming rumours about her, and that her business as a chemist had suffered as a result. But the action failed, the colourful language of the

---

[22] See also the Information Commissioner's Code of Practice which states that '[I]f it is not possible physically to restrict the equipment to avoid recording images from those spaces not intended to be covered by the scheme, then operators should be trained in recognising the privacy implications of such spaces being covered (First and Third Data Protection Principles)'. The Code then gives the example of individuals sunbathing in their back gardens '[who] may have a greater expectation of privacy than individuals mowing the lawn of their front garden'. It is not suggested that surveillance of the former kind should not take place.

[23] *Robertson v Keith* 1936 SC 29.

court recording that there was no proof that 'the watch instructed by the [chief constable] involved any wrongous act of any kind, nor that any trespass, invasion of the pursuer's personal liberty, or nuisance was committed'. Also in Scotland, but much more recently, a complaint was made by Neil Connor about the systematic surveillance of his flat by the police, leading to a search warrant being issued under the Misuse of Drugs Act 1971, and Connor being charged under the same Act. Mr Connor argued that the police conduct violated his rights 'to respect for his private and family life, his home and his correspondence', under article 8 of the European Convention on Human Rights (ECHR). But the High Court dismissed the claim, noting that 'all that could be said of the surveillance operation was that it involved observation of the public street outside the building in which the appellant's flat was one of a number of flats'. As a result, said the court, there was no interference with Mr Connor's rights under article 8 of the Convention.[24]

The Regulatory Framework

Although the English courts have taken a similarly permissive view of surveillance techniques that do not otherwise involve infringements of liberty or violations of property rights, the European Court of Human Rights has typically taken a more robust approach, requiring legal authority before such techniques can be used. The position is now governed by legislation passed by the Westminster Parliament for England and Wales, and similar measures passed by the Holyrood Parliament for Scotland.[25] But RIPA and RIP(s)A respectively impose the most minimal obligations on public authorities, depending on the form of covert surveillance used, of which there are three kinds:

- *directed surveillance*, which essentially involves the kind of surveillance in the *Robertson* and *Connor* cases, where the State is parked outside someone's house to obtain information in relation to an investigation;[26]

---

[24] *Connor v HM Advocate* 2002 JC 255.
[25] Regulation of Investigatory Powers Act 2000, Part II; Regulation of Investigatory Powers (Scotland) Act 2000.
[26] As an aside, directed surveillance could include the use of CCTV cameras by the police. Cambridge City Council takes steps to ensure that any request from the police and other enforcement agencies for CCTV images complies with the foregoing legislation. Cambridge City Council's code of practice also reveals that a monitor is installed in the Control Room at Police Headquarters some 20 miles away. It is further revealed that '[p]ictures from any of the cameras may be relayed to this monitor at the instigation of the CCTV Operator or at the request of the Duty Police Operator'. Under the terms of the legislation regulating surveillance, the use of the CCTV systems for general monitoring purposes would not require authorisation; the use of CCTV systems is likely to run up against the surveillance legislation only in the case of directed surveillance, for the purposes of which

- *intrusive surveillance*, which means for example the use of a listening device placed inside a house or a car, conduct also regulated by the Police Act 1997 as an interference with property; and

- *the use of covert human intelligence sources (CHIS)*, an elaborate term to disguise what is basically the use of various informants, agents, and undercover officers.

In all of these cases, some form of authorisation is now required before the surveillance is undertaken, though there are serious questions about the purposes for which authorisation may be given and the people who may give it, as well as the accountability of all those engaged in the process.

So although it may be true that the need for authorisation places these surveillance techniques at a different level of accountability to the installation and use of CCTV cameras, this is not to make any bold claims about the nature of the authorisation required:

- although the authorisation is to be given only for prescribed statutory purposes, these purposes are not limited to the predictable purposes of national security or preventing or detecting crime, or preventing disorder. In some cases the powers may be used in the interests of public safety, the protection of public health, or other purposes specified by the Home Secretary;[27]

- although authorisation may be required, there is no question of a warrant being required from an independent judicial figure (subject to a number of important exceptions relating specifically to *intrusive surveillance*);[28] authorisation need only be given by someone from within the same agency (and it may even be within the same department);[29] and

- although higher levels of authorisation are required in the case of *intrusive surveillance* this means only that it must be authorised by the most senior officer (such as the chief constable) in the agency in question; it is only in the case of *interference with property* by the police involving homes, offices, or hotel bedrooms, or privileged material that judicial authorisation is required.[30]

And while individuals who are the target of authorised (or unauthorised) surveillance may complain to the Investigatory Powers Tribunal, this is a

---

the surveillance needs to be undertaken in relation to a specific investigation or operation. This would cover watching the movements of a specific individual.

[27] Regulation of Investigatory Powers Act 2000, s 28.

[28] Ibid, ss 28, 29, 32.

[29] Ibid, ss 30, 32.

[30] Police Act 1997, s 97.

body revealed by its own judgments to have limited powers,[31] with the result that there would be no place in the tribunal for Margaret Robertson. Indeed, it remains unclear what remedy—if any—she would now have.[32]

The Exercise of Regulatory Authority

The surveillance regime under RIPA is supervised by the Office of Surveillance Commissioners. Appointed by the Prime Minister,[33] the current Chief Commissioner is Sir Christopher Rose QC, a retired judge of the Court of Appeal, who now commands an army of surveillance commissioners, assistant surveillance commissioners, and surveillance inspectors, with an annual budget of £1.6 million (OSC, 2008). It is only in the most exceptional circumstances, however, that the surveillance commissioners are required to authorise surveillance in advance,[34] and for the most part their job is to review the operation of practice and procedures of the central and local government agencies that engage in this form of activity. The task is a formidable one, for it is one thing for the legislation to confer such wide powers, but quite another to confer these powers on such a wide range of bodies. It is true that the powers relating to *intrusive surveillance* can generally be used only by the police, or the security and intelligence services. But this is not the case in relation to either *directed surveillance* or *the use of CHIS*. There are no fewer than 23 agencies listed in the Act as originally passed (with others added since) permitted to engage in both the latter forms, provided the necessary authorisation is granted for the use of the powers in particular cases. These bodies range from the police, the intelligence services, the armed forces, HM Revenue and Customs, and various government departments. But it also includes local authorities as well as a number of quangos, such as the Environment Agency, the Food Standards Agency, as well as the Post Office. In addition to these bodies which are empowered to use both *directed surveillance* and *CHIS*, there are five other categories of body which are permitted to use *directed surveillance only*. These include the Health and Safety Executive, a wide range of NHS bodies, and the Royal Pharmaceutical Society. Other bodies exercising power under the Act and subject to supervision by the Chief Surveillance Commissioner include

---

[31] *C v The Police* IPT/03/32/H—no power to deal with complaints about surveillance of a retired police officer by his former employer where no criminal conduct suspected.

[32] See *Martin v McGuiness* 2003 SLT 1424.

[33] Regulation of Investigatory Powers Act 2000, s 91.

[34] As under the Police Act 1997, s 97—interference with property where the property consists of a dwelling or a hotel bedroom. See above, pp 61–62. The Commissioners are the judicial figures referred to there.

the BBC, the Healthcare Commission, the National Assembly for Wales, OFCOM, and the Information Commissioner.

Collectively these different agencies make extensive use of their powers, as reported by the Chief Surveillance Commissioner in 2007:

- thus, in 2006–07 the 'number of *directed surveillance* authorisations granted by public authorities other than law enforcement agencies [were] almost double the number of authorisations ... compared with the previous year' (OSC, 2007: paragraph 2.3). So while the use of directed surveillance by the police declined to 19,651 authorisations in 2006–07 (from 23,628 in the previous year), in the case of other public authorities the numbers rose in the same year to 12,494 (from 6,924 in the previous year) (ibid: paragraph 7.3). This increase was explained by the Chief Surveillance Commissioner as being due to 'a better understanding by local authorities and other Government departments of the relevant legislation' (ibid), so that these bodies 'can no longer be regarded as low users, as was the case hitherto' (ibid). There was, however, a 'significant decrease' to 9,535 in directed surveillance authorisations by public authorities in the following year (OSC, 2008: paragraph 7.3), though the figures in relation to law enforcement agencies remained 'relatively stable' (ibid: paragraph 7.2);

- it is also the case that in 2006–07 there had been a slight decline (to 4,373 recruits) in the *use of human intelligence sources* by the law enforcement agencies (from 4,559 in the previous year) (OSC, 2007: paragraph 7.4), rising slightly to 4,498 in the following year (OSC, 2008: paragraph 7.4). But before we are intoxicated by the declining levels of police activity, a sense of sobriety is restored when it is revealed that the use of human intelligence sources declined at the same time as some police forces introduced the concept of the 'tasked witness' for reasons which are not clear, but which has the apparent effect of being a way to get round the legislation. The Chief Surveillance Commissioner reported that he was 'disturbed' by this development, the scale of which he did not reveal. He did, however, say that these individuals who are recruited as 'an apparent alternative to the correct, legally-recognised, term "covert human intelligence source" ... have been engaged in a manner that establishes or maintains a covert relationship'.

The nature of this latter engagement is not explained, but the Chief Surveillance Commissioner also reports that he had not been 'satisfied that the arrangements for their welfare, security and management have been of the standard required by law' (OSC, 2007: paragraph 8.9).

Covert Surveillance: The Problem of Local Authorities

Along with the increase in the use of surveillance is a failure of public bodies to comply with the law, the Chief Surveillance Commissioner expressing 'disappointment' about various failings of surveillance conducted by non-law enforcement agencies in particular (OSC, 2007: paragraph 10.2), with specific concern being expressed about the failings of some local authorities. Sir Christopher Rose's first report as Chief Surveillance Commissioner reveals concern that local authorities had 'failed to act on the recommendations of previous inspections' conducted by his predecessors, noting that a 'funda-mental aim of [his reviews] is to improve standards and assist the authority in protecting its activities from criticism in the courts' (ibid). Apart from what appears to be the stubborn refusal on the part of some authorities to comply with the law, concern was also expressed that 'in a small number of cases, authorities have produced policy—as the result of an earlier inspection—but have failed to implement sufficient oversight to ensure that the policy was followed' (ibid: paragraph 10.3). Ignorance of recent changes to the law led Sir Christopher to 'deduce that some local authorities cannot be relied on to remain conversant with amendments to legislation' (ibid), while he remained concerned about poor quality training on the ground that 'much of it comes from a number of well-meaning but inadequately-informed provid-ers' (ibid: paragraph 10.5), complaining that 'much of the instruction appears superficial and fails to address adequately key areas of compliance' (ibid). He was said to be 'particularly concerned at the lack of dedicated CHIS management capability in some authorities which would clearly benefit from a more professional approach', noting that the 'authorisation of CHIS by local authorities is inconsistent' (ibid: paragraph 10.6), with 'many authori-ties . . . reticent to invest in this area of covert activity because of the need for specialist training' (ibid). The default policy for many authorities is to avoid using CHIS altogether or to rely on the police, though Surveillance Office inspections, 'have identified that some authorities are probably conducting CHIS activity without proper authorisation' (ibid).

Concerns about the Use of Local Authority Surveillance

In the light of the conduct identified by the Chief Surveillance Commissioner, it was inevitable that some of the human stories informing the annual reports would hit the headlines. The first of these involved the surveillance of a family in Poole who had applied to have their child admitted to the pop-ular Lilliput First School, 'where their two elder children, aged six and 10, were educated'. Close to 'the millionaire suburb of Sandbanks', the *Daily Telegraph*, claimed that 'for two weeks the middle-class family was followed by council officials who wanted to establish whether they had given a false address', to secure a place for their three-year-old at the over-subscribed school.[35] The so-called local authority 'spies' were reported as having:

made copious notes on the movements of the mother and her three children, who they referred to as 'targets' as they were trailed on school runs. The snoopers even watched the family home at night to establish where they were sleeping. In fact, the 39-year-old mother—who described the snooping as 'a grotesque invasion of privacy'—had held lengthy discussions with the council, which assured her that her school application was totally in order.

To its credit, the Council told the family that it had been under surveillance, the family finding it 'very creepy when [they] found out that people had been watching [them] and making notes'. When challenged, the Poole Borough Council revealed that it had used RIPA's powers of surveillance 'to spy on the family', arguing that the suspected conduct of the family was criminal for the purposes of the Act, claiming that lying on a school application amounted to fraud'. But even if that is the case, it was nevertheless argued that this 'is a ridiculously disproportionate use of RIPA and will undermine public trust in necessary and lawful surveillance'.[36] According to the *Daily Telegraph*, the Council 'had used the law on two other occasions during the past year and on both had proved that parents had lied about where they lived'.[37]

Apart from shooting RIPA to national prominence (the story made the *BBC News*, *The Times*, *The Guardian*, *The Daily Telegraph* and *The Daily Mail*), the Poole case led the Press Association to conduct an investigation about the extent to which the Act was being used. In a survey of 100 local authorities conducted in April 2008, the PA found that the Act was used mainly to 'combat rogue traders, benefit fraud, counterfeit goods and antisocial behaviour like noise nuisance and criminal damage'.[38] But it also found that the Act was being used 'to find out about people who let their dog foul (at least seven cases), breaches of planning law (one case), animal welfare (one case), littering (at least one case) and even the misuse of a disabled parking badge (one case)'.[39] In other cases Poole Borough Council (again) 'snooped on fishermen to see whether they were illegally catching shellfish'; Conwy council 'had one case where it used the law to spy on someone who was working while off sick'; and

[35] *Daily Telegraph*, 21 October 2008.
[36] *BBC News*, 10 April 2008.
[37] *Daily Telegraph*, 21 October 2008.
[38] *The Guardian*, 23 June 2008.
[39] Ibid.

Newcastle City Council 'used it for one case of "car parking surveillance re suspected contraventions of parking orders"'.[40] Since the PA's survey, another episode which captured the attention of the national press was the infamous case of the Cambridgeshire schoolboys, with village paper-boys being said by the *Daily Mail* to be the new target for the anti-terror spies'.[41] Cambridgeshire bye-laws require paper boys to have a work permit, which must be signed by their parents, their school, and the employer. In this case, the owners of a Spar shop in the village of Melbourn were prosecuted for breaching the bye-laws for failing to obtain work permits for five children. As part of its investigation, the Council had 'sent undercover council officers to lurk outside [the shop] and take notes on the movements of the boys'. The shop owners were found guilty of breaking the bye-law and given a criminal record. Although predictable allegations of the local authority's activities being likened to those of the Stasi are way off target, this is nevertheless another case that raises questions about proportionality in the use of the law, which cannot be used simply because the conduct complained of is allegedly criminal.

Concerns of the Chief Surveillance Commissioner

In light of the national press interest in the use of surveillance powers by local authorities, Sir Christopher Rose returned to this matter in his second annual report. Although much of the media reporting had been 'misguided' (OSC, 2008: paragraph 2.4), he nevertheless remained highly critical of local authority standards:

- there is a 'serious misunderstanding' of the law and in particular 'the concept of proportionality' (OSC, 2008: paragraph 9.2). In a pointed remark, the Chief Surveillance Commissioner said that 'It is not acceptable, for example, to judge, that because directed surveillance is being conducted from a public place, this automatically renders the activity overt or to assert that an activity is proportionate because it is the only way to further an investigation' (ibid); and

- there was concern about the lack of independent oversight by authorising officers. In many cases it seems that the law is little more than a farce, with investigators being authorised by their own heads of department. This is said to be a 'common weakness', with the Chief Surveillance Commissioner reporting that 'If an authorizing officer is too close to the investigation it is difficult to demonstrate the independence and objectivity encouraged by the legislation' (ibid: paragraph 9.7).

[40] Ibid.   [41] *Daily Mail*, 5 December 2008.

Poor oversight in some cases by inexperienced authorising officers was matched by a failure on the part of Chief Executives to understand the risks they run 'if activity is conducted without appropriate management or if activity is being conducted in a disproportionate manner' (ibid: paragraph 9.3).

Although Sir Christopher thought it 'wrong to conclude that all local authorities are performing poorly', it was nevertheless the case that those performing well 'are not yet in the majority' (OSC, 2008: paragraph 9.9), a rather sobering remark as the legislation approaches its 10th anniversary. This judgment was based not only on the use of directed surveillance, but on the use of surveillance powers generally, with Sir Christopher also returning in his second report to the use of CHIS, where he lamented the lack of any 'demonstrable improvement' in local authority investment in 'appropriate' CHIS management facilities (ibid: paragraph 9.5). And while making clear that it was not his role to encourage the use of covert activity, the Chief Surveillance Commissioner expressed the view strongly that 'public authorities empowered to use CHIS must ensure that they possess the capability to conduct the activity in a manner required by the legislation' (ibid). But if local authorities were rightly on the receiving end of the Chief Surveillance Commissioner's ire, the performance of the OSC itself has not passed without criticism. As part of an investigation into *Surveillance: Citizens and the State*, the House of Lords Constitution Committee took evidence from Sir Christopher, among others. The Committee reported as follows:

When we asked Sir Christopher if he would consider investigating specific cases reported by the press such as those in Poole, he answered as follows:
'Certainly not. It would be totally impossible to do that. As I say, there are a very large number of authorities which we inspect, we have a carefully designed programme. I mean, I am not ruling it out absolutely, if there was a well documented manifest abuse of power by a local authority, well then, of course we would try and do something about it, but I am afraid responding to press reports is not always a fruitful activity when you only have a small amount of resources at your disposal.' (Q 653)

This was said to be 'unsatisfactory', for although the Committee understood that 'resources are constrained, it is essential that the regulators overseeing the use of RIPA powers should maintain public confidence in the regime', and 'introduce more flexibility to their inspection regimes, so that they can promptly investigate cases where there is widespread concern that powers under the [Act] have been used disproportionately or unnecessarily' (HL, 2009: paragraphs 256, 257).

Surveillance by the Security Service

There is already emerging in this account of the Surveillance State a number of themes that raise concerns for the constitutional lawyer. Thus, we have encountered (a) procedures that operate without clear legal authority; (b) surveillance operations that are alleged or appear to take place in breach of the law with apparent impunity; and (c) authorisations to invade privacy rights on the authority of the executive rather than the judiciary. This is subject to an exception referred to above whereby under section 97 of the Police Act 1997, the police must seek judicial approval before placing bugging devices in people's homes, hotel bedrooms, or business premises; or to secure various forms of privileged information. It is true that we have also encountered judicial scrutiny of surveillance practices, which is clearly independent of the government. But it is also true that these procedures are not wholly effective (if effectiveness is to be measured by ensuring compliance with the law), and that there has been a huge rise in the use of surveillance devices, raising questions about the need for even greater scrutiny. This question of accountability and scrutiny of the exercise of surveillance powers arises again in the context of security service surveillance and the inadequate steps taken to regulate it. Special powers for this purpose were introduced by the Security Service Act 1989, following a finding that the pre-existing arrangements, operating without any legal authority were in breach of the ECHR.[42] These powers are now to be found in the Intelligence Services

---

[42] *Hewitt and Harman v United Kingdom* (1992) 14 EHRR 657. Indeed, not only did the arrangements in force before 1989 operate without legal authority, they also operated in breach of the law, with the apparent approval of the English courts. In 1987, Peter Wright famously published *Spycatcher*, an account of his time as a member of the security services. Frantic attempts were made by the government to stop the publication of the book, as well as extracts in the British press, all ultimately to no avail. Attempts in Australia failed (Ewing and Gearty, 1990), there was no question of the book being banned in the United States (because of the First Amendment), and attempts to restrain newspapers in this country were frustrated by the ease with which the book itself could enter the country from North America (For the legal proceedings, see *Observer v United Kingdom* (1992) 14 EHRR 153. See further pp 141–143 below). In the course of legal proceedings in the British courts the issue arose about allegations in the book that the security service had been involved in illegal entry to premises in order to place bugging devices. According to Lord Donaldson in the Court of Appeal: 'It would be a sad day for democracy and the rule of law if the [security] service were ever to be considered to be above or exempt from the law of the land. And it is not. At any time any member of the service who breaks the law is liable to be prosecuted. But there is a need for some discretion and common sense. Let us suppose that the service has information which suggests that a spy may be operating from particular premises. It needs to have confirmation. It may well consider that, if he proves to be a spy, the interests of the nation are better served by letting him continue with his activities under surveillance and in ignorance that he has been detected rather than by arresting him. What is the service expected to do? A secret search of the premises is the obvious answer. Is this really "wrongdoing?"' (*Attorney General*

Act 1994, which provides that the security service (MI5), the intelligence services (MI6), and GCHQ may apply for a warrant to 'interfere with property' or wireless telegraphy. This is in addition to the powers of the security service to use intrusive surveillance, directed surveillance, and CHIS, for which provision is made by the grim RIPA, albeit applied differently in the case of the security and intelligence services.

Security Service Surveillance and the Rule of Law

Beginning with the powers of the security and intelligence services in relation to the interference with property, these powers apply where the service 'needs' to enter private property, in order to carry out the widely defined statutory purposes of the respective services.[43] A warrant is necessary for this purpose, but under the 1994 Act the application is made not to an independent judge, but to a minister, who would normally be the Home Secretary, the First Minister in Scotland, the Northern Ireland Secretary, or the Foreign Secretary. This seems an increasingly eccentric procedure in a constitutional system developing a growing love affair with the separation of powers, as reflected most recently in the Constitutional Reform Act 2005. Nevertheless, we thus have a system of issuing warrants by the executive following an application by officials in an executive body for whom the minister is ultimately responsible. As a matter of constitutional law (in light of the so-called *Carltona* principle),[44] it is not far off the mark to say that the procedure is equivalent to the minister granting a warrant to himself, and as a matter of constitutional practice the procedure is not unlike the procedure denounced by the Court of Common Pleas in *Entick v Carrington*.[45] However, although there is thus no *ex ante* scrutiny of the need for a warrant to interfere with property, there is nevertheless a procedure of *ex post facto* scrutiny by a senior judge (the Intelligence Services Commissioner) appointed by the Prime Minister to keep under review the way in which ministers use their powers under the Act. It is also possible for a complaint to be made to the Investigatory Powers Tribunal about interference with

---

v Guardian Newspapers (No 2) [1990] AC 109, at p 190). The answer must surely be yes: 'By the laws of England, every invasion of private property, be it ever so minute, is a trespass' (*Entick v Carrington* (1765) 19 St Tr 1030).

[43] The statutory purpose as set out in s 1 of the 1994 Act, is 'to obtain and provide information relating to the actions or intentions of persons outside the British Islands'.

[44] *Carltona Ltd v Minister of Works* [1943] 2 All ER 560.

[45] (1765) 19 St Tr 1030. A major difference between the powers exercisable then by Lord Halifax (then a minister under George III) and his counterpart today, however, is that the latter is operating under powers which another minister (Douglas Hurd, then a minister under Mrs Thatcher) had the good sense to ask Parliament to endorse (which of course it duly did).

property (for example because there is no ground for issuing a warrant). But the tribunal is required to refer the matter to the Commissioner for investigation, and in any event it is not clear how people will find out that they are subject to this kind of surveillance to enable them to make a complaint in the first place. It is not the practice to inform people that they have been the subject of surveillance, even after the surveillance has stopped.

Turning to the powers relating to intrusive surveillance (other than interference with property), directed surveillance and CHIS, here we find that the writ of the surveillance commissioners does not run as far as the intelligence services.[46] But the latter are governed by RIPA when they use these various forms of surveillance, which means that there must be authorisation for the of the surveillance in question:

- in the case of *directed surveillance* and the use of *covert human intelligence sources*, authorisation is given by someone within the relevant security or intelligence agency (s 30); and
- in the case of *intrusive surveillance*, the authorisation must be given by a minister in the form of a warrant, and the same warrant may authorise action under both the 1994 and 2000 Acts (s 42).

It is not altogether clear, however, how intrusive surveillance under the RIPA 2000 relates to the power to interfere with property under the 1994 Act. On one reading, it would be necessary to obtain both an authorisation in the form of a warrant to use a surveillance device in domestic premises (intrusive surveillance defined to include surveillance 'carried out by means of a surveillance device'),[47] and authorisation in the form of a warrant in order to place the surveillance device (this being an 'interference with property').[48] But very little light is shed on this matter by the Intelligence Services Commissioner. Indeed, the annual reports of the latter shed very little light on anything. The most recent report of the Commissioner amounts to no more than eight pages, no less than five or six of which consist largely of a description of the relevant legislation (not unhelpful in light of the various amendments to the legislation and the powers of the intelligence services), along with an outline of just over a page of his methods of investigation (which involve examining the ministers and the officials involved in the warrant process), together with reassurance that the system is working well. There is thus a marked lack of transparency about the purposes for which the powers are used, the ways in which these powers are used, or the frequency with which the different powers are used (Brown, 2007; Gibson, 2008).

---

[46] Regulation of Investigatory Powers Act 2000, s 62.
[47] Ibid, s 26(3)(b).   [48] Intelligence Services Act 1994, s 5.

Scrutiny by the Intelligence Services Commissioner

The current Intelligence Services Commissioner is Sir Peter Gibson, a retired member of the Court of Appeal. Until recently, the position had been held for some time by Lord Brown of Eaton-under-Heywood while a serving member of the Court of Appeal and subsequently the House of Lords. Lord Brown maintained the practice of his predecessors by refusing to disclose the number of warrants issued annually, and Sir Peter has adopted the same practice. This practice is adopted on the ground that it would 'assist the operation of those hostile to the state if they were able to estimate even approximately the extent of the work of the Security Service, SIS and GCHQ in fulfilling their functions' (Brown, 2007: paragraph 32). Lord Brown's valedictory report teases the reader with the enigmatic remark that the figures are 'of interest' (ibid), but included in 'the confidential annex' to the report, to be seen only by the Prime Minister. But we do not know if the number of warrants is increasing, and if so on what scale. Nor do we know anything about the procedure followed before the warrants are signed, and how much time ministers spend on each warrant placed before them.[49] Similarly, although Lord Brown reports 12 errors 'in respect of RIPA authorisations and ISA warrants and three breaches in one of the agencies' handling arrangements', again it was 'not possible' for him 'to say much about these errors without revealing information of a sensitive nature', leaving them also to be included in the confidential annex for the Prime Minister's eyes only (ibid: paragraph 39). Lord Brown did, however, 'report that the majority of these errors occurred as a result of there being no valid authorisation or warrant in force in respect of surveillance and interference with property' (ibid). There is thus a danger that the work of the Commissioner conceals as much as it reveals, a concern hardly assuaged by his inability to give details of complaints upheld by the Investigatory Powers Tribunal, over which he has an oversight function. In 2005, the tribunal upheld two complaints about conduct which was presumably unlawful, this being the first time in its history that complaints were successful. Yet again no information is provided about the complaints, the Commissioner claiming that on 'the

---

[49] But we are told that 'ministers take considerable care to satisfy themselves that the warrants applied for are necessary for the authorised purposes, and that what is proposed is proportionate. If any of the Secretaries of State felt they needed further information to satisfy themselves that the warrant should be granted then it is requested and given. Outright and final refusal of an application is comparatively rare, because the requesting agencies prepare their submissions with care and senior officials in the Departments of the respective Secretaries of State scrutinise the applications diligently before they are submitted for approval by the Secretary of State. The agencies are fully cognisant of the fact that the Secretary of State does not act as a "rubber stamp"' (Gibson, 2008).

grounds of confidentiality', the Investigatory Powers Tribunal Rules 2000 prohibited him from 'disclosing specific details' about the matter.[50]

It is difficult to know why senior judges agreed to engage with this process, and unclear whether it is appropriate that they do so.[51] Returning to the question of the separation of powers, although there is no suggestion here of personal bias (though it would surely be inappropriate for a serving or retired Intelligence Services Commissioner to sit in a case involving the security services), there is the question of institutional bias, as judges are seen to be close to the authority of the State, and close to practices which traditionally have been viewed with displeasure and distrust, albeit now glamourised and sanitised for popular consumption by the BBC's *Spooks*. Although the judicial role undoubtedly gives credibility to these processes (and may also lead to high standards in their administration, as the Commissioner is at pains to point out) (ibid: paragraph 40), the very credibility that the judges provide may also serve to compromise their own independence (if they are seen to have been co-opted into a process which it is their role ultimately to scrutinise in open legal proceedings). That role is hardly helped by secret reports to the Prime Minister, or indeed by a lack of accountability in the way in which the Intelligence Services Commissioner (who is appointed by and is accountable to the Prime Minister) carries out his duties. Nor is that role helped by the fact that the Intelligence Services Commissioner (like the tribunal he is required by statute to support) was protected from judicial review by as wide an ouster clause as one is likely to encounter on the statute book.[52] Given the outrage created by the Asylum and Immigration Bill when the then government tried to restrict judicial review of the decisions of the Asylum and Immigration Tribunal (Woolf, 2004), it is particularly surprising that judges have been willing to serve under those terms, especially when the ouster of judicial review is seen to be in direct conflict with the rule of law (ibid). It is true that although the Commissioners are senior

---

[50] Lord Brown did, however, report that 'the conduct complained of was not authorized in accordance with the relevant provisions of RIPA nor was it a complaint against any of the agencies or persons whose conduct [he was] responsible for reviewing' (Brown, 2007: para 38). Although compensation was awarded by the tribunal, the enigma continues.

[51] Such concerns may be greatly diminished—but perhaps not eliminated—by the appointment of retired rather than serving judges (for which eventuality express provision is made in the Intelligence Services Act 1994, s 8) to hold the position of Intelligence Services Commissioner, as is the practice with appointments to the position as Chief Surveillance Commissioner and Interception Commissioner.

[52] Intelligence Services Act 1994, s 9: 'The decisions of the Tribunal and the Commissioner under Schedule 1 to this Act (including decisions as to their jurisdictions) shall not be subject to appeal or liable to be questioned in any court.' Section 9 was repealed by the Regulation of Investigatory Powers Act 2000, but the Investigatory Powers Tribunal is protected by a wide exclusion clause (s 67(8)). See also note 58 below.

and distinguished judges who can be trusted rarely to get it wrong, it would not be the first time that a even a House of Lords judge had been successfully challenged in judicial review proceedings in relation to his extra-curial activities.[53]

Telephone Tapping and Email Interception

The wide and general powers considered so far do not confer a specific power to tap phones, as part of the State's surveillance of the British people. There are, however, special powers for this purpose, which can be traced back to the Interception of Communications Act 1985, and now to be found in RIPA. But although this is a special regime to deal with this particular form of surveillance, the principles of the regime will be instantly recognisable, while the concerns to which it gives rise are simply variations on themes already encountered: wide powers to intercept; massively increased use of the powers; and serious concerns about accountability and scrutiny (though here the Interception Commissioner is more forthcoming—and indeed sometimes disarmingly forthright—about his role). The phone tapping regime is in fact the oldest of the three surveillance regimes now in operation, and the legal framework introduced in 1985 was not only a response to a decision of the European Court of Human Rights,[54] but also a substantial enactment in legal form of the administrative procedures that had existed hitherto. The 1985 Act was also to become the template for the Security Services Act 1989 and in turn the Intelligence Services Act 1994, before its repeal and incorporation as part of RIPA. The latter, however, does not deal only with interceptions by the State, but following a more recent decision of the European Court of Human Rights involving the former deputy chief constable of the Merseyside police,[55] it is now unlawful to intercept communications of people at work unless the individuals in question have given their consent to the monitoring of their calls and emails.[56] It is most unlikely that many employees will be in a position of being able to withhold such consent, but the requirement to give it at least puts people on notice of the risks that they run.[57]

---

[53] *R v Lord Saville of Newdigate, ex parte A* [1999] 4 All ER 860. Also *Paul v Butler Sloss* [2007] EWHC (Admin) 408.

[54] *Malone v United Kingdom* (1985) 4 EHRR 14.

[55] *Halford v United Kingdom* (1997) 24 EHRR 523.

[56] Regulation of Investigatory Powers Act 2000, s 1.

[57] Surveillance by the private sector continues to be a massive problem, as reflected for example in the blacklist of trade unionists maintained by the so-called Consulting Association on behalf of the construction industry. See BIS, 2009; Ewing, 2009.

Telephone Tapping and the Rule of Law

Under the 1985 Act, telephone tapping and mail interception could be authorised where necessary in the interests of national security, for the purpose of preventing serious crime, or for the purpose of safeguarding the economic well-being of the United Kingdom. These grounds were somewhat opaque, yet no attempt has been made in the 2000 Act to define what is meant by national security, which will continue to mean what the government says it means (subject to arm's length scrutiny by the courts, though it is difficult to see how this scrutiny could operate, for the courts have been excluded from the operation of this area of law as well).[58] Since the 2000 Act, the power to tap phones and intercept other communications has been extended to cover interceptions necessary to give effect to an international mutual assistance agreement, which means at the request of a foreign government. So although there may be legal authority for the practice of phone tapping and related activities, the wide purposes for which the power may be used are unlikely to present an obstacle to those agencies which seek to use it. Admittedly, interceptions on any of these grounds can take place only with the authority of a warrant. But, the warrant is issued by a minister—the Home Secretary, the Foreign Secretary, the Northern Ireland Secretary, or the Scottish Ministers—rather than by a judge, as is the practice in other countries, even if there is independent judicial oversight of the process by the Interception Commissioner, another senior judge appointed by the Prime Minister to keep the system under review. There is also a right to complain about any improperly authorised interception to the Investigatory Powers Tribunal, though again these complaints can only be speculative as people are never told that they have been the subject of surveillance, even after it has ended. The warrant need only specify the 'interception subject', which would cover all the relevant communication devices used by the person concerned. In the same way, 'all premises warrants' can be issued (that is to say for a 'single set of premises as the premises in relation to which the interception to which the warrant relates is to take place'), which means in some cases that all phone lines into the premises would be covered.[59]

The post of Interception Commissioner is held by Sir Paul Kennedy, a retired Court of Appeal judge who in 2006 replaced Sir Swinton Thomas another retired Court of Appeal judge who had held the position since his retirement in 2000. In his valedictory report (for 2005–06), Sir Swinton pointed out that when he began his work as the Interception Commissioner

---

[58] Ibid, s 67(8), on the exclusion of the Investigatory Powers Tribunal from judicial review.
[59] On 'all premises' search warrants, see pp 39–41 above.

in 2000, there were nine agencies empowered lawfully to intercept communications under RIPA (Thomas, 2007: paragraph 8). Since then, he had been asked by the Home Secretary to undertake inspection of interceptions in prisons, and he had assumed responsibility to review the exercise of powers to acquire communications data—'an extremely powerful and effective investigative tool, [though] not as intrusive as the interception of communications themselves' (ibid).[60] As a result, the Commissioner was now responsible for 786 agencies, as well as the original nine referred to above; these 786 including 52 police forces, 139 prisons, 475 local authorities, and other organisations such as the Serious Fraud Office (Thomas, 2007: paragraph 8). But in addition to the increasing role of the Commissioner, since New Labour came to office in 1997 there has also been a massive increase in the use of the various powers, the exercise of which he is responsible for supervising. In 1988, the Home Secretary and the Secretary of State for Scotland issued a total of 519 warrants (Bradley and Ewing, 2007: 524). By 2005, the numbers had increased dramatically, with no fewer than 2,407 warrants being issued by the Home Secretary and the Scottish Ministers in the 15 months from January 2005 to March 2006 (Thomas, 2007: 19), an increase of almost 400 per cent in 17 years.[61] According to these figures the Home Secretary is now issuing on average more than 30 warrants a week, as well as dealing with requests for modifications, which ran on an average of more than 90 a week, though these latter can be made by senior officials in some cases.[62] That means 24 warrants or modifications every working day on average, raising questions about how much time can be spent considering these requests.[63] Even more spectacular is that 439,054 requests were made for communications data in the 15 months covered by Sir Swinton's last report, despite the fact that the

---

[60] This new power is also governed by the 2000 Act, which provides that designated public authorities may apply to postal or telecommunications companies for information about communications traffic to or from a particular number or destination (s 22). This can be done for a number of predictable statutory purposes (ibid).

[61] In 2007 the numbers remained fairly stable at 2,026 for the 12 month period from 1 January to 12 December (Kennedy, 2008a: para 2.23).

[62] It has since increased to over 100 a week. In 2007, there were 5,577 modifications approved by the Home Secretary and another 367 by the Scottish Ministers (Kennedy, 2008a: para 2.23).

[63] Questions all the more urgent for the fact that the power to issue warrants cannot be delegated; 2000 Act, s 7. The Interception Commissioner refuses to give details of the number of warrants issued, to either the Foreign Secretary or the Secretary of State for Northern Ireland. According to the Interception Commissioner, 'the disclosure of this information would be prejudicial to the public interest' (Thomas, 2007: para 35). It is not known on what scale warrants are issued to these ministers, whether the number has increased or decreased in recent years, and if so to what extent. While it might be expected that the situation in Northern Ireland would lead to a reduction in the number of warrants being issued there, the international situation is such that it might be expected that there would be an increase in the number of warrants issued by the Foreign Secretary.

power to acquire these data was exercised by only 150 of 583 public bodies entitled to make a request (ibid: paragraph 82).[64] Yet the Interception Commissioner appeared troubled that so few bodies were using their powers and reported that 'if this state of affairs continues unexplained, then consideration must be given to removing the powers from them' (ibid: paragraph 26). In other words, they must use them or lose them, a choice which is bound to inflate the levels of surveillance.

Scrutiny by the Interception Commissioner

The role of the Interception Commissioner is to keep the operation of the legislation under review,[65] though he takes a wide view of his statutory responsibilities (ibid: paragraph 7). Thus, according to his annual report, the Commissioner sees his role as being not only to protect people in the United Kingdom from any unlawful intrusion of their privacy, but ominously also to assist the agencies to do the work entrusted to them, something (the giving of advice) that 'occurs quite frequently' (ibid: paragraph 7).[66] In addition to 'assisting' the Executive in this way, the Interception Commissioner also 'advises' ministers and government departments 'in relation to issues arising on the interception of communications' (ibid). In the course of his work, the Interception Commissioner meets with ministers and officials, and has provided a very robust defence of the system of interception, and the procedures in place to monitor it, with little or no criticism of either, and with little sense that it is the function of the judge to protect civil liberties rather than participate in their erosion. The beginning and end points appear to be an acceptance that 'the Interception of Communications is an invaluable weapon in the continuing battle against terrorism and serious crime' (ibid: paragraph 87). According to Sir Swinton, he found 'no evidence whatsoever of any desire within the Intelligence or the Law Enforcement Agencies in this field to act wrongfully or unlawfully' (ibid: paragraph 7). On the contrary, he 'found a palpable desire on the part of all these Agencies to ensure that they do act completely within the four walls of the law' (ibid). Sir Swinton records that he is:

impressed by the quality, dedication and enthusiasm of the personnel carrying out this work on behalf of the Government and the people of the United Kingdom. They have a detailed understanding of the legislation and are always anxious to

---

[64] This rose to 519, 260 requests in 2007: Kennedy, 2008a: para 3.7.

[65] Regulation of Investigatory Powers Act 2000, s 57(2).

[66] The Commissioner also claims that the agencies 'welcome the oversight of the Commissioner and over the years have frequently sought my advice on issues that have arisen, and they have invariably accepted it' (Thomas, 2007: para 7).

ensure that they comply both with the legislation and the appropriate safeguards. All applications made to the Secretary of State are scrutinised by officials in the warrants unit within their respective Department (e.g., the Home Office, the Foreign Office and the Ministry of Defence and by similar officers in departments in the Northern Ireland Office and Scottish Executive). They are all skilled in their work and there is very little danger of any defective application being placed before the Secretary of State. (ibid: paragraph 13)

This satisfaction with the operation of the current law would no doubt reinforce the confidence of the Commissioner in making a number of recommendations, the effect of which would be to reinforce the secrecy and lack of transparency of the existing arrangements relating to the interception of communications. This applies particularly to his rejection of the case for allowing interception material to be admissible in legal proceedings.[67] The admissibility of this material in criminal proceedings (especially in those relating to suspected terrorists) is supported by many civil libertarians (Liberty, 2007), and it would have the advantage of flushing out and exposing the circumstances in which interception was used, thereby adding to the transparency of the process. The taking of such a step was also supported by Lord Lloyd of Berwick who conducted an *Inquiry into Legislation Against Terrorism* in 1996. A former interception commissioner himself (and a judge in the House of Lords at the time of his inquiry), Lord Lloyd recommended that the prosecution should be allowed to use this evidence in national security cases (Lloyd, 1996). However, the recommendation was rejected by the government, and in his last report as Interception Commissioner Sir Swinton Thomas attacked 'sometimes misguided, and often ill-informed, though no doubt well-motivated people' who kept opening this question, with a long and detailed account of why it would not be appropriate (Thomas, 2007: paragraph 44). The use of intercept evidence was said to be 'counter-productive', and in an extraordinary side-swipe this was said perhaps to 'explain why some who tend to act on behalf of defendants in terrorist and serious criminal cases appear to be supporting the concept' (paragraph 46).[68] Sir Swinton also made a number of other recommendations calculated to increase rather than decrease the use of surveillance practices. These included extending the use

---

[67] The position is currently governed by the Regulation of Investigatory Powers Act 2000, s 17.

[68] He gave as an example 'a recent case [where] a Court felt it had to order that 16,000 hours of eavesdropping (not intercept) material must be transcribed at the request of the Defence'. The cost was thought to be 'of the order of £1.9 million' (para 46). A Committee of Privy Councillors has since recommended that intercept evidence should be available for use in limited circumstances with appropriate safeguards (Chilcot, 2008), though the Interception Commissioner has welcomed 'the government's acceptance that if the Chilcot conditions could not be met then intercept evidence should not be introduced' (Kennedy, 2008a: para 2.7).

of telephone tapping to include MPs, a group hitherto exempt because of the Wilson doctrine, so-called after the Prime Minister who announced it (ibid, paras 47–57). This exemption—the removal of which is supported by Sir Swinton's successor (Kennedy, 2008: paragraph 63; 2008a: paragraph 7.2)— was thought to be inconsistent with the rule of law and indefensible in view of the procedures and safeguards now in force.

The National DNA Database

The focus so far has been on *watching people* and *acquiring information* about them. Although it is with some relief that we leave these matters, the respite is short as we turn now to the *storage and use of information* by the State, where an issue of great concern relates to the DNA database, which is used for the purposes of criminal investigation. The United Kingdom boasts the largest DNA database in the world, with the Home Office claiming that 5.2 per cent of the population is on the database, compared to only 0.5 per cent in the United States. This represented over 3.8 million people in the United Kingdom at the beginning of 2007, reflecting in turn a £300 million invest-ment of public money in the previous five years.[69] Although the government has no plans to introduce a universal database (whether compulsory or vol-untary), 'maintaining and developing the database is one of the government's top priorities',[70] with a Home Office minister claiming in the House of Lords that 'we have been able to detect a large number of crimes', there being 45,000 crimes with DNA matches in 2005–06.[71] A remarkable feature of this data-base is that it was not established by Parliament, nor regulated by Parliament, at least directly. Although there is legal authority to take and retain samples which can be used for DNA analysis,[72] there is no statutory authority for the creation of a DNA database, and no specific regulation of who may have access to the database and in what circumstances. Like CCTV cameras, there is effectively self-regulation through the modest requirements of the Data Protection Act 1998 to the extent that the database involves the process-ing of personal data. There is, however, a National DNA Database Strategy Board, chaired by a chief constable, with representatives from ACPO, the Home Office, and local police authorities; the secretary of the Board is also a police officer (NDNAD, 2006: 4). Yet despite its composition, the Board

---

[69] <http://www.homeoffice.gov.uk>.
[70] Ibid.
[71] HL Debs, 8 March 2007, col 318 (Baroness Scotland).
[72] Police and Criminal Evidence Act 1984, s 63.

claims that it is responsible to Parliament 'through its Home Office member-ship', though it does not report to Parliament (ibid: 5). On 25 July 2007, the Home Office announced the establishment of an Ethics Group to provide independent ethical advice to ministers about the operation and practice of the Board.[73] But this too was done without legislation or legislative authority, and although it is not clear by whom the nine member Board was appointed, it is to be assumed that it was by the Home Office itself.

The DNA Database and the English Courts

What is less well known is the role played by the courts in relation to the database, with the procedure giving rise to obvious questions about its com-patibility with article 8 of the ECHR. The right to take samples is provided in the Police and Criminal Evidence Act 1984 (as amended) which authorises non-intimate samples to be taken from anyone who has been arrested for a recordable offence; this may be done without the consent of the individual in question.[74] The Act then provides that once taken the information can be retained and stored, even though the individual in question is subsequently found not guilty and even if the police decide not to prosecute.[75] This is pre-cisely what happened in the case of an 11-year-old boy in South Yorkshire who was charged with attempted robbery but found not guilty; and a 38-year-old man called Michael Marper who was arrested and charged with harassing his partner with whom he was reconciled before the case came to trial, as a result of which charges were dropped. In both cases the police refused to destroy the samples, and in both cases the conduct of the police in retaining and storing the samples was challenged as violating the article 8 rights of the individuals in question. In what must be a blow to those who look to the courts to protect human rights, the House of Lords held that there was no violation of article 8.[76] Indeed, in giving the leading speech, Lord Steyn was of the view that the storage of this information did not engage article 8, but that if it did 'any inter-ference is very modest indeed'.[77] In coming to this conclusion, Lord Steyn endorsed the views of Mr Justice Leveson who had said at first instance that:

---

[73] HL Debs, 25 July 2007, col WS 70 (Lord West of Spithead).

[74] See Criminal Justice and Police Act 2001, ss 80–82. In Scotland, in contrast, the police must destroy samples and profiles from individuals who are not convicted, with an exception which allows for the retention of up to three years where the arrested person is suspected of involvement in sexual or violent crimes.

[75] Ibid.

[76] *R(S) v South Yorkshire Chief Constable* [2004] UKHL 30.

[77] Ibid, para [31].

A person can only be identified by fingerprint or DNA sample either by an expert or with the use of sophisticated equipment or both; in both cases, it is essential to have some sample with which to compare the retained data. Further, in the context of the storage of this type of information within records retained by the police, the material stored says nothing about the physical makeup, characteristics or life of the person to whom they belong.[78]

The only note of dissent to this view came from Baroness Hale, who was unable to see how the retention, storage, or keeping of information is not an interference, when the taking and use of the information is such an interference. In her view, 'It is an interference with privacy for someone to know or have access to private information even if they make no other use of it', adding that 'The mere fact that someone has read my private correspondence or seen my bank accounts is an interference with my privacy even if that person tells no one else what he has seen. That is why access to private information such as that contained in medical records has to be carefully controlled.'[79] Nor was Baroness Hale persuaded by Lord Steyn's point that only a few people can understand the information: in Baroness Hale's view, this does not affect the principle, although it may affect the justification.[80] That said, however, even Baroness Hale 'readily' accepted the argument that even if article 8 was engaged, the conduct of the police could be defended under article 8(2), arguing unequivocally and without apparent hesitation that:

The whole community, as well as the individuals whose samples are collected, benefits from there being as large a database as it is possible to have. The present system is designed to allow the collection of as many samples as possible and to retain as much as possible of what it has. The benefit to the aims of accurate and efficient law enforcement is thereby enhanced.[81]

In a similar vein, Lord Steyn had thought that even if article 8(1) had been engaged, there was plainly an objective justification for the violation under article 8(2) of the Convention, and that the restrictions on article 8(1) rights was in accordance with the law (notwithstanding the issues relating to the database referred to above).

The DNA Database and the Rule of Law

The DNA database thus raises significant rule of law issues. Not only has it been established without statutory authority, but it appears to operate

---

[78] Ibid, para [29].   [79] Ibid, para [73].   [80] Ibid.   [81] Ibid, para [78].

without judicial supervision. Imagine the situation of the individual—the young man at a peace camp—who has been wrongly arrested by the police, and from whom samples have been taken. He might subsequently bring an action for wrongful arrest, assault, and false imprisonment, and may well succeed; but there is no way that he would be able to have his data removed from the DNA database. Although a victim of improper and unlawful police conduct, there is no need to remove the data because the individual has no right not to be on the database in the first place. This is an outcome not far removed from the *Malone* case where telephone tapping without statutory authority was permitted by the courts on the ground that it did not violate any right of the complainant which was then known to or recognised by English law. The eclipse of the rule of law in this situation is compounded by the Data Protection Act 1998, with which the National DNA Database no doubt has to comply, as explained above. However, although those operating the database presumably must register under the 1998 Act, they are exempt from the first data protection principle, which requires data to be processed fairly and lawfully. They are exempt by virtue of the provision in the Act excluding personal data processed for the prevention or detection of crime (s 29), except to the extent that the first principle requires data processors to comply with the conditions in Schedule 2 of the Act (and Schedule 3 in the case of sensitive personal data). But all this requires is that the processing of the data should be undertaken for one of a number of purposes vaguely prescribed, such as the 'administration of justice' or even more generously 'the exercise of any other functions of a public nature exercised in the public interest by any person'. So even though the processing is neither 'lawful' nor 'fair', it is still 'permitted', provided it is necessary. For this purpose, processing data includes obtaining it. This means that rather than being protected from processing by the 1998 Act, data acquired from someone who was unlawfully arrested would appear to be expressly protected for processing by the 1998 Act.

Apart from these basic questions about the application of contitutional principle to the DNA database, this episode in British legal history also raises questions about the role of the judges. These questions arise not only in relation to decisions such as *Marper*, but also as a result of the extra-curial activities of members of the Bench. In a highly publicised intervention, Sir Stephen Sedley claimed that the current system—of including on the database all those who have passed through the hands of the police (whether innocent or guilty)—was indefensible, partly because it discriminated on racial grounds (with 40 per cent of black men,

13 per cent of Asian men, and 9 per cent of white men on the database).[82] Sir Stephen—who had been in the Court of Appeal in *Marper*[83]—also expressed concern that 'a great many people who are walking the streets and whose DNA would show them guilty of crimes, go free', and proposed that there should be a mandatory DNA database which would cover everyone resident in the United Kingdom, as well as everyone visiting the country (even for a weekend).[84] Acknowledging that this would have 'very serious' implications, use of the database would be for the 'absolutely rigorously restricted purpose of crime detection and prevention'. Although he is reported as having expressed these views in the past (in a lecture at Leicester University), Sir Stephen's comments nevertheless caught many people off guard. In his judicial work he had displayed a desire to enhance privacy rights, notably in cases involving celebrities such as Catherine Zeta Jones and Michael Douglas, often the subject of unwanted media publicity. Indeed he was the pioneering judge who proclaimed that 'we have reached a point at which it can be said with confidence that the law recognises and will appropriately protect a right of personal privacy'.[85] But as well as being surprised, very few people were convinced that a universal DNA database would be sustainable, it being claimed by an otherwise sympathetic Home Office minister that Sir Stephen had underestimated both the practical problems with such a proposal, along with the civil liberties implications.[86] This was supported by the House of Lords Constitution Committee, according to which a universal DNA database 'would be undesirable both in principle on the grounds of civil liberties, and in practice on the grounds of cost' (HL, 2009: paragraph 200).

Marper in the European Court of Human Rights

Any ambitions for a universal, national DNA database (which would take us even further out of line with the rest of Europe) have now been scotched by the decision of the European Court of Human Rights in the *Marper* case,[87] which at the time of writing has yet to be implemented. In proceedings

---

[82] See now HAC, 2009b, where it is said that 'the Equalities and Human Rights Commission estimates that over 30% of all black men are on the database compared with about 10% of all Asian men and 10% of all white men' (para 6).

[83] *R (Marper) v Chief Constable of South Yorkshire* [2002] EWCA Civ 1275.

[84] *Guardian*, 5 September 2007.

[85] *Douglas v Hello!* [2001] 2 WLR 992, para [110].

[86] *BBC News*, 5 September 2007.

[87] *Marper v United Kingdom* [2008] ECHR 1581.

before the Court (in a case that was concerned with the taking and storing of fingerprints as well as DNA samples), it was revealed that at least 20 Member States of the Council of Europe 'make provision for the taking of DNA information and storing it on national data bases or in other form'.[88] The countries in question were Austria, Belgium, the Czech Republic, Denmark, Estonia, Finland, France, Germany, Greece, Hungary, Ireland, Italy, Latvia, Luxembourg, the Netherlands, Norway, Poland, Spain, Sweden, and Switzerland, and their number 'is steadily increasing'. The British government was hardly helped, however, by the evidence that in most countries, 'the taking of DNA information in the context of criminal proceedings is not systematic but limited to some specific circumstances and/or to more serious crimes, notably those punishable by certain terms of imprisonment'.[89] Nor was it helped by the evidence that the 'United Kingdom is the only member State expressly to permit the systematic and indefinite retention of DNA profiles and cellular samples of persons who have been acquitted or in respect of whom criminal proceedings have been discontinued.'[90] Nor indeed was the United Kingdom helped by the additional evidence that it was the only Member State of the Council of Europe 'expressly to allow the systematic and indefinite retention of both profiles and samples of convicted persons',[91] with the general rule being that the profiles of convicted persons is allowed but only for limited periods after conviction. But British practice was not only way out of line with European practice, it was also out of line with the practice in other Commonwealth democracies, with the attention of the Strasbourg Court being addressed to a decision of the Supreme Court of Canada which had disapproved of the retention of the DNA of a juvenile first offender as being a grossly disproportionate violation of privacy rights, in the absence of a compelling public interest.[92]

Privacy, Legality, and Proportionality

The first of two questions for the Court was whether the DNA Database violated article 8(1) of the Convention, the issue which had been so casually dismissed by Lord Steyn in the House of Lords. The government had argued that the mere retention of DNA profiles did not fall within the ambit of private life for the purposes of article 8(1); but even if it did, 'the extremely limited nature of any adverse effects rendered the retention not sufficiently serious to constitute an interference',[93] thereby following the

---

[88] Ibid, para [45].   [89] Ibid, para [46].   [90] Ibid, para [47].
[91] Ibid, para [48].   [92] *R v RC* [2005] 3 SCR 99.
[93] *Marper v United Kingdom*, above, para [65].

line of argument that had won favour with Lord Steyn. The Court disagreed in uncompromising terms, noting that 'the concept of private life is a broad term not susceptible to exhaustive definition'; but that the 'mere storing of data relating to the private life of an individual amounts to an interference within the meaning of Article 8'.[94] Applying these principles to the specific question of the retention of DNA samples and fingerprints, the Court thought the concerns of the claimants were legitimate, commenting in agreement with Baroness Hale in the House of Lords that 'samples contain a unique genetic code of great relevance to both the individual and his relatives'.[95] Rejecting the government's claim that a 'DNA profile is nothing more than a sequence of numbers or a bar-code containing information of a purely objective and irrefutable character' intelligible to 'only a limited number of persons', the Court observed that 'the profiles contain substantial amounts of unique personal data', and that 'the DNA profiles' capacity to provide a means of identifying genetic relationships between individuals is in itself sufficient to conclude that their retention interferes with the right to the private life of the individuals concerned'.[96] And although the retention of samples and DNA profiles 'has a more important impact on private life than the retention of fingerprints', also agreeing with Baroness Hale the Court thought that 'the retention of fingerprints constitutes an interference with the right to respect for private life'.[97] It was accepted, however, that 'it may be necessary to distinguish between the taking, use and storage of fingerprints, on the one hand, and samples and profiles, on the other, in determining the question of justification'.[98]

Which brings us to the question of justification, at which point the Grand Chamber of 17 judges parted company with Baroness Hale. In holding that the retention of the DNA and fingerprints in this case could not be justified, it is important to emphasise that the Court did not say that the retention of DNA data cannot be justified under article 8(2) in any circumstances, acknowledging that the 'fight against crime' depends to a 'great extent' on the use of modern scientific techniques of investigation and identification.[99] The Court's concern was with the facts of the case before it, and in rejecting the government's claim that the data of the applicants could be retained, the Court was influenced strongly by the practice of other Council of Europe States, and by the position in Scotland ('as part of the United Kingdom').[100] In the first of two particularly important passages, the Court said that it was:

---

[94] Ibid, paras [66]-[67].   [95] Ibid, para [72].   [96] Ibid, para [75].
[97] Ibid, para [86].   [98] Ibid.   [99] Ibid, para [105].
[100] Ibid, para [109].

struck by the blanket and indiscriminate nature of the power of retention in England and Wales. The material may be retained irrespective of the nature or gravity of the offence with which the individual was originally suspected or of the age of the suspected offender; fingerprints and samples may be taken—and retained—from a person of any age, arrested in connection with a recordable offence, which includes minor or non-imprisonable offences. The retention is not time-limited; the material is retained indefinitely whatever the nature or seriousness of the offence of which the person was suspected. Moreover, there exist only limited possibilities for an acquitted individual to have the data removed from the nationwide database or the materials destroyed; in particular, there is no provision for independent review of the justification for the retention according to defined criteria, including such factors as the seriousness of the offence, previous arrests, the strength of the suspicion against the person and any other special circumstances.[101]

The foregoing is a paragraph that will doubtless inform the government's legislative response, as will the second important passage in the Court's decision where it expressed concern that 'persons in the position of the applicants, who have not been convicted of any offence and are entitled to the presumption of innocence, are treated in the same way as convicted persons'.[102]

Restoring the Rule of Law

The *Marper* case raises interesting questions about the effectiveness of the Human Rights Act as an instrument for the protection of human rights. This is not the first time (whether before or since the introduction of the Act) that the Strasbourg Court has had to intervene to find that the domestic courts had fallen short on Convention rights. It is unlikely to be the last as the flow of cases from London to Strasbourg continues despite the Human Rights Act; and it is unlikely to be the last in light of the strategy of the domestic courts of the United Kingdom to see the Strasbourg jurisprudence as a ceiling rather than a floor. The fact is that the United Kingdom falls short of Convention obligations in a number of areas, and these failings are not failings for which the judges can avoid any responsibility. In the meantime, the Court has given the government a headache on the question of samples, fingerprints and the DNA database, without giving any clear indication of what now needs to be done. Although the government lost comprehensively, it does not follow that it will be impermissible to take samples and store on the database the DNA of anyone who has not been found guilty of an offence. Only five States require information and data to be

---

[101] Ibid, para [119].   [102] Ibid, para [122].

destroyed on acquittal, or on the discontinuance of criminal proceedings; at least ten allow for its retention in limited circumstances, for example where suspicions remain about the person or if further investigations are needed in a separate case, or if there is a risk that the suspect will commit a dangerous offence.[103] It is perhaps significant also that the Court made a specific—and apparently warm—reference to the Scottish position as being of 'particular significance', where the DNA of unconvicted persons may be retained for up to three years in the case of adults charged with a violent or sexual offence.[104] The other question for the government is the period of time for which DNA samples of the guilty as well as the innocent may be retained under any future regime. Although the United Kingdom is the only country in the Council of Europe to allow for indefinite retention, in France 'DNA profiles can be retained for 25 years after an acquittal or discharge'.[105]

While wrestling with these issues, true to form the government cocked a snook at the Court when it was announced only 12 days after the decision that it planned to expand the DNA database by taking samples from prisoners who had been convicted before the national database had been set up.[106] Announcing that the DNA samples of children under 10 would be removed immediately from the database, it was announced that 'the Government [was] also seeking powers to allow police to trawl the country taking samples from serious offenders who have been released from jail', with *The Times* reporting further that the Home Secretary 'wants the police to enter jails in England and Wales and Northern Ireland to start taking DNA samples from rapists and murderers who were convicted before the database was created in 1995'.[107] In the meantime, the Home Secretary announced that a White Paper would be published in 2009 with proposals for 'a more proportionate, fair and commonsense approach', the White Paper to address both the retention of DNA of those not convicted of any offence, as well as the length of retention of the DNA of those who have been so convicted. The early indications are that the Home Office was looking closely at the Scottish model.[108] The implementation of the *Marper* decision will almost certainly need primary legislation, and will provide the opportunity to address a major rule of law question which was raised but elided by the Court in its decision. According to the Court,

it is as essential, in this context, as in telephone tapping, secret surveillance and covert intelligence-gathering, to have clear, detailed rules governing the scope and application of measures, as well as minimum safeguards concerning, *inter*

[103] Ibid, para [47].
[104] Ibid, para [109].
[105] Ibid, para [47].
[106] *The Times*, 17 December 2008.
[107] Ibid.
[108] Ibid.

alia, duration, storage, usage, access of third parties, procedures for preserving the integrity and confidentiality of data and procedures for its destruction, thus providing sufficient guarantees against the risk of abuse and arbitrariness.[109]

Like telephone tapping, secret surveillance and covert intelligence-gathering before it, the DNA database grew up without any statutory authority (though the taking of samples had statutory authority). And like telephone tapping, secret surveillance, and covert intelligence-gathering before it, it has taken a decision of the Strasbourg Court in the face of complacency by the domestic courts to require something to be done.

The National Identity Register and Identity Cards

The Identity Cards Act 2006 introduces a new concern about privacy, with its provisions for a National Identity Register and identity cards. As we shall see, the Act just as significantly also introduces a new concern about the rule of law not hitherto encountered in this chapter, though it does appear elsewhere in this book. This is the role of the executive in the enforcement of the law, and the marginalisation of the judiciary in the process. But before considering such matters, it is necessary first to consider the substance of a law which—if fully implemented—will create a most remarkable invasion of privacy, and which in the process will promote a heightened sense of surveillance, as well as a capacity for detailed personal information to be moved around cyberspace and beyond with relative impunity. The government justified these measures on a number of grounds, from the need to respond to terrorism, to the need to control access to public services by illegal migrants, to the need to address the growing problem of identity theft. According to the biographer of the author of the new law, however, ID cards were 'essentially about controlling immigration and the consequences, such as health tourism and benefit fraud' (Pollard, 2004: 230). Nevertheless, concerns about the impact of the Identity Cards Bill on human rights—along with concerns about the costs of the register and the Bill's original provision for compulsory identity cards—led to strong political opposition. As a result, the government was required significantly to dilute its original proposals which will require fresh legislation if they are to be fully realised. Fresh legislation will also be required if the police

---

[109] *Marper v United Kingdom*, above, para [99].

are to win the power to stop people to check their ID cards.[110] The Identity Cards Act 2006 nevertheless breaks new ground in peacetime. Measures of this kind have only ever been introduced when the nation was at war, with a national registration scheme established by statute during the First and Second World Wars, and a national identity card scheme introduced by statute during the Second World War, and continued for a short time thereafter.[111] The legal regimes introduced in these earlier periods were much different from those constructed by the 2006 Act. Under the National Registration Act 1915, a duty was imposed on local registration authorities to compile and maintain a register of people in their locality, and on every person to 'fill up and sign a form showing [prescribed] particulars' (s 4(1)). Similarly, under the National Registration Regulations 1939, there was a duty on prescribed persons—usually the 'head' of the household—to submit returns as provided for in the regulations.[112]

The Statutory Framework

In contrast, if it is implemented in its present form the Identity Cards Act 2006 will impose a duty on the part of the Home Secretary to establish a register for the 'maintenance of a secure and reliable record of registrable facts about individuals in the United Kingdom' (s 1(3)). The duty is designed to promote a number of statutory purposes, notably the interests of national security, the prevention or detection of crime, the enforcement of immigration controls, the enforcement of prohibitions on unauthorised working or employment, and securing the efficient and effective provision of public services. The Act will also impose a duty on the Home Secretary to enter on the register those people who apply and who are entitled to be entered on the register (s 2). Entitlement will be extended to every individual over the age of 16 resident in the United Kingdom (s 2(2)), subject to a power of the Home Secretary to exclude those with no right to remain in the country, as well as others (s 2(3)). In a supreme act of doublespeak, registration

---

[110] Rather ominously, however, the police and the army in Northern Ireland have retained their statutory power to 'stop a person for so long as is necessary to question him to ascertain his identity and movements' (Justice and Security (Northern Ireland) Act 2007, s 21).

[111] Under the 1939 Act, however, where a constable in uniform could require a person to produce his or her identity card, or if he or she was not carrying the card at the time of the request to produce within a prescribed period of time at the local police station. Moreover, it was revealed as 'obvious' that the police 'as a matter of routine, demand the production of national registration identity cards whenever they stop or interrogate a motorist for whatever reason' (*Willcock v Muckle* [1951] 2 KB 844; Bradley, 1987: 209).

[112] SR&O 1939 No 1248, reg 8.

under the Identity Cards Act 2006 (unlike either of its antecedents) is thus presented not as a duty but as a right of the citizen (who has the attendant right also to pay the costs associated with registration).[113] However, section 4 authorises the Home Secretary to 'designate' certain documents—such as passports—for the purposes of the Act. Where a document is designated, any applicants for such a document will also have to apply for entry to the National Identity Register and to have an ID card (unless they have already done so), whether they want to be on the register or not, and whether they want an ID card or not. This means that while there will be no duty to be registered, nevertheless there will be circumstances where the citizen will be under a duty to exercise his or her right to be on the register. This is at best a jurisprudential solecism, which severely tests the neat classifications of the great jurist Hohfeld, who saw rights and duties as correlatives and not coordinates, with the duty to exercise a right perhaps having no parallel on the statute book. New Labour's doublespeak certainly provides nice material for endless discussions in the jurisprudence class:

Question: When is a right a duty?
Answer: When the citizen is required by the State to exercise it.

Perhaps in time the unforgiving wall that distinguishes rights from duties will crumble. In the meantime, those of us well grounded in doublethink 'remember their original meanings', though we must hope that it is not the case that 'within a couple of generations even the possibility of such a lapse [into Oldspeak] would have vanished'. There is in fact a spectrum of circumstances whereby someone may appear on the register. At one extreme are the 'free'—those improbable individuals who exercising their right to be included just make an application, for no obvious reason, perhaps because they are 'identity challenged', or have an identity crisis. In the middle and likely to be the largest group are the 'hybrids'—those with a duty to exercise their right. And at the other extreme is a third category whom the Act recognises may be included by the Home Secretary, even though they have not applied to be included and whether or not they are entitled to be. These people—the 'coerced', who will be unable to remove themselves despite their unwillingness to be entered—will be in effect under a duty to be on the register if entry would be consistent with the statutory purposes, and if there is information capable of being recorded in an entry for the individual in question 'otherwise available to be recorded' (s 2(4)). We can speculate as to how the State would

---

[113] In a bitter dispute with the London School of Economics, the government contested claims that ID cards could cost as much as £300, though regulations made under s 35 (which must be approved in draft by both House of Parliament) may provide for 'the payment of fees by instalment'. The government has more recently announced that the scheme will cost £5.4 billion to establish and run in its first 10 years.

have recordable information about an individual, though the other forms of surveillance discussed in this chapter provides a good start. But it seems that this last group will include foreign nationals who will be required to register,[114] with the National Identity Register in the first instance being a de facto National Foreigners' Register. Those who are compulsorily registered will be required—on pain of a civil penalty—also to apply for an identity card (s 7). However, for those about to enter the register by whichever of these three routes, some comfort may be found in the words of section 3. This makes it clear that information may be entered on the register 'only if and for so long as it is consistent with the statutory purposes'. Moreover, information may not be recorded on the register unless it is information authorised by Schedule 1 of the Act. The reassuring impression is that there are thus clear statutory limits.

The National Identity Register and the Rule of Law

Any sense of security from the words of the statute would, however, be a false one: the statutory purposes are wide, and the information required by Schedule 1 takes 135 lines to list under nine separate categories, which—incidentally—is much more than was required under the two previous schemes introduced at a time of world war and the threat of invasion. Although this may not be enough to dissuade the most severe cases of 'identity challenge', any lingering sense of security might rapidly evaporate when it is realised that the individual who exercises his or her right to be registered may be required to 'attend at an agreed place and time or (in the absence of agreement) at a specified place and time'; allow his or her fingerprints and other biometric information to be taken and recorded; allow himself or herself to be photographed; and 'otherwise to provide any other information that may be required by the Home Secretary' (s 5). So there is no question about the formalities being completed at home, or by a quick trip to Tesco for a passport photo. To add to the woes, there is little doubt that the work will be privatised, with the government's Explanatory Notes recording at one point that 'private sector organisations may have certain parts of the process contracted out to them' (including the actual production of ID cards), thereby creating yet another opportunity for abuse on a massive scale. Those registered will be given a National Identity Registration Number (s 2(3)) (not yet to be indelibly imprinted or impregnated by tattoo or computer chip), and (except in prescribed circumstances) must be issued with an identity card (s 6). Thereafter, the provision of certain public services may be made

[114] *BBC News*, 26 January 2007.

conditional on an individual producing an ID card, though this does not apply to matters such as the payment of benefit or access to the NHS, except in the case of those who are 'subject to compulsory registration' (s 13(2)). It is also the case that the Home Secretary will be able to share the information on the Register with other government agencies in some circumstances without the consent of the individual concerned, and without the need for a warrant or any other formality (s 17). These agencies include the various security services (MI5, MI6, and GCHQ) and the Serious Organised Crime Agency, the police, HM Revenue and Customs (for various purposes), and other government departments (for carrying out 'prescribed functions').

The use of information in this way raises by now predictable concerns about rights being violated on the say-so of the executive, with the scheme to be supervised by yet another executive appointed commissioner, on this occasion the National Identity Scheme Commissioner, though with limited powers (s 22).[115] The Identity Cards Act 2006, however, raises fresh rule of law concerns in relation to the Surveillance Society, these dealing with the enforcement procedures. Several of the obligations under the Act (such as the duty to supply information to keep the register up to date,[116] which will become a real burden long after the novelty of registration wears off) are to be supported by civil rather than criminal penalties, an arrangement which is a constitutional curiosity as well as a legal oxymoron.[117] What is particularly contestable about the enforcement provisions of the Identity Cards Act 2006 is that the power to impose the penalty rests with the Home Secretary who may exercise the power without a court order in advance. The money (up to £1,000) will then be recoverable by the Home Office 'via the civil courts' (that is to say, by sending in the bailiffs), as the government's Explanatory Notes cheerfully make clear, the executive thus having the authority to demand money by cutting out the judicial middleman and without a court order that the money is due. It is true that the Home Secretary will have to impose penalties in accordance with a Code of Practice (s 34). It is also true that the individual will be able to contest liability by giving notice to the Home Secretary that he or she objects to the penalty, though if this route is chosen, no provision is made for a hearing before the Home Secretary

---

[115] The jurisdiction of the National Identity Scheme Commissioner does not extend to the security services, with the Intelligence Services Commissioner being given an additional role for this purpose (s 24).

[116] Identity Cards Act 2006, s 10.

[117] There are, however, some criminal penalties in the Act: it is an offence to pass on confidential information without lawful authority, a measure addressed principally to those who work with the register, ID cards, or with the Commissioner (s 27). It is also an offence to possess false documents (s 25), and to give false information (s 28).

who will have the power to confirm or increase the penalty (s 32). And it is true too that it will be possible to lodge an appeal in the county or sheriff court (in addition to or instead of an appeal to the Home Secretary), this to take the form of a 'rehearing of the Secretary of State's decision to impose the penalty' (s 33), which also means that the penalty could be increased. Although the use of administrative law to impose quasi-criminal penalties is not unprecedented, it is nevertheless greatly to be regretted. Whatever label is to be given to this procedure (criminal, civil, or administrative), de facto criminal penalties should not be imposed by a minister. It is indeed a first principle of the rule of law that penalties should be imposed, if at all, only after (not before) due process, and only after (not before) a finding by an independent judicial or quasi-judicial body.

Conclusion

Constitutional principle is not something that would have troubled Big Brother: in Airstrip One, 'nothing was illegal, since there were no longer any laws'. Phrases such as the 'rule of law' would have been either abolished in Newspeak, or regarded as a heresy of 'a very crude kind, a species of blasphemy'. Nevertheless, only a person 'well grounded in doublethink' could confidently contend that the current laws and practices relating to surveillance are consistent with the rule of law, in a society where it can now confidently be said by influential people that 'national security is a civil liberty of every citizen' (Carlile, 2009: 5). As in the case of police powers, however, in this chapter too we have confronted the reality of (a) power without legal authority (for example in the use of CCTV cameras, and the establishment and use of the DNA database); and (b) the failure of public authorities to comply with the legal rules by which they are bound (for example in the use of various forms of targeted surveillance), with apparently little fear of any adverse consequences if they get caught taking the risk. More pronounced in the context of surveillance than in the context of police powers is (c) the extent to which public authorities are empowered to determine when to exercise their powers of surveillance, with the most remarkable invasions of privacy being authorised in advance, not by the courts but by a bewildering kaleidoscope of government agents, from town hall clerks, to police officers, to the Home Secretary. More recently, we have seen (d) the introduction of an even more stark kind of executive justice, whereby the executive will be empowered to impose penalties (without a hearing) on those who are alleged to have broken the law, a much more insidious form of administrative intervention than the various forms against which

Dicey (1959) and his disciple Hewart (1929) railed. It is true that there is (e) an equally bewildering array of government appointed judicial commissioners to supervise the operation of much of this legislation, but it is also true that this system has been found wanting for a number of reasons, with one function of the commissioners having been to reinforce the secrecy by which surveillance powers are exercised, while evidently powerless in the face of executive non-compliance with statutory obligations.

So far as the contribution of courts and judges to these developments is concerned, here it may be said that that the latter have oiled the wheels rather than applied the brakes. When given an opportunity in legal proceedings to temper the growing power of the State, they have refused to intervene. The outstanding example is the *Marper* case,[118] in which the House of Lords preferred to see the data of the innocent preserved on the National DNA database along with that of the guilty, leading to an application to the Strasbourg court, which the Human Rights Act has failed to make redundant from a British point of view. This failure on the part of the courts to deal with the threat to personal privacy posed by the State contrasts with the willingness of the same judges to develop a right of privacy to protect celebrities—such as Michael Douglas and Naomi Campbell—from unwanted press publicity.[119] But apart from failing to restrain the surveillance state, the judges have allowed themselves to be used as part of a process of questionable supervision of executive power, as in the case of the various Commissioners established to supervise the different surveillance regimes. In these ways the judges have allowed themselves to become part of the executive branch, working with and advising agencies, rather than operating as part of the judicial branch by authorising in advance (and at arm's length) the various agencies before they invade the privacy of the individual. It is true that *ex post facto* supervision offers some scrutiny over the process of surveillance. But as already argued, it is a weak form of scrutiny, in which the judges have not only reinforced the secrecy of much of what goes on, but have also made recommendations which are calculated to reinforce the secrecy and lead to the greater use of the powers they have been commissioned to monitor.[120] Yet it is not only

---

[118] [2008] ECHR 1581.

[119] 'the right of the media to impart information to the public has to be balanced in its turn against the respect that must be given to private life': *Campbell v MGN Ltd* [2004] UKHL 22, para [106] (Lord Hope).

[120] In 1993 the then Interception Commissioner (Sir Thomas Bingham) questioned whether 'the Secretary of State should circumscribe his discretion to authorise the issue of warrants by reference to an arithmetical norm' (Bingham, 1993a: paras 14–16), with reference to a quota that had existed for many years in relation to the granting of warrants to the police; in 2007 (as we have seen) public authorities were told by the Interception Commissioner that if the low use of the power to secure

while sitting in the courts and operating as judicial commissioners that the judges have distinguished themselves by encouraging rather than restraining the Surveillance State. In 2007, Lord Justice Sedley—a member of the Court of Appeal in the *Marper* case but speaking extra-judicially—made the eyes of even Home Office ministers water when—as we have seen—he proposed that everyone should be entered on the DNA database, including weekend visitors to the United Kingdom.

---

access to communications data 'continues unexplained, then consideration must be given to removing the powers from them' (Thomas, 2007: para 26); and in 2008 the Chief Surveillance Commissioner expressed unease 'about the large number of Local Authorities which are electing not to exercise the powers given them for the use of CHIS', while acknowledging that it was not his role 'to encourage the use of covert activity' (OSC, 2008: para 9.5).

CHAPTER 4

Freedom of Assembly and the Right of Public Protest

Introduction

O N Saturday 15 February 2003, an estimated two million people converged on London to protest against the imminent invasion of Iraq by British and American forces. Organised by the Stop the War Coalition, the Campaign for Nuclear Disarmament and the Muslim Association of Britain, they came by bus, train and car from all over the country to take part in what is thought to have been the biggest demonstration ever held in the United Kingdom. Similar events took place at the same time in other British cities in what was a coordinated global event, with an estimated six to ten million people demonstrating in support of the same cause in an estimated 60 cities throughout the world. According to the BBC, the London march stretched for three and a half miles, doubtless causing huge inconvenience for those in the capital with less worldly concerns, not to mention a great deal of noise as 'a tide of banner-waving protesters . . . cheered, shouted, sounded horns and banged drums, waving signs with slogans "No War On Iraq" and "Make Tea, Not War".' The march ended with a rally in Hyde Park (despite initial resistance from Tessa Jowell, worried about possible damage to the grass), where the protesters were addressed by such notables as Ken Livingstone, Vanessa Redgrave, Tony Benn, Bianca Jagger, Harold Pinter, and Mo Mowlem. Perhaps remarkably, only a handful of arrests were made during the course of the day, mainly for minor public order offences, though attention was also drawn to an incident where 20 protesters held a sit down protest in Trafalgar Square, leading to another four arrests. Nevertheless, there can be no clearer example that liberty is alive and well in Great Britain, and that people are free to protest, march, and assemble, and to do so in great numbers through the centre of our capital city. But as might be expected, the great demonstrations of 15 February 2003 do not tell the whole story about the vigour of freedom of assembly in British law.

As we will see in this chapter, serious concerns remain about the extent to which people may freely assemble and publicly protest, despite the 'constitutional shift' engineered by the Human Rights Act where the right to freedom of assembly is expressly protected.[1] This is also an area where constitutional principle is at times threadbare. There is clear evidence that the police act beyond their powers (as established by the courts); there are persistent allegations that public authorities exercise their powers arbitrarily (whether local authorities in imposing conditions on demonstrations, or the police in the exercise of their powers of arrest) and improperly (as in the case of the police in dispersing groups of peaceful protesters, or in seeking ASBOs to deal with demonstrators); and that steps are taken to avoid any accountability for aggressive and violent policing (for example by resorting to the well known tactic of covering identification numbers on the uniforms of police officers, a controversial issue in the G20 protests in April 2009, but complained about in the past, from the general strike in 1926, to the policing of a student protest in Manchester in 1985). This is an area also where the Human Rights Act appears to be sleeping: if the constitutional gears have shifted, they have yet to engage, as was made clear by the various official reports into the policing of the G20 protests, which were held almost 10 years after the Human Rights Act was introduced (HAC, 2009a; HMIC, 2009), but which raised serious questions about the conduct of the police in facilitating protest in a way anticipated by article 11 of the ECHR. The approach of the judges (even at the highest level) has been inconsistent, using the HRA simultaneously to facilitate and contain the operation of controversial police powers, while also fashioning new private law constraints on the exercise of peaceful assembly. To the extent that the courts have been effective constraints on the exercise of executive power, this has arisen largely as a result of the work of the jury, willing to stand up to the government, the police and the judiciary (Weir, 2007; Morrison, 2008). The experience of the right to freedom of assembly is quite a catalogue of human rights failure.

Rule of Law or Rule by Police?

There are many well-established powers available to the police to seek to ban or to impose conditions on the conduct of marches or demonstrations

---

[1] According to Sedley LJ, the Human Rights Act constituted a 'constitutional shift' in English law with regard to freedom of assembly in particular: *Redmond-Bate v DPP* (1999) 163 JP 789, at p 795.

(Bradley and Ewing, 2007). These typically require the police to secure the approval of democratically elected and accountable bodies (local authorities usually, though the Home Secretary in London), and the decisions of these bodies will normally be subject to judicial review, to ensure that the powers are used for the purposes for which they were intended (even though the courts have typically shown great indulgence to the needs of the police in these situations). However, alongside these statutory powers with accountability built into the manner of their exercise have emerged a body of powers and practices which are exercisable by the police themselves, without reference to any accountable political authority, and which have the effect of circumventing these statutory provisions and the accountability that goes with them. It is true that the exercise of these informal powers and practices may be challenged in the courts. But as we shall see, this will take place after the event, and it offers little by way of a serious threat to the police. In any case, from the point of view of the protester, a right once denied can never be revived. Nor is the denial of the right something for which there can be adequate compensation.

Infiltration of Protest Groups

It begins with the infiltration of protest groups, perhaps using powers of surveillance under the Regulation of Investigatory Powers Act 2000 (and its Scottish sibling) discussed in Chapter 3. On 25 April 2009, the *Guardian* ran a story exposing an attempt by the Strathclyde police to infiltrate the protest group Plane Stupid, which has organised demonstrations against aviation and airport expansion, including high profile events at Stansted airport (where they managed to close the airport by making their way through the security fences onto the runway), and at the House of Commons (where they managed to climb onto the roof of the Parliament building). Police infiltration of political organisations and protest groups is well known, though it is unusual to be presented with such clear evidence as that revealed by the tape recorded interviews between Matilda Gifford and two men presenting themselves as police officers who were trying to recruit her. Arrested on 22 March 2009, Gifford was subsequently released from custody 'without being processed through the court, and without the return of all her confiscated possessions—including the keys of her house'. She was told that these could be picked up from Partick police station on 25 March, where two middle aged men claiming to be plain clothes police officers were waiting to speak to her, one claiming to be a detective constable and the other his assistant. In a subsequent meeting with Gifford, the detective constable sought to reassure her that both men were 'officers from Strathclyde police with warrant cards', who worked for 'the community intelligence section, but the names of people in his department were not available via the main switchboard'.[2]

Apart from the stupidity of the police officers in not taking steps to see whether they were being recorded (though they were alive to the possibility), three factors of importance emerge from the report. The first is the acknowledgement of the police officers that infiltration of groups is widespread. Thus, according to one of the officers:

Look at the big picture—we work with hundreds of people, believe me, ranging from terrorist organisations right through to whatever ... We have people who give us information on environmentalism, leftwing extremism, rightwing—you name it, we have the whole spectrum of reporting.

The point we're making is: they come to us with the concerns, because within the organisations for which they have strong ideologies and beliefs they are happy to go along with that, but what they will not get involved in is maybe where it's gonna impact someone else. That's when they come to us and say 'by the way, so and so—in my opinion—is maybe getting a wee bit too hotheaded'.

Later in the same report it is said that Gifford was 'given the impression that, if she agreed, she would become one of "thousands" of paid informants who work with the police, secretly relaying information about protest groups'.

The second point to emerge from the report is that various inducements were given to secure co-operation, in circumstances that give the appearance of a rather cavalier disregard for the legal obligations of the informer. Inevitably the discussion turned to the question of possible financial inducements, and the conversation took the following turn:

We don't want to stop you doing what you're doing. We're just asking you to consider a proposal. And if you look at it in the light of—I'm gonna use the adage, if you want— almost a business proposal ... It is effectively entering into a business contract. You would assist us. Let's not use the word work—you would assist us. But equally we would be ... assisting you— be it financially or whatever'. He added that the contract would have implications if she were ever arrested.

Gifford said she would be unlikely to be interested if they were talking about '20 quid'. The assistant replied: 'UK plc can afford more than 20 quid'.

After having been told that she would only have to meet her handlers once a week in return, Gifford mentioned something about returning to university, and her loan, whereupon:

'You see exactly what you've said there?' said the detective constable. 'At least you're thinking logically. If you're going back to school you're going to have loans

[2] *The Guardian*, 25 April 2009.

to pay off. So you're going to need money, you'll still be out probably working, doing bits, but wouldn't it also be nice to have tax-free money you'd be getting? You wouldn't pay any tax on it. So you could do with it what you want'.

The interesting features of the *Guardian* report are the suggestions that Gifford would enjoy some kind of protection were she to be arrested, and that she would be paid in such a way as not to pay income tax on her earnings for what was described as 'almost a business proposal'. It is no doubt a naïve thought, but is it not the case that the police ought not be offering to protect sources from the consequences of their actions (the law should apply equally to everyone), or seducing people with tax free payments (with the detective constable's assistant claiming that 'people have been paid tens of thousands of pounds')?

Pre-emptive Action by the Police

The impact of infiltration is to be seen coincidentally in an event that was to occur within weeks of the *Guardian* report about Tilly Gifford and Plane Stupid. On 13 April 2009 police officers raided the Iona independent school in Sneinton, Nottingham, and arrested environmental protesters (unrelated to Plane Stupid). According to *The Independent:*

Shortly after midnight more than 20 riot vans disgorged scores of police officers, backed by dogs, who charged into the car park of a privately owned school off Sneinton Dale, the main thoroughfare running through the suburb. Over the next three hours police rounded up more than 100 people, bundling them en masse into the vans before eventually driving them down to police stations around the city.[3]

In fact 114 people were arrested in what was thought to be 'the biggest pre-emptive raid on environmental campaigners in UK history', the operation being said to involve some 200 police officers.[4] From 'information gathered' the police announced that they believed that 'those arrested were planning a period of prolonged disruption to the safe running of Ratcliffe-on-Soar power station',[5] a coal fired facility owned by E.ON. According to E.ON:

Ratcliffe power station was the planned target of an organised protest during the early hours of this morning. While we understand that everyone has a right to protest peacefully and lawfully, this was clearly neither of those things so we will be assisting the police with their investigations into what could have been a very dangerous and irresponsible attempt to disrupt an operational power plant.

[3] *The Independent*, 14 April 2009.
[4] *The Guardian*, 14 April 2009.
[5] Ibid.

According to the BBC, doors and windows were smashed in the raid,[6] which led to the seizure of specialist equipment as well as the arrests. Those arrested were taken into police custody, and 'a number of premises were searched'.[7]

The police conduct led to speculation that the activists may have been 'penetrated by police agents after years of running rings around law enforcement with bold publicity stunts and meticulously planned operations of their own'. According to press reports:

This is pretty much the first time that the police have been able to pre-empt a mass demonstration and it does raise the prospect that they have used spies', said one veteran activist. 'As the anti-coal movement gathers momentum the police reaction seems to be getting stronger and more aggressive. The same thing happened with the anti-road movement in the 1990s'.[8]

This action was taken by the police in light of earlier demonstrations at Ratcliffe and similar demonstrations at other power stations, notably Drax power station in North Yorkshire and Kingsnorth in Kent, where protesters famously climbed the cooling tower. Although formal details of the proposed action were not released, the press reported campaign veterans who 'speculated that the demonstrators could have been planning to chain themselves to the conveyor belts taking coal into the power plant in an attempt to stop the turbines when fuel ran out'.[9] This was also said to be part of a larger campaign against the coal industry:

It is thought the demonstration was being organised by activists linked to the Climate Camp group, which organised the attempted blockade of Kingsnorth power station in Kent, where large groups of environmental activists were able to defy heavy security to stage publicity demonstrations against some of Britain's most polluting industries. Over the past 12 months direct action groups have stepped up their campaigns against the coal industry. In June last year, 29 protesters stopped a coal train from entering Drax power station in Yorkshire while last year's Climate Camp was held at Kingsnorth power station to highlight opposition to any increased use of fossil fuels.[10]

The police it seems were acting on the basis that the planned action had been taken to prevent a conspiracy to commit an aggravated trespass, and criminal damage. The former is an offence under the Criminal Justice and Public Order Act 1994, s 68 which applies to any trespass on land designed to intimidate people taking part in lawful activities, or to obstruct

[6] *BBC News*, 15 April 2009.
[7] *The Guardian*, 14 April 2009.
[8] *The Independent*, 14 April 2009.
[9] *The Guardian*, 13 April 2009.
[10] *The Independent*, 14 April 2009.

or disrupt such activity, having been introduced originally to deal principally with hunt saboteurs. According to Liberty (2009), however, s 68 'turned demonstrations on private land into a criminal matter even where there is no intended harm to people or property', adding that '[w]hen you add the suspicion of conspiracy to this already problematic offence, a broad discretion for pre-emptive arrests exists. And when restrictive police bail conditions are then imposed on those bailed without charge, the cumulative power of the police to stifle a potentially peaceful protest becomes alarmingly apparent' (ibid). All of those arrested were released on police bail, with the police announcing that it would be some time before any decision was taken to charge any of them. But for the police and for E.ON, their mission had been accomplished: the action was foiled, doubts were cast within the protesters that they had been infiltrated; and a message was sent to the supporters that the police would act aggressively, with more than one press report drawing comparisons between the policing of this incident and the policing of terrorist incidents. It was left to an *Independent* leader to point out, however, that

pre-emptive arrests may sometimes be justified: for instance, if there is evidence that an act of terrorism or other major life-threatening crime is nearing execution. But the evidence has to be persuasive, and it is often hard to convince a jury that a conspiracy to commit a crime existed, as acquittals under such circumstances show. People tend to be uncomfortable with the idea that someone can be arrested before a crime has been committed – and rightly so. It smacks of totalitarian regimes and the thought police.[11]

Preventing Attendance at Demonstrations

A long established tactic of the police is to stop people attending demonstrations, which they decide not to pre-empt. The police, it seems, will decide not only whether an event should take place, but who should be permitted to take part. The issue was brought into sharp focus by the policing of a demonstration at RAF Fairford on 22 March 2003 organised by a group called Gloucestershire Weapons Inspectors. Due notice was given to the police under the Public Order Act 1986 (s 11), and conditions were duly imposed by the police under the same Act (s 12). A number of protest groups including the Wombles—who also posted a message on their website 'couched in violent terms'[12]—advertised coaches to attend the event, which it was estimated would attract a crowd of up to 5,000. The policing operation was said to be 'the largest ever undertaken by the Gloucestershire Constabulary', with police officers:

[11] Ibid.
[12] *R (Laporte) v Gloucester Chief Constable*, [2006] UKHL 55, para [6].

mustered in large numbers, supported by anti-climbing teams, patrols on both sides of the perimeter fence, dog teams, a member of the Metropolitan Police Public Order Intelligence Unit (to recognise those known to be extreme protesters), a facial recognition team, Forward Intelligence Teams, three Police Support Units ('PSUs') and helicopters.[13]

Into this scene travelled Ms Laporte, along with

a diverse group of about 150 campaigners—Quakers, 70-year-old CND members, journalists, anarchists, socialists, and members of a samba band [who] boarded coaches in London to set off for a day at the 'Flowers for Fairford' demonstration at the airbase (Liberty, 2003: 5).

About 10 miles away from RAF Fairford, however, at a place called Lechlade, 'their three coaches were met by police motorcyclists who escorted them into a blockade of at least 70 police officers'. The protesters were 'told that police officers would be using powers under section 60 of the Criminal Justice and Public Order Act 1994 to search them'.[14] After being searched and filmed and after some people had property confiscated, the protesters boarded their coaches. But rather than be allowed to proceed to RAF Fairford, the coach drivers were instructed to follow a police escort all the way back to London.

This latter intervention was made under common law powers authorising the police to take steps to prevent a breach of the peace, the police concerned that the coaches included a number of Wombles and other 'hardcore' protesters. In fact, a metropolitan police officer identified eight Wombles members, while a search of the coaches yielded 'some dust and face masks, 3 crash helmets, hoods, 5 hard hats, overalls, scarves, a can of red spray paint, two pairs of scissors and a safety flare',[15] all of which were seized. These controversial police powers to prevent a breach of the peace have been gradually extended by the courts since the landmark decision in *Duncan v Jones*,[16] and have become a staple part of the diet for dealing with demonstrations and picket lines. The question in the *Laporte* case was whether this rather arbitrary common law power was consistent with the Human Rights Act, and if so whether it had been lawfully used by the Gloucestershire police. The Divisional Court held that it was, but that the police had acted unlawfully in escorting the protesters back to London in the manner that they did. This was said to breach their right to liberty under article 5 of the ECHR, in a decision which was upheld by the Court of Appeal which also upheld the legality of the decision to stop the coaches and prevent their passengers from travelling to the demonstration. In the House of Lords, however, it was held that the action taken against the applicant Laporte was

---

[13] Ibid, para [8].
[14] Section 60 authorises the police to stop and search for offensive weapons. See pp 24–25 above.
[15] *R (Laporte) v Gloucester Chief Constable*, above, para [11].   [16] [1936] 2 KB 218.

unlawful and could not be justified under breach of the peace powers. This is because the power could be used only if the breach of the peace was imminent,[17] the House of Lords rejecting the existence of a wider common law power argued for the police that they could to do whatever was reasonable to prevent a breach of the peace. By their own evidence, the police did not believe that a breach of the peace was about to take place in this case, which—according to Lord Bingham—was very different from *Moss v McLachlan*,[18] a decision said to have 'carried the notion of imminence to extreme limits'.[19] In that case the police were held lawfully to have prevented miners from leaving the M1 to join nearby picket lines.

The crucial distinction for Lord Bingham, it seems, is that the miners in *Moss* were prevented from proceeding immediately to the scene of their picketing. Thus,

With four members of one belligerent faction within less than five minutes of confronting another belligerent faction, and no designated, police-controlled, assembly point separated from the scene of apprehended disorder, as in the centre of Fairford, it could plausibly be held in *Moss* that a breach of the peace was about to be committed by those whose onward progress the police decided to block.[20]

In other words, the police had the power to take steps to prevent an imminent breach of the peace, but at Fairford had misjudged the nature of the power and had intervened too early. It is clear from the speech of Lord Rodger in particular that the position would have been very different if the chief constable had allowed 'the coaches to go on to Fairford where the forces assembled to deal with an anticipated demonstration of up to 10,000 protesters would surely have been able to prevent any breach of the peace which the eight known Wombles were planning'.[21] More significant perhaps is the other possibility suggested by Lord Rodger which 'would have been to target the known Wombles on the coaches and to remove them at Lechlade. There is no evidence to show that this would not have been practicable, given the forces and facilities available to the police there'.[22] The key point about this case, however, is that the existence of the common law power of breach of the peace was confirmed, and in not insignificant terms by Lord Rodger notwithstanding the Human Rights Act, albeit that it applies only 'in an emergency to prevent something which is about to happen'. According to Lord Rodger, the requirement of imminence

[17] *Albert v Lavin* [1982] AC 546.
[18] [1985] IRLR 76.
[19] *R (Laporte) v Gloucester Chief Constable*, above, para [51].
[20] *Ibid*, para [51].
[21] *Ibid*, para [87].
[22] *Ibid*, para [89].

does not mean that the officer must be able to say that the breach is going to happen in the next few seconds or next few minutes. That would be an impossible standard to meet, since a police officer will rarely be able to predict just when violence will break out. The protagonists may take longer than expected to resort to violence or it may flare up remarkably quickly. Or else, as in *O'Kelly v Harvey*,[23] the breach of the peace may be likely to occur when others arrive on the scene and there is no way of knowing exactly when that will happen. There is no need for the police officer to wait until the opposing group hoves in sight before taking action'.[24]

'Kettling' Participants

A sightly less draconian restraining practice used by the police is referred to as kettling, which came to public attention in 2001 when anti-globalisation protesters were detained by the police in Oxford Circus for over seven hours until 9.30 pm in the evening. It was raining and there were no toilet facilities, and no food or drink. One protester was not permitted to leave at 4 pm to collect her 11-month-old baby from a registered crèche, while another was in the area to make a collection from a bank for his employer and was not involved in the protest. The term kettling has been described by Louise Christian, a leading civil liberties solicitor, as when:

the police impose cordons on demonstrators and refuse to let anyone from within the cordon leave for what can be hours. This is a controversial tactic, since the police are effectively imprisoning people who may be behaving perfectly peacefully and lawfully. Moreover such tactics might be thought to encourage violence in some instances by overreaction especially if . . . some of the more violent elements of a crowd are left on the outside of the cordon. Even worse can be if a person's safety is compromised as well as their liberty.[25]

Two of those who had been caught up in the kettling incident on 1 May 2001 brought legal proceedings against the police claiming a breach of their right to liberty under article 5 of the ECHR. But the action failed in the High Court, the Court of Appeal, and the House of Lords, with Lord Hope holding that:

there is room, even in the case of fundamental rights as to whose application no restriction or limitation is permitted by the Convention, for a pragmatic approach to be taken which takes full account of all the circumstances.[26]

---

[23] (1883) 14 LR Ir 105.

[24] *R (Laporte) v Gloucester Chief Constable*, above, para [69].

[25] L Christian, 'G20: Questions Need to be Asked About Kettling', *The Guardian*, 2 April 2009.

[26] *Austin v Metropolitan Police Commissioner* [2009] UKHL 5, para [34]. It remains to be seen—now that the House of Lords has unanimously endorsed the practice of kettling—whether the courts will now intervene to regulate the manner of its exercise in particular cases, following the example of other controversial executive threats to liberty that have been endorsed in recent years.

As already indicated, one of many problems with kettling is that it involves confining people who are exercising their right to freedom of peaceful assembly, along with those who may be pursuing other pleasures. Yet the innocent are lumped in with those who are presumed guilty of an intent to make mischief. Nevertheless, according to Lord Neuberger of Abbotsbury:

> where there is a demonstration, particularly one attended by a justified expectation of substantial disorder and violence, the police must be expected, indeed sometimes required, to take steps to ensure that such disorder and violence do not occur, or, at least, are confined to a minimum. Such steps must often involve restraining the movement of the demonstrators, and sometimes of those members of the public unintentionally caught up in the demonstration. In some instances, that must involve people being confined to a relatively small space for some time.[27]

In such cases, said Lord Neuberger, it was:

> unrealistic to contend that article 5 can come into play at all, provided, and it is a very important proviso, that the actions of the police are proportionate and reasonable, and any confinement is restricted to a reasonable minimum, as to discomfort and as to time, as is necessary for the relevant purpose, namely the prevention of serious public disorder and violence.[28]

But where is the line to be drawn? Suppose the police decide it would be convenient to march the protesters into a large hall nearby, or to take some to the local police stations? Would that also be acceptable because it is for a benign purpose, namely the protection of the protesters and the public? Would it still be 'unrealistic to contend that article 5 can come into play at all'? And what is the difference between this case where people were detained without food and toilet facilities in the open air for seven hours (where there is no deprivation of liberty) and the *Laporte* case where people were detained in the comfort of a moving coach without food and toilet facilities for a shorter period (where there was a deprivation of liberty)?

The practice of kettling attracted further notoriety in April 2009 when it was used again by the police to contain the protesters outside the Bank of England on the occasion of the G20 meeting in London. It was at the policing of that demonstration that Ian Tomlinson died (though there is no evidence that he had been corralled by the police), and it was the use of kettling at this demonstration that led to stinging criticism of the police by the Home Affairs Committee on the ground that inadequate steps were taken to ensure that the lessons learned from the 2001 experience were carried out. In particular, it was 'impossible for [the Committee] to judge whether water and toilets were

---

[27] Ibid, para [59].
[28] Ibid, para [60].

made freely available to protesters'. But 'given the recommendations made after the May Day protests this [was] a question that should not need to be asked; that there remains doubt on this issue is unacceptable' (HAC, 2009a: paragraph 43). There was also the question of people who were refused permission to leave the kettle, with the Committee concluding that there is

no excuse for the police preventing peaceful protesters or other people innocently caught up in a protest from leaving a "contained" area when the police can be sure that they do not pose a violent threat to society. This is doubly true when people are asking to leave for medical (or related) purposes. We are particularly concerned at the evidence we have received suggesting that an explicit order was given to maintain the "cohesion" of the police lines at the expense of peaceful protesters' right to egress and to access medicine. While it may be true that some protesters would falsely claim a medical need to leave a contained area for the purposes of causing disorder, we believe that this is a risk that the police must be prepared to run; the dangers of denying protesters their needed medications are too great (ibid: paragraph 45).

More generally, although not opposed to the use of kettling, the Home Affairs Committee nevertheless appeared more concerned than the courts to ensure that a practice which 'involves a shift in power and control from the protesters to the police' is only used 'sparingly and in clearly defined circumstances', and that these circumstances 'should be codified' (ibid: paragraph 41).

Prosecution or Persecution?

Apart from these various preventive powers, the police also have the power of arrest, and as we have seen there are many offences which confer such a power, beginning with obstruction of the highway (Highways Act 1980, s 137); the use of threatening, insulting, or abusive behaviour (Public Order Act 1986, ss 4, 4A, and 5); and trespass of various forms (trespassory and aggravated) (Criminal Justice and Public Order Act 1994). The importance of arrest is that it opens up the individual and the organisation to the wonders and horrors of the criminal justice process, about which there are many concerns:

- once arrested the individual can be searched, as can his or her home. This can be done without a warrant under the authority of the Police and Criminal Evidence Act 1984 (PACE), sections 32 and 18, with a nice example of the reality of this power in a political context being exposed on the *Guardian* website.[29] There young police officers using

---

[29] See <http://www.guardian.co.uk/environment/video/2009/apr/19/police-activism>.

powers under section 18 of PACE are seen informing the father of an environmental protester who had been arrested that they were looking for material that was 'evidence of his views', and material of a 'political' nature, which did not include a letter from the arrested person's MP. A quantity of material was seized, and subsequently returned;

- once arrested, the individual may be brought before magistrates, where he or she may be remanded in custody, or more likely released on bail. In recent years, however, bail conditions have typically been imposed, that involve a deprivation of the individual's right to engage in any other act of protest. The right of peaceful protest is thus removed, without any finding of guilt and without any guarantee that a prosecution will be brought. At RAF Fairford, for example, Liberty reports that arrested persons were required on bail 'to sleep at their home address and [not to go] within 2 miles of Fairford' (Liberty, 2003); and

- once arrested, the individual may be kept in custody as a form of punishment without the inconvenience of a trial and due process. This is alleged to be the practice in Scotland where peace protesters at Faslane are routinely arrested for breach of the peace, and where protesters were said to have been held overnight so that the Crown 'could decide whether to bring them to court when [it] saw the reports the next day'.[30] But as 'the majority of people were then released with a warning that if they returned they might be prosecuted, it was clearly designed to punish blockaders with a night in custody without the cost and inconvenience of having [them] all in court'.

In some cases, of course, prosecutions will be brought and protesters will feel the full majesty of the law, as in the examples below. But as these case studies show, the door to the criminal justice process is released by very open-textured offences which bestow an enormous degree of discretion on the police officer as gatekeeper, and provide an opportunity for the most arbitrary conduct on the part of the State, against those who are at best a nuisance rather than a threat.

Campaign for the Accountability of American Bases

The Campaign for the Accountability of American Bases 'evolved out of the long campaign of protest at Menwith Hill, near Harrogate, North Yorkshire in 1992; local people having expressed their concerns at the arrival of the US Army at Menwith Hill in 1951' (CAAB, 2009). At one typical campaign

---

[30] *Peace News*, July–August 2008.

event on Saturday 16 December 2000, a leading member of the group was arrested outside RAF Feltwell in Norfolk by the Ministry of Defence police (MDP). Standing at the main entrance to the base, Lindis Percy was holding a 'Stars and Stripes' flag with the words 'STOP STAR WARS' written on it. Arrested for obstructing the highway, Percy was taken to Thetford police station, where she was charged with using threatening, abusive, or insulting words or behaviour or disorderly behaviour within the hearing or sight of a person likely to be caused harassment, alarm, or distress which was racially aggravated, contrary to the Public Order Act 1986, section 5. Percy was released on bail on the condition that she did not to go within 500 yards of the USAF bases at Feltwell, Mildenhall, and Lakenheath.[31] The complaint against her was that she had defaced the American flag, stopped a vehicle in front of which she then placed the flag, on which she proceeded to stand. The people most affected by this conduct were US military personnel who regarded it as 'desecration of their national flag, to which they attached considerable importance', though by the time the case came to trial the racial aggravation element had been dropped from the charge. In finding Ms Percy guilty, the District Judge found that there was a pressing social need in a multicultural society to prevent denigration of objects of veneration and symbolic importance for one cultural group and that it was quite clear that the appellant's conduct which offended against section 5 of the 1986 Act was not the unavoidable consequence of a peaceful protest, but arose from the particular manner in which she chose to make her protest. From this Ms Percy appealed, and in allowing the appeal, the Divisional Court held that from this Ms Percy appealed and in determining whether a restraint on the accused's article 10 right to freedom of expression could be justified, a court was required to take into account a wider range of factors than the single factor considered by the District Judge.

Apart from the question whether Percy's conduct was the unavoidable consequence of peaceful protest, these latter included:

The fact that the accused's behaviour went beyond legitimate protest; that the behaviour had not formed part of an open expression on a matter of public interest, but had become disproportionate and unreasonable; that the accused knew full well the likely effect of their conduct upon witnesses; that the accused deliberately chose to desecrate the national flag of those witnesses, a symbol of very considerable importance to many, particularly those who were in the armed forces; the fact that the accused targeted such people, for whom it became a very personal matter; the fact that the accused was well aware of the likely effect of their (sic) conduct; the fact that the accused's use of a flag had nothing, in effect to do with conveying a message

---

[31] *The Guardian*, 7 September 2002.

or the expression of opinion; that it amounted to a gratuitous and calculated insult, which a number of people at whom it was directed found deeply distressing.

The failure on the part of the District Judge to take these matters into account led to the conviction being overturned, though it is by no means clear if the decision at first instance would have been any different even if all these points had been expressly acknowledged. But while there may be a temptation to see this decision as a vindication for the Human Rights Act, think again. In a review of this and two following cases (Geddis, 2004) comments that the decision in Percy was reached 'only on the narrowest of grounds', echoing the same point made earlier in the *Criminal Law Review* (Ormerod, 2002: 836). There the editor points out that the case was decided simply on the basis that the District Judge attached too much weight to one factor, and that 'in terms of developing a clear picture of the way in which courts should approach section 5 when faced with a freedom of expression plea, the court leaves things in a rather unhelpful state'. The position contrasts all the more unfavourably with the position in the United States where the US soldiers would have had no cause for complaint about flag desecration, with this form of political protest being protected by the First Amendment to the US Constitution, albeit by narrow majorities in the Supreme Court. In *Texas v Johnson*,[32] the Supreme Court equated with speech for the purposes of the First Amendment the burning of the flag by a member of the Revolutionary Communist Party. He was taking part in a demonstration against the policies of Ronald Reagan. According to the Mr Justice Brennan in *Eichman v United States*[33] a year later, 'punishing desecration of the flag dilutes the very freedom that makes this emblem so revered, and worth revering'.[34]

A Pyrrhic Victory?

Although a handsome victory, the free speech standard has not been raised in other section 5 cases (Geddis, 2004). Moreover, the overturning of the section 5 conviction in *Percy* (relying on article 10 rather than 11) cannot by any stretch of the imagination be said to have emancipated Lindis Percy from other statutory control on freedom of assembly and public protest. Significantly, her conviction for obstructing the highway was not reversed

---

[32] 491 US 397 (1989).   [33] 496 US 310 (1990).

[34] The same point was made by Keir Starmer, counsel for Ms Percy (and now the Director of Public Prosecutions), who told the court: 'Flag denigration is a form of protest activity renowned the world over and has been afforded protection in other jurisdictions, for example in the US itself': *The Independent*, 22 December 2001.

by the Divisional Court, while she has been prosecuted for obstruction on at least three occasions since, without any evidence that article 11 of the ECHR can operate as a mediating influence. As the *Guardian* pointed out with great prescience, while the overturning of the section 5 conviction added 'to growing human rights case law in Britain', it was 'likely to face further challenges because of the competing rights of individuals affected by protest'.[35] In January 2002, Percy returned to RAF Feltwell where, it is reported, she 'walked quietly backwards and forwards across at the main gate of the base with the US flag with 'STOP STAR WARS' written on it'. According to the same report, she was eventually arrested for obstruction of the highway by the Ministry of Defence Police, and taken again to Thetford Police Station and charged. Similar bail conditions to those imposed in 2000 were imposed here, this time forbidding her to go within 500 yards of any American airbase in East Anglia. Percy was arrested in the following year (January 2003) for standing in front of a car being used to transport Robin Cook, then Leader of the House. Cook had been in Hull for a BBC Question Time show and was confronted by Percy when he left the event. Percy was holding a US flag with the words 'THE ROGUE STATE' written on and spoke to him about the pending US/UK attack on Iraq. When she stood in front of his car, the police were called and she was arrested for obstruction of the highway, and immediately 'de-arrested' after the car had gone—with none of her details having been asked for by the police.

Much of Percy's activity takes place at RAF Menwith Hill, an intelligence centre near Harrogate in North Yorkshire which provides information for the US and UK governments. A weekly protest is held outside the centre, and this protest has helped to keep the local magistrates' court fully occupied, despite the peaceful nature of the protests. In February 2004, Percy successfully defended a prosecution for obstruction in the Harrogate Magistrates' Court. On this occasion, she had stopped a car leaving the US base at Menwith Hill for 20 seconds and had carried an upside-down US flag with the words 'INDEPENDENCE FROM AMERICA' written on it. A 20 second delay was held to be de minimis and she was found not guilty. Later that year, in which she was arrested at least 12 times, Percy was arrested again for obstruction. This time, she was a lone protester outside the same base at Menwith when a car came out of the base. According to her own report, Percy 'safely stood for a short time, holding the US flag upside down with "SHOCKING AND AWFUL" written on it, in front of the car as it came out of the base, having done this many times during

---

[35] *The Guardian*, 22 December 2001.

the protest'[36] She was arrested and taken to Harrogate Police Station and eventually charged with obstructing the highway. The outcome of that case is not known, but another conviction for obstruction of the highway took place in 2007 following the protest outside a US base at Menwith Hill. On this occasion, she was charged, found guilty and fined £50 by Harrogate Magistrates' Court which refused to accept her claim that 'she had been neither on the highway nor obstructing cars leaving the base at the time of the offences'.[37] But because she refused to pay the fine, Percy was jailed for seven days, with *The Independent* claiming that the case 'raised new questions about the judiciary's inclination to jail protesters who appear to offer no threat to the public'.[38] Equally significantly for present purposes, it also raises old questions about the purpose of the highway, and in particular whether the 'right of peaceful assembly on the highway' crafted by Lord Irvine in *DPP v Jones*[39] on the eve of the Human Rights Act's implementation was simply an eccentric aberration.

The Protests at Faslane Naval Base

The Faslane protesters have been equally prominent, with demonstrations against nuclear weapons taking place there in the early 1960s. The demonstrations have led to hundreds of arrests (including prominent Scottish politicians), the establishment of the Faslane peace camp (near Helensburgh on the Clyde), and Faslane 365 which involved a year long peaceful protest beginning on 1 October 2006, culminating in the big blockade on 1 October 2007. Most of the arrests that have taken place at the Trident base over the years were for breach of the peace, some of which are considered below. Unlike in England and Wales an apprehended breach of the peace does not only give the police the power to take preventive measures; in Scotland a breach of the peace is itself a common law offence. And unlike in England and Wales, the power of arrest is not activated by a fear of imminent violence, but where the conduct in question 'will reasonably produce alarm in the minds of the lieges, not necessarily alarm in the sense of personal fear, but alarm lest if what is going on is allowed to continue it will lead to the breaking up of the social peace'.[40] This was gradually extended, so that in a case in 1949 breach of the peace was said to apply 'where something is done in breach of public order or decorum which might reasonably be expected to

---

[36] Relying on *Hirst v Chief Constable of West Yorkshire* (1987) 85 Cr App R 143.
[37] *The Independent*, 29 January 2007.   [38] Ibid.
[39] [1999]2 All ER 257.
[40] Ferguson v Carnochan (1889) 16 R(J) 93, at p 95 (Lord Justice Clerk Macdonald).

lead to the lieges being alarmed or upset or tempted to make reprisals at their own hand'.[41] By 1982 it had been extended further to apply where 'the proved conduct may reasonably be expected to cause any person to be alarmed, upset or annoyed or to provoke a disturbance of the peace'. [42] Moreover, 'it is not essential for the constitution of this crime that witnesses should be produced who speak to being alarmed or annoyed',[43] while 'positive evidence of actual harm, upset, annoyance or disturbance created by reprisal is not a prerequisite of conviction'.[44] This 'offence of wide and ill-defined scope' (Wallington, 1972) has been the staple diet of the police in dealing with assemblies and protests of various kinds, from the selling of National Front literature outside a football ground, to the conduct of motorway protesters, one of whom was charged with sitting on a felled tree being cut up by chain-saw-wielding contractors.[45]

The type of situation for which breach of the peace could be used is highlighted by the case of Pamela Smith, who had been arrested on 15 February 1999 for conducting herself in a disorderly manner by lying down on the roadway, disrupting the free flow of the traffic, and refusing to desist when requested to do so.[46] This was said to amount to a breach of the peace, to which Ms Smith responded by contending that the charge of breach of the peace was 'too vague' to be consistent with the ECHR and more specifically that it violated article 7 of the Convention. This is perhaps a curious line of argument, article 7 being the prohibition against retrospective criminal offences, though in view of the way in which the offence had developed, there was certainly some substance in the argument that 'a citizen could not know with reasonable certainty what actions would breach the criminal law'.[47] As might be expected, however, the Scottish courts were hardly likely to deprive the Scottish police of one their most important weapons for dealing with pickets and protesters, and it was also to be expected that the court would respond by saying that 'a comprehensive definition which would cover all possible circumstances is neither possible nor desirable'.[48] Nor was it possible to derive a comprehensive definition from a close analysis of the different cases in which it had been held a breach of the peace had been committed.

[41] *Raffaelli v Heatly*, 1949 JC 101.
[42] *Wilson v Brown*, 1982 SCCR 49. In one case at this time, it was enough that someone was caused embarrassment: *Sinclair v Annan*, 1980 SLT (Notes) 55.
[43] *Young v Heatly*, 1959 JC 66. (Lord Justice General Clyde).
[44] *Wilson v Brown*, above.
[45] See respectively *Alexander v Smith*, 1984 SLT 176; *McAvoy v Jessop*, 1989 SCCR 301; and *Colhoun v Friel*, 1996 SCCR 497.
[46] *Smith v Donnelly*, 2001 SLT 1007.
[47] Ibid, at para [6].
[48] Ibid, at para [17].

Although contesting whether the offence had been redefined or modified since *Ferguson v Carnochan* in 1843 (!) the High Court nevertheless appeared to tighten up the scope of the offence, first by emphasising 'what is required' is 'conduct which does present as genuinely alarming and disturbing, in its context, to any reasonable person';[49] and secondly by referring to a passage in *Young v Heatly* that if there is no evidence of actual harm, the conduct must be 'flagrant'.[50] The last was a 'strong word', its use being said to point 'to a standard of conduct which would be alarming or seriously disturbing to any reasonable person in the particular circumstances'.[51] However, the apparent tightening of the scope of the offence was of little comfort for Pamela Smith, found guilty and fined £100.

Another Pyrrhic Victory

The decision in *Smith* was said to have caused chaos in Helensburgh District Court',[52] with some Sheriffs being encouraged to mutter unhelpfully that 'a certain latitude of behaviour must be allowed in bona fide political protest'.[53] These problems for the Crown were also being encountered in Edinburgh Sheriff Court, following a protest by peace activists in the Scottish Parliament on 2 April 2001, demanding that Trident be considered during First Minister's questions. Of the 11 people charged, only Jane Tallents was found guilty, the other trials collapsing 'mainly [because of] the failure of the Crown to show that the demonstrator's actions had caused, or potentially would cause the level of distress and alarm sufficient to establish the breach of the peace charge'.[54] Jane Tallents provided an opportunity for the High Court to look at this matter again, in an appeal which was consolidated with four others, including one by the indefatigable Margaret Jones of Bristol who had been convicted of breach of the peace following her arrest at Faslane on 12 February 2002 on a charge that 'at the south approach road to a naval base at Helensburgh, while acting with others, she conducted herself in a disorderly manner, sat on the roadway while mechanically fastened to a wheelchair and refused to desist when required to do so'.[55] Following her conviction, Dr Jones was said to have 'blasted the Helensburgh District Court for yet again misinterpreting the

---

[49] Ibid.
[50] 1959 JC 66, at p 70.
[51] *Smith v Donnelly*, above, at para [18].
[52] <http://www.banthebomb.org/archives/news/2002/May/notguilt.shtml>.
[53] Trident Ploughshares, 'Crown Admits Defeat on Scottish Parliament Demo Cases', 6 February 2002: <http://www.tridentploughshares.org/article695>.
[54] Ibid.
[55] *Jones v Procurator Fiscal, Dumbarton*, XJ264/03, para [4].

latest ruling from the High Court on Breach of the Peace' in *Smith v Donnelly*, 'having already sat through two other similar trials for blockades of the Faslane Trident base which resulted in convictions. According to Jones, 'the issue was not whether she locked herself to someone's wheelchair, lay in the road and obstructed traffic but whether that behaviour caused anyone to be in fear or alarm or was genuinely disturbing to the community'. To claims by the fiscal that 'her behaviour would have been extremely annoying to base workers who couldn't get to work', Dr Jones replied that 'this was an absurd and illogical argument as the High Court made it quite clear that annoyance was not enough to be a Breach of the Peace' and that if she was convicted on this basis then it would be a distortion of the law.[56]

By the time the case got to the High Court, however, it was accepted that the District Court had correctly applied Smith, the advance in that case perhaps not being quite as significant as had originally been thought, though the *Jones* and *Tallents* cases provided a fresh opportunity to use Convention rights to rein in the scope of the offence. In the *Jones* case it was argued, with reference to article 5, that there could be no offence in the absence of evidence that 'persons were actually alarmed by the conduct complained of'.[57] In rejecting what was dubbed as a 'subjective' test to determine whether conduct is alarming and disturbing, the Court favoured the existing objective test, despite openly acknowledging that there may be no evidence that anyone was alarmed or disturbed. In so doing, the Court was clearly concerned that 'if the crime of breach of the peace were to be limited to cases in which there was evidence of actual alarm or annoyance, whether given by the persons who were alarmed or annoyed or by others, this would represent an unfortunate and unjustifiable narrowing of the common law'. Moreover, 'the safeguard against any undue expansion of the law is provided by the need, which was emphasised by the court in *Smith v. Donnelly*, for the conduct to be genuinely alarming and disturbing to any reasonable person'.[58] In *Tallents* a different approach was taken, arguing on the strength of articles 10 and 11 that there could be no breach of the peace unless there was 'evidence from which an inference could reasonably be drawn of the likelihood of public disorder'.[59] Although not disputing that the Scottish Parliament authorities were perfectly entitled to remove Tallents and her fellow resisters, it was argued on her behalf that it was plainly not enough if her conduct caused persons to be irritated. It was argued strongly on her behalf that, 'in

---

[56] Trident Ploughshares, 'Protestor Accuses Court of Making a Mockery of the Law', 29 October 2002, <http://www.tridentploughshares.org/article369>

[57] *Jones*, above , para [5].

[58] Ibid, para [13].

[59] Ibid, para [16].

the absence of actual alarm, the conduct had to be "flagrant", which created a real likelihood of serious disturbance'.[60] But the appeal against conviction was dismissed on the ground that the sheriff was entitled to conclude that her conduct was of such a nature as to be likely to provoke a reaction of alarm and disturbance among reasonable persons.

New Restrictions and Old Liabilities

It might have been thought that there were more than enough powers to restrain freedom of assembly, with the problem now being not the lack of effective controls, but the existence of too many laws, and too many laws arbitrarily applied. The point is well made by the JCHR, which drew attention to two frivolous uses of breach of the peace powers:

- 'Liberty provided an example of the police citing section 5 of the Act where a young man demonstrating outside the Church of Scientology's London headquarters was issued with a summons by the police for refusing to take down his sign, which read "Scientology is not a religion, it is a dangerous cult". The police alleged that the used of the word "cult" violated section 5, although they did not subsequently proceed with a prosecution' (JCHR, 2009: paragraph 80); and

- 'An Oxford student was arrested for allegedly calling a police horse "gay"' (ibid: paragraph 83). The student in question (Sam Brown) spent the night in the cells, after mounted police officers 'considered the comments to be a breach of the Public Order Act, and took him into custody, calling on two squad cars and six policemen to make the arrest'.[61] Mr Brown was taken to court by the police after he refused to pay an £80 fixed penalty fine. The case was, however, dropped for lack of evidence.[62]

But although concerns have been raised repeatedly about the scope and extent of the existing law, despite sensible proposals for reform made by the JCHR and others, and despite the protection of the right to freedom of assembly in the Human Rights Act, the direction of travel has been all one way—for even more rather than fewer restraints on freedom of assembly. The view of the police it seems is that 'if [people] felt that we were acting inappropriately or making excessive use of our powers then they had the right to challenge us about it' (JCHR, 2009: paragraph 82).

[60] Ibid.
[61] *Oxford Student*, 17 November 2005.
[62] *BBC News*, 12 January 2006.

New Statutory Restraints

According to his website, Brian Haw has been protesting in Parliament Square since 2 June 2001, initially against economic sanctions and the bombing of Iraq.[63] Since 9/11, however, the focus of his protest has changed to a wider protest against the war on terror and the 'terror that the US and UK have inflicted on Afghanistan and Iraq'. The campaign is conducted from a point on the east side of Parliament Square, opposite the main vehicular access to the House of Commons (known as 'Carriage Gates'). It is clearly a source of great irritation to Members of Parliament, but an attempt by Westminster City Council in October 2002 to have it removed was rejected by the High Court, Mr Justice Gray rejecting the claim that the one man demonstration amounted to an obstruction of the highway under section 137 of the Highways Act 1980.[64] Despite the court ruling, the one man demonstration was clearly a threat to the dignity of the House of Commons Procedure Committee, which reported that demonstrations in Parliament Square, opposite the main vehicular entrance to the House of Commons were a 'major issue' (HC, 2003: paragraph 17). In 2003, the Committee reported that:

Complaints that we have received included hindering of access, the appearance of long-standing and visually unattractive demonstrations and the disruption of work in Members' and staff offices by noise from loud-hailers used by demonstrators. Set against this were representations in favour of the right to demonstrate. (ibid)

The recognition of a civil liberties dimension appears here almost as an afterthought to other more trivial concerns, which appear to have been shared by the Sub-Dean of Westminster Abbey who, according to the Committee had made representations that 'the long-term display of placards reduces one of the most important squares in London to an eyesore' (ibid: paragraph 18).

The legal position regarding demonstrations in Parliament Square was set out in a helpful Memorandum prepared for the Committee by the Clerk of the House and the Serjeant at Arms, which refers to orders made by each House of Parliament at the beginning of each session of Parliament directing the police to ensure that the streets leading to the Palace of Westminster 'be kept free and open and that no obstruction be permitted to hinder the passage of Members to and from this House'. The difficulty for the police with these measures, however, is that they do not contain a power of arrest, so that the police are left to rely on general public order powers, including obstruction of the highway and breach of the peace, neither of which was much use for dealing with Brian Haw. In its report, the Select Committee

---

[63] <http://www.parliament-square.org.uk/>.
[64] *The Guardian*, 5 October 2002.

recommended that legislation was needed to deal with the problem of long-term demonstrations in Parliament Square. While graciously accepting that 'demonstrations which do not significantly impede access should be allowed', the Committee less graciously considered whether such demonstrations 'should be limited in duration, and well organised, to avoid long-term occupations which would limit the number of demonstrations and undermine the aesthetic and environmental value of Parliament Square as an important heritage square' (HC, 2003: paragraph 21). To this end, it was recommended that the government should introduce appropriate legislation, a step duly taken in the Serious Organised Crime and Public Order Act 2005, which makes it an offence to organise or take part in an unauthorised public demonstration within one kilometre of Parliament Square.[65] In order to secure authorisation for a demonstration within the designated area, a written application must be made to the Metropolitan Police Commissioner (normally at least six clear days in advance) setting out the date, time, and place of the demonstration, as well as its likely duration. The Metropolitan Police Commissioner is required to give the authorisation (and has no power to refuse), but he may impose conditions which in his 'reasonable opinion' are necessary for a number of purposes set out in section 134 of the Act. These include preventing serious public disorder, disruption to the life of the community, or serious damage to property. The conditions in turn may impose requirements as to the place, times, duration, and numbers of people who may take part. It is an offence to demonstrate without authorisation, and an offence to break any of the conditions of authorisation.

SOCPA 2005 in Operation

The Act came into force on 7 April 2005, and was followed shortly thereafter by an application for judicial review by Mr Haw seeking a declaration that it did not apply to him and that he did not need to seek authorisation for his continued demonstration.[66] By a majority, the Divisional Court obliged, on the ground that the Act provides that it is an offence only where authorisation has not been given 'when the demonstration starts'. In Mr Haw's case, his demonstration started in June 2001 'long before there was any requirement for authorisation under section 134(2) of the Act'.[67] But this conclusion was given short shrift by the Court of Appeal, which unembarrassed by any point under the Human Rights Act overturned the Divisional Court, holding in the process that:

---

[65] Serious Organised Crime and Public Order Act 2005, s 132.
[66] *R (Haw) v Home Secretary* [2006] EWCA Civ 532.
[67] [2005] EWHC 2061 (Admin).

The only sensible conclusion to reach in these circumstances is that Parliament intended that those sections of the Act should apply to a demonstration in the designated area, whether it started before or after they came into force. Any other conclusion would be wholly irrational and could fairly be described as manifestly absurd.[68]

Given the history, the latter is a conclusion with which it is difficult to disagree. The decision of the Court of Appeal was duly followed on 9 May 2006 by a notice issued by the Metropolitan Police to dismantle his protest which by now occupied the whole of the east side of the square, imposing conditions on the demonstration that would confine Mr Haw to a space of 10 feet, which according to the *Daily Telegraph* was enough for a poster and his camp bed.[69] As a result of Mr Haw's failure to comply with these conditions, on 23 May 2006 'police attended the site and removed a number of items on the ground that this was necessary to achieve compliance with the conditions'.[70] This was in fact a night manoeuvre involving 78 police officers at a cost of £7,200 (the cost of overtime along with transport, catering, and the erection of road barriers) to dismantle Mr Haw's protest, 'reducing his permitted protesting space to a 10 foot cube'.[71] The operation was conducted in the dead of night 'to avoid unwanted publicity', with the wreckage from the police operation being carried away in an articulated lorry.[72] In addition to moving about 90 per cent of his posters and other material, criminal proceedings were also brought against Mr Haw for breaking the police conditions, the police explaining that the accused posed a threat as terrorists could hide bombs under his banners and placards.[73] In January 2007, however, District Judge Quentin Purdy held that the conditions imposed on Mr Haw were unlawful because they lacked clarity and because they had not been made by the Metropolitan Police Commissioner as the 2005 Act required, but by a junior officer—Superintendent Terry—to whom Mr Ian Blair was not authorised to delegate. Immediately after the decision, however, Superintendent Terry is said to have handed over an envelope containing new conditions, this time signed by an Assistant Commissioner, aimed at stopping Mr Haw from erecting his former display, which was to find a new home in the Tate Gallery in Millbank not far from Westminster.[74]

---

[68] Ibid, para [23] (Sir Anthony Clarke MR).

[70] *DPP v Haw* [2007] EWHC 1931 (Admin), para [16].

[72] *Daily Telegraph*, 24 May 2006.

[69] *Daily Telegraph*, 11 May 2006.

[71] *Daily Telegraph*, 26 May 2006.

[73] *BBC News*, 22 January 2007.

[74] An appeal by the police against the decision of Judge Purdy was partially successful, on the ground that the Metropolitan Police Commissioner was entitled to delegate, but that the conditions imposed had been unworkable. The limited success of the appeal was, however, to include seeds of misfortune for Mr Haw, with the Lord Chief Justice also pointing out that 'the challenge made on behalf of Mr Haw to the practicality of the conditions imposed may mean that the police will be driven, in the interest of workability, to impose conditions on him that are simpler and more restrictive' (*DPP v Haw*, above, para [42]).

Although Brian Haw has become the most prominent protester against the war in Iraq, he is by no means the only one, and by no means the only one to have been ensnared by the 2005 Act. Four people were arrested on the day the Act was introduced (1 August 2005) for conducting an unauthorised demonstration, at least two of whom were members of Stop the War Coalition, on this occasion protesting against the 2005 Act rather than the war. The two most prominent arrests were those of Maya Evans and Milan Rai, both of whom were arrested on 25 October 2005 near the Cenotaph in Whitehall, well within the designated area, close to the entrance to Downing Street where there is a heavy police presence. Without authorisation, Mr Rai was reading out the names of dead Iraqi civilians, while Ms Evans was reading out the names of dead British service men and women. It is not clear if they had started to ring a bell for each of the dead as they had intended, though it is acknowledged that the demonstration was 'peaceful and good-humoured', and that those involved behaved in a 'peaceful and orderly way throughout'. Both were 'aware that authorisation for the demonstration was required, and [were] aware that it had neither been sought nor given'. Mr Rai was charged with organising an unauthorised demonstration in a designated area, while Ms Evans was charged with participating in such a demonstration, after being detained for five hours in Charing Cross police station. Although given a conditional discharge, Ms Evans is reported as having said that she was not 'doing anything wrong standing there on a drizzly Tuesday morning with a colleague reading names of people who had died in a war'.[75] She also said that she '[did] not agree with the Act', and that 'it's a shame that you can't voice your freedom of speech in this country any more and it is illegal to hold a remembrance ceremony for the dead'.[76] For his part, Mr Rai was also convicted, though in his case he was fined £350, and ordered to pay £150 costs.[77] One of the issues raised by Milan Rai was that the requirements of the 2005 Act violated his human rights, an argument that was rejected by District Judge Nicholas Evans who is reported to have said that 'Parliament had been "very much alive to the need to have the interest of demonstrators and their convention rights protected, particularly in relation to articles 10 and 11", when it framed the legislation'.[78]

[75] *The Independent*, 8 December 2005; also *BBC News*, 9 December 2005.
[76] *BBC News*, 7 December 2005.   [77] *The Guardian*, 12 April 2006.
[78] Ibid. This decision was upheld by the High Court, relying on *Ziliberberg v Moldova*, Application No 61821/00 of 4 May 2004. See also *Blum and Others v DPP* [2006] EWHC 3209 (Admin), and *Tucker v DPP* [2007] EWHC 3019 (Admin).

The Use of Injunctions to Restrain Protest

The concern so far has been with restraints on the right to freedom of assembly imposed by the criminal law. Of emerging importance, however, is the use of injunctions, familiar to trade unions, used in the 1980s against environmental protesters, and refined in the counter-attack by Huntingdon Life Sciences, a company targeted by animal welfare groups because of alleged vivisection. The campaign against Huntingdon Life Sciences was conducted mainly by a group called Stop Huntingdon Animal Cruelty (SHAC), and the campaign was resisted by the company using the Protection from Harassment Act 1997. Introduced initially to deal with stalking, it is an offence under the 1997 Act to pursue a course of conduct which amounts to the harassment of others, with conduct for this purpose including speech. While anyone suspected of causing harassment may be arrested (in England and Wales only), it is possible also for the person being harassed to seek a civil remedy by way of an injunction and damages. Where this is done, it is an offence to breach the terms of an injunction, and an application can be made by the victim to the same court to have the harasser arrested. The Act has been used not only by Huntingdon Life Sciences, but also by its suppliers and customers who have also been targeted by the animal welfare lobby, and as a result there have been several reported cases emerging from this campaign. One of the defendants was the British Union for the Abolition of Vivisection which applied successfully to the High Court to have the injunction amended to exclude them. Although acknowledging the company's complaints about 'a sustained and menacing anti-vivisection campaign directed at itself and its employees', Mr Justice Eady was nevertheless concerned that the 1997 Act was being used to 'clamp down on the discussion of matters of political protest and public demonstration which was so much part of our democratic tradition'. According to the judge, Parliament would have been 'surprised to see how widely [the 1997 Act] was perceived to extend by some people', expressing the view that 'the courts would resist any wide interpretation of the Act'.[79] In other cases, however, there has been only a nod in the direction of 'the rights to freedom of speech and of assembly and association' (without mentioning the Human Rights Act), the courts more concerned with 'the proper protection of the named claimants and the employees of the claimant companies from unlawful harassment'.[80]

The injunctions under the 1997 Act have gradually become more refined since the Act was first used by the animal testing companies and their suppliers and customers. There are now over 30 injunctions posted on

---

[79] *Huntingdon Life Sciences Ltd v Curtin, The Times*, 11 December 1997.
[80] *Daiichi Pharmaceuticals UK Ltd v SHAC* [2004] 1 WLR 1503.

the website of the National Extremism Tactical Coordination Unit (NETCU)–the government body to deal with domestic extremism, including animal rights extremism.[81] Most of the injunctions are directed at SHAC and its leading members, though some (such as that obtained by Harrods) are directed at organisations campaigning against the fur trade. More recently, however, the use of injunctions has expanded well beyond those seeking to control the animal welfare lobby to include environmental campaigners as well. One of the most notorious cases involves 69 year old Dr Peter Harbour who was campaigning on behalf of a body called Save Radley Lakes, a beauty spot near Oxford. He was the subject of an injunction obtained by Npower Ltd in April 2007 under the 1997 Act, senior management in Thames Valley Police giving evidence against him in the proceedings, despite that the fact that the group 'have been complimented [by the local police on the ground] on how we conduct operations' (Harbour, 2009). In evidence to the JCHR Dr Harbour expressed a number of concerns about the how the procedure for obtaining injunctions allows big companies largely to hijack the legal process, concerns with which the JCHR appeared largely to agree:

- First, 'there is something wrong when a company can bring a case to the High Court, give evidence effectively in secret (no notice was given to the defendants), using anonymous witnesses to produce a wide ranging injunction against innocent, law-abiding ordinary people, needlessly preventing them from access to land they have previously been able to enjoy over many years'.
- Secondly, 'by the time an application has been made to the High Court it is impossible for a person of average means to defend themselves because the financial risks are much too large. This is not acceptable. Someone of average means can be injuncted for a long time (in my own case almost two years to date) without a defence being mounted, and without an opportunity to clear their name'.

Dr Harbour was quite properly concerned also that he had no opportunity to refute the allegations made against him, that he was prevented from using an amenity that he greatly enjoyed, and that his name appeared on the NECTU website, thereby suggesting that he was a 'national extremist' (ibid).

---

[81] <http://www.netcu.org.uk/default.jsp> According to the website NECTU is funded by the Home Office and reports to ACPO, providing tactical guidance 'on policing extremist protest activity and its associated criminality'.

A Constitutional Shift?

In an era of a so called 'constitutional shift' in favour of freedom of assembly, these injunctions make remarkable reading, and suggest that freedom of assembly will be protected if it is intermittent conduct of a largely passive population which causes little inconvenience. The injunctions show little stomach for demonstrations which are persistent, aggressive and damaging to commercial interests. Thus, one SHAC injunction in force at the time of writing (issued on 19 March 2007), is designed to prevent harassment as defined by the 1997 Act of protected persons, defined by the injunction to mean employees of the company, their families, servants or agents, and any person seeking to visit the company's premises (other than protesters). As such the injunction is addressed not only to named defendants associated with SHAC, but also 'any other person, whether by himself his servants or agents, who is acting in concert with the Defendants with a view to exposing, deterring, obstructing or preventing the conduct of experimentation on live animals by [HLS]'. Under the terms of the order, the protesters were restrained from various forms of conduct, to by no means all of which could exception be taken, such as assaulting, harassing or molesting a protected person or making threatening or abusive communications to a protected person. But it also included a restriction on picketing within 50 yards of the any residence of a protected person, publishing personal details of a protected person, or seeking to persuade a protected person against his will to do something he is entitled or required not to do. The injunction also creates an exclusion zone around the premises of the company, the adjoining land, and adjoining roads, from which the protesters are prohibited from entering for the purposes of conducting a demonstration or protest. This is subject to an exception permitting a demonstration at a designated spot once a week, not to exceed six hours, with no more than 30 people to be present. Advance notice (24 hours) is to be given to the police of any such demonstration, along with the registration number of any cars that are to be parked in the immediate vicinity. However, no cars are to be parked within half a mile of the designated area, and noise restrictions prohibit the use of megaphones or similar devices 'save that one megaphone may be used for verbal amplification only and at a noise level not exceeding 7 in the course of the demonstration between 12.00 pm and 1.00 pm, with such use subject to reasonable direction by attending police officers'.

One other exception is permitted, allowing processions or assemblies to take place once every three months on the public highway within the exclusion zone, provided it takes place at the weekend or on a bank holiday. The other conditions are that it complies at all times with the Public Order

Act 1986, sections 11–14, that there be compliance with all reasonable directions given by the police, and that notice of the procession or assembly is given 14 days in advance to Huntingdon Police Station. Although presented as an authorisation of assemblies in the exclusion zone, these latter terms are in fact a qualification to what is in effect a ban on the right to peaceful assembly, with the introduction of a new extra-statutory qualification (14 days' notice) in those cases where the exception applies. Yet these extraordinary powers of the 1997 Act to impose obligations in excess of those required by the Public Order Act 1986 are to be seen in the other injunctions issued against SHAC and other animal rights groups, including those obtained by Oxford University to stop the protests in Oxford about the building of new laboratories where animal testing is to be conducted. In one injunction upheld by the Court of Appeal in August 2006,[82] the protection extends to employees, members and former students of the university (as well as their respective families, servants and agents), as well as contractors' employees and shareholders (as well as their respective families, servants and agents). The restrictions to protect these 'protected persons' apply to picketing within 100 rather than 50 yards of a protected person's home, with an additional restriction on picketing within 50 yards of a contractor's business premises. A demonstration within the exclusion zone around university is permitted once week for three hours on a Thursday afternoon, with a peaceful procession permitted once a month on the public highway within the exclusion zone, provided that it complies with the Public Order Act 1986. In this case, however, there is no additional extra-statutory notice requirements. These injunctions obtained by Oxford University led to contempt proceedings and more importantly for our purposes raise questions about how such wide restraints on freedom of assembly could be imposed so soon after the 'constitutional shift' engineered by the Human Rights Act. Yet although the Human Rights Act was placed before the court, it was fairly easily sidestepped',[83] and not even cited in the decision of the Court of Appeal upholding these remarkably wide injunctions.

The Exercise of Police Power

Apart from preventing demonstrations from taking place on the one hand, and the use of various offences that may be committed in the course of a protest event, the other problem facing demonstrators will be the conduct

---

[82] *Oxford University v Broughton* [2004] EWHC 2543 (QB); [2006] EWCA Civ 1305.
[83] [2004] EWHC 2453 (QB), at para [82].

of the police, and the manner in which they exercise their powers. This does not always give rise to difficulty, but it does so often enough to continue to give rise to serious concerns, both in terms of the operation of constitutional principle on the one hand, and respect for human rights on the other. The first problem highlighted in recent years is the excessive numbers of police officers present at demonstrations, with Liberty pointing out in 2003 that the peace demonstrations at RAF Fairford 'were characterised by the very large number of police officers on duty to deal with a relatively small number of protesters' (Liberty, 2003). The same complaint is made by other groups, with CAAB reporting to the JCHR that:

The police presence at the major demonstrations has been and continues to be excessive, with Home Office police forces being 'bused' in from all over North Yorkshire and beyond. They have been accompanied by police horse, officers on quad bike and pedal bikes. The ratio of police to protesters is sometimes: 1 protester to 10 officers. (CAAB, 2009)

Similarly, CAAT, complained—also to the JCHR—that 'Today, significant numbers of police attend even the small vigils, which are no different in size or nature from those in earlier times. For instance, 34 officers were present on the occasion of the Reed Elsevier AGM in April 2005.' Although 'most of the police sit in vans, not doing anything', 'their presence in such numbers is, however, unnerving for protesters, as well as tying up a large amount of police time and resources' (CAAT, 2009). The presence of large numbers of police officers is, however, only the start of it.

Surveillance of Protesters

Apart from excessive numbers, concern has also been expressed about the use of Forward Intelligence Teams by the police to photograph protesters. These FIT teams appeared in the 1990s and are designed for the purpose of evidence gathering, the police having relied in the past on requiring newspapers to hand over photographs of incidents that may have been taken by journalists. This is a form of surveillance that raises lots of concerns, it being claimed by more than one activist group in evidence to the JCHR that 'the standard use of the Forward Intelligence Team to record every person and movement on a demonstration is often very intimidating and always extremely intrusive' (Voices in the Wilderness UK, 2009). Another has revealed the indiscriminate use of this practice even in relation to indoor meetings as well as outdoor processions, with CAAT reporting to the same JCHR inquiry that:

On 13 September 2005 CAAT held an 'alternative conference' at Toynbee Hall, London in the evening following a demonstration at the DSEi arms fair. About an hour after the conference started, Forward Intelligence Team officers began looking through the windows and pointing a camera in. After closing the curtains, a colleague went outside, asked the officers why they were there and was told it was because CAAT was 'a group known to do direct action'.

But apart from the intimidatory and indiscriminate use of FITs, there is the related problem of its storage and use, with the *Guardian* reporting that the information gathered in this way is stored for up to seven years, and that:

- activists 'seen on a regular basis' as well as those deemed on the 'periphery' of demonstrations are included on the police databases, regardless of whether they have been convicted or arrested;
- names, political associations, and photographs of protesters from across the political spectrum—from campaigners against the third runway at Heathrow to anti-war activists—are catalogued; and
- police forces are exchanging information about protesters stored on their intelligence systems, enabling officers from different forces to search which political events an individual has attended.[84]

Police surveillance activities were considered by the Court of Appeal in *Wood v Metropolitan Police Commissioner*[85] where a photographer had been sent to cover the AGM of Reed Elsevier in 2005, following information that there might be a protest by the Campaign Against Arms Trade. Andrew Wood, a press officer for CAAT, attended the meeting which was held in the Grosvenor Hotel, London. He was not involved in any unlawful activity, but was nevertheless photographed by the police, and his photographs were retained against his wishes. In judicial review proceedings he complained that the retention of the photographs violated his Convention rights, a claim that was rejected at first instance and upheld only by a majority of the Court of Appeal. An interesting feature of this case highlighted by Lord Collins is not only did the police have 'no reason to believe that any unlawful activity had taken place, and still less that Mr Wood had taken part in any such activity', but Mr Wood

was followed by a police car [as he made his way with another man from the meeting to a nearby tube station,] and then questioned about his identity by four police officers, two of whom then followed him on foot and tried to obtain the assistance of station staff to ascertain Mr Wood's identity from his travel card.[86]

---

[84] *Guardian*, 7 March 2009.   [85] [2009] EWCA Civ 414.
[86] [2009] EWCA Civ 414, para [92].

Lord Justice Dyson had previously noted that the police had discovered Mr Wood's identity 'by discovering the names of the new shareholders in Reed and working out by a process of elimination that the person photographed [by the police] was the appellant', raising questions about (a) how they got the details of Reed shareholders, (b) what personal data are stored in relation to these people, and (c) by whom. On the facts, it was held that the retention of the photographs for more than a few days was not justified, principally it seems because it involves 'the images of persons who have committed no offence and are not suspected of committing an offence'.[87]

The decision in the *Wood* case is a slender victory on a modest point. It does not mean that the police cannot photograph demonstrations; nor does it mean that they cannot retain the photographs. This practice of the police has not gone unchallenged, with a group called Fit Watch having emerged to counter the conduct of the police, and operating by taking photographs of the surveillance crews and blocking the cameras of the crews by the use of posters and banners. In a notorious incident in August 2008, two members of Fit Watch (Emily Apple and Val Swain) were present at Kingsnorth power station in Kent where they challenged a police officer (from the West Midlands Police Force) 'over his failure to display a badge number'. That proved to be a rash move:

Both Swain and Apple were pinned to the ground in restraint positions for around 15 minutes. Apple had her head pushed into the ground by an officer without a badge number. Moments later, the same officer placed one hand around her neck in a stranglehold position, apparently attempting to show her face to the police camera. He then pressed his fingers on pressure points in her neck to move her across the road.

Several metres away, Swain was also being pinned to the ground. The footage captured her groaning in pain and telling an officer to stop standing on her foot. The camera panned down to show the officer's boot clamped on top of Swain's foot. The officer said: "I am not on your foot." .... S[wain] was turned on her side while officers removed her shoes. Her legs were bound with black leg restraints before several officers carried her into back of a police van.

Their indignity continued when the pair were (i) denied bail (allegedly on the ground that their release would cause 'physical or mental injury' to police officers), (ii) detained for four days (three of which were in HMP Bronzefield), (iii) before being released without charge.[88]

---

[87] Ibid, para [100].

[88] *The Guardian*, 21 June 2009. For a video recording of the incident, see <http://www.guardian.co.uk/environment/video/2009/jun/21/fit-watch-kingsnorth-arrests>

Interference with the Press

The activities of FITs has been an issue in connection with a yet further concern about the policing of protests in recent years, namely the relationship between the police and the press. The role of the latter is crucial for obvious reasons, relating to the need to report on what is happening for the benefit of the public (there being no point in conducting a protest which is denied any publicity), and to monitor the behaviour of the police and the protesters (albeit this is a secondary concern). Yet, the National Union of Journalists identifies three problems encountered by its members in covering protests and demonstrations (NUJ, 2009), the first of which is the problem of obstruction by the police. This is a problem that is said to be most acute in the protected zone near Parliament following the SOCPA 2005 amendments, which according to the NUJ have 'led to a deterioration in relations between photographers and police, and also increased the hazards of covering protests because of the different atmosphere it has created between police and demonstrators' (ibid). Three complaints in particular have been made:

- 'At various events where demonstrators have been penned in on the edge of a pavement, for example . . . . opposite Downing Street and in Parliament Square, the police have set up a traffic-free area in front of the protesters, and then denied press access to this zone, making it hard to photograph the protest'.

- 'While covering marches police at times order photographers/camera crews away from the marchers—as happened during the march up Whitehall by Stop the War/CND on 8 October 2007. Police often use the explanation that they could not distinguish the photographers from the protesters and, therefore, treated them identically'.

- 'On various occasions when marchers or static demonstrations have been surrounded by police, journalists have been prevented from leaving the demonstration, being treated by the police exactly as if they were demonstrators, despite showing a valid press card' (ibid).

The second complaint made by the NUJ relates to the surveillance of journalists by FITs, with the General Secretary writing to the Home Secretary to express 'serious concerns' about the activities of the Metropolitan Police's FIT Team in monitoring and recording the activities of bona fide journalists, especially photographers.[89] According to Mr Dear, a number of members of

---

[89] The letter, dated 22 May 2008, is reproduced in NUJ (2009).

the union 'alleged that the police's surveillance action amounts to virtual harassment and is a serious threat to their right to carry out their lawful employment'. At a lobby against the SOCPA restrictions on 1 March 2008, for example, 'all members of the press present were catalogued by the FIT team'. Using the Data Protection Act 1998, the union had been able to establish that once photographed, the images of the journalists concerned are retained on the police database, the individual then being given a four-figure Photographic Reference Number. Mr Dear also claimed that intimidation continues in other forms even after entry on the database:

members of the FIT team who know individual journalists by name still follow them and film them all the time they are working. The journalists have provided their Press Cards to FIT team members, have asked why they are under surveillance and have reminded police officers of their lawful right to carry out their work. Despite this the surveillance continues.

This activity of the police raised questions about the purpose of the database and the identity of those who have access to it. In evidence to the JCHR, the NUJ complained that surveillance and intimidation 'means people are less likely to go out and cover protests', leading in turn to the undermining not just of press freedom (which is bad enough) but to the right of peaceful protest: '[if] publicity is one of the reasons for protest, actually what the police are doing here is undermining that freedom of the media and the ability of the protesters to be able to get their message across via the media' (JCHR, 2009a: para 193).

The third problem relates to the gratuitous interference by the police with the work of the press, in a way that sometimes would be fitting in a totalitarian regime. Although not the only explanation of police conduct, it has been suggested that the police are using their powers of arrest to gain access to journalistic material (which would include a camera memory card) which enjoys protection as special procedure material under the Police and Criminal Evidence Act 1984.[90] One such case referred to by the NUJ in its evidence to the JCHR is that of Lawrence Looi, a staff photographer with news agency News Team who had been sent 'to cover a protest on public roads outside the International Conference Centre in Birmingham when he was approached by a police constable who objected to having been photographed' (NUJ, 2009). The officer is alleged to have held Mr Looi by the upper arm, before asking him 'to delete any photographs that had been

---

[90] Speaking at the 2007 NUJ Photographers' Conference, a leading solicitor said: 'The police are arresting journalists, seizing their equipment, treating them as suspects, looking at their photographs, taking copies, perhaps returning them to them, taking no further action often (but not always) and they've got, straight away, what they want' (NUJ, 2009).

taken of police officers'. He was then approached by a sergeant who asked to see the photographs, and told him that unless he deleted the photographs, the sergeant would do it himself. This was said to be only one of a 'long list of controversial incidents where police have been accused of misusing their powers to try to control press photographers' (ibid), which included:

- August 2006: During a terror alert, police at Heathrow Airport forced two staff press photographers to delete images from their camera memory cards. All photographers arriving at the airport were banned from taking pictures of the incident.

- September 2006: *Milton Keynes News* staff photographer Andy Handley [wa]s arrested for obstruction after refusing to hand over his equipment after photographing a traffic accident. Police later apologise[d], and describe[d] his arrest as 'a serious misjudgement'.

- October 2006: Photographer Marc McMahon [wa]s arrested for breaching the peace while photographing an incident on Newcastle's Tyne Bridge where a man was threatening to commit suicide. Despite showing his press card, police unlawfully told McMahon he could not take photographs, and when he continued to do so, he was arrested.[91]

Dispersal of Protesters

Recent events have also given rise to complaints about the abuse of police powers to disperse protests and demonstrations, the issue arising in the particular context of the G20 demonstrations in April 2009. There is no formal power of dispersal in either common law or statute, and no specific regulation of the circumstances in which an assembly can be dispersed. Traditionally, it must be assumed that if an event was getting out of control and public disorder was expected in the shape of a breach of the peace, the police officer on the spot could take pre-emptive action to disperse the crowd or part of it; or where there were two rival factions, to disperse one of them. There appears, however, to have been a move in recent years in the sense that the police now rely on the Public Order Act 1986, section 14 for this purpose, at

---

[91] See also the affair of Marc Vallee (Vallee, 2009). Even more remarkable is the claim made by CAAT to the JCHR that 'on 24 July 2007 and again on 6 May 2008, anti-arms-trade campaigners in Nottingham protested at the premises of an arms manufacturer. Campaigners sent press releases to local media, which initially expressed interest in covering the demonstration. The campaigners involved have told CAAT that, shortly after reporters contacted the company for a statement, the media outlets received telephone calls from Nottinghamshire Police advising them that it would be "irresponsible" of them to cover the demonstration. Most of these media outlets decided to drop the story as a result. Individual reporters told the campaigners about the police intervention' (CAAT, 2009).

least in some circumstances. This enables the police to take steps in relation to a public assembly, where there is a risk of serious public disorder, serious damage to property, serious disruption to the life of the community, or intimidation of others. Under section 14, the police may give instructions about the numbers, locations and duration of an assembly with a view to addressing the anticipated disorder or other concern, with the utility of this power being greatly enhanced when the definition of a public assembly was changed by Mr Blair's government so that it now applies to all assemblies of two or more people. As originally introduced by Mrs Thatcher's government, section 14 applied only to assemblies of 20 or more people. There is nevertheless still no formal or express power of dispersal in the Act, though the view of the police (apparently shared by HMIC) is that 'since the Act gives the police the power to impose a condition defining the 'maximum duration' of a public assembly, a police direction bringing an existing assembly to an end is likely to be found lawful under the Act' (HMIC, 2009: 20).

The use of s 14 for the purposes of dispersal was clearly evident and openly acknowledged during the G20 protests on 1 April 2009, when the police were presented with demonstrations at four different location in central London. One of these was the Climate Camp at Bishopgate, near Liverpool Street station, which commenced at 12.30 pm, with the intention of remaining for 24 hours. At 7.00 pm, however, the police began the process of dispersing the 5,000 or so kettled demonstrators at the Bank of England, and as pointed out by HMIC, while 'the 4,000– 5,000 protesters at Bishopsgate were relatively peaceful, the 4,000–5,000 protesters at the Bank of England were not', and the police did not want the Climate Camp to be hijacked (HMIC, 2009: 52). Steps were taken by the police not only to prevent the Bank of England protesters from joining the Climate Camp, but also to begin a dispersal of the latter, using powers under section 14 'in order to prevent serious disorder and serious disruption' (ibid: 53). Steps to disperse the crowd began to be taken shortly after 9.30 pm, though it appears that protesters heard 'no intelligible announcements', and that 'to the protesters being dispersed it seemed as if the police, without warning had began to use force to clear a peaceful protest' (HAC, 2009a: para 27). Some protesters claim in evidence to the Home Affairs Committee to have suffered extreme violence without warning:

at about 9.00 or 9.30 the police line just decided to advance and charge us. There was no warning given. There was no request to move. There was no indication of what was going to happen. We were sat on the floor. The police advanced on us. They pressure pointed my girlfriend on the neck, which is extremely painful, and dragged her backwards off me. Whilst this was happening an officer leant over the top of her and punched me directly in the face. At this point I was sat on the floor pretty much being pushed onto my back with my hands above my head and he punched me square in the face for no valid reason that I could see whatsoever. My girlfriend was dragged off me. I was pulled up, pushed back towards the crowd by the police as they descended upon me with the sides of their shields on the side of my head, again just basically striking me with shields. Again, there was no request to move, no indication of what was happening or why. My girlfriend had been dragged behind me with her wrists bent behind her back, threatened to be broken and was pulled back behind the police line. She was then thrown back by officers head first with her hands behind her back and landed on the floor. Whilst this was happening I was being struck on the side of the head by the sides of shields.[92]

Concerns about the use of section 14 were expressed forcefully by the Home Affairs Committee in its G20 report. The Committee referred to 'inappropriate use' of section 14 (HAC, 2009a, para 62), being used against journalists and protesters, the Committee having received evidence 'showing police threatening press photographers with arrest under section 14, with instructions 'to clear the photographers from [a particular] area, in contravention of laws around freedom of the press and without any apparent imminent threat to police or press on the scene' (Defend Peaceful Protest, 2009). Apparently, the police 'later apologised for this inappropriate use of section 14 of the Public Order Act' (ibid), though by that time their purpose had been achieved, and the moment could never be recaptured. The Committee reported that it was not 'certain' that either the protesters or the journalists 'posed a threat of "serious public disorder, serious damage to property or serious disruption to the life of the community"' (HAC, 2009a: para 62). This led the Committee to express 'concern' that 'the police view section 14 of the Public Order Act as a handy "catch-all" tool to be used whenever they wish to move people on from a given area' (ibid). As the Committee also pointed out, 'this would be an abuse of the rights of protesters to demonstrate in a peaceful manner and a misuse of the powers granted to the police'. Part of the problem encountered at Climate Camp on 1 April related to the lack of adequate training about the 'suitable legal application' of this power, a deficiency which the Home Affairs Committee found 'odd' in view of the 'importance' with which section 14 is viewed by the police (ibid). The report by HMIC also exposed failings in police training, though quite whether the need for better training is on its own a sufficient response to the 'levels of force used by the police to disperse the protest' on the day must be questioned, with the physical force involved including 'shield and

---

[92] Home Affairs Committee, 12 May 2009, HC 418-II (2009), Q 130.

baton tactics' (HMIC, 2009: 54). The question neatly sidestepped by HMIC was whether this was a lawful use of the section 14 power.

Allegations of Excessive Force

Allegations about the use of excessive force by police officers at demonstrations have been made since time immemorial: during the General Strike in the 1920s, during the anti fascist demonstrations in the 1930s, during the anti war and peace movement demonstrations in the 1950s and 1960s, during anti-racism demonstrations in the 1970s and 1980s, during poll tax demonstrations more recently still, to say nothing of the indelible image of baton wielding militarised police officers smashing the unprotected heads of striking miners at the battle of Orgreave in 1985. Allegations about the excessive use of force were raised again with by a number of high profile policing events since 1997, including the policing of the Countryside Alliance demonstration in London in 2004, the G8 party for international politicians and celebrity guests at Gleneagles in 2005, and most recently the G20 protests in London on and around 1 April 2009. The last brought back memories of a demonstration in London in 1979 when a protestor (Blair Peach) died, in circumstances so far unexplained, with the report of an internal police investigation still unpublished some 30 years later. The policing of the G20 demonstrations will forever be remembered as the event at which newsvendor Ian Tomlinson died after a confrontation with a police officer, in which he was struck by a truncheon as Mr Tomlinson was moving away from a police officer. Mr Tomlinson had not participated in the demonstration, but was trying to make his way home after work, inadvertently encountering a period of heightened aggression between the dispersal of the kettle at the Bank of England and the containment and subsequent dispersal of the Climate Camp at Bishopsgate further to the east.[93] It will also be remembered as the event in which the police are alleged to have attempted to deflect attention and responsibility for their role in this matter by blaming protesters. The policing of that demonstration will be remembered further for the alleged assault by a police officer on Nicola Fisher who attended the vigil following the death of Mr Tomlinson.

Like the incident involving Mr Tomlinson, the slap inflicted on Ms Fisher was broadcast all over the world. It was followed by an alleged baton attack by a police officer, as explained by Ms Fisher in evidence to the Home Affairs Committee:

---

[93] For video footage of the blow to Mr Tomlinson, see <http://www.guardian.co.uk/uk/video/2009/apr/07/G20-police-assault-video>

- **Q187 Mr Winnick:** We saw the incident on television and we have had other reactions to that. So you were slapped across the face. What happened next?

Ms Fisher: After he slapped me I was shocked and angry and I shouted at him.

- **Q188 Mr Winnick:** Did you swear at him?

Ms Fisher: I shouted at him, "What are you doing hitting a **** woman?" I did swear then. I also pointed out to him that there were two film crews next to me filming him. I was trying to point out what are you doing hitting a woman and there are film crews filming you.

- **Q189 Chairman:** What happened after that, Ms Fisher?

Ms Fisher: Straight after that he got his stick out—

- **Q190 Mr Winnick:** The same police officer?

Ms Fisher: Yes.

- **Q191 Chairman:** He got his what out?

Ms Fisher: His stick and hit me twice. He hit me over the back of my leg and I stumbled backwards, someone caught me and my leg went up and he hit me again and caught me at the bottom of my leg.

- **Q192 Mr Winnick:** So during this incident you were hit three times?

Ms Fisher: Yes.

- **Q193 Mr Winnick:** What injuries did you receive as a result of being slapped on your legs? Were you in hospital?

Ms Fisher: I went to the local hospital, St Bart's Minor Injuries Unit and got some painkillers. I went to my doctor's the next day. I had a seven-inch by three-inch bruise at the top of my leg and a two-inch by four-inch bruise at the bottom of my leg.[94]

There were many other allegations of excessive force by police officers at the G20 event, including 'cases of head injury, cuts and bruising from batons, broken limbs from batons or being pushed to the ground during "kettling" operations, threats of severe force (breaking fingers or arms) as part of restraint techniques and other violence and intimidation' (Defend Peaceful Protest, 2009). In evidence to the Home Affairs Committee, it was claimed that the 'most unjustified and disproportionate acts of force

---

[94] Home Affairs Committee, 20 May 2009, HC 418-II (2009).

were deployed, largely by TSG elements' (ibid), with one eye-witness claiming that

protesters sat down at police lines being hit with batons as the police moved in. This caused the crowds to surge down the street. Consequently what ensued was chaos and panic as people tried to grab belongings. People were being pushed over and trampled upon by both police and fellow protesters due to the speed and force at which the police moved with their shields. These shields were not being used to protect the officer holding them, but more as a weapon to forcefully shove people forward (ibid: Appendix).

The use of force by the police is governed by the Criminal Law Act 1977, which provides that a 'person may use such force as is reasonable in the circumstances in the prevention of crime [but not disorder], or in effecting or assisting in the lawful arrest of offenders or suspected offenders or of persons unlawfully at large'. Those present at the G20 protests, however, have claimed that this does not cover 'Repeatedly punching, batoning and using edges of riot shields on peaceful demonstrators in a non-violent situation'.[95] In the case of Nicola Fisher, the Home Affairs Committee reported that from 'the evidence [it] received the use of force against Nicola Fisher was a first, rather than last resort' Although the Committee did 'not know whether it was justified', 'equally [it did] not know whether it was needed; Nicola Fisher never got the chance to obey the officers' orders' (HAC, 2009a: paragraph 56).[96]

Conclusion

So what then of Lord Justice Sedley's 'constitutional shift' in favour of freedom of assembly? Just what does it mean in practice? The welcome decision in *Laporte* should not be allowed to obscure the fact that little appears to have changed, and that the contribution of the HRA to the right of peaceful assembly has been little more than a mirage. Despite concern in the 1980s and 1990s about the accumulation of more and more common law and statutory restraints on freedom of assembly to deal with the latest wave of protesters, not a single law has been consigned to the dustbin as a result of the Human Rights Act. The common law powers of the police

---

[95] See also HMIC, 2009: 141.

[96] The HAC noted that 'police trained in crowd control are taught that a slap across the face or a baton strike to the leg (as inflicted on Nicola Fisher) are appropriate actions to prevent an escalation of violence, and a textbook example of "distraction" tactics' (para 57). For a fuller account of police training in different violence techniques (sanitised with the synonym 'distraction'), see HMIC (2009).

remain intact, with even the notorious offence of breach of the peace in Scotland evading two separate challenges based on articles 6 and 11 of the Convention. At best, the common law has stalled for the time being, with the House of Lords in *Laporte* unwilling to extend police powers still further, though it is hard to see why the Human Rights Act was necessary to induce such restraint. Similarly, not a single piece of legislation restraining freedom of assembly has been challenged, with the most significant decision on free-dom of assembly to have been made by the House of Lords in the *Jones* case before the Human Rights Act came into force. But that was in a distant era – before the fetish of separation of powers would exclude the Lord Chancellor from sitting in such cases (surely an example of the liberals cutting their noses to spite their faces, given the seminal contribution of Irvine in this case), and before the events of 9/11 shattered the lens through which civil liberties are now to be seen (raising questions about the impact in practice of *DPP v Jones*, given the ease with which an assembly could be deemed to be an unreasonable use of the highway). At best, the proceedings in the *Percy* case (reinforced by *Gillan*, discussed fully in chapter 6) suggest that these statutory powers will have to be used with greater circumspection than might otherwise have been the case, though with how much circumspec-tion remains to be seen. What is clear, however, is that the Human Rights Act has not prevented the extravagant use of some of the pre 1998 statutory powers; nor indeed has it stopped the process of granting still more powers to control and restrain demonstrations, which increasingly must have a de facto licence from the public authorities (in the sense that they have to be informed, may impose conditions, and otherwise do not object).

But just as the Human Rights Act has not pushed back the rising tide of restraint, it has failed to silence the chorus of critics of police conduct at marches and demonstrations. So although the anti-war protests on 15 February 2003 were carried out in relative peace, the same cannot be said about other events before and after. These include the anti-globalisation protesters who were corralled in Oxford Street for seven hours by the police on 1 May 2001, the House of Lords in *Austin* holding that the common law power of breach of the peace remains in rude good health. They also include the anti-royalist demonstrators who were put on a London bus by the police and driven around London to stop them disrupting the Queen's birthday celebrations in 2002; the anti-war protesters who claim to have been the victims of over-enthusiastic and arbitrary policing at RAF Fairford and elsewhere; and the pro-hunt lobby who found themselves on the wrong end of police batons in Parliament Square in 2004. Further concerns about policing were encountered during the G8 meeting at Gleneagles in July 2005. A five mile 'ring of steel' at a cost of £1 million was erected around the hotel site, the fence reinforced by 'sensitive CCTV cameras'. An airship was to act 'as a spy in the sky' over the hotel 'to spot troublemakers and allow police to move in and arrest them',[97] while the Tayside police took delivery of two helicopters 'fitted with public address systems, searchlights, infra-red systems and video cameras' to 'assist in the overall policing operation'.[98] The police would also be using 'the Automatic Number Plate Recognition network of traffic cameras, which would enable them to 'read number plates, scan the intelligence database and the police national computer and advise police patrols'. Otherwise, an 'intensive intelligence operation' had been in place, with the Tayside police working in co-operation with MI5, Special Branch and the Metropolitan Police,[99] with policing costs being estimated to exceed £50 million. With 10,600 police officers to be on duty (of whom 6,000 were drafted in from England and Wales), the preparations seemed more appropriate for a major civil insurrection than a political demonstration.

[97] *Scotland on Sunday*, 3 July 2005.   [98] *The Scotsman*, 29 June 2005.
[99] *Scotland on Sunday*, 3 July 2005.

CHAPTER 5

Free Speech and the National Security State

Introduction

At common law, people are free to say and print what they like, provided that it is not otherwise unlawful. The problem with this formula is that the law makes unlawful various forms of speech—and has done so since time immemorial, through the medium of devices such as seditious libel, blasphemous libel, and obscene libel. The nature of the restraints on speech has changed, but on the eve of the implementation of the Human Rights Act 1998 (HRA), the scope and scale of restraint was massive. There were statutory restrictions in the Obscene Publications Acts 1959–1964 aimed at—but not limited to—restricting the publication of pornography; in the Contempt of Court Act 1981, preventing news reports that might prejudice a fair trial; and in the Conservative government's controversial Official Secrets Act 1989, protecting some forms of government information from disclosure. There was also a battery of common law restrictions preventing the publication of information acquired in confidence, prohibiting the publication of information about the conduct of government, as well as the publication of defamatory material, a sword by the scrupulous to seek recompense for malicious personal attacks, as well as for the unscrupulous who used the threat of defamation to prevent the publication of uncomfortable truths. It might have been expected, of course, that the incorporation of the European Convention on Human Rights (ECHR) would transform the landscape and remove or dilute the many restraints on free speech. Indeed, article 10 of the Convention provides clearly enough in paragraph one that 'everyone has the right to freedom of expression', and that 'this right shall include freedom to hold opinions and to receive and impart information and ideas without interference by public authority and regardless of frontiers', though this is not to 'prevent States from requiring the licensing of broadcasting, television or cinema enterprises'. But although the right to freedom of expression is now formally recognised in British law in a statutory form, it does not come without limitations.

Events since the enactment of the HRA in 1998 are all the more curious for the parallels that can be drawn with the Thatcher governments in the 1980s. That was also an era in which there was a high profile war against a small nation (this time about the Falkland Islands), and controversial (but not directly related) conduct by the security service (this time to deal with dissent on the home front). It was also an era of leaks to the press and elsewhere about secret government activity, which were duly published often to the great embarrassment of the government at the time. These leaks and press reports led in turn to a spate of criminal prosecutions and civil actions as the government tried to limit the damage, which the litigation succeeded only in escalating. This chapter gives an account of these modern day parallels to the bleak days of the Thatcher government, and as such takes us on a journey from the protection of journalistic sources, defamation (of government no less), official secrecy, contempt of court, and parliamentary privilege. The range of issues covered thus reveals that there are several ways by which free speech can be curtailed beyond the simple expedient of press censorship and banning certain forms of publication, a stage of development beyond which we have largely passed. Now the restraints are slightly more subtle and more focused, targeting information that the government does not want in the public arena, or criticism from certain quarters that it does not want to hear. So the manner of restraint may be said principally to take the form of (a) penalising the public official who places the information in the public arena; (b) attacking and discrediting the media outlets who criticise the government; and (c) taking action against those (including those in prominent positions) who use the information that has been leaked to them. In several of these developments the courts and judges have played a prominent part (both in their judicial and extra-judicial capacities), though in this chapter we also encounter the failings of others with a constitutional duty to protect free speech, as well a violation of constitutional principle of a most spectacular kind.

The Thatcher Legacy

The relationship between free speech, official secrecy, and national security has long been a controversial one, and much of the difficulty related to the much criticised Official Secrets Act 1911, section 2. This made it an offence for a civil servant or government contractor to communicate information to an unauthorised person, when there was no duty to communicate the information in question in the interests of the State. It was also an offence to receive such information unless it could be shown to have been received by the recipient against his or her wishes, while a separate offence would be committed if the third party were then to pass on the information to someone else. So it was thus unlawful for an official to provide information to a journalist, an offence for the journalist to receive it, and an offence for a newspaper to publish it. The only safeguard against the stupid as opposed to the oppressive use of these provisions lay in the requirement that the consent of the Attorney General was necessary before a prosecution could take place, though this consent was not required before an arrest warrant for an offence under section 2 was issued or executed. While the repeal of section 2 had been recommended in 1972 (Franks, 1972), it was to survive another 17 years, often in controversial circumstances. Indeed, section 2 was significant not only as a source of restraint on those who would publish official information without authorisation, but also for contributing to the development of new areas of media restraint. A good example is provided by a prosecution under section 2 in 1978 when a witness was allowed to be referred to in court only as Colonel B. The name of the witness was published by the *Leveller Magazine* which was then prosecuted for contempt of court. Although the contempt was not made out on the facts, it was nevertheless held to be unlawful at common law deliberately to interfere with the administration of justice.[1] So began a courtship between the law of contempt and the Official Secrets legislation that continues to flourish.

The Official Secrets Act 1911

As already suggested, it was during the Thatcher years that section 2 of the 1911 Act assumed great prominence, with the emergence of practices by government that were shocking then but easily recognisable and mimicked today. The first of three notorious cases was the case of Sarah Tisdall, a young Foreign Office official who in 1983 leaked to the *Guardian* two documents which provided information about the proposed arrival of US Cruise Missiles at RAF Greenham Common in Oxfordshire. The documents had been addressed by the Foreign Office to a number of senior ministers and their purpose was to let the recipients know that a parliamentary statement would be made only after rather than before the US missiles had arrived. The purpose it seems was to withhold this information from Parliament until it suited the government's convenience. Following the leak

[1] *Attorney General v Leveller Magazine Ltd* [1979] AC 440.

of the documents (which were published by the *Guardian*), the government brought proceedings for their return, a claim which the *Guardian* resisted on the ground that it was protected by the Contempt of Court Act 1981, section 10, which provides that:

No court may require a person to disclose, nor is any person guilty of contempt of court for refusing to disclose, the source of information contained in a publication for which he is responsible, unless it be established to the satisfaction of the court that disclosure is necessary in the interests of justice or national security or for the prevention of disorder or crime.

However, both the High Court (Mr Justice Scott) and the Court of Appeal dismissed the *Guardian's* claim that section 10 applied and the document was duly returned. Following forensic tests on the document, Ms Tisdall was identified as a suspected source of the leak, at which point she confessed. Subsequently charged under the Official Secrets Act 1911, section 2, Tisdall was found guilty and sentenced to a short period in prison. In a subsequent appeal by the *Guardian* (which would have been rather too late for the hapless Ms Tisdall had it succeeded), the House of Lords held by a majority of 3:2 that the High Court had been correct to order the return of the documents to the Foreign Office.[2]

At about the same time the House of Lords was beginning to hear the *Guardian* appeal, the government was embarrassed by another leak, this time by Clive Ponting, a senior civil servant in the Ministry of Defence, in connection with the controversial sinking of an Argentine cruiser—the General Belgrano—during the Falklands war in 1982. This leak also concerned two documents, the first a draft answer written by Ponting in response to a parliamentary question by Tam Dalyell MP, and the second an internal document giving instructions that certain information about the rules of engagement were to be withheld from the Foreign Affairs Committee of the House of Commons. Having leaked both documents to Dalyell, Ponting is said to have confessed to an internal investigation, and to have claimed that he had acted as he had done because ministers were not prepared to 'to answer legitimate questions from a member of Parliament about a question of considerable public concern, simply in order to protect their own political position'. So like Tisdall before him, Ponting could reasonably claim that he was moved by a sense of outrage about the failure of government to comply with good constitutional practice, though in this case the civil servant's claim was strengthened by the fact that he leaked to an MP rather than a hostile newspaper. Ponting was also charged with an

---

[2] *Secretary of State for Defence v Guardian Newspapers* [1985] AC 339.

offence under section 2 of the 1911 Act, but on this occasion he advanced a cunning argument. Thus, under section 2, there was a defence where the accused had acted either (a) with authority, or (b) in accordance with his or her duty in the interests of the State. The trial judge, however, quickly scotched any suggestion that the latter could be used to justify the conduct of all manner of public spirited civil servants, taking the view that for these purposes the interests of the State are the interests of the State as determined by the government of the day. But despite being left little wriggle room by the judge, the jury nevertheless returned a verdict of not guilty, in the process delivering a fatal blow to section 2, which was by now hanging by only a slender thread.[3]

Breach of Confidence

The power of the jury in Official Secrets' prosecutions is a phenomenon that was to recur in the 21st century. But in the meantime, a third major incident in the 1980s revealed ingenuity on the part of government for dealing with situations where the writ of the Official Secrets Act 1911 did not run. This was the infamous *Spycatcher* case which concerned the publication in Australia of the memoirs of a retired MI5 official, Peter Wright, who was then living in Tasmania. The book contained some allegations about the operational activities of the Security Service, its relationship with government, and the government's relationships with foreign governments. Mr Wright clearly could not be prosecuted by the British government in Australia, and for legal reasons he could not be extradited to the United Kingdom to stand trial here. So the government resorted to the ill-advised and ill-fated strategy of civil proceedings in the New South Wales courts seeking an injunction to restrain the publication of material that had been obtained by Mr Wright in confidence during his service with the Crown. The action failed at first instance before Mr Justice Powell and on appeal to the New South Wales Court of Appeal, which in a majority decision refused the injunction: first because this was in reality an action to enforce the penal law (Official Secrets Act 1911) of a foreign country (the United Kingdom), and secondly because the injunction could only be granted if it was in the public interest, and the court in Australia had no way of knowing what was in the public interest in the United Kingdom. This decision was unanimously upheld by the High Court of Australia, in a comprehensive 7:0 decision.[4] In the meantime, however, the British newspapers were beginning to pick up bits and

---

[3] *R v Ponting* [1985] Crim L Rev 318.
[4] (1987) 8 NSWLR 341; (1987) 75 ALR 353; (1988) 78 ALR 449.

pieces of information from the proceedings in Sydney. The reporting of this information led in June 1986 to an injunction being sought and obtained in the English courts against the *Guardian* and the *Observer* to restrain them from publishing any of the allegations made by Mr Wright about his time in the service of the Crown. So set in motion a train of litigation that led to three decisions of the House of Lords and a decision of the European Court of Human Rights.

The first of these cases arose when the *Guardian* and the *Observer* applied to have lifted the temporary injunctions against them. This was done on the ground that the book had been published in the United States, with thousands of copies being brought into the United Kingdom, with the result that there was no longer any confidentiality in the information which the injunctions were designed to protect. In what was perhaps one of the most extraordinary free speech decisions of an English court, the House of Lords disagreed, taking the view that the injunctions remained necessary in the public interest, despite the fact that the exceptionally dull book itself was now freely available all over the world to those who wanted it.[5] This was followed by a second decision in which proceedings for contempt of court were brought against the *Times* newspapers and its editor for publishing material which had been covered by the injunctions against the *Guardian* and the *Observer*. Although they had not been a party to the injunctions in question, they were held nevertheless to have been bound by them and to be guilty of contempt of court by deliberately publishing material that would frustrate their terms.[6] The liability for contempt was confirmed, despite the outcome in the third case, which was the refusal by the House of Lords to uphold the Crown's request for a permanent injunction to restrain the publication of Wright's allegations in the United Kingdom. This was decisively rejected on the ground that general publication of the book and its allegations would not cause any damage beyond that which had already been done, with details of the allegations now being available to the agents of whatever foreign powers wanted to have them.[7] The episode was not closed, however, until the European Court of Human Rights had an opportunity to address the first of these three cases, taking the view that the continuation of the temporary injunctions against the newspapers breached article 10 of the ECHR, in light of the US publication and distribution of the book itself.[8] As has happened before and since,

---

[5] *Attorney General v Guardian Newspapers Ltd* [1987] 3 All ER 316.
[6] *Attorney General v Times Newspapers Ltd* [1992] 1 AC 191.
[7] *Attorney General v Guardian Newspapers Ltd (No 2)* [1990] 1 AC 109.
[8] *Observer v United Kingdom* (1992) 14 EHRR 153.

the British press thus had to be protected from the English common law by the Strasbourg court.

Persecution without Prosecution

The leaks in the 1980s led in due course to the enactment of the Official Secrets Act 1989, which replaced the blunderbuss with the sniper's rifle. But although it restricted the scope of the criminal law in this area, the new law did not seriously restrict the capacity of governments to undermine freedom of expression. One of the most remarkable attacks on freedom of expression in the Blair years was to be found in the circumstances relating to Dr David Kelly, a distinguished government weapons inspector, whose apparent suicide caused great anxiety in government. Although none of the actors in the Kelly affair appear to have done anything unlawful, the BBC was condemned for its journalism, while the government committed British troops to a war in Iraq of doubtful legality, on the basis of what has so far transpired to be false information. The starting point was a broadcast on the BBC's *Today* programme on 29 May 2003 casting doubt on claims made in a government dossier of 24 September 2002. This was an important document containing a foreword by the Prime Minister who 'wanted to share with the British people' the reasons he believed why the issue of *Iraq's Weapons of Mass Destruction* was a 'current and serious threat to the UK national interest' (Prime Minister's Office, 2002). A passage in the dossier which was to prove to be particularly controversial was the claim that 'Iraq's military forces are able to use chemical and biological weapons, with command, control and logistical arrangements in place', and that the 'Iraqi military are able to deploy these weapons within forty five minutes of a decision to do so' (ibid). The 45 minute claim was repeated in the executive summary after a sentence stating that Iraq has 'military plans for the use of chemical and biological weapons, including against its own Shia population', a sentence preceded in turn by another to the effect that 'despite sanctions and the policy of containment, Saddam has continued to make progress with his illicit weapons programmes' (ibid). Government dossiers about Iraq were later established as being 'dodgy', with a document of February 2003 alleged to have been plagiarised from an American student's thesis and alleged to have been about 12 years out of date (Prime Minister's Office, 2003). In the case of the September 2002 dossier, much of it appears to be pure fiction: to the horror of the US and British governments, there were no weapons of mass destruction, never mind a 45 minute capacity to deploy them.

The Foreign Affairs Committee Inquiry

Some concerns about these claims appear to have been expressed by Dr Kelly in discussions he had with a number of BBC journalists (Hutton, 2004). A meeting with Andrew Gilligan in the Charing Cross Hotel on 22 May 2003 led Mr Gilligan to report on 23 May 2003 that 'the senior officials in charge of drawing up [the September 2002] dossier', told him that 'the government' 'probably' 'knew that that forty five minute figure was wrong, even before it decided to put it in' (ibid). Mr Gilligan reported, moreover, that a week before the document was published, it was thought to have been 'a bland production' and that according to his unnamed source Downing Street 'ordered it to be sexed up, to be made more exciting and ordered more facts to be discovered'. The 45 minute claim had not been in the original text, and apart from being 'probably the most important thing that was added', its inclusion was said to have made the intelligence services 'unhappy' (ibid). This is because it came from only one source whereas most of the other claims were from two, while 'the intelligence services say they don't really believe it was necessarily true because they thought the person making the claim had actually made a mistake' (ibid). A report on BBC News by Gavin Hewitt on 29 May 2003 claimed that the dossier was 'toughened up' following a request by Downing Street, that the 45 minute claim was based on a single uncorroborated source, and that there were murmurings in the intelligence community about the wording of the document. The source of this information was Dr Kelly, to whom Mr Hewitt spoke earlier in the day (ibid). On the following day, Dr Kelly spoke to Susan Watts of BBC *Newsnight* which reported on 4 June 2003 that 'a senior official intimately involved with the process of putting together the original weapons dossier' 'felt considerable discomfort' over the 45 minute claim (ibid). The same source was reported as having said that the inclusion of the 45 minute claim was a mistake, with an emphasis that 'turned a possible capability into an imminent threat and a critical part of the Government's case for war' (ibid). Mr Gilligan also published an article in the *Mail on Sunday* in which he claimed that it was the Prime Minister's Director of Communications (Mr Alastair Campbell) who had 'sexed up' the document.[9] The claims were strongly denied by the government which furiously demanded an apology for the impression that the government had taken the country into war on a false basis.

The temperature around this affair was raised on 3 June 2003 when the House of Commons Foreign Affairs Committee announced its intention to conduct an inquiry into the decision to go to war in Iraq. As part of that

[9] *Mail on Sunday*, 1 June 2003.

inquiry, on 19 June the Committee took evidence from Andrew Gilligan who was accused of making very serious allegations against the government and the Joint Intelligence Committee. In a wide-ranging session, there was some discussion of meetings generally between journalists and members of the intelligence community, as well as legal measures such as the Official Secrets Act 1989. In the course of the exchange, Mr Gilligan did not identify his source and he did not appear to have been pressed very hard to do so. He did, however, paint 'a picture of frequent contacts, both official and unofficial', and 'alleged that one of his four unofficial contacts showed him a Defence Intelligence Staff paper classified *Top Secret*', while 'another showed him a JIC paper' (FAC, 2003: paragraph 150). At this stage, however, this was a sideshow, with the Committee concluding in its report published on 7 July that 'the 45 minutes claim did not warrant the prominence given to it in the dossier, because it was based on intelligence from a single, uncorroborated source' (ibid: paragraph 70), the government being asked to 'explain why the claim was given such prominence', and whether it believed it still to be accurate (ibid: paragraph 71). It was also concluded (though—as the BBC was later to point out—only with the casting vote of the Committee's Labour chairman) that Mr Alastair Campbell 'did not play any role in the inclusion of the 45 minutes claim in the September dossier' (ibid: paragraph 77), and that 'the claims made in the September dossier were in all probability well founded on the basis of the intelligence then available' (ibid: paragraph 86). A long and detailed list of recommendations included the recommendation that '*Andrew Gilligan's alleged contacts be thoroughly investigated*' (ibid: paragraph 154),[10] and that 'the Government review links between the security and intelligence agencies, the media and Parliament and the rules which apply to them' (ibid). Both the government and the BBC sought vindication of their respective positions, with the latter claiming that it was justified in running the *Today* and *Newsnight* stories, both of which were said to have been in the public interest. The BBC also drew attention to another of the Committee's conclusions, that the language used in the dossier 'was in places more assertive than that traditionally used in intelligence documents' (ibid: paragraph 100).

Ordeal by Foreign Affairs Committee

Pending the publication of the FAC report, Dr David Kelly wrote to his line manager in the Ministry of Defence on 30 June 2003 to say that he had met Andrew Gilligan on 22 May 'to privately discuss his [ie Gilligan's] Iraq experiences and definitely not to discuss the dossier', with Dr Kelly claiming that he

---

[10] Emphasis added.

would not have met Mr Gilligan for such a discussion. Dr Kelly denied any attempt to undermine government policy (which he supported), but recognised that Mr Gilligan's description of a meeting he gave to the Foreign Affairs Committee 'matches my interaction with him'. Dr Kelly could only conclude three things: 'Gilligan has considerably embellished my meeting with him; he has met with other individuals who truly were intimately associated with the dossier; or he has assembled comments from both multiple direct and indirect sources for his articles' (Hutton, 2004). At this point Dr Kelly was drawn into the investigatory processes of the Ministry of Defence, being reminded that he had acted in breach of regulations by having unauthorised contacts with journalists, but being informed that no disciplinary action would be taken against him 'on the ground that there had been no malicious intent' and 'no reason to believe that classified material had been revealed'. It was also made clear that no question arose under the Official Secrets Act 1989. However, investigations at the highest level within the defence and security community (which involved the Prime Minister) led to the conclusion that Dr Kelly was the likely source of Mr Gilligan's claim, and matters were complicated by the report and recommendations of the Foreign Affairs Committee on 7 July 2003. At this point it was decided in government that Dr Kelly's identity should not be withheld from the press, and it was later decided that he should be offered as a witness to both the Intelligence and Security Committee, and the Foreign Affairs Committee, both of which held special sessions, the latter in public. Although this is a decision that led to some criticism of the administration, a controversial inquiry appointed by the Prime Minister into the death of Dr Kelly by Lord Hutton (a senior judge) nevertheless concluded that the government was entitled to behave as it did. This is because there was a need to avoid (a) any allegations of a cover up if it had failed to inform the Committee that Dr Kelly had come forward before its report had been published; and (b) 'a serious political storm' if it had refused to permit Dr Kelly to appear before the FAC (Hutton, 2004).

Dr Kelly was thus put forward despite the advice of the permanent undersecretary of state in the Ministry of Defence, with Lord Hutton taking the view that the decision to reject this advice could not be validly criticised. This is despite the claim made by one member of the FAC that Dr Kelly had been 'treated absolutely uniquely', in being 'made a public figure', and that he had been 'thrown to the wolves'.[11] Yet Dr Kelly was a model of loyalty in proceedings in which he had a torrid time. His claim never to have had any meetings or conversations with BBC journalist Gavin Hewitt was

---

[11] House of Commons Foreign Affairs Committee, Minutes of Evidence, 15 July 2003, HC 390-i (2003-04), Qq 155, 160 (Mr John Stanley).

directly contradicted by Hewitt who gave evidence to Hutton that he had spoken to Kelly on 29 May and that this conversation had informed Hewitt's broadcast on the BBC News Bulletin that day (Hutton, 2004). Similarly, Dr Kelly was evasive in his responses to the Foreign Affairs Committee about his dealings with Susan Watts of BBC's *Newsnight* programme, effectively denying that he had used words in a conversation which were subsequently revealed to have been tape recorded. This recording tended to contradict Dr Kelly's claim before the Committee that he knew about the 45 minute claim only after the publication of the dossier. When he declined to provide details about the identity of journalists with whom he had spoken, Dr Kelly was tormented by one member of the Committee, who barked that 'this is the High Court of Parliament and I want you to tell the Committee who you met'.[12] The same inquisitor was to further humiliate Dr Kelly as 'chaff', thrown up to divert the Committee's probing.[13] Dr Kelly's torment at the hand of parliamentarians was not concluded by his appearance before the Select Committee, with a Tory front bench spokesman tabling a series of parliamentary questions demanding to know about Dr Kelly's contacts with Andrew Gilligan, what civil service rules had been broken by Dr Kelly, and what disciplinary measures were to be taken against Dr Kelly, who was found dead the day after he had been notified of these questions. Although there were thus no legal or disciplinary proceedings against Dr Kelly, his death did not prevent Lord Hutton from concluding that his meeting with Andrew Gilligan was unauthorised and that he had acted in breach of the Civil Service rules in meeting Mr Gilligan and in discussing intelligence matters with him. However, Lord Hutton concluded that Dr Kelly had not claimed that the government probably knew the 45 minute claim to have been wrong (Hutton, 2004).

Protecting the Government's Reputation

Although the main victim of the entire affair was unquestionably Dr Kelly, the BBC was the main casualty of an inquiry which became an inquiry into the ethics of BBC journalism as much as an inquiry into the death of Dr Kelly. It transpired that Mr Gilligan's notes of his meeting with Dr Kelly did not support his conclusions about the government knowing the 45 minute claim to be inaccurate at the time they were made. Indeed, Lord Hutton went further and found that the allegation that the government 'probably knew that the 45 minutes claim was wrong before the Government

[12] Ibid, Q 107.   [13] Ibid, Q 167.

decided to put it in the dossier was an allegation which was unfounded' (Hutton, 2004: paragraph 467). Also unfounded was the allegation that the reason why the 45 minutes claim had not been put in the original draft is because it was from a single source which was not thought to be reliable. In fact, according to Lord Hutton, the real reason why this information had not been included is because it was not received until very late in the day (29 August 2002). Nor was Lord Hutton prepared to accept that the dossier had been 'sexed up'—'a slang expression, the meaning of which lacks clarity'—but one which was subject perhaps for the first time to a forensic definition. From all of this, a number of conclusions were then to cascade. Thus,

- the BBC failed to ensure proper editorial control over Mr Gilligan's unscripted broadcast on 29 May;
- the BBC management was at fault in failing to investigate properly and adequately the government's complaints that the report was false;
- the BBC management failed to make an examination of Mr Gilligan's notes to see if they supported the allegation he had made on 29 May;
- the BBC management failed to appreciate that Mr Gilligan's notes did not fully support his most serious allegation when the notes were finally examined in June;
- the BBC management failed to appreciate the gravity of the allegations against the government made by Mr Gilligan; and
- the BBC governors should also have made more detailed investigations into the extent to which Mr Gilligan's notes supported his report.

These findings had a hugely dramatic effect on the BBC, leading to the resignation of Mr Gilligan, Mr Greg Dyke (the Director General of the BBC), and Mr Gavyn Davies (the Chairman of the Governors).[14] We thus have an extraordinary list of casualties which included the source, the journalist, and the broadcaster; the casualty list being all the more extraordinary for the fact that this remarkable affair took place under the protection of a legal system more fully committed to freedom of expression than at any time in the past. Whatever the rights and wrongs of the conduct of the various actors in this drama, two matters in particular stand out so far as freedom of expression is concerned.

No Protection for Journalists' Sources

The first issue which was not adequately considered by either the FAC or Lord Hutton is the duty of journalists to protect their sources. This is

---

[14] *BBC News*, 28–30 January 2004.

a fundamental principle fully acknowledged by the European Court of Human Rights in *Goodwin v United Kingdom* where it was said that:

Protection of journalistic sources is one of the basic conditions for press freedom, as is reflected in the laws and the professional codes of conduct in a number of Contracting States and is affirmed in several international instruments on journalistic freedoms. Without such protection, sources may be deterred from assisting the press in informing the public on matters of public interest. As a result the vital public watchdog role of the press may be undermined and the ability of the press to provide accurate and reliable information may be adversely affected.[15]

The Court went on to say that in view of the importance of the protection of journalistic sources for press freedom in a democratic society, any failure to respect this principle can be justified only 'by an overriding requirement in the public interest'.[16] This principle is recognised in English law, with the Contempt of Court Act 1981 protecting journalists from having to identify their sources unless disclosure is necessary in the interests of justice or national security, or for the prevention of disorder or crime.[17] British judges have a poor record in applying these provisions to protect journalists, and the protection tends easily to yield to its exceptions.[18] Nevertheless, what is striking in the way in which Andrew Gilligan was pursued first by the Foreign Affairs Committee and then by Lord Hutton was the failure even to engage with this question. Thus, after the publication of the FAC report on 7 July, Gilligan was asked to supply the Committee in writing with the identity of his informant. When he refused to do so, he was summoned to appear for a second time, and at the hearing on 15 July the Chairman (Donald Anderson) began gravely in the following vein:

It is only fair that you be informed of the seriousness of the current situation and of the powers available to a Select Committee of the House. You have refused to answer a question put by me in writing on behalf of the Committee in your last letter. That is why essentially you are here today. You will be aware that a witness appearing before a committee of Parliament is bound to answer all questions which the committee sees fit to put to him or to her and that no witness may excuse himself or herself because of the adherence to a professional code, or indeed on any other ground. Therefore, the committee has the power, if it sees fit, to make a report to the House of Commons of the circumstances of a refusal to answer a question put by it and the powers of the House in dealing with such a matter are considerable. I thought it only fair to make this point to you before we

---

[15] (1996) 22 EHRR 123, p 143.   [16] Ibid.   [17] See pp 141–142 above.
[18] As for example in the *Guardian* case, at pp 142–143 above.

start, before the questioning begins. Can you at the outset confirm that you have fully understood the meaning and significance of what I have said?[19]

Happily, the foregoing statement was as hollow as it was pompous, with Mr Gilligan refusing to name or identify his source, the Committee left to report to the House that Gilligan's conduct revealed that witnesses were free to make allegations against third parties 'who then has no recourse to a legal remedy'. The Committee concluded that it was 'unsatisfactory that a witness who enjoys the full protection of parliamentary privilege should be free to make an allegation against a third party, however serious, without revealing the source for that allegation', and invited the House 'to consider this matter, and to offer guidance to its committees and to their witnesses' (FAC, 2003a: paragraph 6). Not only did this reveal the ridiculous nature of Anderson's statement, it was also a ridiculous claim to make in the context of this par-ticular case, as Gilligan had said nothing before the Committee that was not already in the public domain. It is true that the Committee noted that Gilligan's refusal to discuss any detail about his contacts with his source was based on 'what he calls "a necessary principle of free journalism"', and that 'journalists regard the maintenance of this principle as being fundamental to their ability to carry out their work' (ibid: paragraph 3). Nevertheless, the Committee was clearly concerned to assert the position that the duty of witnesses to answer questions put by a Select Committee is not 'qualified by reference to any professional code' (ibid: paragraph 5).[20] In contrast, however, it is significant that the Committee did not bare its dentures against the government which was guilty of an even more egregious failure to provide information, in a manner which more seriously prevented the Committee from carrying out its functions. Thus the Committee complained that it had 'attempted, so far in vain, to explain to Ministers that for the FAC to discharge effectively its role of scrutinising the policies of the FCO, it will on occasion require access to intelligence material and, on rare occasions, to the agencies themselves' (FAC, 2003: paragraph 61), and that it regarded 'the Government's refusal to grant us access to evidence essential to our inquiries as a failure of accountability to Parliament' (ibid: paragraph 163), This led the Committee to conclude rather feebly that 'continued refusal by Ministers to allow [it] access to intelligence papers and personnel, on this inquiry and more generally, is hampering it in the work which Parliament has asked it to carry out'; and to recommend that 'the Government accept the principle that it should be prepared to accede

[19] House of Commons Foreign Affairs Committee, Minutes of Evidence, 15 July 2003, HC 390-i (2003-04), Q 182.
[20] The only alternative would be to remove the protection of privilege from witnesses, hardly a sensible solution.

to requests from the Foreign Affairs Committee for access to intelligence, when the Committee can demonstrate that it is of key importance to a specific inquiry it is conducting and unless there are genuine concerns for national security' (ibid, paragraphs 168–169). No silly attempts here to bully the government in the way that an attempt had been made to bully Gilligan.

The Defamation of Government

The second area where serious freedom of expression concerns arise relates to Lord Hutton's attack on the BBC. This is not to deny that the issue of freedom of expression was addressed, with Lord Hutton acknowledging unequivocally that the 'communication by the media of information (including information obtained by investigative reporters) on matters of public interest and importance is a vital part of life in a democratic society'. He went on to say, however, that 'the right to communicate such information is subject to the qualification (which itself exists for the benefit of a democratic society) that false accusations of fact impugning the integrity of others, including politicians, should not be made by the media' (Hutton, 2004: paragraph 467). Lord Hutton was clearly exercised greatly by Gilligan's claim that the government probably knew that the 45 minute claim was untrue at the time it was made. In his report, Lord Hutton referred to these as 'very grave allegations in relation to a subject of great importance', and in an article in *Public Law* he wrote that:

The report in the Today programme that 'the government probably knew that the forty five minute figure was wrong, even before it decided to put it in' was the report of an allegation that the government had deliberately misled the country by putting in the dossier, against the wishes of the Intelligence Services, intelligence which the government probably knew was wrong. This was an extremely grave allegation which attacked the integrity of the government and the integrity of the Joint Intelligence Committee, the main function of which is to provide ministers and senior officials with intelligence assessments on a range of issues. (Hutton, 2006: 809–810)

This was followed by the startling claim that 'If true, the allegation would have led to the resignation of the Prime Minister and probably to the fall of the government' (ibid: 810). On the question of the integrity and reputation of executive bodies, however, it is a matter of particular concern that in the *Public Law* article Lord Hutton openly acknowledged that his loadstar was the House of Lords decision in *Reynolds v Times Newspapers Ltd*,[21] in which the former Irish Prime Minister successfully sued for libel, recovering only one penny in damages. This is significant because Lord Hutton had allowed himself to be drawn into protecting the reputation of the government, from

---

[21] [2001] 2 AC 127.

attack by the BBC, and in the process of doing so had employed a standard appropriate for civil actions brought by named individuals, using it in the context of a general and non-specific attack on the government.

Such an approach is open to question for two reasons. In the first place, it empowered Lord Hutton to require a standard of behaviour from the press in its dealings with government which is very high in comparative terms, thereby imposing unduly onerous burdens. The position in English law as developed by the House of Lords in *Reynolds* is thus in sharp contrast to the position in the United States where there is a much greater emphasis on 'a profound national commitment to the principle that debate on public issues should be uninhibited, robust, and wide-open, and that it may well include vehement, caustic, and sometimes unpleasantly sharp attacks on government and public officials'.[22] Not only that, but 'erroneous statement is inevitable in free debate', and 'must be protected if the freedoms of expression are to have the breathing space they need to survive'.[23] It is true of course that the writ of the First Amendment does not run as far as England, at least not directly. First Amendment jurisprudence was, however, also relevant to the second concern about Lord Hutton's approach, which is that reliance on *Reynolds* allowed him to elide the First Amendment inspired rule of English law that the government cannot be defamed, a point established in a leading House of Lords' case in 1993. In *Derbyshire County Council v Times Newspapers Ltd*,[24] it was recognised that 'it is of the highest importance that a democratically elected governmental body, or indeed any governmental body, should be open to uninhibited public criticism'.[25] In the same way, only three years earlier the Privy Council expressed the view that:

it would on any view be a grave impediment to the freedom of the press if those who print, or a fortiori those who distribute, matter reflecting critically on the conduct of public authorities could only do so with impunity if they could first verify the accuracy of all statements of fact on which the criticism was based.[26]

This reflected a similar point made by the US Supreme Court in *New York Times Co v Sullivan* where it was said that a 'rule compelling the critic of official conduct to guarantee the truth of all his factual assertions' would lead to self censorship in which 'would-be critics of official conduct may be deterred from voicing their criticism, even though it is believed to be true and even though it is in fact true'.[27]

---

[22] *New York Times v Sullivan*, 376 US 254 (1964), p 270.

[23] Ibid, p 272.   [24] [1993] AC 534.   [25] Ibid, p 547.

[26] *Hector v Att Gen of Antigua* [1990] 2 AC 312, p 318.

[27] 376 US 254 (1964), p 280.

Persecution by Prosecution: Revival of the Official Secrets Act

The Kelly affair revealed a range of measures available to protect official information, apart from the criminal law in the form of the Official Secrets Acts 1911–1989. But given the intense concern about the government's conduct of the war in Iraq, it was unlikely that this legislation would remain locked up indefinitely. It is true that the use of the Act got off to a bad start in the case of GCHQ employee Katherine Gun. Shortly before the invasion of Iraq started, Ms Gun (along with many others at GCHQ) received an email (since published in the press)[28] from Frank Koza in the US National Security Agency in Washington. According to press reports, the email is said to have 'requested British help with what amounted to a dirty tricks campaign: a plan for the bugging of offices and homes in New York belonging to UN diplomats from the six "swing states",[29] countries whose support would be vital if Washington and London were to win a Security Council resolution authorising the invasion of Iraq'.[30] Several days after receiving the email, Ms Gun leaked it to the *Observer* which published it on 2 March 2003. Shortly thereafter, she informed GCHQ that she was responsible for the leak, following which she was arrested and questioned by the police, as might be expected. She was sacked in June 2003 and charged in the following November with an offence under section 1 of the 1989 Act for an unauthorised leak of information obtained in the course of her employment as an employee of GCHQ. In a surprise move on 25 February 2004, however, the case against Ms Gun was dropped when the prosecution offered no evidence. In view of the claims in the press that Ms Gun had admitted leaking the document, this gave rise to speculation about the motive of the Attorney General, whose consent is required for a prosecution under the 1989 Act, one suggestion being that the government was concerned about a request that had been made by the defence for the Crown to produce the Attorney General's highly controversial advice to the government about the legality of the Iraq invasion.

The *al Jazeera* Memorandum

Katherine Gun's good fortune was shared by neither David Keogh nor Leo O'Connor. The former was a civil servant in the Whitehall communications centre located underneath the Ministry of Defence building in Whitehall,

---

[28] *The Observer*, 2 March 2003.
[29] The countries in question were Angola, Bulgaria, Cameroon, Chile, Guinea, and Pakistan.
[30] *The Guardian*, 26 February 2004.

who had been asked to 'photocopy and distribute' a four page document for 'a select group of mandarins', but having read it 'felt morally obliged to get it into the public domain'.[31] Written by Matthew Rycroft, the Prime Minister's private secretary on foreign affairs, the memo was 'only supposed to be circulated to those "dealing directly with British policy in Iraq"',[32] and was marked 'extremely sensitive', to be seen only by those with 'a really need to know'.[33] Although the 33 recipients included the Prime Minister's director of communications and his official spokesman, it was never intended by the government that the document should be made public.[34] Sometime in April or May 2004, however, Mr Keogh gave a copy of a memo to Mr O'Connor, a researcher for Anthony Clarke, the anti-war Labour MP for Northampton South. The exchange took place in the improbable setting of the Northampton Labour Club, and Mr O'Connor then passed the document to Mr Clarke. Although the four page document was not even disclosed in subsequent legal proceedings (part of which were held *in camera*), it was said to have been the note of a meeting between George Bush and Tony Blair at the White House on 16 April 2004, about the war in Iraq and in particular an American assault on the city of Fallujah, which had given rise to international condemnation. According to press reports, Mr Keogh's intention was to have the contents of the memo raised in the House of Commons, and to be used by US presidential candidate John Kerry; but the plan backfired when according to the reports of the trial, Mr Clarke quickly notified the police on becoming aware of the contents of the document, earning Mr Clarke a personal letter of thanks from Mr Blair. According to his parliamentary colleague Peter Kilfoyle (a former junior minister in the MOD), Mr Clarke 'agonised and was very nervous', before deciding that 'the right thing to do was to return it'.[35]

Both David Keogh and Leo O'Connor were identified by the police quite quickly, as the source of the leak. Nevertheless, it was another 15 months before charges were brought, with the reasons for the delay never having been explained. Following the arrest of O'Connor, however, it is alleged that Mr Clarke and Mr Kilfolyle sought to make the contents of the document known in the United States.[36] According to the *Guardian*, the pair:

decided in October 2004 to reveal the contents of the transcript of the Blair–Bush meeting to John Latham, a Democrat supporter living in San Diego, California. They hoped to influence the impending 2004 US election, Mr Kilfoyle said.

---

[31] *BBC News*, 10 May 2007.
[32] *BBC News*, 20 April 2007.   [33] Ibid.   [34] Ibid.
[35] *The Guardian*, 9 January 2006.   [36] Ibid.

In San Diego, Mr Latham, 71, a retired electrical engineer and a 'contributing member' to the Democrat National Committee, told the *Guardian* that the MPs also wanted him to send letters with the information to newspapers in Los Angeles and New York. At a meeting at the House of Commons, he had been introduced to Mr Clarke by Mr Kilfoyle. Mr Latham, a British expatriate, and Mr Kilfoyle had attended the same school.

Mr Latham said he had never met Mr Clarke before. He added: 'He mentioned that the document was a transcript of a meeting in Washington DC between Bush and Blair. There had been a proposal to take military action against *al-Jazeera* at their headquarters in Qatar. This was defused by Colin Powell, US secretary of state, and Tony Blair.' Mr Latham decided not to write to US newspapers at the time.[37]

Mr Clarke was subsequently to write about being investigated by the police, with his parliamentary offices being searched (albeit with his consent), and with both he and Mr Kilfoyle being interviewed under caution for periods of up to four hours each. According to Mr Clarke 'one of the worrying aspects of [the] case' was that the police told him that 'the member of the Democratic Committee we had met had had his computer seized over in the US to try and retrieve emails sent to and from Parliament'.[38] But neither MP was arrested, to the evident bemusement of Mr Kilfoyle, who is reported as having said that:

It's very odd we haven't been prosecuted. My colleague Tony Clarke is guilty of discussing it with me and I have discussed it with all and sundry.[39]

Prosecution and Conviction

In contrast to the fate of the MPs, David Keogh was eventually charged under section 3 of the Official Secrets Act 1989 with making a damaging disclosure of a government document as a Crown servant without lawful authority; while Leo O'Connor (who gave the document to an MP it will be recalled) was charged under section 5 of the same Act with making a damaging disclosure of a document passed to him unlawfully. The damage alleged related to defence and to international relations. In a further twist, however, shortly after the two men were charged but before the trial, *The Mirror* published details of what was said to be contained in the contested document. Under an 'exclusive' tag and a headline proclaiming:

[37] Ibid.

[38] <http://www.opendemocracy.net/blog/ourkingdom-theme/tony-clarke/2008/12/01/questioned-by-the-met-an-mps-experience>.

[39] *The Guardian*, 9 January 2006.

'BUSH PLOT TO BOMB HIS ARAB ALLY', it was reported that the President planned to bomb the Arab television station, *al Jazeera*, based in Qatar, a country which was an ally of the United States, and that he was talked out of this course of action by Tony Blair, 'who said it would provoke a worldwide backlash'. According to *The Mirror*:

The attack would have led to a massacre of innocents on the territory of a key ally, enraged the Middle East and almost certainly have sparked bloody retaliation. A source said last night: 'The memo is explosive and hugely damaging to Bush.' He made clear he wanted to bomb *al-Jazeera* in Qatar and elsewhere. Blair replied that would cause a big problem. 'There's no doubt what Bush wanted to do—and no doubt Blair didn't want him to do it.'[40]

These alleged plans were said to have been a direct response to *al Jazeera's* reporting of the US assault on Fallujah.[41] *al Jazeera* was also said to have 'infuriated Washington and London by reporting from behind rebel lines and broadcasting pictures of dead soldiers, private contractors and Iraqi victims'. According to *The Mirror* the memo called into question US claims that earlier attacks on *al Jazeera* staff and offices (including strikes on its Kabul and Baghdad offices) were military errors, and it was also claimed that any such action would have been 'equivalent to bombing the BBC in London and the most spectacular foreign policy disaster since the Iraq War itself'.[42]

It is unclear whether *The Mirror* disclosed the full content of the memo, which was said also to contain information about troop movements. However, *The Mirror* did give No 10 notice of its intention to run the story, and although no steps were taken by the government to prevent the publication, the paper was threatened by the government 24 hours later with proceedings under section 5 of the Official Secrets Act 1989, whereby it is an offence for the press to disclose information which has been leaked to them in breach of the Act. It was also alleged that the Attorney General had threatened other newspapers with prosecution if they reported the contents of the documents.[43] But the threat was an empty one, unlike the real threat hanging over the heads of Keogh and O'Connor who, after a trial lasting three weeks in April and May 2007, were both convicted at the Old Bailey,

---

[40] *The Mirror*, 22 November 2005. See <http://www.mirror.co.uk/news/top-stories/2005/11/22/exclusive-bush-plot-to-bomb-his-arab-ally-115875-16397937/>. The report continues: 'A Government official suggested that the Bush threat had been "humorous, not serious". But another source declared: "Bush was deadly serious, as was Blair. That much is absolutely clear from the language used by both men"'.

[41] Ibid.

[42] *The Mirror* also commented that 'Dozens of *al-Jazeera* staff at the HQ are not, as many believe, Islamic fanatics. Instead, most are respected and highly trained technicians and journalists'.

[43] *The Guardian*, 9 January 2006.

with Keogh being jailed for six months and O'Connor for three.[44] Keogh had claimed that the disclosure was embarrassing for the United States rather than damaging to the United Kingdom, as the law required. This was met with the response that

international diplomacy [is] based on trust and if the contents of confidential discussions between Britain's Prime Minister and another world leader were to leak out it would undermine Britain's ability to conduct international relations.[45]

O'Connor had claimed that he had always intended to hand over the material to his boss (Mr Clarke), that he had no intention of going to the press or other MPs with it, and that he was confident that Clarke (a special constable) would hand it in to the authorities.[46] It appears, however, that the jury took a different view, the convictions leading to Peter Kilfoyle's claim that the whole affair had been about 'protecting the name of President Bush and possibly Prime Minister Blair' rather than national security.[47] In the light of the indulgence shown to others, it certainly seemed a flimsy prosecution, and O'Connor in particular seems to have a grievance that section 5 was used only against him, but not also against some of the other parties in the drama. The legal action against Keogh and O'Connor seems to have been designed *pour encourager les autres*; action against MPs was merely postponed.

Protecting the Government's Information

The challenge to freedom of expression did not end with the threat of prosecution, or the conviction of the whistleblower and the man who passed on the information to an MP. Steps were also taken not only to conduct some of the trial in secret, but also to prevent the full reporting of aspects of the case that were conducted in public.[48] The trial judge (Mr Justice Aikens) imposed two orders under the Contempt of Court Act 1981. The *first order* was made under section 4(2) and provided that *'No report of the question and answer given by the defendant David Keogh at about* 10.46 *a.m on* 30 *April* 2007 *whilst giving evidence in chief in the witness box should be published in any form'*. This was done following a mishap whereby evidence was given in open court that ought to have been given only *in camera*. The *second order* was more detailed and was made under section 11 of the same Act, apparently addressed to the memo itself, it being directed that

[44] *BBC News*, 10 May 2007.
[45] *BBC News*, 2 May 2007.
[46] *BBC News*, 1 May 2007.   [47] Ibid.
[48] *Times Newspapers Ltd v R* [2007] EWCA Crim 1925.

1. There cannot be publication in connection with these proceedings of any material which would or might reveal evidence or statements concerning:
   a. the content of a letter dated 16 April 2004 from Mr Matthew Rycroft (the Prime Minister's Private Secretary for Foreign Affairs at the time) to Mr Geoffrey Adams of the Foreign and Commonwealth Office ('the letter');
   b. the actual, possible or alleged damage resulting from any alleged unauthorised disclosure of the letter.
2. For the avoidance of doubt, this Order does not apply to the following matters:
   a. The date of the letter;
   b. The 'Secret-Personal' marking on the letter or other markings on it;
   c. The heading of the letter, viz. 'Iraq: Prime Minister's Meeting with President Bush';
   d. The contents of the first paragraph of the letter;
   e. The identities of the intended recipients of the letter, as set out in the last paragraph of the letter;
   f. Subject to any order made under section 4(2) of the Contempt of Court Act 1981, evidence given or statements made in open court during the course of the proceedings.

The Court of Appeal and the First Reporting Restriction

These orders were treated with some dismay by various press sources, and were thought by the *Guardian's* Richard Norton-Taylor to mean that 'the media cannot comment on previous allegations about what the document said about Bush', though they can 'report on allegations already in the public domain—so long as [they] don't connect these allegations to the document'. Remarkably, however, such reports 'should be on a separate page to any report on the Keogh/O'Connor secrets trial (where any discussion and evidence about the contents of the document was heard in closed court without the media or the public present)'. According to Norton-Taylor,

This would all be Alice in Wonderland stuff were it not so deadly serious. There are serious principles at stake, the erosion of free speech and openness, by a government determined to cover up embarrassing disclosures by hoisting the flag of 'national security', a term to which judges, even in their present angry mood, can almost always be relied on to defer.[49]

It is thus no surprise that both of these orders were challenged in the Court of Appeal, and although in both cases the appeals were successful, the victory

---

[49] *The Guardian*, 24 May 2007.

was largely pyrrhic, despite inevitable claims in the press that a partial victory had been secured.[50] So far as the first order is concerned, the Court of Appeal agreed that the trial judge had no power under the 1981 Act, section 4(2) to make such an order.[51] Section 4(2) provides that:

the court may, where it appears to be necessary for avoiding a substantial risk of prejudice to the administration of justice in those proceedings, or in any other proceedings pending or imminent, order that the publication of any report of the proceedings, or any part of the proceedings, be postponed for such period as the court thinks necessary for that purpose.

Reviewing the jurisprudence, the Court of Appeal concluded that there was a difference between 'prejudicing the administration of justice in a particular case and prejudicing it generally', and that section 4(2) was addressed to the former rather than the latter. Indeed, according to Lord Denning in one leading case, the purpose of section 4 had been not to restrict the freedom of the press but to liberate it by removing uncertainties that had previously troubled editors.[52]

In this case, the Court of Appeal found it impossible to accept that the order 'with indefinite effect [to apply] after the trial had been completed fell within the jurisdiction conferred by [section 4(2)]'.[53] That, however, was not the end of the matter for the Court of Appeal also rejected the argument that 'once the question had been posed and the answer given in open court, the evidence was in the public domain and publication could not be prevented'.[54] Although the order could not lawfully be made under section 4(2) of the 1981 Act, it had been open to the trial judge to have made a similar order under section 11 of the same Act. This provides that:

in any case where a court (having power to do so) allows a name or other matter to be withheld from the public in proceedings before the court, the court may give such directions prohibiting the publication of that name or matter in connection with the proceedings as appear to the court to be necessary for the purpose for which it was so withheld.[55]

Quite apart from the power to make an order under section 11, the Court of Appeal appeared to conclude that the judge could also have resorted to little-used residual common law powers of contempt of court to deal with the situation:

---

[50] *Press Gazette*, 31 July 2007.
[51] [2007] EWCA Crim 1925, para [21].
[52] *R v Horsham JJ ex p Farquharson* [1982] 1 QB 762.
[53] [2007] EWCA Crim 1925, para [21].
[54] Ibid, para [22].
[55] To be read with *Attorney General v Leveller Magazine Ltd* [1979] AC 440.

it would have been open to the judge, having made it plain that the question and answer had been given in open court in breach of his *in camera* direction, to have made it plain that to publish the question and answer would be a contempt of court. This it would have been as it would have constituted the frustrating of an order lawfully made by the court.[56]

So although the section 4(2) order was quashed, Lord Phillips announced that 'the judge had jurisdiction to prevent publication of the question and answer and that it was proper to exercise that jurisdiction, albeit that an order under section 4(2) was not the correct way of achieving this'.[57] It was also announced that the Court would 'consider submissions from counsel as to the appropriate order that we should make in these circumstances'.[58]

The Court of Appeal and the Second Reporting Restriction

Revived common law powers—the uncertain scope of which were expressly protected by section 6(c) of the 1981 Act—and the futility of litigation were to be a feature of the second order as well. Here it was also accepted that there was no power to make the order in the wide terms that it was made, and in particular no power to make an order under section 11 of the 1981 Act that prohibited publications that would reveal not only what was given *in camera*, but also that which might have been given *in camera*. Such an order was thought to go too far because section 11 only allows the prohibition of publication of a 'name or matter', which did not include speculation that was wholly inaccurate. But, the Court of Appeal continued:

That is not, however, the end of the story. Such publications would be attempts, albeit unsuccessful, to flout the order made by the court and would be seen by the public as a violation of the order of the court. We consider it likely that any such attempt would, itself, constitute a contempt of court at common law. In making the order that he did under section 11, Aikens J had the praiseworthy object of removing from the media any uncertainty as to what they were or were not permitted to publish having regard to the provisions of section 12(1)(c) of the [Administration of Justice Act 1960]. His order removed uncertainty and provided the media with mandatory guidance as to how to involve any risk of being in contempt of court, but it went beyond the powers conferred by section 11.[59]

The Court of Appeal thus amended the order made under section 11 by deleting the words 'or might', and reminded the media of the risk they will run 'if they speculate about the content of the evidence that was given *in*

---

[56] [2007] EWCA Crim 1925, para [24].
[57] Ibid, para [25].   [58] Ibid.   [59] Ibid, para [32].

camera'.[60] Yet despite this setback, as we have seen the Court of Appeal decision was said to have been a partial victory for the 17 press outlets which had launched the appeal to defend freedom of speech. But the concessions secured did not include the right to publish Keogh's comments, but only that 'Keogh is reported to have said the contents of the document were "abhorrent" and "illegal" and that he felt the document revealed Bush to be a "madman"'. It was a curious kind of success.

The second order was by far the more important, for as the BBC pointed out the memo at the heart of the case 'will remain secret for many years to come', so that by the time it is released, 'its contents will no longer be embarrassing or damaging for those involved'.[61] Apart from the general concern about secrecy of such information on grounds of principle, there was the particular concern identified—again by Richard Norton Taylor—that 'the Iraq war has been masked by a confection of official spin and disinformation, [and] now we are being prevented from hearing the truth behind the fiction and discovering what Blair and Bush really said behind closed doors'.[62] It was also pointed out that while the British press was muzzled, 'American and European newspapers [could] say rather more'. So could websites, while the British press were unable even to 'report—or link to—what Larry Miller said about the trial and the document in his Letter from London for the American channel and website, CBS'.[63] This evokes memories of the dark days of the Thatcher regime when—as we have seen—the then government pursued Peter Wright to the ends of the earth to prevent the publication of his memoirs as an MI5 officer, leading to an injunction against two British newspapers (held to extend to all British newspapers even though they were not parties to the proceedings) as the government tried in vain to prevent the publication of the memoirs in Australia.[64] When copies of the US publication of the book began to saturate the British book buying market, it was clear to all (though not the government or the British courts) that the injunctions were unsustainable, with the European Court of Human Rights ruling that the continuation of the injunctions constituted a breach of the right to freedom of expression.[65] It is hard to see how the orders in the Keogh and O'Connor case are not similarly in breach of Convention rights, though the fact that the question has not seriously been pursued—and not even addressed by the Court of Appeal in that case—tells us a great deal about the limited scope of these rights. This is a matter to which we return.[66]

[60] Ibid, para [33].   [61] *BBC News*, 10 May 2007.   [62] *The Guardian*, 24 May 2007.
[63] Ibid.   [64] See pp 142–143 above.
[65] *Observer v United Kingdom* (1992) 14 EHRR 153.
[66] See pp 173–177 below.

Subverting Thatcher's 'Reforms': New Restraints and New Targets

One of the threads left hanging by the Keogh and O'Connor case was the threat to the MPs who spoke out against the government or who put into the public domain government information which could be used to damage the government politically. That thread was picked up in perhaps the most audacious attack on free speech under New Labour, with the breaking of new ground in the Damien Green affair. This not only saw the government's guns trained on its political opponents, but in the process saw the police develop instruments of control which seem deliberately designed to replace the criminal law which a Conservative government had removed in 1989. Conservative MP for Ashford, Mr Green had benefited from leaks from someone close to the Home Secretary over several years, the source of the leak being revealed as Christopher Galley, a 26-year-old civil servant, who worked in the office of Jacqui Smith. According to the BBC, the information in question included the following, which Mr Galley claimed he had passed onto Mr Green because it was in the public interest to do so:

- an e-mail from the Home Secretary's private secretary in July 2007 which showed that 'licences had been granted to security guards who were illegal immigrants';
- a memo to Home Office minister Liam Byrne in February 2008, which revealed that 'an illegal immigrant had been employed as a cleaner in the House of Commons'; and
- a draft Home Office letter to Downing Street in August 2008, in which the Home Secretary 'warned that a recession could lead to a rise in crime'.

The leaks led eventually to an investigation initiated by senior civil servants which led in turn to the arrest on 19 November 2008 of Mr Galley (at 5.30 am) and on 27 November 2008 of Mr Green.[67] The arrest of an MP—required to provide a DNA sample,[68] and threatened with life imprisonment[69]—gave rise to a great division of opinion, with the red corner arguing that MPs are not above the law and that they enjoy no freedom from arrest when they commit a crime, and the blue corner arguing that it was a deliberate attempt

---

[67] *BBC News*, 27 November 2008. Both men were held for 17 and 9 hours respectively. See also *The Guardian*, 17 April 2009.

[68] *The Guardian*, 17 April 2009, where it is reported that 'The Metropolitan Police did not rule out the return or destruction of the forensic evidence, saying a senior officer had discretion to do so in exceptional circumstances if an individual requested it.'

[69] Ibid.

to frustrate the ability of an MP to do his job to hold the government to account. In what looked like a late after-thought, however, the government claimed to have been moved by considerations of national security, with the Cabinet Secretary telling the House of Commons Public Administration Committee that

when we started the inquiry the reason for it was our worry that certain information was getting out which potentially was very damaging to national security and that the kind of person who had access to some of the other things that had come out in the newspapers might also have access to secret stuff.[70]

But this too seems a poor excuse for what happened, particularly in view of the fact that the police action was not taken under the Official Secrets Acts, which would clearly have been called for if the leaked information was potentially *very* damaging to national security as claimed.

A Fragile Basis for Police Conduct

In addition to Mr Green's arrest, a number of premises were also searched, including his home, his constituency office, his London residence, and his parliamentary offices. Although it had been mistakenly thought that four warrants had been issued for these purposes, it subsequently transpired that just three warrants had been issued, with the Commons search having been 'consensual', albeit not with the consent of Mr Green (in contrast to the search of Anthony Clarke's office several years earlier). When asked about this, a Scotland Yard spokesman said there had been 'no deliberate attempt to mislead'.[71] Nevertheless, the arrest of Mr Green and the search of his parliamentary offices were as controversial as they were unprecedented. Controversial not least because they had been made under vague common law powers that had not been devised for the purposes for which they were now being used. Thus, the police were reported by the BBC as saying that 'Mr Green was held on suspicion of "conspiring to commit misconduct in a public office" and "aiding and abetting, counselling or procuring misconduct in a public office"—an obscure and little-used offence under common law'.[72] Geoffrey Robertson QC waded in to point out that 'the offence of "misconduct in public office" was invented by Lord Mansfield in 1783 to convict a deceitful army accountant', and has been 'superseded by more modern

---

[70] House of Commons Public Administration Committee, Minutes of Evidence, 11 December 2008, HC 83-I (2008-09), Q 5. See also *BBC News*, 11 December 2008, which highlights the Cabinet Secretary's 'surprise' at the arrests.

[71] *BBC News*, 3 December 2008. [72] *BBC News*, 28 November 2008.

statutory offences of bribery, corruption and theft'.[73] Robertson made two other extremely important points. First, were the charge to stick, it would mean that any 'public watchdog'—editor, journalist or MP—who enthusiastically receives a leak from a civil servant, would be liable (incredibly) to a maximum sentence of life imprisonment, without any public interest defence'. Secondly, the charge had been used in modern times only against police officers who 'recklessly fail in their duty',[74] and had never been used against a watchdog until the Sally Murrer case, the Milton Keynes journalist who had been charged with 'aiding and abetting misconduct in public office'.[75] But as Robertson pointed out the Murrer trial had collapsed on 25 November 2008. Yet 'two days later the Met Police arrested the MP (and obtained entrance to Parliament) on a charge they must therefore have known was legally questionable', on the ground that it is 'probably incompatible with the Article 10 [of the European Convention on Human Rights] right to receive and impart information'.[76]

The legal basis of the police action was controversial not only because of the apparently flimsy legal basis on which it was constructed, but also because it appeared so conspicuously to get round the limits introduced by the Official Secrets Act 1989. The latter had been introduced to limit the role of the criminal law in dealing with the leaking of government information which had previously been caught by the hugely discredited Official Secrets Act 1911, section 2. The new law provided that the use of criminal sanctions to deal with leaks would be confined to areas of intelligence, foreign relations, and defence. In a letter to *The Times* on the day before the letter by Geoffrey Robertson referred to above, it was pointed out by Maurice Frankel of the Campaign for Freedom of Information that:

The 1988 White Paper that announced the reform made clear that disclosures that were merely 'undesirable, a betrayal of trust or an embarrassment to the Government' would not be punishable by the criminal law. Introducing the new legislation Douglas Hurd, then the Conservative Home Secretary, explained that it 'will remove the protection of the criminal law from the great bulk of sensitive and important information—including policy documents, Cabinet discussions on education, on health and on social security, and economic information and budget

---

[73] *The Times*, 5 December 2008. Modern authority (relied on by the DPP) is to be found in *Attorney General's Reference (No 3 of 2003)* [2004] EWCA Crim 868.
[74] Coincidentally, the BBC News reported on 8 December 2008 that a police officer in Newcastle-upon-Tyne faced such a charge in connection with prostitution. She was suspended from duty. See <http://news.bbc.co.uk/1/hi/england/tyne/7771166.stm>.
[75] On which see the chilling piece by Nick Cohen, 2008. See further *The Guardian*, 28 November 2008; *The Times*, 28–29 November 2008. See also *Press Gazette*, 5 February 2008.
[76] *The Times*, 5 December 2008.

preparations. None of them will any longer have the protection of the criminal law.' Such disclosures might lead to disciplinary action—but not prosecution.[77]

As Frankel also pointed out, 'the disclosures that the Home Office civil servant are alleged to have made not only fall within the broad class of information deliberately removed from these criminal sanctions but in some cases are likely to be disclosable under the Freedom of Information Act'.[78] So although the government may have had cause to have been irritated and angry with both Galley and Green, the answer lies in better recruitment practices and better enforcement of the *Civil Service Code* which provides clearly enough that civil servants must not 'misuse [their] official position, for example by using information acquired in the course of [their] official duties to further [their own] private interests or those of others'. But the *Civil Service Code* is not a criminal statute and does not give rise to criminal liability directly; nor should it give rise to such liability indirectly as the government seeks to enforce its own rules of behaviour in the courts, under a common law offence calculated to undermine the intention of Parliament in 1989.

Police Conduct and Parliamentary Privilege

The doubtful legal basis for the government's action was duly confirmed on 17 April 2009 when the DPP announced that there would be no prosecution.[79] In the meantime, however, there was another issue to consider, notably the 'privileges' of Members of Parliament designed to enable them to carry out their duty to represent the people of their constituencies and in Mr Green's case to hold government to account. These privileges include the right to freedom from arrest and the right to freedom of speech, as well as the right of the House to control its own internal proceedings. There is a great deal of uncertainty about how far these principles extend, and it has been rightly pointed out that they do not give the MP a complete immunity from legal

---

[77] *The Times*, 4 December 2008.   [78] Ibid.

[79] The DPP's published text giving his reasons stated that 'The documents leaked undoubtedly touched on matters of legitimate public interest and Mr Green's purpose in using the documents was apparently to hold the government to account. The extensive coverage of the issues by the national press, along with comments from Government and Opposition sources is evidence of this. The information contained in the documents was not secret information or information affecting national security: it did not relate to military, policing or intelligence matters. It did not expose anyone to a risk of injury or death. Nor, in many respects, was it highly confidential. Much of it was known to others outside the civil service, for example, in the security industry or the Labour Party or Parliament. These examples are not an exhaustive list of the types of information that may be damaging for the purposes of the offence of misconduct in public office' (paras 32 and 33). The text is reproduced in full in the *Daily Telegraph*, 16 April 2009.

liability. But although the freedom from arrest is actually quite limited (and is unlikely to cover the facts in the Damien Green case), the scope of the right to freedom of speech is much more uncertain. Protected expressly by the Bill of Rights of 1688, article 9 provides that 'the Freedome of Speech and Debates or Proceedings in Parlyament ought not to be impeached or questioned in any Court or Place out of Parlyament'. The principal question here—in terms of the scope of article 9—is what is meant by 'proceedings in Parliament', a term which is not confined to words spoken in the course of a parliamentary debate. This was made clear in the famous case of Duncan Sandys in 1938, which was given considerable publicity while the Green controversy was in full spate. Mr Sandys was a Conservative MP for Norwood (in south London) and the son-in-law of Winston Churchill. In 1938 he had been interviewed by the Attorney General and threatened with prosecution under the Official Secrets Act 1911 unless he revealed the source of information that he had included in a proposed parliamentary question, a draft of which he had sent to the Secretary of State for War in advance. The question contained information about the United Kingdom's lack of preparedness for the imminent war with Germany, information which the War Office believed could only have come from an official in breach of the Act. When the matter was raised in the Commons, the House took the unusual step of setting up a Select Committee to consider some of the legal issues relating to the threat made to Sandys.

In an important report, the Select Committee pointed out that freedom of speech is 'not confined to words spoken in debate or to spoken words', but extends to all proceedings in Parliament'. Moreover, although the term 'proceedings in Parliament' in the Bill of Rights had never been construed by the courts, it was said to cover:

both the asking of a question and the giving written notice of such question, and includes everything said or done by a member in the exercise of his functions as a member in a committee of either House, as well as everything said or done in either House in the transaction of parliamentary business.[80]

And quite independently of any question of privilege, the Select Committee also pointed out that 'any action which, without actually infringing any privilege enjoyed by members of the House in their capacity as members, yet obstructs or impedes them in the discharge of their duties, or tends to produce such results, even though the act be lawful, may be held to be a contempt of the House'.[81] The issue here relates not to the arrest of Mr Green, which would have raised separate questions of proportionality on the part

---

[80] HC 101 (1938–39), para 3.   [81] Ibid, para 18.

of the police, in the event that there were reasonable grounds to suspect that a credible offence had been committed by Mr Green. Rather, the main issue relates to the entry and search of Mr Green's office in the House of Commons and the seizure of his computer which is likely to have contained information and files other than those relating specifically to the subject matter of the police inquiries. At the very least, the conduct of the police raises questions about whether conduct of this kind would fall within the general principles expressed in the Sandys case (even supposing that there was a credible investigation underway). These questions are underlined by jurisprudence from other Westminster democracies where it has been accepted by some judges that the removal of material from parliamentary offices may well fall within the scope of the free speech privilege as relating to a proceeding in Parliament (Groves and Campbell, 2007).

Protecting the Government from Embarrassment

So much then for Damien Green MP's right to free speech, whether under article 10 of the ECHR or article 9 of the Bill of Rights. As we have seen, this was not the first time that free speech had been failed by Parliament, with the lack of respect for journalistic privilege in the case of Andrew Gilligan being quite inexplicable.[82] But it was the first time that Parliament had failed one its own members in quite this way, and the first time in living memory it had failed to protect one of its own members from the police. Nevertheless, in a statement to the Commons on 3 December 2008, the Speaker said that on 26 November 2008, the police had told the Serjeant at Arms that an arrest of an unnamed MP was contemplated. The Speaker was told by the Serjeant at Arms, who was again approached by the police at 7.00 am on the next morning when Mr Green's identity was disclosed along with the background to the case. The Serjeant at Arms again informed the Speaker who was also told that a search might take place of Mr Green's offices in the House, though according to the Speaker he was not told that 'the police did not have a warrant'. Nor did the police explain, as the Speaker claimed they were required to, 'that the Serjeant was not obliged to consent, or that a warrant could have been insisted upon'. The embattled Speaker continued by saying:

I must make it clear that I was not asked the question of whether consent should be given, or whether a warrant should have been insisted on. I did not personally

---

[82] See pp 149–152 above.

authorise the search. It was later that evening that I was told that the search had gone ahead only on the basis of a consent form. I further regret that I was formally told by the police only yesterday, by letter from Assistant Commissioner Robert Quick, that the Hon Member was arrested on 27 November on suspicion of conspiring to commit misconduct in public office and on suspicion of aiding and abetting misconduct in public office.[83]

The Speaker continued in a widely criticised statement to make it clear that in future 'a warrant will always be required when a search of a Member's office, or access to a Member's parliamentary papers is sought', and that every case will have to be referred to the Speaker for his personal decision, as it was his 'responsibility'.[84]

Parliamentary Privilege and Search Warrants

At a time when many Members of Parliament felt that they had been let down by a failure of the Commons authorities to defend their ancient rights and privileges, this statement was poorly received by some, and it is a matter of regret that these rights and privileges were not taken more seriously by MPs on the government side. Concern about the hapless Speaker's performance was matched only by a sense that it was all too late: the stable door was being closed after the horse had bolted. It was the responsibility of the Speaker to protect the privileges of Mr Green as well as MPs in the future, and on this occasion he may be said to have been found wanting, not only in the face of serious questions about the legal basis on which the police acted, but also in terms of his response. In a letter to the Home Secretary by Assistant Commissioner Robert Quick (on the same day as the Speaker's statement to the House), the police claimed—for example— that they were entitled to act without a warrant by virtue of the Police and Criminal Evidence Act 1984 (PACE), section 8, which provides that the police may apply to a magistrate for a search warrant to enter and search premises where they believe there may be evidence relating to an indictable offence. By virtue of section 8(1)(e), however, a warrant may only be granted if any of the conditions in section 8(3) apply, these being:

(a) that it is not practicable to communicate with any person entitled to grant entry to the premises;

(b) that it is practicable to communicate with a person entitled to grant entry to the premises but it is not practicable to communicate with any person entitled to grant access to the evidence;

---

[83] HC Debs, 3 December 2008, col 2.   [84] Ibid, col 3. See also HAC, 2009: para 25.

(c) that entry to the premises will not be granted unless a warrant is produced;

(d) that the purpose of a search may be frustrated or seriously prejudiced unless a constable arriving at the premises can secure immediate entry to them.

The police took the view that section 8(3)(c) means that a magistrate 'may not issue a search warrant' if 'entry to the premises will be granted without a warrant (ie by consent)'. In this case there was no basis for believing that consent would be refused,[85] and that as a result it was 'not open to a constable to make an application' (HAC, 2009: paragraph 22).

This is a contentious reading of section 8(3) of PACE: it does not follow from the fact that condition (c) does not apply that other conditions in section 8(3) do not apply. In particular there is the question of condition (b): while the House of Commons authorities may be empowered to give permission to enter the premises and indeed even Mr Green's office, it is far from clear that they are 'entitled to grant access to the evidence', which takes the form of Mr Green's private property, namely his correspondence and his computer equipment. This, however, may be a distraction, as pointed out in yet another letter to *The Times*, on this occasion from Mark Lomas QC, who wrote in trenchant terms that 'the Queen herself does not have the right to enter the House of Commons without the invitation of the Speaker and the House itself'. So far as a warrant authorising the police to enter Parliament is concerned, 'Neither a magistrate nor a High Court judge, nor any other officer of the Crown has th[e] power [to issue a warrant]', with the result that 'the talk of warrants is a complete irrelevance'.[86] To which the Director of Legal Services of the Metropolitan Police responded by claiming that Mr Lomas was conflating the chamber of the House of Commons with the precincts of Parliament.[87] Mr Lomas may have the better of the argument. The case law is quite clear that, as a matter of parliamentary privilege, the House of Commons is entitled to control its own internal proceedings, which extends well beyond the chamber of the House. In one case, for example, an application was made to summons 15 members of the House of Commons for serving liquor without a licence. The application was dismissed by the Chief Metropolitan Magistrate, as was an appeal to the Divisional Court. According to the latter, the magistrate was entitled to say that this was a matter 'which fell within the area of the internal affairs of the House', and that any tribunal would feel 'an invincible reluctance to interfere'.[88]

---

[85] <http://news.bbc.co.uk/1/hi/uk_politics/7765081.stm>. See also HAC, 2009: para 22.

[86] *The Times*, 5 December 2008.   [87] *The Times*, 8 December 2008.

[88] *R v Graham-Campbell, ex p Herbert* [1935] 1 KB 594.

Failure of the Parliamentary Authorities

On this basis the ordinary courts have no authority to grant a search warrant, whatever the Speaker may claim about the precincts of the House not being 'a haven from the law'.[89] The question then arises about the extent to which the Speaker could authorise a search without a warrant. The power of the House of Commons authorities to grant access to the precincts and the premises probably arises by virtue of the power of the House to control its own proceedings. That power of the Commons authorities was to be seen in 1985 during the 'Zircon' affair when the Speaker banned the showing of a film in the House of Commons which was the subject of a High Court injunction, the House of Commons having been regarded as a safe haven from the injunction. But even if the House authorities do not have the legal authority to grant access to Mr Green's office at Westminster, there is not much that he could do about it, given the refusal of the courts to intervene in matters relating to the internal affairs of Parliament. That reluctance to intervene was seen in the Charles Bradlaugh affair in the 1880s when the courts refused to stop the properly elected Mr Bradlaugh from being ejected from the chamber by the Serjeant at Arms because as an atheist he was unable to swear the parliamentary oath (which has since been changed).[90] All of which tends to suggest that for one reason (*de jure*) or another (*de facto*), the member is unlikely to have any redress against the Commons authorities if they allow access to his or her office and removal of his or her private property. This, however, will not necessarily authorise the police to seize the propery of an MP for the purposes of a criminal investigation. It is true that under the Police and Criminal Evidence Act 1984 the police have the power to seize evidence of a criminal offence they are investigating when lawfully on any premises. But even if it could be argued that they were lawfully on the premises in the Green case, it is not clear how far the 1984 Act would allow them to remove personal computers; and more to the point, it is not in any event clear if they could rely on PACE for authority to do so. If parliamentary privilege prevents the issuing of a summons to enforce the criminal law (and by a logical extension the issuing of warrants under PACE to investigate a breach of the criminal law), it is not clear why the same privilege would not also prevent the use of powers of seizure without a warrant, for similar reasons.[91]

---

[89] HC Debs, 3 December 2008, col 2. Compare, *ex p Herbert*, ibid.

[90] *Bradlaugh v Gossett* (1884) LR 12 QBD 271.

[91] By the same token, given that parliamentary privilege was claimed for most of the documents seized from Mr Green's parliamentary office, it is not clear by what authority the DPP thought it appropriate to have 'read and reviewed all of the relevant documents recovered from the searches' (from the DPP's 'decision' not to prosecute Green or Galley, para 2—see note 79 above), if it was the case that they ought not to have been seized in the first place. It is also to be noted that the CPS was

According to Mark Lomas QC, 'what occurred in the House of Commons was a gross breach of parliamentary privilege permitted by the very person whose office exists to uphold it, and some of whose predecessors have gone to the Tower to protect it'.[92] If that is the case, it is not clear that the Speaker's statement to the House on 3 December adequately addresses the problem. There is no case for saying that if criminal conduct has been committed that MPs should be beyond the law; such a position would be an affront to constitutional principle. But in any democracy, there is a need to protect MPs from the eccentric activities of the police, whether moved by real or imaginary national security concerns. That principle is already reflected in the so-called Wilson doctrine which gives MPs a de facto exemption from telephone tapping by the police or the security services, a privilege which (rightly) they vigorously defend (HAC, 2008: paragraph 331). As the Speaker's statement acknowledges, so far as the search of MPs' offices is concerned, there is a need to ensure that there is a prima facie case that there is relevant material in parliamentary offices which relate to the commission of a crime the police are investigating. There is no point, however, in the Speaker saying that a warrant should be required if no one has the lawful authority to grant a warrant. What may be necessary then is a change in the law, so that an order could be made by a High Court judge establishing that a prima facie case has been made out to justify the entry and search of an MP's offices and the seizure of relevant evidence. But that should be done on the basis of an *inter partes* hearing in the same way that an application is made in the case of confidential business records, medical records, or journalistic material.[93] MPs should not have privileges from the criminal law, but they should at least have the same protection as businessman, doctors, and journalists. Such a judicial order granted in relation to the criminal investigation of an MP should be no more than an order to be granted subject to the approval of the Speaker who should be required to provide a fresh examination of the matter, not to determine whether there is sufficient evidence to grant the order in the first place (that is the job of the judge),

---

consulted and informed before the start of the police operation: House of Commons Home Affairs Committee, Minutes of Evidence, 10 February 2009, HC 157 (2008–09), Q 263. A more robust House would have had both the police and the DPP before them to justify their actions with reference to parliamentary privilege. On the contrary, Assistant Commissioner Bob Quick of the Metropolitan Police was treated with kid gloves when he appeared before the Home Affairs Committee, with the issue of privilege appearing in only two exchanges, one of which he initiated. As to the other, Mr Quick was asked ever so politely: 'Can you explain to us—I do not need to remind you of just how sensitive it is to parliamentarians and parliamentary privilege—the process by which you sought permission?': House of Commons Home Affairs Committee, Minutes of Evidence, 10 February 2009, HC 157 (2008–09), Q 235.

[92] *The Times*, 5 December 2008.   [93] PACE, ss 9–14.

but to determine whether a consent to the order on the Speaker's part would be consistent with the privileges of the House. That should be done by an amendment to the Standing Orders of the House with which the Speaker would be expected to comply in all cases.

The Invisibility of the Human Rights Act

The attack on free speech has thus been wide ranging and far reaching. It has caught journalists, the BBC, civil servants, MPs' researchers, and now senior Opposition MPs. There can be hardly anyone left to drag into this net. Yet this was supposed to be the era of human rights, with the Human Rights Act promising to stop the abuses of the kind that we witnessed during the Thatcher years. If anything, matters have deteriorated. Although civil servants (Tisdall and Ponting) were prosecuted and although the BBC (Zircon) and its journalists (Campbell) were persecuted, it was on a qualitatively different scale, while there was no evidence then of MPs being arrested, questioned under caution, or having their homes or offices searched with (Anthony Clarke) or without (Damien Green) their consent. So whatever happened to the Human Rights Act? In light of the foregoing, it is hard to believe that the question of freedom of expression and official secrecy has now occupied the attention of the House of Lords not once but three times since the Human Rights Act came into force. These cases have provided the highest court with the opportunity to say something important about freedom of expression in the national security state, and to use the Human Rights Act to redress the balance between liberty and security, which many thought had tilted too far in the direction of the latter during the Thatcher years. There is certainly no shortage of rhetoric, with Lord Bingham proclaiming loudly in the *Shayler* case that:

Modern democratic government means government of the people by the people for the people. But there can be no government by the people if they are ignorant of the issues to be resolved, the arguments for and against different solutions and the facts underlying those arguments. The business of government is not an activity about which only those professionally engaged are entitled to receive information and express opinions. It is, or should be, a participatory process. But there can be no assurance that government is carried out for the people unless the facts are made known, the issues publicly ventilated.[94]

[94] [2002] UKHL 11, para [21].

Official Secrecy, the Human Rights Act, and Freedom of Expression in Practice

Yet despite the recognition of the need to make the facts known and to ventilate the issues, there is little evidence of this important principle being translated into practice, not even in the *Shayler* case where this powerful rhetoric was expressed. David Shayler had joined MI5 in 1991 and resigned in 1996, shortly thereafter disclosing to the *Mail on Sunday* information that he had obtained during his service for the Crown. This was said to include '28 files on seven topics, including several on Libyan links with the IRA and Soviet funding of the Communist Party of Great Britain', documents 'said to be "chock-a-block" with agents' names, [with] the prosecution claim[ing that] 50 had their lives placed at risk' as a result.[95] Concerned by Shayler's disclosures, the government had moved on 4 September 1997 to seek injunctions against both Shayler and Associated Newspapers Ltd, the publishers of the *Mail on Sunday* and the *Evening Standard*.[96] These injunctions were designed to restrain Shayler from publishing:

any information obtained by him in the course of or by virtue of his employment in and position as a member of the Security Service (whether presented as fact or fiction) which relates to or which may be construed as relating to the Security Service or its membership or activities or to security or intelligence activities generally.[97]

The wide terms of the injunction were subject to a number of provisos, the first of which excluded information 'in respect of which the Attorney General stated in writing that the information is not information whose publication the Crown seeks to restrain'; the other proviso covered the information previously disclosed in a *Mail on Sunday* article published on 24 August 1997.[98] There matters lay until 1999 when *Punch* magazine decided that they would like to hire Shayler as a columnist, writing as an 'insider' about security and intelligence matters. After the publication of the eighth piece by Shayler, however, the Treasury Solicitor wrote to the magazine's editor on behalf of the Attorney General, reminding him of the content of the injunctions (about which the editor already knew), and claiming that some of the articles were damaging national security. The Treasury Solicitor also invited the magazine to take advantage of the first proviso to

---

[95] *Independent*, 6 November 2002.
[96] *Attorney General v Punch Ltd* [2002] UKHL 50.
[97] Ibid, para [8].   [98] Ibid, para [9].

the injunction, to which its editor testily replied that the government was attempting to force *Punch* to 'submit to government censorship'.[99]

The dispute between the government and *Punch* came to a head in July 2000 (before the HRA had been brought into force) when the latter published an article by Shayler about an IRA bomb in London in 1993. Because of concerns about its content, the editor of *Punch* faxed a copy of the magazine to the Treasury Solicitor on Friday 21 July, anxious to receive a speedy response. By midday on the following Monday, the Treasury Solicitor replied to say that the article would damage national security and that no steps should be taken to publish it until all relevant government departments had had a chance to comment on it. The editor then consulted Shayler and a number of amendments were made before the article was sent off for printing, before the Treasury Solicitor faxed the government's proposed amendments on Tuesday 25 July. Following publication of the article, the Attorney General commenced contempt of court proceedings against *Punch* and its editor; both were found guilty and fined £20,000 and £5,000 respectively. The convictions were reversed by the Court of Appeal but upheld by the House of Lords which rejected the editor's defence that he thought the purpose of the injunctions was to protect national security, that it was not his intention to damage national security, and that he did not think that he had. The House of Lords also rejected the claim accepted by the Court of Appeal that the need to get government clearance before a piece was published smacked of government censorship. According to Lord Nicholls, the effect of the proviso was to add to rather than subtract from the rights of the respondents—it set out a 'simple, expeditious and inexpensive procedure which avoids the necessity of an application to the court' to have the injunction varied on a case-by-case basis.[100] Lord Nicholls did accept, however, that orders of this kind created an unsatisfactory state of affairs:

an interlocutory injunction in the wide form used in the present case may well in practice have a significant 'chilling' effect on the press and the media generally, inhibiting discussion and criticism of the Security Service. Parts of the media may well be discouraged from publishing even manifestly innocuous material which falls within the literal scope of the order. A newspaper may be unwilling to approach the Attorney General, the plaintiff in the action in which the order was made. An application to the court for a variation of the order may involve delay and expense. Even less attractive is the prospect of proceeding to publish without further ado, at the risk of having to face contempt proceedings and penal sanctions. The ability to defend such proceedings, on the basis that

---

[99] Ibid, para [13].   [100] Ibid, para [59].

disclosure of the material had no adverse effect on the administration of justice, will not usually afford much consolation to a journalist.[101]

Official Secrecy, the Human Rights Act, and the Public Interest

This subordination of free speech to the interests of national security is to be seen also in the second House of Lords' decision to arise out of the Shayler affair, which takes us back to the Official Secrets Act 1989. One of the controversial features of the government's proposals when they were made in 1989 was that there would be only two defences (that disclosure was authorised and that it was not damaging) but not a third (that disclosure was in the public interest) to a charge under the Act. The government attracted a great deal of criticism for rejecting a public interest defence, but explained that it had done so on the ground that such a defence would undermine the desire 'to achieve maximum clarity in the law and its application' (Home Office, 1988: paragraph 60), and that in any event what is now the 1989 Act is 'designed to concentrate the protection of the criminal law on information which demonstrably requires its protection in the public interest' (ibid). An early opportunity to revisit this issue under the Human Rights Act was provided by *R v Shayler*,[102] which concerned the prosecution of Shayler on three counts under the 1989 Act. Shortly before the *Mail on Sunday* article was published, Shayler dramatically fled the country (though only as far as Paris rather than Hobart), where he remained for the best part of three years, successfully fighting off British attempts for his extradition, a request which was refused by the French because he was wanted to stand trial for political offences. In August 2000, however, Shayler just as dramatically returned to the United Kingdom, ostensibly to clear his name and to allow a jury of 12 of his fellow citizens to judge him, claiming that any disclosures he made 'were in the public and national interests'. The key to the success of this high risk strategy was a recognition by the courts that such a defence existed, a matter sufficiently important to occupy the attention of the highest court. All too predictably, however, the House of Lords unanimously held that there was no such defence, and that none could be created.

It is true that the speeches contain some vigorous commitments to the importance of freedom of expression, as the passage from Lord Bingham's speech quoted above makes clear.[103] But it is also true that the Lords were at pains to point out that the right to freedom of expression is not unlimited, with article 10(2) heavily laden with exceptions and qualifications.

---

[101] Ibid, para [62].   [102] [2002] UKHL 11.   [103] See p 172 above.

And although the 1989 Act undoubtedly places limits on the right of free speech, it was nevertheless directed to legitimate objects of a kind fully anticipated by article 10(2) of the ECHR. The overriding consideration of the House of Lords in this case was thus not the right to freedom of expression, but the needs of the security service. Lord Bingham was influenced by the fact that there was much domestic legal authority pointing to the need 'for a security and intelligence service to be secure',[104] feeling it necessary also to remind the reader that 'the commodity in which such a service deals is secret and confidential information'.[105] In any event, there were less harmful ways by which the concerns of former security officials could lawfully be brought to official attention without the need to resort to unauthorised public disclosure. These were first through the staff counsellor who was created for this purpose in 1989; secondly (in the case of unlawful conduct) by way of a disclosure to the Attorney General, the DPP, or the Metropolitan Police Commissioner (though quite whether someone in Mr Shayler's position could command an audience with any of the above without a public disclosure is seriously open to question); or in the case of irregularity, maladministration, or incompetence by way of a disclosure to the Home Secretary, the Foreign Secretary, the Prime Minister, the Cabinet Secretary, or the Joint Intelligence Committee (where a right of audience might be even more remote than in the case of law officers and the Metropolitan Police Commissioner). Should any of this fail, it was suggested that it would always be possible for the official to ask his or her supervisor to authorise disclosure, the supervisor being constrained by the threat of judicial review to consider any request fairly.

Conclusion

Decided in the shadow of 'the horrific events of 11 September 2001',[106] the outcome in *Shayler* was perhaps hardly surprising. Nevertheless, the extent to which the House of Lords has institutionalised a requirement of prior restraint is a particularly disappointing feature of the jurisprudence on official secrecy. If a security and intelligence officer (and presumably a civil servant too) feels the need to put information in the public domain (perhaps about the subversion of democratic government), he or she must first seek approval (perhaps from those who are busy doing the subverting). And if information of this kind comes its way, the newspaper will be encouraged to behave responsibly and to speak to the service or the department concerned; indeed, in the *Shayler* case the *Mail on Sunday* sent back some 29 of

---

[104] Ibid, para [25].   [105] Ibid.   [106] Ibid, para [67] (Lord Hope).

Shayler's papers because they were too hot,[107] while in the *Punch* case the magazine sought approval in advance in the light of concerns about compromising agents. The *Punch* case is disappointing, however, in the sense that the House of Lords upheld a High Court order which—despite what the House of Lords says—effectively requires the press to seek approval prior to publication. Yet although an elegant attempt to reconcile conflicting interests, the idea that the head of the service would seek ministerial approval to authorise such a disclosure, and the idea that all this activity of requests and their consideration would take place under a meaningful threat of judicial review may strike some as implausible.[108] As Lord Hope recognised:

There must, as I have said, be some doubt as to whether a whistle-blower who believes that he has good grounds for asserting that abuses are being perpetrated by the security or intelligence services will be able to persuade those to whom he can make disclosures to take his allegations seriously, to persevere with them and to effect the changes which, if there is substance in them, are necessary.[109]

Yet despite Lord Hope's injunction to be 'realistic',[110] at no point is there any recognition that the circumstances may be so grave (which may or may not have been the situation in the *Shayler* case—it was not permissible to ask the question) that unauthorised disclosure is the only way by which the public interest will be served.[111] To have recognised the principle, while holding it inapplicable on the facts, at least would have been a step forward—a small victory for the Human Rights Act, and an even bigger victory for its credibility.[112]

---

[107] Ibid, para [4].

[108] On judicial self-confidence about the effectiveness of judicial review in this context, in the light of strong scepticism by the appellant, see paras [32]–[33] (Lord Bingham); paras [75]–[79] (Lord Hope); and paras [107]–[115] (Lord Hutton).

[109] Ibid, para [70].

[110] Ibid. Lord Hope also pointed out that 'Institutions tend to protect their own and to resist criticism from wherever it may come' (ibid).

[111] Lord Hope—who seemed the most responsive to the appellant's arguments—also threw in his lot with relief via a request for authorisation to go public, with judicial review as a remedy lurking in the background.

[112] *Shayler* was all the more disappointing for the powerful rhetoric of Lord Bingham, especially poignant in light of subsequent events relating to the invasion and occupation of Iraq: 'Sometimes, inevitably, those involved in the conduct of government, as in any other walk of life, are guilty of error, incompetence, misbehaviour, dereliction of duty, even dishonesty and malpractice. Those concerned may very strongly wish that the facts relating to such matters are not made public. Publicity may reflect discredit on them or their predecessors. It may embarrass the authorities. It may impede the process of administration. Experience however shows, in this country and elsewhere, that publicity is a powerful disinfectant. Where abuses are exposed, they can be remedied. Even where abuses have already been remedied, the public may be entitled to know that they occurred. The role of the press in exposing abuses and miscarriages of justice has been a potent and honourable one. But the press cannot expose that of which it is denied knowledge' (para [21]).

Under the Human Rights Act, Britain thus remains a nation obsessed with the secrecy of official information, with the use of neither the Official Secrets Act 1989 nor its partner the Contempt of Court Act 1981 being in any way affected by the human rights culture. No pre-existing statutory or common law restraint has been removed to give effect to the new legal regime, there is little evidence that existing restraints are being applied with any less rigour than before, and new restraints in the form of emerging privacy laws have been developed by the courts no less, further to restrict what might be published, especially about so-called celebrities, who like to enjoy a somewhat one-dimensional relationship with the media. This is not to deny that there has been lots of impressive rhetoric from the courts acknowledging the importance of freedom of speech as an essential precondition of a democratic society.[113] Nor is it to claim that the courts offer no threat to official secrets prosecutions in particular. But as suggested by the Katherine Gun case, the continuing threat of the courts comes not from judges, but from juries and their real or anticipated reactions to the facts brought before them. According to the BBC, in that case 'the government had made a political calculation that a random selection of a dozen jurors would be likely to be so instinctively anti-war that an acquittal would be likely'.[114] This would have had implications beyond the instant prosecution, and lead to the reputation of the Act itself being irrevocably damaged.[115] It is thus not human rights law or human rights lawyers that offers protection for free speech but the extraordinary and unknown response of 12 lay people moved by a sense of justice rather than legality, though as David Keogh and Leo O'Connor discovered, juries will not always put justice before legality. The invisibility of the Human Rights Act in this sensitive area—where it is so badly needed—and the lottery of the criminal justice system suggest that there is no alternative to an amendment to the Official Secrets Act 1989 to complete the business that was left unfinished during Mrs Thatcher's tenure in Downing Street. This would be to do what the *Shayler* court refused to do, namely modify the 1989 Act by a third—a public interest—defence, to protect the official, the journalist, and the press.

---

[113] See *R v Shayler* [2002] UKHL 11, esp para [21], citing *Attorney General v Guardian Newspapers Ltd* [1987] 1 WLR 1248, pp 1269, 1320; *Attorney General v Guardian Newspapers Ltd (No 2)* [1990] 1 AC 109, pp 178, 218, 220, 226, and 283; *R v Home Secretary, ex p Simms* [2000] 2 AC 115, p 126; and *McCartan Turkington Breen v Times Newspapers Ltd* [2001] 2 AC 277, pp 290–291.

[114] *BBC News*, 25 February 2004.

[115] For the official reason for discontinuing the prosecution, see HL Debs, 26 February 2004, col 339.

CHAPTER 6

A Permanent Emergency and the Eclipse of Human Rights Law

Introduction

O N 7 July 2005, London was rocked by a series of bomb explosions
timed to take place simultaneously as commuters were travelling to
work. Four bombs exploded, three in the underground system and one on a
bus, ironically outside the headquarters of the British Medical Association
in Tavistock Square. In total, 56 people were killed including four of the
bombers, and another 700 were injured and maimed, making this the largest single terrorist attack in the United Kingdom since Pan-Am Flight 103
exploded over Lockerbie, killing 270 people in 1988. The principal perpetrators of the London attacks were suicide bombers killed in the carnage
they created, but a number of alleged accomplices were successfully tracked
down by the police and arrested on suspicion of having been involved in the
commission, preparation, or instigation of acts of terrorism. These included
the widow of one of the bombers (Mohammad Sidique Khan), but she was
released without charge.[1] The events of 7 July were quickly followed by an
incident on 21 July 2005 when another four bombs were detonated on the
London transport system, though on this occasion the bombs failed to
explode. A massive police manhunt led within just over a week to the arrest
of the would-be suicide bombers and to their prosecution for attempted
murder. Four men were convicted and sentenced to 40 years' imprisonment
for what the trial judge called 'a viable . . . attempt at mass murder'.[2] The
police manhunt in a climate of heightened anxiety also led to the shooting dead by the police of the young Brazilian electrician—Jean Charles de

---

[1] *BBC News*, 15 May 2007.
[2] *BBC News*, 11 July 2007.

Menezes—in shocking circumstances at Stockwell tube station on 22 July, the victim wrongly mistaken for one of the would-be suicide bombers.[3] But although 7/7 and 21/7 are perhaps the most notorious incidents in recent years, there have been others, including the incident on 29 June 2007 when two cars were found in central London containing bombs which were ready to detonate. By chance, the vehicles were identified as being suspicious and disabled before exploding.

On the following day an unsuccessful attempt was made to drive a vehicle loaded with explosives into the main terminal building at Glasgow airport. But this too failed, with the only serious casualty being one of the participants in the incident, who later died in hospital as a result of burns suffered at the scene when his vehicle burst into flames. These latter events also led to prosecutions, with Bilal Abdulla convicted for conspiracy to commit murder, and jailed for 32 years.[4] Given the nature and scale of the problem, there are few who would deny that real powers are necessary to deal with these and other incidents since 9/11. However, the issue for this chapter is to examine the extent to which the State's response has inevitably intruded upon established civil liberties and contradicted the spirit of the human rights culture that the Human Rights Act (HRA) was designed to presage. This has been a regular complaint since the first anti-terrorism powers were taken in the Prevention of Terrorism (Temporary Provisions) Act 1974, in the wake of the Birmingham pub bombs. The temptation to fail to properly address the human rights dimension is real, with the United Kingdom having been pulled up by the European Court of Human Rights on a number of occasions in the past. The alarm now is not only that the State has introduced permanent powers of an exceptional nature to deal with what remains essentially criminal activity (sometimes of the most grave and heinous kind), but that these powers are growing to feed what presents as an insatiable appetite, with four major pieces of anti-terrorist legislation—the Anti-terrorism, Crime and Security Act 2001 (ATCSA 2001), the Prevention of Terrorism Act 2005, the Terrorism Act 2006, and the Counter-Terrorism Act 2008—having been introduced since 9/11 to complement the already wide-ranging and far-reaching Terrorism Act 2000. Yet it seems unlikely that the 2008 Act will be the last word on the matter, as the government continues to push for fresh powers, having lost the parliamentary battle to detain terrorist suspects for up to 90 days (2006) and then 42 days (2008) without trial.[5]

---

[3] See pp 17–18 above.

[4] *BBC News*, 17 December 2008.

[5] On the defeat of the government's proposals for 90 day detention, see HC Debs, 9 November 2005, col 386. The Terrorism Act 2000 had provided for detention following arrest for terrorist-related offences for up to 48 hours, and a further detention with the approval of a designated magistrate of up

Banning Political Organisations

The Terrorism Act 2000 begins with a major assault on freedom of association, making detailed provision for the banning of political organisations. The banning of organisations has a long pedigree in Britain, and can be traced back at least to the days of the French Revolution when prosecutions for seditious conspiracy were brought against the members of the United Scotsmen and the United Irishmen. Other 19th century terrorists include Thomas Muir and other Scottish radical insurrectionists of the 1820s, while prosecutions for sedition were brought during the Chartist campaign of 1848.[6] More recently, the Communist Party was effectively outlawed, its members deemed to be engaged in a seditious conspiracy (Ewing and Gearty, 2000), while during the Second World War the Defence of the Realm Regulations permitted the locking up of members of organisations which were subject to foreign influence or control, or controlled by people who were sympathetic to the system of government of any power with which the country was at war (Simpson, 1992: 425). More recently still, the events in Ireland and later Northern Ireland led to the banning of a number of organisations. The origins of these latter measures was traced recently in the House of Lords by Lord Bingham in *R v Z*[7] where he pointed out that a 'scheme for proclaiming associations to be dangerous was established by the Criminal Law and Procedure (Ireland) Act 1887, and in 1918 five associations were proclaimed to be dangerous'.[8] 'After Partition', continued Lord Bingham, 'similar provision was made', referring to the Civil Authorities (Special Powers) Act (Northern Ireland) 1922.[9] Introduced by the newly created Government of Northern Ireland, this 'criminalised membership of any of a number of organisations',[10] which included the IRA, the Irish Republican Brotherhood,

---

to seven days in total (s 41; Sch 8). There was no suggestion that the period for detaining suspects for questioning should be extended in the wake of 9/11 which saw the introduction of a range of other anti-terror powers. The position was, however, revisited in 2003 when the seven days were doubled by the Criminal Justice Act 2003. Needless to say, the government's proposal to extend police powers still further to detain for questioning for up to 90 days were widely criticised (JCHR, 2005a: para 87). Under the Terrorism Act 2006, s 24, amending Terrorism Act 2000, Sch 8, detention before charge may now be authorised for up to 28 days, replacing the pre-existing power to hold for up to 14 days in terrorist cases. Authorisation under the 2006 Act must be given by a High Court judge where it is sought on the ground that it is necessary 'to obtain relevant evidence whether by questioning [the suspect] or otherwise', or to preserve relevant evidence, or 'pending the result of an examination or analysis of any relevant evidence'. According to the JCHR, 2009a, on 24 June 2009, the power to detain for more than the standard 14 days had not been used for two years (para 6). Lord Carlile has described the use of the power to detain for longer than the standard 14 days as 'rare' (Carlile, 2009: 27).

[6] *HM Advocate v Cumming* (1848) J Shaw 17.
[7] [2005] UKHL 35.   [8] Ibid, para [3].
[9] Ibid.   [10] Ibid.

the Irish Volunteers, the Cumann na m'Ban, the Fianna na h'Eireann, and later the UVF. Amendments made in 1967 extended the ban to include 'republican clubs or any like organization howsoever described'. These powers have traditionally been widely construed by the courts, most notably in *McEldowney v Forde*,[11] a leading decision of the House of Lords, though one strongly criticised at the time (MacCormick, 1970). In a case not without contemporary parallels, the House of Lords rejected the argument that the 1967 Regulations were void for vagueness, with Lord Hodson able to understand why the Minister 'in order to avoid subterfuge, was not anxious to restrict himself to the description "republican" seeing that there might be similar clubs which he might seek to proscribe whatever they called themselves'.[12]

The Statutory Power of 'Proscription'

The banning (or 'proscription' to use the sanitised language of the Act) of political organisations is now to be found in the Terrorism Act 2000. As might be expected, the 2000 Act addresses the Troubles in Northern Ireland, with no fewer than 14 organisations associated with Northern Ireland being expressly listed in the Act as 'proscribed', and with the Home Secretary being given the power to add to the list any other organisation he believes is concerned in terrorism. These 14 groups associated with events in Northern Ireland did not include the Real IRA, which splintered from the Provisional IRA in 1997, and which was responsible for atrocities such as the Omagh bombing on 15 August 1998. In *R v Z*,[13] however, the House of Lords had to decide in an appeal from the Northern Ireland Court of Appeal whether someone believed to be a member of the Real IRA could be convicted of being a member of a proscribed organisation when the Act proscribed only the Irish Republican Army. Although 'the Real IRA and other groups within the IRA family are separate in their membership and distinct in their aims',[14] and although a 'person should not be exposed to criminal liability if the law does not clearly define the offence he is said to have committed at the time of his committing it',[15] the Irish Republican Army as used in the Act was interpreted by the court to be 'a blanket description to embrace all emanations, manifestations and representations of the IRA, whatever their relationship to each other'.[16] The House of Lords has thus consistently interpreted provisions banning Irish republican organisations in a way that benefited those wishing to ban them, and in a way that is unsympathetic to the principle of

---

11 [1971] AC 632.   12 Ibid, p 645.
13 [2005] UKHL 35.   14 Ibid, para [22].
15 Ibid, para [23].   16 Ibid, para [19].

freedom of association. The 2000 Act does not, however, deal only with the banning of political organisations associated with Northern Ireland. By 31 July 2008, the power of proscription had been used to ban what the Home Office refers to as 45 international terrorist groups, of which two were added as a result of amendments to the law made in the Terrorism Act 2006, which allow for proscription on the grounds of glorifying terrorism.[17]

All the 43 organisations on the list before 2006 were banned because they were believed to be concerned in terrorism for reasons other than glorification, 21 of the organisations being listed in the first ministerial order which was laid before Parliament on 28 February 2001,[18] the rest being added in four subsequent tranches.[19] The 45 groups include al-Qaeda, as well as organisations concerned with Kurdish independence, political reform in Iraq, the overthrow of the Egyptian government, the establishment of a radical Sunni Islamic state in Somalia, the establishment of an Islamic state in the southern Philippines island of Mindanao, and the independence of Kashmir. The Terrorism Act 2000 makes it an offence to be a member of any of these 'proscribed' organisations, or to claim to be a member. Said to be a provision of 'extraordinary breadth',[20] conviction carries potentially heavy penalties of up to 10 years' imprisonment (s 11). It is also an offence carrying the same penalty on conviction to solicit support or organise a meeting for a terrorist organisation, as well as to address a meeting of such an organisation. For these purposes, the meeting need be attended by only three (or more) people, and may be a public or a private meeting (s 12). The other provision of the Act aimed at terrorist organisations makes it an offence to wear an item of clothing, or wear, carry, or display an 'article' where this is done 'in such a way or in such circumstances as to arouse reasonable suspicion that [the wearer] is a member or supporter of a proscribed organisation' (s 13). On this occasion the offence is committed only where the forbidden activity takes place in public, and on this occasion the maximum penalty on conviction is limited to six months' imprisonment, though no doubt the display of membership could lead in turn to a conviction under section 11 and the higher penalties which this attracts. But although the penalties under section 13 are thus limited by comparison with sections 12 and 13, this should not obscure the scope of the legislation which was used in one Scottish case to convict a man for wearing a ring bearing the letters UVF.[21]

[17] For the full list, see <http://security.homeoffice.gov.uk/legislation/current-legislation/terrorism-act-2000/proscribed-groups>. A controversially proscribed 46th group was after a long campaign eventually de-proscribed using procedures under the Act. See below, pp 185–190.
[18] SI 2001 No 1261.
[19] SI 2002 No 2724; SI 2005 No 2892; SI 2006 No 2016; and SI 2007 No 2184.
[20] *Attorney General's Reference (No 4 of 2002)* [2004] UKHL 43, para [47] (Lord Bingham).
[21] *BBC News*, 1 June 2004.

Flawed Procedures for Challenging 'Proscription'

These procedures thus have devastating consequences for the organisations to which they relate, and give rise to serious restrictions on freedom of association, assembly, and expression, as well as (as we shall see) respect for property rights. Yet despite the wide scope for banning organisations under the Act, and despite the dramatic consequences of a ban, powerful complaints have been made about the lack of adequate safeguards before the powers are exercised. It is true that a banning order must be laid by the minister before Parliament. But ministerial orders can only be accepted or rejected, and cannot be amended. This is a matter of some importance when the order contains more than one organisation—as in the case of the first order laid by the Home Secretary which contained 21 organisations. As one solicitor with experience in this field pointed out, 'if you wanted to proscribe al-Qaeda, you had to proscribe [other organizations] as well. If you wanted to keep [a particular organisation] off the list, you were accused of not wanting to proscribe al-Qaeda.'[22] Quite apart from the lack of effective parliamentary scrutiny, doubts have been raised about the lack of adequate judicial review of ministerial decisions. Thus, the decision to proscribe an organisation is taken without any notice of intent being given to the organisation in question and without the organisation being given an opportunity to be heard and to contest the reasons for the minister's proposed proscription. Yet until the point of proscription, the organisation is a perfectly lawful organisation to the extent that it is engaged in this country in lawful activities. Nevertheless, in judicial review proceedings brought by three banned organisations (the Kurdistan Workers' Party (PKK), Mujaheddin e Khalq (PMOI), and Lashkar e Tayyaba (LeT)), the High Court took the view that the minister's decision is not subject to judicial review, and that the organisations in question must use only the 'de-proscription' procedure provided for in the Terrorism Act 2000.[23]

This latter procedure involves making an application to the Home Secretary to de-proscribe the organisation in question. But in view of the fact that he has just proscribed the applicant association and in view of the fact that he has just secured parliamentary approval, the chances of any such application succeeding are very slim. In any event, the Home Secretary has 90 days under the Act to consider the application, during which time Convention rights will have been suspended for the body in question. It is only against the decision not to de-proscribe (and

---

[22] <http://iranjustice.org/content/view/32/28/>.
[23] *R (Kurdistan Workers' Party) v Home Secretary* [2002] EWHC 644 (Admin).

not against the decision to proscribe) that an appeal can be made by the organisation to another of the ragbag special tribunals set up to deal with terrorism, on this occasion the Proscribed Organisations Appeal Commission (POAC), from which a further appeal may lie on a point of law to the Court of Appeal in England and Wales or the Court of Session in Scotland. But by the time it has applied to be de-proscribed, the organisation is illegal, and anyone bringing a case on its behalf to the POAC will reveal himself or herself as a member or supporter and run the risk of prosecution under section 11 of the Act, the procedure in this sense in danger of being a honey trap. According to the leading solicitor already referred to, however, POAC may be a hive without honey, being described as 'quite inadequate' for having proscription set aside.[24] In addition to some of the concerns already identified, Stephen Grosz (who acted for PMOI) drew attention to some of the problems encountered by PMOI in its early dealings with the Commission, some of which are encountered in the next chapter in relation to detention without trial and control orders:

PMOI were denied access to large swathes of material, which were said to have formed the basis of the Secretary of State's decision. A special advocate was appointed, who did see the material, but he could only talk to the representatives of the [National Council of Resistance to Iran] before he saw that material. He could invite them to tell him anything they wanted which might be relevant to the submissions he might make to POAC on the subject of de-proscription, but once he had seen that material, he was not allowed to share anything with them. In order to make sure that he did not let anything slip out, he was not allowed to talk to them at all. So PMOI were unable to see or to meet the substantial part of the case which the Secretary of State was advancing simply because they did not know what it was.[25]

PMOI: A Rebuke for the Home Office

PMOI was in the first tranche of 21 organisations proscribed with effect from 29 March 2001.[26] On 5 June 2001 the organisation applied to be de-proscribed, but the Home Secretary refused the application, and an appeal was then lodged by PMOI to the POAC. For reasons that are not clear, that appeal hearing was not scheduled to take place until 30 June 2003. In the meantime, the unsuccessful judicial review proceedings had come

[24] <http://www.maryam-rajavi.org/index2.php?option=com_content&do_pdf=1&id=218>.
[25] Ibid.   [26] SI 2001 No 1261.

and gone,[27] and a second application for de-proscription was made to the Home Secretary, this time on 13 March 2003, bringing forward fresh information that had been made available in the judicial review proceedings. But this too was refused in a decision of the Home Secretary dated 11 June 2003. No appeal was made against this second decision of the Home Secretary, and the appeal against the first decision was withdrawn. PMOI thus pulled out of 'what appeared to them to be a hostile environment' rather than pay lawyers 'to go through [with] something which was effectively a charade'. A representative of PMOI 'appeared in front of POAC at the final hearing to read a statement explaining why they were not going to go ahead', a decision said to be 'an entirely right one' by solicitor Stephen Grosz in view of 'the hostility which exuded from the bench when [the] statement [was made]'.[28] This apparent lack of confidence in the POAC suggests that PMOI at least may not have shared the views of the government's independent reviewer on terrorism that the 'inevitably confidential processes used to determine whether an organisation should be proscribed are generally efficient and fair' (Carlile, 2006: paragraph 45). Lord Carlile's fourth report on the operation of the 2000 Act was also notable not only for highlighting that the power of proscription was designed to send out a clear signal that the United Kingdom does not welcome terrorists, but also for his remark that there 'is some concern that the UK government occasionally is inflexible in its attitude to changing situations around the world, with reference to proscription' (ibid: paragraph 43), raising directly consequential questions about the legality of the government's conduct. Lord Carlile gave the specific example of PMOI, which 'claim to have disarmed in 2003 to become a political organisation dedicated to the reform of government in Iran' (ibid).

PMOI in the Proscribed Organisations Appeal Commission

Acknowledged as having 'significant Parliamentary support across parties at Westminster', Lord Carlile was 'sure' that the review group set up by the government regularly to examine the case for continuing proscription of the proscribed organisations 'will give serious examination to whether the PMOI really should remain proscribed' (ibid). Whether or not the review group gave serious examination of the PMOI's proscription,

---

[27] *R (Kurdistan Workers' Party) v Home Secretary*, above.

[28] See <http://mujahedin-e-khalq.org/MEK-MKO/index.php?Itemid=7&id=32&option=com_content&task=view>. See also *Lord Alton of Liverpool v Home Secretary*, PC/02/06 (30 November 2007), para [9].

however, the Home Secretary again refused to give effect to a fresh request for de-proscription which was brought on 13 June 2006. On this occasion, however, the application was not made by the organisation itself but by a group of 35 of its parliamentary supporters using powers under the 2000 Act, section 4(2)(b) which allows an application to be made by 'any person affected by the organisation's proscription'. The 16 MPs and 19 peers (including a retired Law Lord and five QCs) complained that they 'have been prevented from being in contact with the PMOI, and carrying out [various] activities in [its] support'. But the parliamentarians not only made the request to the Home Secretary for the ban to be lifted, they also lodged an appeal before the POAC when he refused to do so, and this time a hearing took place.[29] Indeed the hearing led to a comprehensive victory for PMOI, the 145 page decision of the POAC providing a revealing insight into the procedures for proscription and de-proscription, and a desire by the government to stretch already draconian powers well beyond their legal limits, to which the POAC responded robustly, greatly to its credit. The decision was revealing also for the fact that it was not made on the ground that Convention rights had been violated—indeed the Human Rights Act was barely mentioned in any of the 145 pages. On the contrary, it was made on the ground that the minister's conduct was ultra vires and perverse having regard to the normal principles of administrative law, the POAC being directed by the Terrorism Act 2000 to 'allow an appeal against a refusal to deproscribe an organisation if it considers that the decision to refuse was flawed when considered in the light of the principles applicable on an application for judicial review'.[30]

According to the POAC, PMOI is an organisation committed to establishing democracy in Iran. It opposed the Shah and was not tolerated by the theocracy that replaced him.[31] It set up a base in Iraq where it had a considerable arsenal of weapons, and from where it supported the then government during the Iraq–Iran war in 2001. Since 2001, however, PMOI had not been engaged in armed activity and in 2003 it surrendered its weapons to the armies of the invading coalition. In refusing to lift the proscription in 2006, however, the Minister of State—who took the decision on the advice of officials—said that 'even though there has been a temporary cessation of terrorist acts, I am not satisfied that the organization and its members have permanently renounced terrorism', and also that the 'mere cessation of terrorist acts do[es] not amount to renunciation of terrorism.

---

[29] *Lord Alton of Liverpool v Home Secretary*, above.
[30] Terrorism Act 2000, s 5(3).
[31] *Lord Alton of Liverpool v Home Secretary*, above, para [14].

Without a clear and publicly available renunciation of terrorism by the PMOI, I am entitled to fear that terrorist activity that has been suspended for pragmatic reasons will be resumed in the future'.[32] This was said to be unlawful for three reasons, in the first place because the minister had misdirected himself as to the law, which required him to consider whether the proscribed organisation is concerned with terrorism at the date of the application for de-proscription, not whether it has been so concerned in the past. In this case, there was 'no material available which could properly and reasonably lead to the belief that the PMOI had engaged in any form of terrorist acts or otherwise prepared for terrorism since (at the latest) May 2002'.[33] Secondly, it was found that there was a failure to take into account all relevant considerations when making the decision, POAC finding that 'the Secretary of State did not have before him all the material relevant to his decision and that the advice from his officials did not adequately set out all relevant considerations which might affect [his] decision'.[34] And thirdly, the decision was so flawed as to be perverse, POAC concluding that 'the only belief that a reasonable decision maker could have honestly entertained ... is that PMOI no longer satisfies any of the criteria necessary for the maintenance of their proscription'.[35] In September 2006, PMOI was thus not 'concerned in terrorism'.

PMOI in the Court of Appeal

Notwithstanding this quite remarkable rebuke, the Home Secretary nevertheless appealed to the Court of Appeal where it was argued that the POAC had erred on a number of grounds, with the appeal focusing on two points in particular. The first was the level of scrutiny to which the minister should be subject, it being argued that decisions about proscription were like decisions about national security. As a result, the intense level of scrutiny deployed by POAC was inappropriate, and POAC should have confined itself to the *Wednesbury* test,[36] showing deference to the minister in the process. The Court of Appeal disagreed, noting that in any event 'the approach to POAC's review, debated at such length, proved academic, for POAC held that even the application of the conventional *Wednesbury* test led to the conclusion that the applicant's decision was flawed'.[37] The second was on the interpretation of the phrase "concerned in terrorism", but again the Court of Appeal agreed with POAC that 'an organisation that has no capacity to carry on terrorist

---

[32] Ibid, para [31].   [33] Ibid, para [336].
[34] Ibid, para [344].   [35] Ibid, para [349].
[36] *Associated Provincial Picture Houses Ltd v Wednesbury Corporation* [1948] KB 223.
[37] *R (Home Secretary) v Lord Alton of Liverpool* [2008] EWCA Civ 443, at para [44].

activities and is taking no steps to acquire such capacity or otherwise to promote or encourage terrorist activities cannot be said to be 'concerned in terrorism' simply because its leaders have the contingent intention to resort to terrorism in the future'.[38] In so upholding POAC, the Court of Appeal drew comparisons with the Northern Ireland (Sentences) Act 1998 which required the Secretary of State to specify an organisation which he believed was (a) 'concerned in terrorism connected with the affairs of Northern Ireland, or in promoting or encouraging it', and (b) had not established or was not maintaining a complete and unequivocal ceasefire.[39] In contrast to the 2000 Act, the latter was said to draw 'a distinction between being concerned in terrorism and being concerned in promoting or encouraging terrorism', while also making clear that 'an organisation can be so concerned, notwithstanding that it is inactive in consequence of a ceasefire'.[40] While a helpful distinction for the purposes of this case, it is to be hoped nevertheless that the Court of Appeal has not wittingly or unwittingly indicated to the government how the 2000 Act could be amended in order to continue the proscription of groups like the PMOI which have given up terrorism and are banned only because there are fears that it might be revived.

Although the Home Office lost in the *PMOI* case, it can take comfort from the fact that it has been saved embarrassment that the near moribund POAC is at least independent of those who created it. Indeed, the *PMOI* decisions (the first since 2000) led the government's independent reviewer on terrorism to enthuse that the case shows 'the POAC system of law to be sound', with the POAC decision providing 'robust guidance for the future' (Carlile, 2008: paragraph 47). Other organisations wishing to be deproscribed were advised to be 'mindful of the POAC system', for 'by clearly and genuinely removing itself from any terrorism purpose, over a significant period and with unlimited future intent, deproscription can be achieved even by a formerly terrorist group' (ibid). It is unlikely, however, that organisations will be queuing up in the footsteps of the PMOI, though an unsuccessful application was made on behalf of Liberation Tigers of Tamil Eelam (LTTE) (campaigning for self-determination by the Tamils in Sri Lanka) in 2007, a decision not pursued to appeal. There are few if any who could demonstrate the same quality of establishment support as PMOI, and while PMOI succeeded, its success does not address the procedural failings of the system that were identified by Stephen Grosz at the end of the first hearing. Despite the outcome of the *PMOI* case, Lord Carlile continues to

---

[38] Ibid, para [37].
[39] Northern Ireland (Sentences) Act 1998, s 3(8).
[40] *R (Home Secretary) v Lord Alton of Liverpool*, above, para [34].

report that 'Amnesty International, Liberty and other respected lobby and campaign groups continue to take a very straightforward view of POAC', that 'international and European human rights law do not permit of a juris-diction in which an individual or organisation is not told the nature of all the evidence to be deployed against them' (ibid: paragraph 64). To which Lord Carlile replies that such an 'approach begs certain obvious questions about national security and the need for the continuing use of material gained from hard-won intelligence in relation to alleged terrorists' (ibid).[41] There is, however, a more fundamental question, begged this time by Lord Carlile rather than by the critics of proscription. Thus, if 'the value [of proscription] is limited' in the sense that it 'provides little in terms of protection of the public from terrorists', on what basis can it be said to be 'proportionate and necessary' (Carlile, 2009: paragraphs 51–52)?

Terrorist Property and Freedom of Expression

One of the perfectly legitimate targets of the government is the money that might be used for terrorist purposes. However, 'terrorist finance presents particular challenges for law enforcement', with the Newton Committee set up to review the ATCSA 2001 pointing out in 2003 that the 'funds in question may not derive from illegal activities; the sums involved can be small, and the individuals who use those funds may avoid conspicuously expensive lifestyles in seeking to retain effective cover for their operations' (Newton, 2003: 35). Terrorist finance also presents a particular challenge for human rights, as revealed by section 16 of the Terrorism Act 2000, sand-wiched between section 15 which deals with 'fund-raising' and sections 17 and 18 which deal with 'funding arrangements' and 'money laundering' respectively. Section 16 deals with 'use and possession', and makes it an offence to possess money or other *property* with the intention that it should be used (or with reasonable cause to suspect that it may be used) for the purposes of terrorism. Property for this purpose is widely defined in section 121 of the Act to 'include property wherever situated and whether real or personal, heritable or moveable, and things in action and other intangible or incorporeal property'. It seems a long stretch from the context of sec-tion 16 to suggest that it might apply to magazines and literature (whatever provision may be made elsewhere in the Act for terrorist propaganda). But it does, while section 1(5) of the Act provides expressly that a reference to

---

[41] Quite whether these concerns are as strong in relation to groups like LTTE as they are in the case of al-Qaeda is unclear.

action taken for the purposes of terrorism includes a reference to action taken for the benefit of a proscribed organisation, thereby greatly expanding not only the consequences of proscription, but also the impact on freedom of expression. So it would be an offence (a) to possess literature such as a magazine or a newspaper published by a proscribed organisation (for literature would clearly fall within the definition of property), with a view to (b) selling it in order to raise money for the organisation, even though the literature itself does not advocate the use of violence or other terrorist activity (for this would nevertheless fall within the definition of the purposes of terrorism). It does not, however, appear to be an offence to print, circulate, or read such literature, though the risk that it might should not be wholly discounted.

Confiscation of Political Literature

It was into this rather hopeless legal snare that Rory O'Driscoll was plunged when he returned to the United Kingdom from Belgium on 5 January 2002.[42] Mr O'Driscoll's car was stopped at Dover by Customs and Excise officers, and a search revealed that he was carrying 1,001 copies of *Vatan*, a magazine said to be used to raise funds for an organisation called the Revolutionary Peoples' Liberation Party—Front (Devrimci Halk Kurtulus Partisi—Cephesi) (DHKP-C), which according to the Home Office 'aims to establish a Marxist-Leninist regime in Turkey by means of armed revolutionary struggle', and according to the Special Branch was 'a left wing Turkish terrorist group which uses violence, including murder', one of its victims said to be the British businessman Andrew Blake in 1991. Although some miles removed from the Islamic groups against whom the so-called war on terror is said mainly to be directed (about which the same could also be said in relation to PMOI), DHKP-C is a proscribed organisation under the 2000 Act (and has been since 2001, with a request for de-proscription in that year having been refused by the Home Office), and appears on a list of terrorist organisations maintained by the US State Department.[43] Following the search of the vehicle, Mr O'Driscoll was arrested under section 41 of the 2000 Act which provides rather disarmingly that '[a] constable may arrest without a warrant a person whom he reasonably suspects to be a terrorist'. A terrorist for these purposes is defined in section 40 to mean anyone who has committed an offence under the various provisions of the Act (including section 16), or anyone who 'is or has been concerned in the commission, preparation or instigation of

---

[42] *R (O'Driscoll) v Home Secretary* [2002] EWHC 2477 (Admin).
[43] <http://www.state.gov/s/ct/list/>.

acts of terrorism'. Having been arrested on suspicion of having committed an offence under section 16, Mr O'Driscoll was then detained overnight, and released the next morning, after having been interviewed. Invoking powers under Schedule 7 of the 2000 Act and section 22 of the Police and Criminal Evidence Act 1984 (PACE), the police nevertheless retained Mr O'Driscoll's property, notably the 1,001 copies of *Vatan*, along with 23 pre-recorded videos, 26 CD Roms and other documents relating to human rights abuses in Turkey. All but the magazines was returned several months later.

So clear was the legal authority under which the police were acting that permission to seek judicial review was refused on 3 May 2002, with a renewed application rejected on 8 November in the same year. Yet the grounds for the application were not that the police had insufficient powers of arrest, search, or seizure, or that in the exercise of their discretion to exercise these powers they had violated established principles of judicial review. Rather, the principal arguments were based around the Human Rights Act, with this case providing what appears to have been one of the first indications of the extent of the collateral damage the war on terror was to inflict on human rights. The main ground for challenging the legality of these events, however, was not that there had been an unlawful deprivation of property in breach of article 1 of the First Protocol to the Convention, but that section 16 of the 2000 Act breached article 10 of the European Convention on Human Rights (ECHR). Although the government accepted that section 16 could have such an effect, it also argued that section 16 could be justified under article 10(2) of the ECHR as containing restrictions which were prescribed by law and necessary in a democratic society in the interests of national security. But while that might be incontestable in principle, it does not follow that all police conduct under section 16 could be justified under article 10(2). In other words, although there may be a strong case for legislation attacking the use of funds for terrorist purposes, it does not follow that all uses of property for terrorist purposes would meet the requirements of article 10(2), particularly if—say—the definition of terrorist purposes is over-broad or disproportionate. In this case, however, it was assumed that because the law could in principle be defended, it must therefore follow that its application was also unchallengeable. In the words of Lord Justice Kennedy: 'If there is no question about the terrorist nature of the organisation it is difficult to see why section 16 should be regarded as disproportionate, bearing in mind the need for proof of a guilty mind and the extent of the criminal court's powers in relation to sentence.'[44]

---

[44] *R (O'Driscoll) v Home Secretary*, above, at para [26].

Implications for Political Literature

In this case, there was thus no analysis as to whether the material in question could be said to fall within article 10(2), the court appearing to accept the contested evidence of a police officer that *Vatan* was used by the DHKP-C as a means of raising money for the purposes of its activities as a proscribed organisation. This is despite the claim by Mr O'Driscoll that *Vatan* was 'a "left wing radical publication" first published in August 1999', which 'did not incite violence or support terrorism or fund-raise for terrorist organisations', but was 'mainly concerned with human rights abuses in Turkey'.[45] More to the point was the acknowledgement by Lord Justice Kennedy that the translation of *Vatan* magazine seized by the police revealed that 'there is no overt advocacy of violence, merely the expression of political views which, [the claimant] contends, people should be free to express'.[46] Even more to the point, Mr O'Driscoll submitted evidence that 'to his knowledge there is no relationship of any kind between *Vatan* and DHKP-C. About two-thirds of the magazine's income was spent on the cost of publication, and the remainder went on the running costs of the office and staff of the magazine'.[47] Nor was the court persuaded by the argument that even if some part of the proceeds did go to a proscribed organisation

then the offence created by the statute should have been confined to an attack on that part of the proceeds. To create any wider offence was and is disproportionate, just as it was disproportionate to seize and retain, albeit only for a limited time, items which were in the claimant's car and which were plainly not connected with terrorism or providing funds for terrorism, such as literature concerned with the abuses of human rights.[48]

In despatching the claim, however, Lord Justice Kennedy concluded bizarrely that section 16 'is not about freedom of expression', but about 'knowingly providing money or other property to support a proscribed organisation'.[49] And so far as concerns about the seizure and detention of 'superficially innocent material' are concerned, these were dismissed on the ground that 'there can be no sensible criticism of [such] a power',[50] while the failure to return some of what was taken 'as quickly as it should have been', was 'not a matter which merits further investigation by means of proceedings for judicial review'.[51] There was no appeal: the Human Rights Act had failed at one of its first hurdles.

[45] Ibid, para [13].   [46] Ibid, para [14].
[47] Ibid, para [13].   [48] Ibid, para [15].
[49] Ibid, para [26].   [50] Ibid, para [27].
[51] Ibid.

Whatever one may think about the DHPK-C or its literature, this is a decision which points to the implications of the 2000 Act (and in this case section 16 in particular) for other organisations and for issues other than Marxism–Leninism in the unlikely setting of Turkey. In particular, section 16 does not apply only where property is possessed for the purposes of a proscribed organisation, but rather where it is used or possessed 'for the purposes of terrorism'. This could cover the literature of an organisation not yet proscribed but which is under consideration with a view to its proscription, as well as an organisation that is openly tolerated despite meeting the criteria for proscription. This throws us back to section 1 of the 2000 Act where terrorism for this and other purposes is defined in terms that would stray well beyond the boundaries of DHPK-C, al-Qaeda, or other proscribed groups to include a group of people intent on breaking windows at an anti-capitalism demonstration, to say nothing of those who would oppose dictatorship by armed struggle, wherever that dictatorship might be—from Spain under Franco, to South Africa under Forster, to Zimbabwe under Mugabe, and to Burma under Than Shwe. This is because section 1(1) of the Act defines terrorism to mean the use or threat of action that falls within section 1(2), if this action is used to influence the government or to intimidate the public or a section of the public, and the use or threat is made for the purpose of advancing a political, religious, or ideological cause. Much of this is the stuff of democratic politics—seeking to influence government (though perhaps not seeking to intimidate the public), for the purpose of advancing a political cause. The crucial section 1(2) provides that political action becomes unlawful if, for example, it involves (a) serious violence against a person, or (b) serious damage to property,[52] thereby ensuring that the Act would thus cover armed struggle or insurrection against the most vile regimes wherever they may be. This is because it is expressly provided that the government against whom such action may not be directed is not only the British government, but also a government other than that of the United Kingdom.

Freezing Terrorist Assets: No Rebuke for the Chancellor

Just as it is perfectly proper to target fund-raising for terrorist purposes, so it is equally proper to put out of reach any money that might be used for

---

[52] In addition, s 1(2)(c) applies to action that endangers a person's life, other than that of the person committing the action, (d) to action that creates a serious risk to the health or safety of the public or a section of the public, and (e) to action designed seriously to interfere with or seriously to disrupt an electronic system.

such purposes. Thus, if anyone is convicted of an offence under any of the fund-raising provisions of the 2000 Act, the court may order the confiscation of the money. In addition, the ATCSA 2001 introduced new powers to seize terrorist cash in cases where no one had yet been convicted of an offence. Under the ATCSA 2001, cash (widely defined) may be seized by the police, customs, or immigration authorities where there are reasonable grounds to believe that it is terrorist cash. Once seized, the cash may be detained for no more than 48 hours without prior authorisation, which may be provided for renewable periods of three months (up to a maximum of two years) by a magistrates' court (or in Scotland a sheriff court). Where a request is made for such an authorisation, notice must be given to those affected by the notice, including surely the person from whom the cash was taken and anyone else who claims ownership of it. Where a request for authorisation is made, it may be granted only if one of three conditions are met. These include reasonable grounds for suspecting that the cash is intended to be used for the purposes of terrorism and its detention is justified while criminal investigations are pursued. Quite apart from these notice requirements and the conditions for retention, the money must be paid into an interest bearing account if it is held for more than 48 hours, with the interest being added to the amount seized when the money is either released or forfeited. This procedure does not harvest much by way of terrorist cash, and it is open to criticism on a number of grounds: the fact that authorisation can be given in the first instance by a justice of the peace rather than a court, as if this was no more than a request for a search warrant; the fact that money can be seized without limit on reasonable suspicion alone; and the fact that the money can be not only seized but also forfeited without anyone being charged or convicted of an offence.

Freezing of Assets: the 2001 Act, and Human Rights

For all its faults (and there are many), it nevertheless remains the case that minimum standards of procedural fairness are in place under the foregoing arrangements before property is taken. This contrasts with two other provisions aimed at the assets of terrorist organisations. The most extraordinary of these—in the light of human rights obligations—is to be found in Part 2 of the Anti-terrorism, Crime and Security Act 2001, which replaces equivalent but much narrower wartime powers previously contained in emergency laws made in 1964. The new powers allow the Treasury to issue a confiscation order if two conditions are satisfied:

- the first is that it reasonably believes that action detrimental to the British economy is about to be taken, or that action is about to be taken that will constitute a threat to the life or property of one or more British nationals or residents;

- the second is that *the person taking the action or likely to take the action is a foreign government, or a resident of a foreign country.* The effect of the freezing order would be to prevent a bank or anyone else from making funds available to or for the benefit of the person or persons named in the order.

These powers can thus be used for purposes extending well beyond the war on terror, and were used controversially in October 2008 to 'give effect to a freeze on funds in relation to the Icelandic bank Landsbanki, including those owned, held or controlled in relation to that bank by the relevant Icelandic Authorities or the Government of Iceland'.[53] Moreover, this extraordinary executive power can be exercised without any prior judicial authority or approval to justify the deprivation of property on what could be a grand scale, and no need for a warrant before the power can be invoked. The only scrutiny is from Parliament, in the sense that any order must be laid before Parliament and approved within 28 days. But at no point in this procedure is the person who is the subject of such an order to have the right to be notified that the order is to be made, or to be given the opportunity to make representations before it is made. Nor do any affected financial institutions have any such rights, even though they too will be directly affected.

It may well be appropriate that such a procedure should apply in the case of orders freezing the assets in the United Kingdom of a foreign power with whom Britain is at war, though even then it is difficult to see why this power should not need to be approved by a judge. But it is difficult to see how such a procedure is appropriate in the case of the freezing of the assets of an individual British citizen (albeit resident overseas), to whom these provisions apply in the same way that they apply to alleged 'international terrorists' (and now the banks of small nations). In the first place, the very notion of *ad hominem* legislation (primary or secondary) of this kind is a constitutional outrage, perhaps unprecedented in the United Kingdom in modern times (though not in other parliamentary democracies—where its use is criticised (Allan, 2003)). Secondly, the appropriate forum for the confiscation of private property in such circumstances is a judicial one, where cause should be established on the basis of legal principles rather than political expediency. And thirdly, there is also the question of Convention rights, with article 1 of the First Protocol to the ECHR providing that 'every natural or legal

---

[53] SI 2008 No 2668 (Explanatory Memorandum).

person is entitled to the peaceful enjoyment of his possessions', and that 'no one shall be deprived of his possessions except in the public interest and subject to the conditions provided for by law and by the general principles of international law'. Some of the human rights implications of these measures were addressed by the Joint Committee on Human Rights (JCHR) in 2004 as part of its scrutiny of the ATCSA 2001. Although the Committee had not previously expressed concern about these measures, by 2004 it had 'subsequently become clear that freezing orders may have human rights implications' (JCHR, 2004: paragraph 41). According to the Committee:

They would be made by the Treasury, rather than by a judge, and would freeze the assets of named people. They would engage the right to peaceful enjoyment of property under Article 1 of Protocol No. 1 to the ECHR, and the Human Rights Act 1998. They would also engage the right to honour and reputation of the people named, which arises under ECHR Article 8 (which is part of UK law) as well as under Article 17 of the [International Covenant on Civil and Political Rights] (which does not form part of municipal law in the United Kingdom but which binds the United Kingdom in international law). (ibid)

Freezing of Assets: UN Resolutions, and Human Rights

The confiscation powers of the 2001 Act thus raise important questions about constitutional propriety and human rights, though the powers in question have only once been used. This is not because the government is embarrassed about such powers, but because it has found other vehicles to get to the same destination more quickly. These other vehicles are to be found principally in the Terrorism (United Nations Measures) Order 2006 (replacing similar powers made in 2001) (Order 1),[54] and the al Qaeda and Taliban (United Nations Measures) Order 2006 (Order 2),[55] which are made under the authority of the United Nations Act 1946. This provides by section 1 that the government may by Order in Council give effect to a decision of the UN Security Council under article 41 of the UN Charter, and in the course of doing so take steps that appear 'necessary or expedient for enabling those measures to be effectively applied'. The 2006 Orders were made to give effect to various Security Council resolutions on the funding of terrorism, and they have the advantage over the 2001 Act procedures that they apply to British residents as well as to others, and that once the Order in Council has been laid before Parliament, it is not necessary for the Treasury to seek parliamentary approval when it plans to freeze someone's assets. Nor remarkably, is it necessary to secure judicial approval either. Under Order 1, a direction for this

---

[54] SI 2006 No 2657.   [55] SI 2006 No 2952.

purpose can thus be given where there are reasonable grounds for suspecting that the person is or may be 'a person who commits, attempts to commit, participates in or facilitates the commission of acts of terrorism' (article 4(2)). What happens next is explained lucidly by Ben Hayes in an article not inappropriately entitled 'Britain's Financial Guantanamo':

> Once informed of your 'designation', you have 14 days to provide the Treasury with full details of all your assets—properties, rental income, bank accounts, employment status, the employment status of your wife, any benefits either of you receive, and any other 'economic resources' held by you or on your behalf. Failure to provide this information is a criminal offence. All of your assets are then frozen by the Treasury. After this, you and your family can apply to the Treasury for a licence to permit access to your assets or income for 'basic expenses' only.
>
> It is now a criminal offence, punishable by up to seven years in prison, for anyone who knows of your designation to provide you with any funds or economic resources outside the terms of a Treasury licence. The details of around 40 people designated by the Treasury have been published, whilst an unknown number of designations remain entirely secret. These designations are known only to those affected, to financial institutions with access to a password controlled Treasury website, and to other individuals and organisations who the Treasury decides to notify in writing—typically family members, friends, associates, employers and social services. If you have the misfortune to have been personally notified of a designation, it is a criminal offence to disclose the details to anyone else, even your partner. In cases where designations have been publicised via the Treasury website, anyone providing funds or economic resources to a designated individual will be presumed to know of the designation, and therefore liable to prosecution.
>
> Following designation, there is no immediate provision for the now obviously destitute designees, or their families, to access any funds at all. Entitlement to welfare benefit suddenly stops. Unless a designated individual understands what are extremely complex procedures, only a solicitor can lawfully prevent them starving, by petitioning the Treasury for a licence. These licences typically permit designated individuals who are married to receive a maximum of £10 per week in cash. The remainder of their benefit entitlement is paid, under licence, to their spouses. The spouse may only spend this money on basic expenses for the family. Unmarried designees are permitted basic expenses for themselves. (Hayes, 2008)[56]

The use of these procedures has raised major human rights hackles, criticised by both the JCHR (2004: paragraph 42) and the courts,[57] and being described as 'draconic' and as giving 'something as close to absolute power as any department of state could hope for'.[58] It was also recognised by the courts

---

[56] See also *A v H M Treasury* [2008] EWCA Civ 1187, para [27].
[57] Ibid, especially per Sedley LJ; also [2008] EWHC 869 (Admin) (Collins J).
[58] Ibid, per Sedley LJ, para [128].

that the orders were 'indeed oppressive in nature and that they are bound to have caused difficulties for the applicants and their families'.[59] Overturning the High Court, the Court of Appeal nevertheless upheld both Orders, though by a majority in the case of the Terrorism (United Nations Measures) Order 2006,[60] and albeit with a modification in that case. It was held that there was no objection to a direction being made on the ground only of reasonable suspicion that the individual in question was a terrorist, but exception was taken to a direction being made in respect of someone who it is reasonably suspected 'may be' a terrorist, which was said to go beyond what the Security Council Resolution required, and therefore to be ultra vires. Unlike the High Court, however, the Court of Appeal declined to quash the Order, an outcome that would be 'contrary to common sense',[61] the majority preferring instead to excise the words 'or may be', and to leave the rest of it standing. It is true that the steps taken against the applicants were quashed as a result, because they had been made on the ground that the Treasury had reasonable grounds for suspecting the individuals in question 'are, or may be, a person who facilitates the commission of acts of terrorism'. It remains to be seen, however, whether this is more than yet another Pyrrhic victory, in the sense that it is open to the Treasury to impose designations within the narrower terms of the Order, provided of course that there are grounds to do so. And while these designations can be challenged in judicial review proceedings, the Court of Appeal also dismissed concerns raised by Mr Justice Collins in the court below about the lack of procedural safeguards for applicants in such proceedings, noting that this provided no basis for taking the dramatic step of quashing the order,[62] as it would be open to the courts to address these concerns on a case-by-case basis. By Part 6, the Counterterrorism Act 2008 has, however, now provided a statutory framework of minimal procedural protection (which applies also to freezing orders under the 2001 Act), though as with the proscription of political organisations discussed above, there is still no due process before a direction is made, but only a right of challenge after the event on traditional judicial review grounds.[63]

[59] Ibid, at para [25] (Sir Anthony Clarke MR).

[60] The other Order did, however, give rise to a strong difference of opinion between the members of the Court, with Sedley LJ particularly forceful in his concerns, with not all of which Wilson LJ could agree.

[61] [2008] EWCA Civ 1187, para [51] (Sir Anthony Clarke MR).

[62] Ibid, para [78]. This compares unfavourably with the more robust approach of the European Court of Justice in *Joined Cases C-402/05 P and C-415/05 P Yassin Abdullah Kadi and Al Barakaat International Foundation v Council of the European Union*, 3 September 2008.

[63] Concern has been expressed in the European Court of Justice that prior notification and a right to be heard at this stage would be 'liable to jeopardise the effectiveness of the freezing of funds': *Joined Cases C-402/05 P and C-415/05 P Yassin Abdullah Kadi and Al Barakaat International Foundation*, above.

Counter-terrorism and Police Powers

Apart from targeting terrorist organisations in terms of their members, property, and resources, the terrorism legislation also targets what might be referred to as terrorist activity, and to this end important powers have been given to the police. Although many of these powers are unexceptional in principle, they are rendered less so by the manner of their exercise, which continues to be extremely controversial. The area where the citizen is most likely to encounter counter-terrorism legislation is in relation to police powers of stop and search, as was the experience of a group of my King's College London first year students as they made their way from Waterloo station in central London to one of my nine o'clock Public Law lectures (coincidentally on civil liberties) one morning in February 2008. For once they had a good excuse for being late, as with some bemusement they revealed the form that they had been given by the police as a souvenir of their experience. These undergraduates discovered that section 44 of the Terrorism Act 2000 enables the police at senior levels to grant an 'authorisation' which must be confirmed by the Home Secretary if it is to exceed 48 hours. Once an authorisation is granted, police officers are empowered to stop and search any vehicle or any person in the area in question, thereby adding a further exception to the common law rule considered in Chapter 2 above that the police have no pre-arrest powers of stop and search. These undergraduates were later to learn (though this time in the classroom rather than on the street) that the territorial scope of authorisations may be very wide, and indeed may cover the whole of the London metropolitan area (in relation to which a rolling programme of renewed authorisations has been in force continuously since shortly after the Act was introduced).

Exercising Stop and Search Powers

It is true that the power to grant an authorisation may be used 'only if the person giving it considers it expedient for the prevention of acts of terrorism'; that an authorization may be issued for no more than 28 days; and that stop and search powers may be exercised 'only for the purpose of searching for articles of a kind which could be used in connection with terrorism'. But it is also true that there is no limit to the number of occasions an authorisation can be renewed; and that the power of stop and search 'may be exercised whether or not the constable has grounds for suspecting the presence of articles of [a kind which could be used in connection with terrorism]'.[64] Little wonder

---

[64] Terrorism Act 2000, s 45(1).

then that a great deal of concern has been expressed about the misuse of these powers, concern by no means confined to bemused undergraduates leaving Waterloo Station on that February morning in 2008, even if their treatment by the police proved to be a more effective 'learning experience' than the one subsequently 'facilitated' in lecture halls on the same subject. They are not alone. A much better known example of alleged misuse is the case of Walter Wolfgang, the Labour Party member forcibly ejected from the Labour Party Conference in 2005 for gently heckling Jack Straw, then Foreign Secretary. When Mr Wolfgang tried to re-enter the Conference, he was stopped and detained (but not searched) by a Sussex police officer purporting to exercise section 44 powers.[65] But although this attracted a great deal of ridicule, it was only the latest in a number of alleged misuses of this particular power, another having been highlighted by Liberty in a report about the policing of a peace protest outside RAF Fairford in Gloucestershire in 2003. According to the Liberty report, authorisations were issued by the Gloucestershire Chief Constable to cover the whole of the county when the anti-Iraq war demonstrations were at their peak in 2003, though 'the number of terrorists apprehended by police after eight weeks of stopping and searching was zero' (Liberty, 2003: 9). Indeed, it was claimed that 'in most cases officers conducting searches cheerfully acknowledged that the protestors they were searching had nothing to do with terrorism', leading to concern that the power was now being used 'regularly at lawful peace protests at any military base' (ibid).

Home Office ministers claimed that at RAF Fairford, 995 stop and searches had been made between 21 February and 11 April 2003, with Liberty reporting that 'on a typical day', 'a protestor could expect to be stopped and searched about half a dozen times by different groups of police officers' (ibid). But not only that—there are allegations that section 44 stop and searches were made in circumstances which went beyond the powers conferred by the Act, which are limited to articles to be used for the purposes of terrorism. According to Liberty (ibid: 9)

The reasons given for conducting searches often had nothing to do with the prevention of terrorism. Reasons recorded on search forms by police officers included 'looking for prohibited articles (tents) under s.44 of terrorism act', 'wearing material which may cause damage to military establishment', 'following on fence line, seen walking around fence on private property', and 'seen putting something in bag'. Documents such as driving licences and credit cards were inspected and personal details were noted by officers who had inspected such documents. On occasion, personal diaries and correspondence were opened and read and even videoed.

---

[65] *BBC News*, 29 September 2005. Mr Wolfgang was subsequently elected to Labour's once-important National Executive Committee.

More specifically the Liberty report claims that (ibid: 9-10)

Adele Perret, a resident at the Gate 10 Peace Camp was subjected to a minutely detailed search of her possessions during which police officers searched through dirty underwear in a bag she was carrying and lifted up her skirt while conducting a body search. The whole search was filmed by a police video crew. Another camper, Gareth Teasdale, was ordered by officers to strip down to his vest and wait in the cold for twenty minutes during a search on a night when the temperature fell to −4°C.

Protesters walking on their own were particularly vulnerable and in some cases were searched by large groups of police officers. Juliet McBride was searched by a group of eight police officers who confiscated a tape recorder being used to record details of the incident and then prevented other protesters from joining her while she was searched. Kerstine Rodgers and her eight year old daughter were detained with friends for 45 minutes by police who wished to stop and search them, but were eventually released without being searched. Television film crews from media companies were sometimes allowed to film protesters being searched.

Questioning Stop and Search Powers

In 2005, the government's independent investigator of terrorist legislation repeated scepticism expressed in earlier annual reports, questioning 'why section 44 authorisations are perceived to be needed in some force areas but not others with strikingly similar risk profiles' (Carlile, 2006: paragraph 97). Lord Carlile accepted that section 44 was a 'necessary and proportional' response to 'the continuing and serious risk of terrorism' (ibid: paragraph 100), but claimed that there 'is little or no evidence that the use of section 44 has the potential to prevent an act of terrorism as compared with other statutory powers of stop and search' (ibid: paragraph 98). He also pointed out that, although these powers are available to the police in Scotland, they have never been used by a Scottish police force, not even during the meeting of the G8 summit at Gleneagles.[66] Yet London apart, Lord Carlile doubted whether there was 'evidence that Scotland is less at risk from terrorism than other parts of the country' (ibid: paragraph 96). This lack of use in Scotland was said to 'perpetuat[e] the question of why section 44 is needed in England

---

[66] The reference to the G8 is a telling one, given that the meeting of world leaders at Gleneagles in July 2005 (preceded by the Make Poverty History march in Edinburgh on 2 July 2005) presented the Scottish police with their biggest ever challenge. The protest events were attended by thousands of people from all over the world; the planning and preventive measures taken by the police in terms of the use of intelligence and sophisticated modern technology were extraordinary and far reaching; and violence on a large scale was widely expected (and those looking for it were not to have been disappointed) as the Scottish Blood Transfusion Service called on Scots to donate an extra 20,000 pints of blood ahead of the summit. See Ch 4 above.

and Wales if it is not required in Scotland', and to demonstrate 'that other powers are on the whole perfectly adequate for most purposes' (ibid). It is true that changed after the events at Glasgow airport in June 2007, when all eight Scottish police forces applied for section 44 authorisations, which in the unkind words of the *Daily Record* were duly 'rubber stamped' by the Home Secretary.[67] But it appears also to be the case that these authorisations were not renewed after the initial 28 day period, and it appears that section 44 continues to be used 'sparingly' in Scotland (Carlile, 2009: paragraph 235). The fact that Scottish police can use these stop and search powers so sparingly also raises questions about why the British Transport Police need to use them so actively at Scottish railway stations. So although the powers were used for only 28 days to stop and search seven people by the Strathclyde police,[68] they were renewed by the British Transport Police, and in the period from 1 July to 14 December 2007, used by them on roughly 14,000 occasions, in almost 10,000 cases at railway stations, and in 12 per cent of cases against members of ethnic minorities (though ethnic minorities constitute only about 2 per cent of the Scottish population).[69]

More recently, Lord Carlile has expressed serious criticism about the use of section 44, noting in his 2009 report that the use of the power is now 'controversial', and that 'examples of poor or unnecessary use of section 44 abound' (Carlile, 2009: paragraph 140). Having previously accepted that 'London is a special case, [with] vulnerable assets and relevant residential pockets in almost every borough, and fairly extensive use is understandable' (Carlile, 2006: paragraph 100), in 2009 Lord Carlile confessed to frustration that 'the Metropolitan Police still does not limit their section 44 authorisations to some boroughs only, or parts of boroughs, rather than to the entire force area'. He was unable to see any 'justification for the whole of the Greater London area being covered permanently', noting that 'the intention of the section was not to place London under permanent special search powers'. The 'alarming numbers of usages of the power (between 8,000 and 10,000 stops per month as we entered 2009)' was said to 'represent bad news', but more importantly to indicate that 'section 44 is being used as an instrument to aid non-terrorism policing on some occasions', something which Lord Carlile found to be unacceptable (Carlile, 2009: paragraph 147). These growing concerns about the misuse of this power raise two questions, the first being the robustness of the procedures relied

---

[67] *Daily Record*, 3 July 2007. Although policing is a devolved matter, terrorism is not.

[68] <http://scotland.indymedia.org/node/3529>; quoting Scotland against Criminalising Communities.

[69] *BBC News*, 15 December 2007.

on by the courts as a barrier to impropriety. But before considering this matter, the second question prompted by these concerns is whether the power is really needed in the first place. According to Lord Carlile, 'there is little or no evidence that the use of section 44 has the potential to prevent an act of terrorism as compared with other statutory powers of stop and search', and that 'none of the many thousands of searches has ever resulted in conviction of a terrorism offence' (ibid: paragraph 148). These remarks echo those of Assistant Commander Andy Haymen, said by the BBC to have 'questioned the value of stop-and-search powers', observing that 'few arrests or charges arose from such searches'.[70] According to reports of a Metropolitan Police Authority's inquiry into counter-terrorism, Haymen said that 'It is very unlikely that a terrorist is going to be carrying bomb-making equipment around with them in the street.'[71] Lord Carlile was nevertheless not in favour of repealing section 44, still taking the view that it remained 'necessary and proportional to the continuing and serious risk of terrorism' (ibid: paragraph 150), for reasons that remain unclear in the light of the foregoing.

Stop and Search: No Rebuke for the Police

So what about the courts? There have been few judicial triumphs recorded so far in this chapter. Those which have arisen (*PMOI* and to a lesser extent *A*) arose under old-fashioned judicial review principles of illegality or irrationality, with little evidence of Convention rights making a difference. The alleged mis-use of section 44 provided an opportunity to test the mettle of the Human Rights Act, given the challenge which stop and search presents potentially to a number of Convention rights, and given its use in non-terrorist contexts. The leading case involves a Sheffield PhD student and a freelance journalist who were stopped and searched following a section 44 authorisation while trying to join a demonstration against an arms fair being held in Docklands, East London.[72] The student was stopped and the search of his rucksack yielded a sandwich, a notebook, and printouts from websites which the police confiscated after consulting 'central command'. It is not known what was in the sandwich. The journalist was stopped and searched, and detained (she claims) for half an hour, despite wearing a photographer's

---

[70] *BBC News*, 12 December 2006.

[71] Ibid. This led him to question 'what purpose' the stop and search power serves, 'especially as it upsets so many people, with some sections of our community feeling unfairly targeted. It seems a big price to pay.'

[72] *R (Gillan) v Metropolitan Police Commissioner* [2006] UKHL 12.

jacket and having a press pass. So shaken was the latter by the experience that she went home, a living example of Lord Carlile's concern that these powers were 'a substantial encroachment into the reasonable expectation of the public at large that they will only face police intervention in their lives (even when protesters) if there is reasonable suspicion that they will commit a crime' (Carlile, 2006: paragraph 100). The High Court held that there had been no violation of the applicants' Convention rights, while the Court of Appeal appeared to be critical of the way in which the police had used the powers, although accepting that in principle the stop and search powers did not breach the ECHR.[73] But despite its reservations about the way the police had conducted the operation, the appeal court was beset by a lack of evidence on which to make a finding, partly because the nature of the applicants' case had changed as the proceedings progressed. The focus was now more on the issue of principle (on which they failed) rather than on their particular circumstances at this particular event.

The Legality of Stop and Search Powers

So to the House of Lords on the issue of principle, where it was held resoundingly and unanimously that the police conduct was not unlawful and that there was no breach of Convention rights. The House of Lords considered several arguments about the scope of section 44, the first addressing what were seen to be wide powers which allow restraints to personal liberty of a kind quite unprecedented, points acknowledged by Lord Bingham though he did not appear necessarily to agree with them. At first instance, however, these powers were described as being 'extraordinary' and as 'sweeping and far beyond anything ever permitted by common law powers', while it was said in the Court of Appeal that section 44 'confers an extremely wide power to intrude on the privacy of members of the public'.[74] The concern here was that an authorisation can be given where it is deemed 'expedient' to prevent acts of terrorism, a very low threshold for interfering with common law rights, which the applicants argued should be construed in line with the higher standard of necessity. But this argument was firmly rejected by the House of Lords, with Lord Bingham saying that '"Expedient" has a meaning quite distinct from "necessary"', and that 'Parliament chose the first word … not the second'. In his view there is 'no warrant for treating Parliament as having meant something which it did not say', a view reinforced by examination of the statutory context which was said to show that 'the authorisation and exercise of the power are very closely

[73] [2004] EWCA Civ 1067.
[74] [2006] UKHL 12, para [8].

regulated, leaving no room for the inference that Parliament did not mean what it said'.[75] Lord Bingham continued with a comprehensive response to the applicants by saying that:

There is indeed every indication that Parliament appreciated the significance of the power it was conferring but thought it an appropriate measure to protect the public against the grave risks posed by terrorism, provided the power was subject to effective constraints. The legislation embodies a series of such constraints. First, an authorisation under section 44(1) or (2) may be given only if the person giving it considers (and, it goes without saying, reasonably considers) it expedient 'for the prevention of acts of terrorism'. The authorisation must be directed to that overriding objective. Secondly, the authorisation may be given only by a very senior police officer. Thirdly, the authorisation cannot extend beyond the boundary of a police force area, and need not extend so far. Fourthly, the authorisation is limited to a period of 28 days, and need not be for so long. Fifthly, the authorisation must be reported to the Secretary of State forthwith. Sixthly, the authorisation lapses after 48 hours if not confirmed by the Secretary of State. Seventhly, the Secretary of State may abbreviate the term of an authorisation, or cancel it with effect from a specified time. Eighthly, a renewed authorisation is subject to the same confirmation procedure. Ninthly, the powers conferred on a constable by an authorisation under sections 44(1) or (2) may only be exercised to search for articles of a kind which could be used in connection with terrorism. Tenthly, Parliament made provision in section 126 for reports on the working of the Act to be made to it at least once a year, which have in the event been made with commendable thoroughness, fairness and expertise by Lord Carlile of Berriew QC. Lastly, it is clear that any misuse of the power to authorise or confirm or search will expose the authorising officer, the Secretary of State or the constable, as the case may be, to corrective legal action.[76]

The uncompromising demolition of the applicant's first argument was followed by an equally robust rejection of the second. This was the argument based on the nature of the authorisation, and the fact that it covered indiscriminately the entire area of the metropolitan police, and that authorisations which were intended to be for periods of no more than 28 days to deal with particular threats were now de facto permanent by virtue of what looked like a rolling programme of renewal since 2001. The House of Lords apparently thought the latter of these two submissions to be the stronger, the former being rejected on the ground that the authorisations had been made on the basis that the risk was thought to be London-wide; that this assessment was based on security service intelligence; and that the appellants had been offered but had declined an opportunity to review that evidence on a confidential basis. In these circumstances, said

---

[75] Ibid, para [14].   [76] Ibid.

Lord Bingham, 'the House has before it what appear to be considered and informed evaluations of the terrorist threat on one side and effectively nothing save a measure of scepticism on the other', this being an insubstantial basis 'on which the respondents' evidence can be rejected'.[77] In any event Lord Carlile had regarded London as 'a special case, having vulnerable assets and relevant residential pockets in almost every borough', though Lord Carlile is now pressing for the blanket London-wide ban to be rather more focused in its scope.[78] So far as the concern about the state of permanent authorisation was concerned, this too was dismissed, this time on the ground that the authorisations were all made in accordance with the Act, the court influenced by evidence from the police and a civil servant in the Home Office which was said to contradict 'the inference of a routine bureaucratic exercise'.[79] Although it was acknowledged that Parliament may not have envisaged 'a continuous succession of authorisations' when legislating pre 9/11, it was nevertheless 'clearly intended that the section 44 powers should be available to be exercised when a terrorist threat was apprehended'.[80] Moreover, the pattern of renewals since 9/11 was said to be 'a product of Parliament's principled refusal to confer these exceptional stop and search powers on a continuing, countrywide basis'.[81]

Stop and Search Powers and Convention Rights

So what about the Human Rights Act? Here we find the Lords just as uncompromising in their rejection of the appellant's arguments. So far as the ECHR is concerned, there was no breach of the right to liberty in article 5: although a person stopped and searched could be regarded as being 'detained in the sense of kept from proceeding or kept waiting', he or she could not to be regarded as 'being detained in the sense of confined or kept in custody'.[82] Nor was there a breach of article 8, with Lord Bingham doubting 'whether an ordinary superficial search of the person can be said to show a lack of respect for private life'.[83] The contention that the powers breached articles 10 and 11 of the Convention were given even shorter shrift, Lord Bingham finding it 'hard to conceive of circumstances in which the power, properly exercised in accordance with the statute ... could be held to restrict [freedom of expression or assembly] in a way which infringed either of those articles'. But even if it did, he expected 'the restriction to fall within the heads of justification

---

[77] Ibid, para [17].   [78] See pp 203–204 above.
[79] [2006] UKHL 12, para [18].   [80] Ibid.
[81] Ibid.   [82] Ibid, para [25].
[83] Ibid, para [28].

provided in articles 10(2) and 11(2)', as he had previously found in relation to article 8. Having thus found that there was no breach of any Convention right, the House of Lords nevertheless proceeded to consider whether the provisions of section 44 were compatible with those provisions of articles 5, 8, 10, and 11 that require any violation of Convention rights to be prescribed by law (articles 5, 10, and 11) or in accordance with the law (article 8). These measures were said to address 'important features of the rule of law', in the sense that the 'exercise of power by public officials, as it affects members of the public, must be governed by clear and publicly-accessible rules of law', and the 'public must not be vulnerable to interference by public officials acting on any personal whim, caprice, malice, predeliction or purpose other than that for which the power was conferred'.[84] It had been argued that although the stop and search powers were set out in the legislation, the rule of law was breached by the fact that the authorizations to activate the powers were not made public, with the result that the member of the public has no way of knowing that the police officer conducting the stop and search was authorized to stop and search him or her. Moreover,

when, unknown to a member of the public, the power had been conferred on a constable, the constable's discretion to stop and search was broad and ill-defined, requiring no grounds of suspicion and constrained only by the condition that the power could be exercised only for the purpose of searching for articles of a kind which could be used in connection with terrorism.[85]

These powerful arguments—which resonate with matters discussed in Chapter 1 above—were, however, swept aside, with Lord Bingham taking the view not only that 'it would stultify a potentially valuable source of public protection to require notice of an authorization or confirmation to be publicized prospectively', but also that the efficacy of the legislation would be 'gravely weakened if potential offenders were alerted in advance'. In Lord Bingham's view, anyone stopped and searched 'must be told … all he needs to know' by the constable who will be subject to civil suit if he acts arbitrarily. The Act did not authorise the stopping and searching of people who were obviously not terrorist suspects, which would be 'futile and time-wasting'.[86] The power to stop and search without the need for suspicion was simply to protect the police officer where he or she 'does suspect' someone of being a terrorist suspect but cannot show reasonable grounds for that suspicion. In like manner, Lord Brown thought the stop and search powers 'can scarcely be said to constitute any very substantial invasion of our fundamental civil liberties',[87] a judgment all the more surprising for the fact that the powers in

---

[84] Ibid, para [34].   [85] Ibid, para [32].
[86] Ibid, para [35].   [87] Ibid, para [74].

question are used in a discriminatory manner, and indeed it is suggested by Lord Brown that they can only be used lawfully if used in a discriminatory manner. In the words of the latter, it is 'inevitable' that:

so long as the principal terrorist risk against which use of the section 44 power has been authorised is that from al-Qaeda, a disproportionate number of those stopped and searched will be of Asian appearance (particularly if they happen to be carrying rucksacks or wearing apparently bulky clothing capable of containing terrorist-related items).[88]

Nevertheless, to target the use of the power against the members of the Muslim community was not to be regarded as discriminatory, while the use the power against 'those regarded as presenting no conceivable threat whatever' would itself constitute 'an abuse of the power'.[89] There is something singularly unpleasant about a power that can lawfully be used only in a discriminatory way, though there is also something singularly unpleasant about powers which appear incapable of use except on an industrial scale. Although it is apparently not in the public interest for us to be provided with information about the 'reasons and events' which have precipitated the use of section 44 powers, on the day the Gillan and Quinton appeals opened in the House of Lords it was reported that the 'number of people stopped and searched each year has soared since the Act came into force in 2001, when 10,200 people were stopped. It rose to 33,800 in 2003–04.'[90] In 2008, however, the power was used between 96,000 and 120,000 occasions (Carlile, 2009).

Terrorist Offences and Freedom of Expression

A battery of offences is to be found in the Terrorism Act 2000, and few could take exception to many of them (including weapons training and directing terrorist organisations), though much terrorist activity involves conduct for which the criminal law already makes provision (such as murder and manslaughter). However, much of the controversy about the human rights implications of powers against terrorism has not been concerned with provisions of this kind, but with the operation of sections 57 and 58 and the impact they have on freedom of expression in particular:

- under section 57 it is an offence to possess an article 'in circumstances which give rise to a reasonable suspicion that [its] possession is for a

---

[88] Ibid, para [80].   [89] Ibid, para [92].
[90] *The Independent*, 25 January 2006.

purpose connected with the commission, preparation or instigation of an act of terrorism'; and

- under section 58 it is an offence to (a) collect or make a record of information of a kind likely to be useful to a person committing or preparing an act of terrorism, or (b) possess a document or record containing information of that kind.

The onus is on the defendant to prove that he or she did not possess the material for a forbidden purpose, and failure to do so could lead to a sentence of up to 10 years in prison. Again, few could take exception to the use of these provisions against people who are in possession of explosives or chemicals or other bomb-making material. Questions begin to arise, however, when these measures are turned on people like Samina Malik, the self-styled lyrical terrorist—because she thought it was 'cool'—who wrote poetry celebrating martyrdom. Convicted by a jury under section 58 (collection) and found not guilty under section 57 (possession),[91] the 23-year-old shop assistant was said by the prosecution to have had 'a library of material that she had collected for terrorist purposes. That collection would be extremely useful for someone planning terrorist activity.'[92] Titles found on her computer were said to include *The Mujaheddin Poisoner's Handbook, Encyclopaedia Jihad, How to Win in Hand-to-Hand Combat*, and *How to Make Bombs*.[93] Even more serious questions begin to arise when these measures are turned on those who possess literature or propaganda for academic or political purposes related to terrorism but not for the purposes of terrorism, as in some of the cases discussed below.

'Terrorist Literature', Human Rights, and Student Radicals

The *Malik* case reveals just how far reaching and wide ranging are the offences in the 2000 Act: for use against the fantasist as well as the fanaticist. The scope of sections 57 and 58 are highlighted further by the prosecution of Aitzaz Zafar, three other Bradford University students, and a London schoolboy, also under section 57 of the 2000 Act.[94] The articles which formed the basis of the prosecution were, in the words of the Court of Appeal, 'documents, compact discs or computer hard drives on which material had been electronically stored'. The material included

ideological propaganda as well as communications between the appellants and others which the prosecution alleged showed a settled plan under which the

---

[91] *The Guardian*, 9 November 2007.   [92] Ibid.
[93] Ibid.   [94] *R v Zafar* [2008] EWCA Crim 184.

appellants would travel to Pakistan to receive training and thereafter commit a terrorist act or acts in Afghanistan [against the government of Afghanistan].⁹⁵

According to the BBC:

In one of the first trials of its kind [Mohammed Irfan] Raja [19], Awaab Iqbal [20], Aitzaz Zafar [20], Usman Malik [21], and Akbar Butt [20], have been jailed for downloading and sharing extremist terrorism-related material. Raja and his co-accused had watched videos of men blowing themselves up in Iraq and elsewhere—films where the suicide bomber often appears ecstatic in his final moments, edited to rousing music before being posted online. They had dipped into the classic jihadi texts passed around on the internet, including an infamous call to arms urging men to 'Join the Caravan' and become mujihadeen warriors for Afghanistan.⁹⁶

Radicalised by internet use, the students argued in their appeal against conviction (and imprisonment) that an offence under this section—which had been introduced specifically to allow action to be taken against a person who is found in possession of articles which, though perhaps commonplace in normal circumstances, are well known to be used in the manufacture of bombs (Lloyd, 1996: paragraph 14.4)—could only be committed 'if there was a direct connection between the article possessed by the defendant and an intended act of terrorism', and that in this case there was no such connection and indeed could not have been in view of some of the material in question (literature stored on computer discs).⁹⁷

The Court of Appeal agreed, though in doing so it read section 57 widely to mean that 'possessing a document for the purpose of inciting a person to commit an act of terrorism falls within the ambit of [the section]'.⁹⁸ But although reading the scope of section 57 widely, the Court of Appeal also insisted that there had to be 'a direct connection between the articles possessed and the acts of terrorism'.⁹⁹ It was not enough that the

extremist material was collected and possessed by each defendant in order to guide, inspire and sustain the group which they had formed by using the material and which had, because of the material, become indoctrinated.¹⁰⁰

So although there was evidence that

lent support to the prosecution case that the appellants had formed a plan to go to Pakistan to train and then to Afghanistan to fight, there was nothing that

⁹⁵ Ibid, para [1].
⁹⁶ *BBC News*, 26 July 2007.   ⁹⁷ [2008] EWCA Crim 184, para [13].
⁹⁸ Ibid, para [31].
⁹⁹ Ibid, para [32]. See also *R v K* [2008] EWCA Crim 185.
¹⁰⁰ *Zafar*, para [32].

evidenced expressly the use, or intention to use, the extremist literature to incite each other to do this.

As a result there was no case under section 57 'that could properly have been left to the jury',[101] and those who appealed were acquitted. Others may not be so fortunate, for it is not clear how a case on similar facts would now be decided following a very tough construction of sections 57 and 58 by the House of Lords in the more recent *R v G*.[102] As a result of its expansive reading of section 57, the House of Lords held that the offence could be committed by a mentally ill prisoner who collected 'terrorism' stuff while in custody, in order simply to wind up the prison officers who he thought were provoking him.[103] According to the House of Lords 'on no view could a desire to wind up prison officers in this way be a reasonable excuse for collecting and recording the information'.[104] And in indicating still further the now wide scope of sections 57 (possessing) and 58 (collecting), the House of Lords suggested that benign possession or collection of a document such as the al-Qaeda Training Manual simply out of curiosity would not necessarily be lawful, as revealed by the following passage:

there was much discussion of a hypothetical situation where the defendant downloaded and stored information falling within section 58(1) "out of curiosity". But the question as to whether he would have a reasonable excuse under section 58(3) is not one that can be answered in the abstract, without knowing exactly what the defendant did and the circumstances in which he did it. In an actual case where the issue arose, the specific facts of the case would inform the decision as to whether the defendant's excuse for doing what he did either could or should be regarded as reasonable in the circumstances.[105]

'Terrorist Literature', Human Rights, and Academic Study

It was a case against another student that revealed more clearly the unacceptable scope of these provisions, and the unacceptable power they give to the police. In justifying the proceedings against Malik who denied that she was a terrorist, the police said that she 'held violent extremist views which she shared with other like-minded people over the internet. Merely possessing this material is a serious criminal offence.'[106] The implications of this approach of the police were subsequently to be seen in the notorious case involving Nottingham University when on 14 May 2008 two

---

[101] Ibid, para [37].   [102] [2009] UKHL 13.
[103] Ibid, para [87].   [104] Ibid
[105] Ibid, para [87].   [106] *The Guardian*, 9 November 2007.

people (Rizwaan Sabir (a 22-year-old PhD student studying terrorism) and Hicham Yezza (a 30-year-old employee of the university)) were arrested under section 41 of the Terrorism Act 2000 for downloading a copy of an al-Qaeda training manual from a US Department of Justice website. Section 41 empowers a police constable to 'arrest without a warrant a person whom he reasonably suspects to be a terrorist', while section 40 defines a terrorist as someone who has (a) committed one or more of the various offences in the 2000 Act, or (b) 'has been concerned in the commission, preparation or instigation of acts of terrorism'. The 1,500 page document in question had been sent by Sabir to Yezza for printing, and apart from the fact that it is openly accessible on a government website, it was reported that 'an extended version of the same document (which figures on the politics department's official reading list) was also available on Amazon'.[107] According to press reports, the university nevertheless contacted the police who arrested the men, searched university property, and maintained a uniformed presence on the campus, in what was said to be a 'low key operation in conjunction with the Midlands Counter-Terrorism Unit',[108] albeit one that 'involved 'dozens of officers, police cars, vans, and scientific support agents'.[109] The police also searched Sabir's family home, seized the computers and mobile phones of both Sabir and Yezza, and applied successfully for warrants to extend their detention for questioning beyond the statutory 48 hours. Unlike in the case of a PACE arrest during which the police have 36 hours to question before charge or release without judicial approval of further detention (up to a maximum of 96 hours), in the case of arrests under the 2000 Act, the corresponding period of detention is 48 hours without judicial approval (now up to a maximum of 672 hours) , and in this case Yezza was detained for six days.

During his detention, Yezza claims that he was not told why he was a suspected terrorist for 48 hours, that he was kept in solitary confinement in a cold cell, that he was not allowed to contact his parents, and that he was subject to 20 hours of 'intense interrogation', while

entire days were being completely wasted by the police micro-examining every detail of [his] life: [his] political activism, [his] writings, [his] work in theatre and dance, [his] love life, [his] photography, [his] cartooning, [his] magazine subscriptions, [his] bus tickets.[110]

---

[107] *The Guardian*, 18 August 2008. See <http://www.amazon.co.uk/Al-Qaeda-Training-Manual-1/dp/1414507100>.

[108] *BBC News*, 20 May 2008.

[109] *The Guardian*, 18 August 2008.

[110] Ibid.

Questions were also asked about the robustness of the procedures for authorising detention beyond 48 hours, which had been characterised by Lord Carlile as a 'genuine judicial inquisition' by judges (Carlile, 2008: paragraph 88).[111] According to Yezza (2008), however,

... through a perverted but pervasive circularity in the logic, lack of evidence becomes the very justification for requesting 'more time'. The government claims that checks and balances will ensure extensions to detention periods are based on verifiable and compelling arguments. I beg to differ: in my case, the judge was simply bullied by streams of technospeak until she had no option but to grant extra time.

Although Sabir was released without charge after six days, Yezza (an Algerian who has been in this country for 13 years) was re-arrested on immigration charges and detained at Colnbrook detention centre with a view to his early deportation,[112] his life shattered by what looks like an extraordinary reaction on the part of the university. But although raising questions about (a) the overexcited use of overbearing arrest powers, and (b) the adequacy of judicial scrutiny of requests for further detention, it should not be overlooked that at its heart this affair was about freedom of expression and the ability of the police to determine what is an appropriate subject of academic study in a liberal democracy, Sabir having been read a statement while in custody 'confirming [that the document he had downloaded] was an illegal document which shouldn't be used for research purposes'.[113] If that is genuinely the case it is not clear why both Sabir and Yezza were not prosecuted under the 2000 Act.

Glorification of Terrorism: A Rebuke for the Home Office

The draftsman is rarely idle, and the government's desire to adapt the 2000 legislation drafted on the back of Irish terrorism to deal with international terrorism has led to the introduction of yet more terrorist offences. Particularly controversial are the provisions of the Terrorism Act 2006 which introduced a number of new restraints on freedom of expression. Although it is most notable for the extension of the period of time that terrorist suspects could be kept in police custody before being charged or

---

[111] Lord Carlile also claims that, 'the Metropolitan Police view is that the judges involved are far from acquiescent, but rather are aware of the implications of their orders and scrutinise carefully the material placed before them', noting also, however, that 'defence lawyers are less confident in their general comments about the degree of scrutiny of applications' (Carlile, 2008: para 88).
[112] *The Guardian*, 18 August 2008.   [113] Ibid.

released, the Act is important also for implementing the government's 2005 manifesto undertaking to 'introduce new laws to help catch and convict those involved in helping to plan terrorist activities' (Labour Party, 2005: 53). The government's initial proposal was for two new offences, one of which involved the encouragement of terrorism and carried a penalty of seven years in prison, the other involving the glorification of terrorism and carrying with it a penalty of five years. Following strong opposition, however, the two offences were melded into one by the time the Bill was introduced to the House of Commons, though the submerging of glorification into the body of encouragement did little to assuage parliamentary and other critics, and the government's proposals were heavily amended as a result of parliamentary pressure. At the conclusion of a very impressive second reading debate in the House of Commons, the (so far) admirable Tory spokesman Dominic Grieve noted correctly that the 'tenor of the contributions' in that debate had shown that many MPs (of all parties) felt 'the most serious disquiet about the impact of the proposed legislation on civil liberties in this country'.[114] A number of concerns were also expressed in an excoriating report by the (usually admirable) Joint Committee on Human Rights, which was persuaded of the need for a new offence though strongly critical of its content. Like Mr Grieve, however, a few Commons' members of the Committee voted for the Bill at second reading, the Bill being carried by a handsome majority. Nevertheless, a number of significant amendments were made, so that the Bill as enacted was very different in a number of respects from the Draft Bill published several months earlier.

A New Offence: Parliamentary Concerns

It ought to be said initially that although there was support for the need for a new offence (with even the JCHR persuaded), by no means everyone was convinced. A notable source of dissent was Kenneth Clarke, who suggested that 'the body of law we have in this country protects us quite adequately against such extremes'.[115] This is an argument strengthened considerably by the decision of the Court of Appeal in *R v El-Faisal*,[116] where the accused was convicted for soliciting to murder under the Offences against the Person Act 1861, section 4 which was widely construed to cover 'exhortations [in print or by speech] of a general kind which solicited killing on

114 HC Debs, 26 October 2005, col 407.
115 HC Debs, 2 November 2005, col 856.
116 [2004] EWCA Crim 456.

an indiscriminate basis in areas other than the battlefield'.[117] According to the JCHR, '[in] view of the breadth of the offence of solicitation to murder and of common law incitement, the strict necessity for a new offence might be thought to be questionable' (JCHR, 2005a: paragraph 25). This is a judgment which was shown to be well founded when several months later a controversy erupted about a demonstration that was held outside the Danish Embassy in London on 3 February 2006. The demonstration had been held to protest about cartoons that had been published in the Danish press satirising the prophet Muhammed, and was attended by activists who carried placards bearing legends such as 'Butcher those who mock Islam', 'Behead those who insult Islam', 'Europe, you'll come crawling when Mujahideen come roaring', and 'Kill those who insult Islam'. Others called for British soldiers to be brought back from Iraq in body bags, while one protester dressed as a suicide bomber. Following complaints from members of the public and pressure from MPs, the police announced a month later that arrests were imminent under the Public Order Act 1986.[118] In the end, several men were charged with offences under the 1986 Act but others were also charged with soliciting murder, and following their conviction sentenced to six years' imprisonment. The would-be suicide bomber was immediately returned to jail for breaching the terms of his parole.

But although most MPs were persuaded by the government of the need for a new offence to restrict free speech (including the JCHR), many of these MPs were nevertheless concerned about the scope of the government's proposals. Occupying the legal high ground, the JCHR took the view that the new legislation did not comply with the ECHR because of its lack of certainty and proportionality:

we consider that the offence in clause 1 is not sufficiently legally certain to satisfy the requirement in Article 10 that interferences with freedom of expression be 'prescribed by law' because of (i) the vagueness of the glorification requirement, (ii) the breadth of the definition of 'terrorism' and (iii) the lack of any requirement of intent to incite terrorism or likelihood of such offences being caused as ingredients of the offence. (JCHR, 2005a: paragraph 36)

In the course of the parliamentary history of the Bill, a number of more practical concerns were also expressed by MPs who drew attention to the glorification of terrorism (as defined by the Bill) by George Orwell in *Homage to Catalonia*, and to the justification for terrorism expressed by Nelson Mandela at his trial in 1964. In a debate littered also with references of support for armed resistance against contemporary dictators in

---

[117] Ibid, para [44].   [118] *BBC News*, 7 March 2006.

Burma, Uzbekistan, and Zimbabwe, a powerful contribution was made by the senior Labour backbencher Tony Lloyd:

All but the pacifists in our society have always accepted that sometimes, very sadly, although we can use phrases such as "as a last resort", faced with families being slaughtered in Burma, when the Burmese army are moving into the villages of the Karen people, when they are raping women and children and brutally murdering the whole population, when they are ethnically cleansing, it is not illegitimate to say that recourse to defence by force of arms is the only course available. We are pious and nonsensical if we pretend otherwise.[119]

In a similar vein, from the other side of the House, Douglas Hogg (the man with the moat) was heard to ask: 'Do we really want people to be made criminals if they urge an armed insurrection against the military regime in Burma? ... Is that really what we are bringing this society to?'[120]

The Substance of the New Offence

Although the Bill was heavily amended in Parliament (mainly around issues of intent and recklessness), the Act as passed does not appear to meet the basic concerns of the JCHR, and it remains to be seen whether these other practical concerns have been properly addressed. Section 1 is drafted in wide but barely comprehensible terms, with MPs complaining that it is 'almost impossible to read and understand', and that it was 'breathtakingly badly drafted'.[121] First, it applies to

a statement that is likely to be understood by some or all of the members of the public to whom it is published as a direct or indirect encouragement or other inducement to them to the commission, preparation or instigation of acts of terrorism,[122]

acts of terrorism being defined on the basis of the wide definition in the Terrorism Act 2000 which has been widened further by the 2006 Act. Secondly, a person commits an offence if he or she publishes such a statement and intends members of the public to be 'directly or indirectly' to be encouraged to commit, prepare, or instigate acts of terrorism, or is reckless as to whether they do so. Thirdly and most controversially, for these purposes

---

[119] HC Debs, 26 October, 2005, col 364.

[120] Ibid, col 368. The less reverent were also heard to ask whether 'recent remarks by Cherie Blair and Jenny Tong expressing understanding of the motives for terrorism in some parts of the world would be very likely to be caught by this offence'.

[121] HC Debs, 2 November 2005, col 834 (Dominic Grieve and John Bercow respectively).

[122] Terrorism Act 2006, s 1(1).

the statements that are likely to be understood by members of the public as indirectly encouraging the commission or preparation of acts of terrorism or Convention offences include every statement which glorifies the commission or preparation (whether in the past, in the future or generally) of such acts or offences;

and 'is a statement from which those members of the public could reasonably be expected to infer that what is being glorified is being glorified as conduct that should be emulated by them in existing circumstances'. Fourthly and finally, it is no defence that no one was 'in fact encouraged or induced by the statement to commit, prepare or instigate any such act or offence',[123] though it is a defence that the statement in question clearly neither expressed the views nor had the endorsement of the person making it.

Section 2 of the 2006 Act extends liability to apply not only to those who make an offending statement, but also to those who disseminate publications which—among other things—glorify terrorism. Dissemination for this purpose means distributing, circulating, giving, selling, offering for sale or loan a terrorist publication, as well dissemination by electronic means. Serious concerns about the scope of this provision were expressed on behalf of academics and librarians, worried that it could restrict teachers 'who wish to distribute materials to their students on courses such as those concerning terrorism, history or international relations' (JCHR, 2005a: paragraph 45), a propitious concern in light of the subsequent events at Nottingham under the 2000 rather than the 2006 Act. The government responded by claiming that the defences built into section 2 were adequate, and would 'ensure legitimate librarians, academics teachers and others are protected', while 'still allow[ing] the offence to operate effectively' (JCHR, 2006). This, however, hardly met the overall concern of the JCHR about the scope of the section 2 offence, which in its view is

unlikely to be compatible with the right to freedom of expression in Article 10 ECHR in the absence of an explicit requirement that the dissemination of such publications amounts to an incitement to violence and is both intended and likely to do so' (JCHR, 2005a: paragraph 49).

And although not attracting the same degree of attention, it is important not to overlook the potentially chilling provisions of sections 3 and 4 of the 2006 Act, which in effect give to the police the power to close down or censor internet sites by intimidating site owners or internet service providers. Thus, where a constable 'declares that, in [his or her] opinion ... [a] statement or the article or record is unlawfully terrorism-related', he or she may require the relevant person 'to secure that the statement or the

---

[123] Ibid, s 1(5)(b).

article or record, so far as it is so related, is not available to the public or is modified so as no longer to be so related'.[124] This can be done without any prior legal formality, that is to say without the need for a warrant or other judicial authorisation, an amendment to require which being unconvincingly rejected by the government.[125]

Conclusion

It is clear from the foregoing that the terrorism legislation gives the government wide powers to pursue and to punish those engaged in terrorist activity, as well as those who are not. These wide powers are used expansively and aggressively. So although the statistics indicate that a large number of arrests are made under the terrorism legislation, they also reveal that a surprisingly small proportion of those arrested are prosecuted, and that an even smaller proportion are convicted of terrorism legislation offences alone. For example, in 2007 almost a half (126) of the 257 people arrested were released without charge, a figure said by the government's independent reviewer to 'seem a high proportion', but explicable on the ground that 'the nature of terrorism investigations means that those associated with or accompanying a suspect may well find themselves arrested out of an abundance of caution by the authorities' (Carlile, 2008: paragraph 102).[126] An aggressive (rather than cautious) use of these powers is to seen in a number of high profile incidents, including the search of two adjoining houses in the Forest Gate area of East London in June 2006 with the authority of a warrant issued under the 2000 Act, in the course of which one man was shot in the shoulder by a police officer, two men were arrested, ten people were taken to police stations (and though not arrested had DNA samples taken), and over 150 allegations were made against the police. Both of the arrested men (Mohammed Abdulkahar and Abul Koyair) complained that they had been assaulted by the police, as

---

[124] If the relevant person fails to comply with the police instruction to remove or amend the offending material within two days, he or she will be taken to have endorsed the material in question and be liable to prosecution as a result.

[125] HL Debs, 7 December 2005, col 676.

[126] Nevertheless, the high level of arrests relative to the number of charges was said to be 'proportionate to perceived risk, especially when set against the high level of vigilance operated by the statutory services' (Carlile, 2008: para 102). Although 185 of the 257 were arrested under the Terrorism Act 2000, just 45 were charged with Terrorism Act offences only, with another 19 charged under the Act and with other offences. In the same year only four people were convicted under the Act, while another four were convicted of offences under the Act and for other offences. Ten were convicted of other offences, while another 43 were awaiting trial for Terrorism Act offences and another 22 awaiting trial for other offences (ibid: Annex D).

well as being shot (in Abdulkahar's case). According to the Independent Police Complaints Commission (IPCC, 2007), 'the police were extremely robust with the occupants', in a raid which involved a number of armed police officers in protective clothing and 'hundreds of unarmed police officers on standby'. But having already dismissed the shooting as an 'accident', the IPCC seems to have been unable to find evidence against any officer in relation to the alleged assault on Abdulkahar. And although an officer was identified for the assault on Koyair, this was excused 'taking into account the circumstances of the operation and the perceived threat' (ibid). Although the two men were detained for six days, no one was charged, the police it seems acting on faulty intelligence.

The exceptional powers considered in this chapter—and the manner of their exercise—bite deeply into constitutional principle and established civil liberties. They entail extensive State powers to ban political organisations, powers which are not subject to judicial review; the use of secret evidence against people who are stripped of financial resources; and the arbitrary and excessive deployment of law to interfere with freedom of movement and freedom of expression, on a scale clearly never intended when the laws in question were introduced. All of this has the stamp of judicial approval, again sometimes at the highest level, with two major decisions of the House of Lords reading these powers widely.[127] In the process, there are now grave challenges to core freedoms—freedom of association (the proscription of a growing number of organisations), freedom of assembly (the misuse of stop and search), and freedom of expression (the ban on 'glorifying' terrorism)—that few could have anticipated ever arising in this country.[128] On the other hand, it is true that we now have yet another galaxy of accountability mechanisms to deal with the various threats to civil liberties perpetrated by human rights abusers in the name of national security and public safety: the courts, specially created quasi-judicial commissions (such as the Proscribed Organisations Appeal Commission), the government's independent reviewer of terrorism legislation, a committee of Privy Counsellors, various parliamentary committees (including the JCHR), the Independent Police Complaints Commission, and the several judicial commissioners we encountered in Chapter 3. But as we have seen in the course of this chapter, while these different agencies sometimes score notable hits, at other times they often appear to have been supplied with tools they appear unwilling

---

[127] *R v Z*, above, pp 182-183, and *R (Gillan) v Metropolitan Police Commissioner*, above, pp 204-210.
[128] See pp 182-191; 201-210; and 215-219.

to use.[129] It is also true of course that underpinning much of this framework of accountability is the Human Rights Act, designed to help shape the boundaries of permissible State action. But the HRA—though not necessarily the courts[130]—has often been AWOL in the battle to protect human rights in the 'war against terror'. Yet it is in its response to precisely these challenges that the Act must be judged: there is no purpose to be served by a Human Rights Act for the good times, only to crumple at the first sign of bulging government muscle.

---

[129] The reports of the government's independent reviewer are laced with terms such as 'proportionate', 'necessary', and 'fit for purpose' to describe the Terrorism Act 2000 and its provisions, though there are frequently expressed concerns about the manner of exercise of some of these powers. Carlile also offers support for extending the 28 day period of detention without charge, provided certain safeguards are put in place (2008: para 275).

[130] Significantly the judicial triumphs have been by using established old-fashioned tools such as judicial review and the principles of statutory interpretation.

CHAPTER 7

From Detention—to Control Orders—to Rendition

Introduction

B ritain has long been a source of refuge for thousands of people fleeing persecution in their native lands. Different waves of refugees have settled on these shores at various times, and are widely believed to have contributed immeasurably to British life. However, successive British governments have also long exercised the power to deport people on grounds of national security. Under the Immigration Act 1971, someone who is not a British citizen is liable to be deported if the Home Secretary deems his or her deportation 'to be conducive to the public good'. This power was used in a number of high profile cases over the years to deport people on the grounds of national security, including US journalists Philip Agee and Mark Hosenball, and Lebanese peace activist Abbas Cheblak.[1] These cases led to litigation in the courts, which exposed the difficulty of using the law to prevent deportations on national security grounds. Although the decision to deport could not be appealed in a judicial forum, the government had for some time allowed those served with notice of deportation to 'make representations to an independent advisory panel'. At the time of the Cheblak deportation in 1991, the panel consisted of a Court of Appeal judge (who was also deputy chairman of the Security Commission), a recently retired president of the Immigration Appeal Tribunal, and a retired senior civil servant who had worked in the Home Office and the Northern Ireland Office. Anyone seeking to use judicial review proceedings against the panel encountered a number of obstacles in their path:

---

[1] See *Agee v Lord Advocate*, 1977 SLT (Notes) 54, *R v Home Secretary, ex p Hosenball* [1977] 3 All ER 452 , and *R v Home Secretary, ex p Cheblak* [1991] 2 All ER 319.

- the first was the reluctance of the courts to question any decisions on the grounds of national security, said to be 'the exclusive responsibility of the Executive'.[2] This meant that any challenges to the decisions to deport would have to be made on procedural grounds;

- the second was that the normal rules relating to fair hearings did not apply. So it was permissible that the complainant did not know the source of the allegation against him or her, was given 'inadequate information' on which 'to prepare or direct' his or her defence, and was not entitled to be legally represented before the panel;

- the third and final obstacle to judicial review was that the Home Office was not required to give reasons for the deportation other than 'national security', making it very difficult to mount an effective challenge, quite apart from these other concerns.[3]

In light of the foregoing, it is perhaps not surprising that these procedures should be challenged—successfully—under the European Convention on Human Rights (ECHR) as violating article 5(4)'s guarantee that

everyone who is deprived of his liberty by arrest or detention shall be entitled to take proceedings by which the lawfulness of his detention shall be decided speedily by a court and his release ordered if the detention is not lawful.

It is true that the Strasbourg Court did not question the claim of the English courts that the advisory panel provided 'independent quasi-judicial scrutiny', and indeed acknowledged that it 'undoubtedly provided some degree of control'. In *Chahal v United Kingdom*,[4] however, the Court was troubled by the fact that the complainant was

not entitled to legal representation before the panel, that he was only given an outline of the grounds for the notice of intention to deport, that the panel had no power of decision and that its advice to the Home Secretary was not binding.

As a result, Mr Chahal's deportation to India on national security grounds was found to breach the Convention on this and other grounds. The government responded by creating the Special Immigration Appeals Commission (SIAC) to deal with asylum and immigration decisions taken in the interests of national security.[5] The Commission has the same status as the High Court (which means that it can issue declarations of incompatibility under

---

[2] According to Geoffrey Lane LJ (a future Lord Chief Justice), in the event of conflict between liberty and security, 'the alien must suffer, if suffering there be, and this is so on whichever basis of argument one chooses': *R v Home Secretary, ex p Hosenball*, above, at p 462.

[3] *R v Home Secretary, ex p Cheblak*, above.

[4] (1996) 23 EHRR 413.

[5] Special Immigration Appeals Commission Act 1997.

the Human Rights Act 1998 (HRA)), and is chaired by a High Court judge, who sits with a second member who is an immigration judge, and a third member (not a lawyer) with detailed knowledge of the intelligence community. Plus ça change?

Detention without Trial

In the new global environment post 9/11, *Chahal* was to prove a major problem for the British government in dealing with people resident in the United Kingdom who were believed to be involved in international terrorism and whom the government wanted to remove. The difficulty was that many of these people would not be welcome in their 'own' countries, from which they may have escaped persecution, and in which they risked being mistreated by the authorities. Acting as a restraint, *Chahal* confirmed a line of authority that it was not lawful under the Convention to deport someone to another country where he or she would be subjected to torture or inhuman or degrading treatment or punishment. In its decision—involving an attempt to deport a Sikh separatist to India—the European Court of Human Rights was influenced by evidence, including that of the United Nations' Special Rapporteur on Torture, that in India torture was 'endemic' and 'inadequate measures are taken to bring those responsible to justice'. Others pointed to the 'widespread, often fatal, mistreatment of prisoners'. Nor was the Court persuaded by diplomatic assurances given by the Indian government that Mr Chahal would not be maltreated. While not doubting the good faith of the Indian Government in providing these assurances, in the view of the judges 'the violation of human rights by certain members of the security forces in Punjab and elsewhere in India is a recalcitrant and enduring problem'.[6] Consequently, the Court was not persuaded that the assurances would provide Mr Chahal with an adequate guarantee of safety. As we shall see, both of these issues— torture and diplomatic assurances— were to be central in more recent debates in the United Kingdom about the removal of people the government wished to expel.

Internment of Suspected Terrorists

In the meantime, however, the understandable panic generated by 9/11, produced an overwhelming sense in government that a response of some kind was necessary. One of the concerns whipped up by the press and others was that Britain was now harbouring terrorists cut from the same cloth as those

---

[6] *Chahal v United Kingdom*, above, at p 463.

responsible for the events in New York and Washington. One of the more restrained articles of this kind appeared in *The Times* a few days after 9/11, it being noted that:

Despite fine promises and emergency legislation, Britain is still home to hundreds of extremists who have made this country one of the centres for the violent transnational network that inspired and encouraged the barbarism in New York and Washington.[7]

According to the Home Secretary, this was 'just one of hundreds of statements' that had been made in the weeks since 9/11 'about what people perceive to be the situation in our country. Again and again, people—including people in the United States—have illustrated the real dangers that exist, and it is [for these reasons that the government] felt it necessary to act'. That determination was reinforced by events since 9/11, with the Home Secretary recalling 'the interviews given and the video recordings made by bin Laden and the al-Qaeda group, which have spelt out their determination not simply to threaten once, but to threaten the civilian populations of the United States and those working with it'.[8] Yet although the people in question were alleged to be involved in terrorism, there does not appear to have been evidence sufficient to convict them of having committed any offence. So unable to deport people it appears to have been unable to prosecute, the government decided to lock them up instead. In order to do this, however, it would be necessary to take statutory powers to detain individuals without the individuals in question being charged with or convicted of having committed a crime.

Statutory powers were duly taken in section 23 of the Anti-terrorism, Crime and Security Act 2001, which provided that a suspected international terrorist could be detained indefinitely under immigration powers if his or her removal or departure from the United Kingdom was prevented by legal obligations arising under international law (in this case the ECHR). Someone who was detained under these powers could appeal to the Special Immigration Appeals Commission to challenge the Home Secretary's decision to issue a certificate that the individual in question was a suspected international terrorist. If the appeal succeeded, the certificate would be cancelled and the individual would have to be released from internment, though there was also an intermediate stage between liberty and detention, in the sense that SIAC was empowered also to grant bail to those who had been certified, and to impose bail conditions. It is true that these sweeping powers attracted

[7] *The Times*, 15 September 2001.
[8] HC Debs, 19 November 2001, col 25 (David Blunkett).

a great deal of criticism and concern in Parliament and elsewhere (Zander, 2001). Remarkably, however, they were carried at Second Reading by 458 votes to five, with four rebel Labour MPs being joined by a lone Tory (though two other Tories acted as tellers for the dissidents). All it seems were overwhelmed by the power of the Home Secretary's argument that the measures were 'rational, reasonable and proportionate steps to deal with an internal threat and an external, organised terrorist group that could threaten at any time not just our population, but the populations of other friendly countries'.[9] But as is often the case in these situations there was at least one brave voice willing to be heard above the din, with Jeremy Corbyn rising to ask.

Does the Home Secretary accept that many people who are obviously appalled at what happened on 11 September believe that the answer is not to suspend traditional legal rights such as the right of access to courts in this country, but to use the criminal law against those planning or perpetrating criminal acts? Many people are deeply disturbed about this piece of emergency legislation, and believe that it will be no more effective than the Prevention of Terrorism (Temporary Provisions) Act 1974. Peace eventually came to Ireland through a political process, not a legal process.[10]

Internment and Derogation

Powers of the kind found in section 23 of the Anti-terrorism, Crime and Security Act 2001—the indefinite detention of suspects without trial—would almost certainly breach article 5 of the ECHR, incorporated into domestic law by the Human Rights Act 1998. Article 5 of the Convention provides that everyone has the right to liberty, and the right not to be deprived of his or her liberty except in prescribed circumstances, such as 'the lawful detention of a person after conviction by a competent court' (article 5(1)(a)). There is nothing in article 5 that would allow for the indefinite detention of individuals—not even foreign nationals, and not even when suspected of international terrorism. It is true that article 5 also allows for individuals to be detained where action is being taken against them 'with a view to deportation or extradition'. But in the case of the British-based 'international terrorists', the individuals were not being detained *with a view to* their deportation, but because they *could not* be deported. As a result, it would be necessary to derogate from one of the core provisions of the ECHR, with little more than a year having passed since the HRA had been introduced as a monument to the new human rights culture sought by New Labour.

---

[9] Ibid.
[10] Ibid (Jeremy Corbyn).

Such derogation is permitted under article 15 of the Convention, but only in time of war or when there is a public emergency threatening the life of the nation. Where the power of derogation is used, the government effectively says that it will not be bound by those Convention obligations to which the derogation relates. So much then for the commitment to human rights, which was soon to wilt at the first sign of stress, and soon to fail its first major test.

Although derogation is thus permitted under article 15, this is not without limits, with derogation not allowed from some Convention rights, and allowed from others only to the extent 'strictly required by the exigencies of the situation'. The former include article 3, which is why the government could not derogate from it and send the Home Secretary's certified international terrorists to countries where they might be tortured or killed. But the former do not include article 5, which is why the government could derogate from it, to the limited extent necessary to intern foreign nationals without trial. So, on 18 December 2001, the British government, alone of all 47 members of the Council of Europe (including those—such as Spain—that had experienced a major terrorist incident), notified the Secretary General of the Council of Europe of its intention to derogate to the extent that the provisions of the 2001 Act were inconsistent with article 5(1)(f) of the Convention. As we have seen, the latter allows the government of a Member State to detain some-one without trial for the purpose of deportation, but only where the action is being taken with a view to deportation. According to the government, a public emergency threatening the life of the nation existed from the presence of an unspecified number of foreign nationals,

who are suspected of being concerned in the commission, preparation or instiga-tion of acts of international terrorism, of being members of organisations or groups which are so concerned or of having links with members of such organisations or groups, and who are a threat to the national security of the United Kingdom.[11]

The threat to national security was thus synonymous with the existence of a public emergency.

Secret Evidence, Torture, and Special Advocates

The 2001 Act came into force on 14 December 2001, following which eight men were taken from their homes in the early hours five days later and removed to high security prisons where they were held as category A prisoners.

---

[11] Declaration contained in a Note Verbale from the Permanent Representative of the United Kingdom, 18 December 2001, registered by the Secretariat General on 18 December 2001.

According to Birmingham-based solicitors Tyndallwoods, the men were 'immediately locked up in solitary cells for 22–23 hours a day', noting that for some 'it took about 3 months just to get access for family visits or telephone calls as family members and telephone numbers had to be security cleared' (JCHR, 2006a: App 10). Moreover, the men 'were not taken to a police station for questioning and were not questioned by anyone, they did not have any allegations put to them and they were not told the reasons for their internment' (ibid). Over the course of the following months, another nine people were rounded up, amounting to 17 in total, most of them detained at Belmarsh prison, a high security prison 'on the windswept Thames marshlands on the edge of London'.[12] Dubbed 'Hellmarsh', conditions there were said to be just as bad as Camp Delta in Guantanamo Bay, with internees spending so much time locked up in tiny cells they seldom saw the daylight.[13] Apart from this physical hardship, complaints were also made about the arrangements for family visits, it being alleged that family members were roughly strip-searched before and after visits,[14] even though the men had not been convicted of any offence, and even though no physical contact was permitted between the men and their families who were separated by a partition.[15] All those interned were from Arab States, and according to London-based solicitors Birnberg Pierce, 'all were refugees in this country; a number had directly experienced torture in their countries of origin from which they had fled' (JCHR, 2006a: App 7, paragraph 4). The individuals in question included Abu Qatada (an Islamic preacher—said by western governments to be 'Al Qaeda's spiritual ambassador in Europe'—whose taped sermons are alleged to have been watched by 9/11 hijackers) and Abu Rideh, a Palestinian refugee. The others—from countries such as Algeria, Egypt, Libya and Tunisia—were known only by letter—including A, B, C, D, E, G, H, I, K, P, Q, and X—stripped of all dignity as a result, though doubtless in part in their own interests. By December 2004, nine of the men remained interned, another three were in Broadmoor because of mental health problems, while another had been released on bail suffering from terminal cancer. Two had been freed and another two had left for Morocco and France respectively, their liberty in these countries raising questions about why they had to be detained without trial in Britain.

---

[12] *The Times*, 17 December 2004.
[13] Ibid.   [14] Ibid.
[15] Ibid.

Procedural Fairness

As we have seen, those detained under the 2001 Act were entitled to challenge their detention before the SIAC which was empowered to quash the certificate if there were no reasonable grounds for issuing it. SIAC was also empowered to release internees on bail, and was required to conduct regular reviews of the detentions, and bail was in fact granted to some of the internees because of the mental illness induced by their detention. The procedures for challenging the detentions were nevertheless subject to withering criticism by prominent lawyers who represented the internees. In evidence to the House of Commons Constitutional Affairs Committee, Gareth Pierce referred to it as 'this shoddy process' where 'you are not told the evidence, where it is heard in secret, where your lawyers cannot investigate, where you will never know what is happening, you will never know the length of sentence and you will never know how you can progress'.[16] Under the procedure, SIAC could order that part of the proceedings should be held in private (with the applicant and his legal team excluded), while express provision was made for closed evidence to be supplied by the Home Office, meaning that it would not be disclosed to the applicant, who thus would not have full details of the case against him. In view of the inaccuracy of some of the open evidence, this was a major concern, raising questions about 'the reliability of the secret evidence that the detainees have never been allowed to see'.[17] In one case, the evidence against the detainee was said to come from a man who was offered a lenient sentence in return for evidence, and in another case the Home Office was 'forced to concede' that the money allegedly used by the internee for terrorist purposes was 'sent to orphanages in Afghanistan run by a Canadian priest'.[18]

The other concern with the closed material is that it may have contained information or evidence supplied by foreign intelligence services extracted under torture. SIAC was permitted by law to admit evidence that would not normally be admissible in legal proceedings. This raised questions about whether the Home Secretary could produce

---

[16] House of Commons, Constitutional Affairs Committee, Minutes of Evidence, 22 February 2005, HC 323-II (2004–05), Q 2. Compare: ' . . . the legal records of the case, and above all the actual charge-sheets, were inaccessible to the accused and his counsel, consequently one did not know in general, or at least did not know with any precision, what charges to meet in the first plea; accordingly it could be only by pure chance that it contained really relevant matter. . . . In such circumstances the Defence was naturally in a very ticklish and difficult position. Yet that, too, was intentional. For the Defence was not actually countenanced by the Law, but only tolerated, and there were differences of opinion even on that point, whether the Law could be interpreted to admit such tolerance at all' (F Kafka, *The Trial* (1975 ed), p 128).

[17] *The Independent*, 6 January 2005.

[18] Ibid.

evidence obtained by torture. The Home Secretary's position was that he would not use evidence that he knew had been produced in this way, but that he was 'willing to accept and act upon information whose origin is obscure and undetectable, in the knowledge that it may have come from countries that use torture'.[19] According to the Home Secretary, it was 'for the party who objects to its use on the ground that torture was used to make good his objection'.[20] For its part SIAC took the view that the fact that 'evidence had, or might have been, procured by torture inflicted by foreign officials without the complicity of the British authorities was relevant to the weight of the evidence but did not render it legally inadmissible'.[21] It was not until after the legislation was repealed that the House of Lords had an opportunity to question this approach in relation to torture evidence. When it was given this opportunity the House of Lords fluffed its lines: unable to speak with a consistent voice, the dominant position would allow evidence to be admitted unless it could be established on a balance of probabilities that it had been obtained by torture.[22] This is a standard condemned by one of the minority as placing on the detainee 'a burden of proof which, for reasons beyond his control, he can seldom discharge'.[23] Moreover, Lord Nicholls thought that 'in practice' the position taken by the majority would 'largely nullify the principle, vigorously supported on all sides, that courts will not admit evidence procured by torture', thereby paying only 'lip-service to the principle'.[24] Little wonder then that the ruling would not 'impede the executive in its vitally important task of safeguarding the country [except] to a very limited extent indeed'.[25]

Legal Representation

A particularly controversial feature of the procedure before SIAC was the role of the Special Advocate, an office created by the 1997 Act (and extended to other areas since: HC, 2005) on the back of the *Chahal* ruling. As the government has pointed out, it is the function of the Special Advocate to act in the interests of the appellant in deportation cases in relation to material about the appellant which is withheld from him or her on national security grounds. But as the government is also at pains to point out,

---

[19] *A v Home Secretary (No 2)* [2005] UKHL 71, at para [115] (Lord Hope).
[20] Ibid.   [21] Ibid, para [9] (Lord Bingham).
[22] *A v Home Secretary (No 2)* [2005] UKHL 71.
[23] Ibid, para [80]   [24] Ibid.
[25] Ibid, para [66] (Lord Brown).

a Special Advocate acts only in the best 'interests' of an appellant to whom he is appointed. He does not 'act' for the appellant and the appellant is not his client. He owes an appellant no duty of care in relation to the role he undertakes. This is an important point to bear in mind as it has implications for the Special Advocate in relation to the taking of what could be considered to be 'instructions' and represents a significant departure from what counsel or solicitors will be used to insofar as their professional and ethical duties are concerned (Special Advocates' Support Office, 2006: 5).

Indeed, the 1997 Act could not be clearer, providing expressly that the Special Advocate 'shall not be responsible to the person whose interests he is appointed to represent'.[26] Nevertheless, the position of Special Advocate is now being used in an expanding range of circumstances, despite the office being acknowledged by the Law Lords to present 'ethical problems' for the lawyers involved. In a leading case unrelated to terrorism it was said that,

a lawyer who cannot take full instructions from his client, nor report to his client, who is not responsible to his client and whose relationship with the client lacks the quality of confidence inherent in any ordinary lawyer–client relationship, is acting in a way hitherto unknown to the legal profession.[27]

The concerns about these arrangements were addressed directly by the House of Commons Constitutional Affairs Committee which identified a number of problems with a procedure that falls far short of what might be said to be a 'fair trial'. Some of these concerns were in fact made in a memorandum of evidence submitted to the Constitutional Affairs Committee by a group of nine of the 13 Special Advocates, while evidence was given separately by Mr Ian MacDonald who had resigned as a Special Advocate rather than continue to give 'some kind of fig-leaf of respectability and legitimacy' to a process which he found to be 'odious'.[28]

In their submission to the Select Committee, the Special Advocates acknowledged that the nature of the role they play means that they must be security cleared and that as a result 'an appellant will never have a completely free hand in choosing who should represent him or her' (HC, 2005a: paragraph 21). However, the regime gave the appellant 'no choice whatsoever' (ibid), leaving the Special Advocates to conclude that 'it would not be surprising' if appellants had little or no confidence in people who are 'selected at the discretion of a Law Officer who is a member of the executive which has authorised [their] detention' (ibid). The Special Advocates complained

[26] Special Immigration Appeals Commission Act 1997, s 6(4).
[27] *R v H* [2004] UKHL 3, at para [22].
[28] House of Commons Constitutional Affairs Committee, Minutes of Evidence, 22 February 2005, HC 323-II (2004–05), Q1.

that they were untrained and inadequately resourced, being instructed by a solicitor employed by the government which is the respondent to the appeal. Quite apart from this anomaly, the instructing solicitor is not security cleared and is therefore unable to carry out a number of tasks that would normally be performed by a solicitor on behalf of a barrister, adding significantly to the burdens of the Special Advocate who is also denied access to independent interpreters to translate material which may be in a foreign language. Not only are they compelled to rely on experts and interpreters provided by the Home Office, the situation is said to give rise to a 'serious inequality of arms' (ibid: paragraph 18). This problem is compounded by the fact that the Special Advocates are permitted to have little contact with the appellant or his or her solicitor after they have been supplied with the confidential information on which the government's case is based. As the Special Advocates explained in their evidence to the Committee:

Under the SIAC (Procedure) Rules 2003, Special Advocates are permitted to communicate with the appellant and his representatives only before they are shown the closed material . . . Once the Special Advocates have seen the closed material, they are precluded by r. 36(2) from discussing the case with any other person. Although SIAC itself has power under r. 36(4) to give directions authorising communication in a particular case, this power is in practice almost never used, not least because any request for a direction authorising communication must be notified to the Secretary of State. So, the Special Advocate can communicate with the appellant's lawyers only if the precise form of the communication has been approved by his opponent in the proceedings. Such a requirement precludes communication even on matters of pure legal strategy (i.e. matters unrelated to the particular factual sensitivities of a case) (ibid: para 9).

The Constitutional Affairs Committee made a number of recommendations to improve the position (HC, 2005), though these fell some way short of recommending full legal representation for terrorist suspects.

Round One: Legal Challenges to Detention Powers

In light of the foregoing criticism, it is hardly surprising that the detention of the suspected international terrorists should be challenged in the courts. In fact, proceedings were brought by nine detainees before the SIAC, challenging 'every aspect of the action of the [Home Secretary] which resulted in their being detained'. Despite the government's derogation from article 5, SIAC found that there had been a breach of article 14 of the Convention which provides that the rights and freedoms set forth therein should be enjoyed without discrimination on a number of defined grounds, including national origins.

The Commission quashed the derogation order and issued a declaration under section 4 of the Human Rights Act 1998 that section 23 of the 2001 Act was incompatible with articles 5 and 14 of the ECHR to the extent that it authorised detention without trial in a manner that discriminated against foreign nationals. However, this decision was reversed by the Court of Appeal, in which the Lord Chief Justice (Lord Woolf) sat with Lord Justices Brooke and Chadwick. According to the Lord Chief Justice, 'the emergency which the government believes to exist justifies the taking of action which would not otherwise be acceptable', noting that the ECHR 'recognises that there can be circumstances where action of this sort is fully justified'. Despite their detention, the respondents could be comforted by the fact that because of the HRA they now enjoyed 'substantial additional protection', as well as the 'important point' that 'the courts are able to protect the rule of law'.[29] Apparently feeling neither comforted not protected (substantially or otherwise), the internees appealed to the House of Lords where in what was then an extremely unusual move, a Bench of nine judge was assembled to hear what was to be the first of a number of major decisions on this issue.

Public Emergency Threatening the Life of the Nation

As we have seen, the government could derogate under article 15 of the Convention only if there was a public emergency threatening the life of the nation. If the House of Lords were to hold that there was no such emergency, the whole basis on which the internment powers were constructed would collapse. The government obviously claimed that there was such an emergency, though the arguments the other way seemed very powerful and persuasive. First, there was the case law of the European Court of Human Rights which has emphasised the need for an emergency which was not only actual or imminent but which threatened the 'continuance of the organised life of the community'. Secondly, there are the Siracusa Principles on the Limitation and Derogation Provisions in the International Covenant on Civil and Political Rights (ICCPR) dealing with the similar power to derogate from the ICCPR (also ratified by the United Kingdom, though not enforceable in the domestic courts). These raise the bar even higher than the jurisprudence of the Strasbourg Court, by providing that a threat to the life of the nation must be one that:

(a) affects the whole of the population and either the whole or part of the territory of the State; and

[29] A v Home Secretary [2002] EWCA Civ 1502 (Lord Woolf).

(b) threatens the physical integrity of the population, the political independence or the territorial integrity of the State, or the existence of
basic functioning of institutions indispensable to ensure and protect
the rights recognised in the Covenant.

Added to the above, thirdly, are the views of the different organs of the
Council of Europe which have said that the current fears about terrorism
should not be used to justify a derogation on the part of Member States
under article 15 of the ECHR. Indeed, as many others have pointed out, only
the United Kingdom has found it necessary to derogate, even though other
Council of Europe states were also at risk of terrorist attack, and despite the
failure of the British government to provide any evidence to justify its decision to derogate.

Yet notwithstanding the above, the House of Lords held that there was
a public emergency threatening the life of the nation, with Lord Bingham
upholding the government on this point on three grounds. The first is that
it had not misdirected itself as to the law, despite the fact that the decision
was based to some extent on closed material which was not available to the
appellants, and which *the House of Lords did not see*. Secondly, it was held
to be consistent with the test adopted by the European Court of Human
Rights in *Lawless v Ireland*,[30] the very first case on article 15, well before the
jurisprudence became more sophisticated in more recent decisions referred
to by the Lords. And thirdly, it was held that on matters of national security,
the courts must defer to the judgment of the government and Parliament.
According to Lord Bingham, this is because they were:

called on the exercise a pre-eminently political judgment. It involved making a
factual prediction of what various people around the world might or might not
do, and when (if at all) they might do it, and what the consequences might be if
they did. Any prediction about the future behaviour of human beings (as opposed
to the phases of the moon or the high water at London Bridge) is necessarily
problematical. Reasonable and informed minds may differ, and a judgement is
not shown to be wrong or unreasonable because that which is thought likely to
happen does not happen. It would have been irresponsible not to err, if at all, on
the side of safety. As will become apparent, I do not accept the full breadth of the
Attorney General's argument on what is generally called the deference owed by
the courts to the political authorities. It is perhaps preferable to approach this
question as one of demarcation of functions of what Liberty in its written case
called 'relative institutional competence'. The more purely political (in a broad
or narrow sense) a question is, the more appropriate it will be for political resolution and the less likely it is to be an appropriate matter for judicial decision.

---

[30] (1961) 1 EHRR 15.

The smaller, therefore will be the potential role of the court. It is the function of political and not judicial bodies to resolve political questions. Conversely, the greater the legal content of any issue, the greater the potential role of the court, because under our constitution and subject to the sovereign power of Parliament it is the function of the courts and not of political bodies to resolve legal questions. The present question seems to me to be very much at the political end of the spectrum.[31]

These remarks, of course, beg the question of what is a purely political question, what is a purely non-political question, and what is a mixed political and non-political question. It also begs the question of when—if ever—a decision by a politician may be said to be a non-political question, and the additional question of when a legal question is not also a political question. Nevertheless, the European Court of Human Rights subsequently agreed with the House of Lords that there was a public emergency threatening the life of the nation.[32]

Disproportionate and Discriminatory Detention

Happily this was not the end of the matter, as it may have been in the past. Although there was a 'public emergency threatening the life of the nation', the House of Lords was required to consider whether the measures taken to deal with it (indefinite internment) were 'strictly required by the exigencies of the situation', within the terms of article 15. Here the House of Lords (by an 8:1 majority) upheld the arguments for the appellants which were based on three major points of substance. The first was that the legislation applied only to foreign nationals, when there was just as great a threat from al-Qaeda trained British citizens. Secondly, the legislation was too broad in the sense that it applied not only to al-Qaeda—who were said to be the source of the threat—but to all suspected international terrorists. And thirdly, 'it permitted foreign nationals suspected of being al-Qaeda terrorists or their supporters to pursue their activities abroad if there was any country to which they were able to go'.[33] At the heart of the matter, however, was the following claim:

If the threat presented to the security of the United Kingdom by UK nationals suspected of being Al-Qaeda terrorists or their supporters could be addressed without

---

[31] *A v Home Secretary*, above, para [29].
[32] *A v United Kingdom* [2009] ECHR 301.
[33] *A v Home Secretary*, above, para [31].

infringing their right to personal liberty, it is not shown why similar measures could not adequately address the threat presented by foreign nationals.[34]

The House of Lords accepted these arguments that the legislation was disproportionate and a separate argument that it was discriminatory because it applied only to foreign nationals. It is clear, however, that the discriminatory nature of the legislation was a central plank in the proportionality argument, with Baroness Hale emphasising the importance of the discrimination angle in the following way: 'No one has the right to be an international terrorist. But substitute "black", "disabled", "female", "gay", or any other similar adjective for "foreign" before "suspected international terrorist" and ask whether it would be justifiable to take power to lock up that group but not the "white", "able-bodied", "male" or "straight" suspected international terrorists. The answer is clear.'[35]

Would it have made any difference if the power to detain had been confined to people suspected of having been trained by al-Qaeda and if the power applied to both British and foreign nationals until such times as they were deemed not to be a threat? We may never know. But what we do know is that in repudiating the decision of the Court of Appeal, the House of Lords delivered one of the most important public law decisions since *Entick v Carrington* in 1765, and the great judgment of Lord Chief Justice Camden. The decision in *A* is important not only for the fact that the House of Lords stood up to the government on a highly contentious political issue, but also for their manner of doing so. The powerful rhetoric of Lords Hoffmann and Scott was particularly notable, not least for the biting criticism it drew from *The Times* and others. According to Mr Peter Riddell of the former, Lord Scott (who compared the key sections of the 2001 Act with France before and during the Revolution, and with Soviet Russia in the Stalinist era) indulged in 'agitprop grandstanding of the worst kind',[36] while Lord Hoffmann (who asserted that the 'real threat to the life of the nation comes not from terrorism but from laws such as these') was accused of preferring 'sententious grandiloquence to legal precedent', which may make his Lordship 'Liberty's Judge of the Year', but also fails to address how the State should tackle terrorism.[37] But it was not only Mr Riddell who was exercised

---

[34] Ibid.

[35] Ibid, para [238].

[36] *The Times*, 21 December 2004.

[37] *The Times*, 17 December 2004. Lord Hoffmann had himself said only three years earlier that the events of 9/11 'are a reminder that in matters of national security, the cost of failure can be high. This seems to me to underline the need for the judicial arm of government to respect the decisions of ministers of the Crown on the question of whether support for terrorist activities in a foreign country constitutes a threat to national security. It is not only that the executive has access to special

by the rhetoric of the Lords. According to Lord Carlile QC (now the government's independent reviewer of terrorism legislation), the remarks of some of the Lords had 'more of the timbre of the political chamber than the judicial bench'.[38] In truth, however, the hyperbole is open to criticism not because of its content, but because it is not matched by the substance of the conclusion or its consequences, masking a decision which was reached on the narrowest of grounds and which did not seriously challenge certain contestable assumptions on which the government's anti-terrorism agenda is based. Had outcomes matched rhetoric, we might not now be facing the problem of control orders which are equally offensive to human rights.

From Detention to Control Orders

The decision of the House of Lords on 16 December 2004 did not lead to the release of the detainees. Indeed it was not until 10 and 11 March 2005 that they were released, following the enactment of the Prevention of Terrorism Act 2005 and the repeal of section 23 of the 2001 Act under which they had been interned. The individuals in question were initially released on 'conditional bail', and on 12 March the certification that they were international terrorists was lifted, though in each case control orders were imposed. The circumstances of their release were said by Birnberg Pierce to give rise to 'many and various practical and often exasperating difficulties'. Birnberg Pierce drew attention in particular to the problems of the three detainees who had been released from Broadmoor, explaining that:

Each had already expressed his nervousness at re-entering the world abruptly; each expressed his concern that he would not be able to cope with that experience. (Broadmoor in relation to all other patients has a carefully organised gradation when discharge is anticipated, involving close liaison with local mental health professionals and social workers attached to the relevant local authority). In the case of these detainees no such liaison or gradation was satisfactorily achieved; . . . and . . . , both single men, both mentally ill . . . . were taken by police and placed alone in premises that were in no way adapted for their particular needs. . . . suffered a complete mental breakdown during his first night of release from Broadmoor, and was admitted to the psychiatric department of the Royal Free Hospital where he remained as an inpatient for five months . . . (JCHR, 2006a: App 7).

---

information and expertise in these matters. It is also that such decisions, with serious potential results for the community, require a legitimacy which can be conferred only by entrusting them to persons responsible to the community through the democratic process. If the people are to accept the consequences of such decisions, they must be made by persons whom the people have elected and whom they can remove': *Home Secretary v Rehman* [2001] UKHL 47, para [62].

[38] *The Guardian*, 21 December 2004.

But it was not only those detained at Broadmoor who experienced difficulty and apparent inhumanity. According to Tyndallwoods:

The process of releasing the men in March 2005 and serving the Control Orders was chaotic and showed a complete lack of humanity. My client was released at 10:30 pm and taken to his accommodation address. He was released without any money and there was no food at the address. He remained without food and without money until approximately 4:30 pm the following day. He was supposed to have access to a Home Office telephone number. There was no landline installed in the accommodation and it took weeks to get it. He had no access whatsoever to the telephone. The terms of the Control Order prohibited the use of mobile phones, public call boxes and the internet. You have no means of contacting the outside world. My client was not allowed to meet anyone by arrangement or have visitors who had not been cleared by the Home Office. He was allowed to leave the accommodation between 7am and 7pm, but was cut off from all normal social contact as, unless he happened to bump into somebody by chance, he was not allowed social interaction (ibid: App 10).

Concerns about Scope

Far from alleviating the plight of the internees, the Prevention of Terrorism 2005 Act simply displaced it, with a new regime of control orders (applicable to British and non British citizens alike) introducing powers also unprecedented in peacetime. A control order is defined in the 2005 Act to mean an order 'against an individual that imposes obligations on him for purposes connected with protecting members of the public from a risk of terrorism'.[39] These orders are of two kinds: the first are what are referred to as derogable orders, and the second as non-derogable orders. The former are orders which involve a breach of the right to liberty in article 5 of the ECHR and would include house arrest.[40] At the time the Bill was passed (and in response to severe parliamentary pressure), the government indicated that it would seek further parliamentary approval before using these powers. However, the latter could be almost as severe and cover a wide range of orders of a most remarkable kind which can be imposed where there are '*reasonable* grounds for suspecting that the individual is or has been involved in terrorism related activity'.[41] The range of restrictions which the Act permits in the case of a non-derogable control order on the weak grounds of reasonable suspicion only, is as follows:

(a) a prohibition or restriction on his possession or use of specified articles or substances;

[39] Prevention of Terrorism Act 2005, s 1(1).
[40] Ibid, ss 1(2)(b), 4(1)(a).
[41] Ibid, s 2(1)(a) (emphasis added).

(b) a prohibition or restriction on his use of specified services or specified facilities, or on his carrying on specified activities;

(c) a restriction in respect of his work or other occupation, or in respect of his business;

(d) a restriction on his association or communications with specified persons or with other persons generally;

(e) a restriction in respect of his place of residence or on the persons to whom he gives access to his place of residence;

(f) a prohibition on his being at specified places or within a specified area at specified times or on specified days;

(g) a prohibition or restriction on his movements to, from or within the United Kingdom, a specified part of the United Kingdom or a specified place or area within the United Kingdom;

(h) a requirement on him to comply with such other prohibitions or restrictions on his movements as may be imposed, for a period not exceeding 24 hours, by directions given to him in the specified manner, by a specified person and for the purpose of securing compliance with other obligations imposed by or under the order;

(i) a requirement on him to surrender his passport, or anything in his possession to which a prohibition or restriction imposed by the order relates, to a specified person for a period not exceeding the period for which the order remains in force;

(j) a requirement on him to give access to specified persons to his place of residence or to other premises to which he has power to grant access;

(k) a requirement on him to allow specified persons to search that place or any such premises for the purpose of ascertaining whether obligations imposed by or under the order have been, are being or are about to be contravened;

(l) a requirement on him to allow specified persons, either for that purpose or for the purpose of securing that the order is complied with, to remove anything found in that place or on any such premises and to subject it to tests or to retain it for a period not exceeding the period for which the order remains in force;

(m) a requirement on him to allow himself to be photographed;

(n) a requirement on him to cooperate with specified arrangements for enabling his movements, communications or other activities to be monitored by electronic or other means;

(o) a requirement on him to comply with a demand made in the specified manner to provide information to a specified person in accordance with the demand;

(p) a requirement on him to report to a specified person at specified times and places.[42]

For the avoidance of doubt, it is expressly provided that 'power by or under a control order to prohibit or restrict the controlled person's movements includes, in particular, power to impose a requirement on him to remain at or within a particular place or area (whether for a particular period or at particular times or generally)'.[43]

More Procedural Concerns

As with the detention without trial regime, control orders give rise to procedural as well as substantive concerns. These procedural concerns begin with the extent to which the judges have again been incorporated by the government into a process that presents serious threats to the right to liberty, right to privacy, the right to freedom of expression, the right to freedom of association and assembly, the right to family life, and the right to freedom of movement. When the Prevention of Terrorism Bill was introduced, the Home Secretary proposed that he would be the person responsible for issuing the control orders, without the help of the judges. There is nothing unusual in this, given that we have Home Office authorisation for warrants to tap telephones, open mail, place bugging devices, and burgle property (unlike search warrants which need judicial approval in the form of a magistrate's warrant).[44] It was also the case that the power to detain suspected international terrorists was exercised on the say-so of the Home Secretary, without the need for prior judicial approval. But because of political pressure in the case of control orders, the government yielded and by a brilliant manoeuvre (intended or otherwise) succeeded in giving this remarkable provision an enhanced respectability, with High Court judges having been offered a central—but limited—part in the drama. Thus, control orders are normally to be made by the decision of the Home Secretary with the permission of the High Court which must be granted (on a low standard of proof) before the order comes into force. In some cases—urgency and specifically the foreign nationals who were involved in the *A* case—the

---

[42] Ibid, s 1(4). Control orders can be made for renewable periods of 12 months (s 2(4)); the government's independent reviewer has called for a limit (of two years) on the length of time an individual can be made subject to a control order (Carlile, 2008a: para 50).

[43] Ibid, s 1(5).   [44] See Chapter 3 above.

order may be made by the Home Secretary before being approved by the High Court. In these cases, however, the order must be approved retrospectively, and this must be done within seven days.[45] In deciding whether to grant permission (in the standard case) or to confirm the order (in the special cases), the High Court is confined to ensuring that the Home Secretary's decision is not 'obviously flawed',[46] a diluted standard that falls some way below the normal standard for judicial review.

Alongside these requirements of approval and confirmation are the remarkable new procedures for dealing with the judicial proceedings under the Act. Introduced by the Civil Procedure (Amendment No 2) Rules 2005, these impose an overriding objective on the courts in cases involving control orders to ensure that information is not disclosed contrary to the public interest.[47] The procedure thereafter departs significantly from the standards set out in article 6 of the ECHR, which seeks to guarantee the right to a fair and public hearing, and the right of the individual to know 'the nature and cause of the accusation against him', as well as to 'examine or have examined witnesses against him'. Thus, under the new rules, hearings in cases involving non-derogable control orders may be heard in private, in the sense that the person to be controlled and his or her legal representative may be excluded from a hearing or part thereof, 'in order to secure that information is not disclosed contrary to the public interest'.[48] Moreover, the court may conduct a hearing or part of a hearing in private 'for any other good reason'.[49] As in the case of internment which the control orders replace, a Special Advocate may be appointed to 'represent the interests' of the person to be controlled. For this latter purpose, the Special Advocate may make submissions at hearings from which the individual to be controlled is excluded, cross-examine witnesses at such hearings, and make written submissions to the court. After the Home Secretary has served closed material on the Special Advocate, however, the latter 'must not communicate with any person about any matter connected with the proceedings', with a number of exceptions which do not include the person to be controlled, his or her solicitor, or indeed other Special Advocates.[50] In other departures from normal procedure, the court may admit evidence that ordinarily would be inadmissible,[51] and the judgment of the court may 'withhold any

---

[45] Prevention of Terrorism Act 2005 ss 2–3.
[46] Ibid, s 3 (10),(11).
[47] Ibid, Sch, para 2(b).
[48] Civil Procedure (Amendment No 2) Rules 2005, r 76.22(1).
[49] Ibid, r 76.22(2).   [50] Ibid, r 76.25.
[51] Ibid, r 76.26(4).

or part of its reasons if and to the extent that it is not possible to give reasons without disclosing information contrary to the public interest'.[52]

The Impact of Control Orders

Information about the use of the power to make control orders is provided by Lord Carlile, the Liberal Democrat peer, appointed by the Home Office to conduct an annual review the operation of the 2005 Act. According to Lord Carlile, 18 control orders were made between the coming into force of the Act (11 March 2005) and the end of 2005, though by that point only nine were still in force, of which only one related to a British national (Carlile, 2006a). In terms of the continued use of this power, Lord Carlile has reported that at the end of 2008 there were 15 control orders in force, with another 23 people having been but no longer subject to a control order, and with 38 being the total number of people ever served with such an order (Carlile, 2009a). So far as the content of control orders is concerned, the nature of the restrictions should vary from individual to individual, though they have many common features, as explained by the Lord Chief Justice (Phillips):

Each respondent is required to remain within his 'residence' at all times, save for a period of 6 hours between 10 am and 4 pm. In the case of GG the speci-fied residence is a one bedroom flat provided by the local authority in which he lived before his detention. In the case of the other five applicants the specified residences are one bedroom flats provided by NASS.[53] During the curfew period the respondents are confined in their small flats and are not even allowed into the common parts of the buildings in which these flats are situated. Visitors must be authorised by the Home Office, to which name, address, date of birth and photographic identity must be supplied. The residences are subject to spot searches by the police. During the six hours when they are permitted to leave their residences, the respondents are confined to restricted urban areas, the larg-est of which is 72 square kilometres. These deliberately do not extend, save in the case of GG, to any area in which they lived before. Each area contains a mosque, a hospital, primary health care facilities, shops and entertainment and sporting facilities. The respondents are prohibited from meeting anyone by pre-arrangement who has not been given the same Home Office clearance as a visitor to the residence.[54]

[52] Ibid, r 76.32(1).
[53] NASS is a reference to the National Asylum Support Service, a Home Office body responsible for looking after asylum seekers.
[54] *Home Secretary v JJ* [2006] EWCA Civ 1141, para [4].

Control Orders and Personal Liberty

So under the control order regime, suspected international terrorists are no longer to be detained in a prison with three walls (in the shockingly memorable analysis of the government's lawyers in the Belmarsh case), but in a small one-bedroomed flat cut off from the rest of the world. Although not a deprivation of liberty in the sense of being incarcerated, there are many who would see this regime as a denial of liberty in light of the severe restraints imposed on the controlled persons. Thus, it is clear from the information provided by Lord Carlile that the obligations under the control order regime are 'extremely restrictive' (Carlile, 2006a: paragraph 43), while evidence produced to the Joint Committee on Human Rights (JCHR) suggests that Lord Carlile's claim that control orders 'inhibit normal life considerably' was a massive understatement (ibid). This evidence—which the Joint Committee found to be 'disturbing' (JCHR, 2006a: paragraph 18)—was provided by solicitors who represent controlled persons (Birnberg Piece and Tyndallwoods), and by organisations that provide support (Peace and Justice in East London; Campaign Against Criminalising Communities; and Scotland Against Criminalising Communities). According to the submission of one of these groups, control orders 'amount to virtual house arrest', with the government 'in effect re-creat[ing] internment, pending a judicial process which could last for many years' (JCHR, 2006a: App 4). The same witness wrote of the homes of controlled persons being turned into 'domestic prisons', and of 'collective punishment' being visited upon the families of controlled persons. Others tell harrowing tales of inhumanity, isolation, and illness, as well as the humiliation and indignity of controlled persons and their families, shown contempt at all levels by public authorities, and others acting on behalf of the public authorities. An unforgettable vignette is provided by the report that one of the men, who has no arms below his elbows, lived for five months with little furniture and his belongings unpacked around him as no one could enter his home to assemble his flat-packed wardrobes (JCHR, 2006a: App 9).

But there are other concerns, chief amongst them being the impact of the control order regime on the lives of the families of controlled persons, given the complaints already referred to about the homes of controlled persons being turned into 'domestic prisons', and of 'collective punishment' being visited upon the families of controlled persons (ibid: App 4). Before the 'release' of the controlled persons from indefinite imprisonment, their wives and children were—of course—free to meet with people and to have visitors at home. Now *all* visitors must be approved by the police, with few people being willing to go through this process of approval, to be branded as a 'known associate of a terror suspect', an intimidating label calculated to promote the isolation of the controlled persons and their families.[55] According to one witness:

Many people are still waiting months after applying for vetting and in particular Muslim friends of the men—that is the friends who are willing to go through rigorous vetting procedures. Not everyone wants to put themselves in the spotlight like this. Many Muslims are afraid because, as mentioned above, they will be classified as a known associate of a terrorist suspect—a very onerous burden for Muslims, particularly without citizenship, in the current climate in Britain. (ibid: App 9)

These problems are compounded where the controlled persons are refugees and where their friends are also refugees: 'no one in their circle would want to risk being tarred with the same brush of suspicion and fear is strong in the community on such matters' (ibid: App 8). According to the Campaign Against Criminalising Communities many people are 'intimidated, especially friends or relatives who do not hold UK citizenship and so rightly feel more vulnerable to persecution' (ibid: App 4). And while they are permitted to have one landline into their homes, contact with others is said nevertheless to be further inhibited by claims that 'on their small finances they cannot afford to make calls to their families'. In any event, 'some cannot even afford a phone connection and have no social contact at all' (ibid: App 9).

Privacy and Other Concerns

Bad enough though this is, control orders do not only have an impact on the liberty of the individual, his family, and other third parties. There are also major concerns about privacy, with complaints made about the tagging of people and the entering of their homes at 'anytime of the day or night' by police and private tagging companies. In evidence to the JCHR, it was claimed by Scotland Against Criminalising Communities that:

They live in total seclusion under very strict conditions. They exist with the certainty that they will eventually be arrested again and they suffer severe depression and post traumatic stress disorders due to their previous harrowing experiences and arrests at dawn. Their wives sleep fully clothed in trepidation of their doors being broken down in the middle of the night. The monitoring company can visit their homes at any time of the day or night and often their tagging equipment does not function properly and the families pay a distressing price for this. I know of two families living under Control Orders who had malfunctioning boxes which gave them sleepless nights without limit. The box emits a sound like a smoke alarm and their children are constantly awakened by the noise. They live in fear of their neighbours too as the constant visits from the police and tagging

---

[55] *The Independent*, 15 December 2005.

people alert them to their situation. Their children live in trepidation. They have witnessed their fathers' arrests on more than one occasion and they are severely traumatized. The constant visits from the police and monitoring company, often in the middle of the night (5 police officers and 3 tagging people) alert their neighbours to their living conditions and the children are stigmatized at school. Some of the families endure the indignity of searches of their homes at any time of the day or night. (ibid: App 9)

It is not only the invasion of privacy in the home that is an issue, compounded as it is by the frequent attention of the tagging companies. As one witness pointed out, the internees are 'dictated by the monitoring company, security services and the Home Office' (ibid). So they have to tell the monitoring company when they are going out, where they are going, and where they have been.[56]

There were also complaints about the failure to respect the obligations of religious worship, with one controlled person expressing concern that he had not been permitted access to the mosque, and was therefore unable to perform Friday prayers there, a right that had been respected while he had been in prison. Other concerns relate to physical ill-health, with visits by medical practitioners having to be approved in advance, not all doctors willing to be subject to this procedure. In one case:

The man concerned suffered from polio and has had mental health issues in recent years as a direct result of his indefinite detention and harsh conditions. He has been out of prison now for three months under bail conditions. During this time his physiotherapist has not been cleared to see him for the essential work on his legs. She has been his physio for many years and cleared on previous occasions but new clearance was asked for the new conditions. Lack of treatment has brought about deterioration—he's now confined to a wheelchair instead of being able to walk on crutches. He uses plastic leg splints—all hospital appointments to do with these have to be requested by solicitor and given clearance. One such essential visit has been cancelled in the last few days because clearance was not given in time. The GP is only 10 minutes away but is not allowed to visit, each visit has to be cleared by the Home Office. (ibid: App 8)

Other witnesses write about the taking away and destruction of property, the inability to use libraries (as they have internet connections), the inability to attend college courses (because all classmates have to be vetted), and of the constant harassment by the authorities. Perhaps even more compelling, however, are the tales of fear—fear of being arrested, fear of being deported, and fear from neighbours and local communities, with one public-spirited

---

[56] As pointed out by the same witness, the controlled persons 'are not allowed to write to people outside Britain so they cannot write to their families and friends abroad' (JCHR, 2006a: App 9).

local newspaper publishing details of a controlled person's family home (ibid: App 8). And even more compelling still are the reports of mental illness among the detainees and their families, and the tales of traumatised families, fearful that husbands and fathers would be rearrested.

Round Two: Legal Challenges to Control Orders

In light of the foregoing, it is hardly surprising that various control orders should also be challenged in the courts. In fact, there has been a spate of cases, with a number of these ending up in the House of Lords. The decisions in three of the cases were delivered on the same day (31 October 2007), and were concerned with different aspects of the control order regime:

- in *Home Secretary v JJ*,[57] the Home Secretary appealed against decisions of the Court of Appeal in relation to six controlled persons in which it was held that their control orders violated their right to liberty under article 5 of the Convention; and
- in *MB and AF v Home Secretary*,[58] the question before the House of Lords in an appeal by two controlled persons (MB and AF) was whether the procedure for granting control orders was compatible with the right to a fair trial in article 6 of the ECHR.

The third and final of this bunch of cases is *Home Secretary v E*,[59] which also raised questions under article 5 rather than article 6. Collectively these cases represent what is in effect Round Two in the battle between the government and the courts on this issue, though on this occasion the House of Lords appeared to beat a retreat from the apparently bold position adopted in *A*. Perhaps the first sign of retreat is that the level of intensity of that judicial scrutiny was much diminished, in the sense that there was no procession of nine judges to consider the issues (though there was in a more recent control order case), which were dealt with by a more standard Bench of five, with the same five sitting in all three cases. This, however, is overshadowed by the second and much more important (but perhaps concealed) sign of judicial retreat, which is that—unlike the indefinite detention powers they replaced—the control order regime survived largely unscathed. The decisions are thus remarkably paradoxical, in the sense that while two of the three applications to challenge the control order regime were successful, the rulings are more important for what they appeared to permit rather than what they purported to prohibit.

---

[57] [2007] UKHL 45   [58] [2007] UKHL 46.
[59] [2007] UKHL 47.

Control Orders and the Right to Liberty

The key decision on whether a control order results in a deprivation of liberty within the meaning of article 5 of the ECHR is *JJ* where, by a 3:2 majority, the House of Lords dismissed the appeal by the Home Secretary. At one extreme of three different positions adopted by the five judges are the judgments of Lord Bingham and Baroness Hale in the majority. Applying dicta of the European Court of Human Rights in *Guzzardi v Italy*[60] (by which all members of the House of Lords appear to have considered themselves to have been bound), the latter approached the question whether there was a deprivation of liberty, as distinct from a restriction of freedom of movement,[61] as requiring consideration of 'the concrete situation of the particular individuals',[62] taking into account 'a whole range of factors such as nature, duration, effects and manner of execution or implementation of the penalty or measure in question'.[63] Applying these principles, both judges found that the control orders which bound JJ and others to an 18 hour daily curfew resulted in a deprivation of liberty.[64] Agreeing with Mr Justice Sullivan, the trial judge, Lord Bingham observed that:

The judge's analogy with detention in an open prison was apt, save that the controlled persons did not enjoy the association with others and the access to entertainment facilities which a prisoner in an open prison would expect to enjoy.[65]

At the other extreme are the dissenting judgments of Lords Hoffmann and Carswell. For both judges, it was 'essential not to give an over-expansive interpretation to the concept of deprivation of liberty',[66] curiously on grounds relating to the unqualified character of article 5 in contrast to the qualified rights in the other articles.[67] This concept, according to Lord Hoffmann (with whom Lord Carswell agreed),[68] deals with 'literal physical restraint'[69] with '(t)he paradigm case of deprivation of liberty ... being in prison, in the custody of a gaoler'. For Lord Hoffmann, it was 'impossible' to say that the

---

[60] (1980) 3 EHRR 533 ('*Guzzardi's Case*').

[61] *Home Secretary v JJ*, above, at para [12] (Lord Bingham).

[62] Ibid, para [15].

[63] Ibid, para [16] (references omitted).

[64] Ibid, paras [24] (Lord Bingham); [63] (Baroness Hale).

[65] Ibid, para [24] (Lord Bingham).

[66] Ibid, para [44] (Lord Hoffmann). See also ibid, at para [69] (Lord Carswell).

[67] Ibid, paras [32]–[33] (Lord Hoffmann) (emphasis in original).

[68] On this point, his Lordship, like Lord Hoffmann, drew support from the dissenting judgment of Judge Fitzmaurice in the *Guzzardi's Case*: ibid, paras [77]–[78].

[69] *Home Secretary v JJ*, above, para [36] (Lord Hoffmann).

controlled persons were 'in prison'.[70] To characterise their conditions in this way would, according to his Lordship, be 'an extravagant metaphor'.[71]

Splitting the difference between these two positions is the majority judgment of former Intelligence Services Commissioner Lord Brown of Eaton-under-Heywood,[72] who found that 'these appeals fall to be decided as a matter of pure opinion'.[73] In the event, he found that by imposing a curfew of 18 hours, the control orders deprived the controlled persons of their liberty within the meaning of article 5. Unlike Lord Bingham,[74] Baroness Hale,[75] and Lord Carswell,[76] Lord Brown ventured to suggest the point at which a curfew under a control order would result in a deprivation of liberty. According to his Lordship, while an 18 hour curfew would amount to a deprivation of liberty, '12 or 14-hour curfews . . . *are* consistent with physical liberty'.[77] Importantly, he added that he considered the '*acceptable* limit to be 16 hours',[78] though later in his judgment Lord Brown stated that a 16 hour curfew 'should be regarded as the *absolute* limit'.[79] With 16 hours thus being the defined centre of gravity, the other two cases were fairly easy to dispose of: in *Home Secretary v E*,[80] the House of Lords unanimously concluded that a control order that imposed a 12-hour daily curfew did not involve a deprivation of liberty; and in *Home Secretary v MB and AF*,[81] it was unanimously concluded that the control order that subjected AF to a 14-hour daily curfew did not deprive him of his liberty. According to Lord Bingham in *E*, 'the core element of confinement' arising from a 12 hour control order was not sufficiently severe to constitute a deprivation of liberty,[82] while at the higher level of 14 hours in *AF*, Lord Bingham thought that 'on balance' there was 'no deprivation of liberty'.[83] Although *JJ* may thus have been unwelcome for

---

[70] Ibid, para [45] (Lord Hoffmann).

[71] Ibid.

[72] See pp 72–74 above.

[73] *Home Secretary v JJ*, above, para [102] (Lord Brown). See also ibid, para [17] (Lord Bingham).

[74] Ibid, para [16] (Lord Bingham) (references omitted).

[75] Ibid, para [63].

[76] Ibid, para [84] (Lord Carswell).

[77] Ibid, para [105] (Lord Brown) (emphasis in original).

[78] Ibid (emphasis added).

[79] Ibid (emphasis added).

[80] [2007] UKHL 47.   [81] [2007] UKHL 46.

[82] [2007] UKHL 47, at para [11].

[83] [2007] UKHL 46, at para [11]. The conclusions of Lord Bingham are surprising, not least because the impact of the control order in AF's case was more severe than that in E's situation. AF was subject to a 14-hour daily curfew while a 12-hour daily curfew applied in E's case. In AF's case, he was 'cut off from the outside world' (ibid, at para [8] (Lord Bingham)), while E was found to have been 'left with wide opportunities, and in fact does engage in everyday activities' (*Home Secretary v E* [2007] 3 WLR 1, at para [67] (Court of Appeal, Pill, Wall, and Maurice Kay JJ)).

the government, it was pointed out that the 'ruling has no practical effect on any suspect currently held, as the 18-hour curfews have all been reduced by the Home Secretary, Jacqui Smith'. Indeed, despite being on the losing end, the decision emboldened the government perversely to consider 'strengthening some existing orders' with a view to increasing the period of detention of those who were being detained for less.[84]

Control Orders and the Right to a Fair Trial

In contrast to *JJ* and *E*, the issues in *MB and AF* were concerned principally with article 6 rather than article 5. Here, the first issue was whether control order proceedings involve the determination of a criminal charge and whether the procedures adopted in the cases was in breach of article 6. The court unanimously found that control order proceedings did not involve the determination of a criminal charge and, hence, were not subject to the more stringent safeguards guaranteed by article 6. The principal reason according to Lord Bingham—with whom the rest of the court agreed[85]—was that control orders are 'preventative in purpose, not punitive or retributive'.[86] It was necessary nevertheless that the control order procedures would generally provide 'such measure of procedural protection as is commensurate with the gravity of the potential consequences'.[87] But here the Lords were unclear about what would be required to 'prevent significant injustice to the controlled person' in breach of article 6,[88] in view of the role of the judges and Special Advocates in the procedure.[89] Lord Hoffmann went the furthest by concluding that the procedures would always be article 6-compliant because the 'special advocate procedure provides sufficient safeguards to satisfy article 6'.[90] In both *MB* and *AF*, however, the gist of the case for the control orders was in closed material and was not disclosed to the controlled persons. Nevertheless, only Lord Bingham was willing to conclude that article 6 was breached in these situations,[91] with Lords Carswell[92] and Brown[93] perhaps

[84] *The Guardian*, 1 November 2007.
[85] *Home Secretary v MB and AF*, above, para [48] (Lord Hoffmann); para [56] (Baroness Hale); para [79] (Lord Carswell); para [90] (Lord Brown).
[86] Ibid, para [24] (Lord Bingham).
[87] Ibid.
[88] Ibid, para [35] (Lord Hoffmann).
[89] Ibid, para [70] (Baroness Hale); para [85] (Lord Carswell); para [90] (Lord Brown).
[90] Ibid, para [54] (Lord Hoffmann).
[91] Ibid, paras [41], [43] (Lord Hoffmann).
[92] Ibid, paras [86]–[87] (Lord Carswell).
[93] Ibid, para [92] (Lord Brown).

inclined to the same conclusion, but reluctant to proffer a definitive view. Baroness Hale was even more equivocal and stated that:

It is quite possible for the court to provide the controlled person with a sufficient measure of procedural protection even though the whole evidential basis for the basic allegation, which has been explained to him, is not disclosed.[94]

Because of his view that control order proceedings are always article 6-compliant, Lord Hoffmann refused to find a breach of article 6 in these cases.[95] But declining to declare the procedure incompatible with Convention rights, the majority sent the matter back to the lower court, with the House of Lords using section 3 of the HRA to subject the duty of the courts to prevent 'disclosure contrary to the public interest', to the condition 'except where to do so would be incompatible with the right of the controlled person to a fair trial'.[96]

But just as the decision in *JJ* made only a limited impact on the permissible length that someone could be subject to a curfew under a control order (and did not seriously challenge the power to impose control orders with tight conditions), so *MB* and *AF* made only a very limited impact on the procedural burdens that taint the procedural process which must be followed by anyone who wishes to challenge a control order or its content. Indeed, real progress was not made until the decision of the European Court of Human Rights in *A v United Kingdom*.[97] That was the case in which some of the Belmarsh detainees brought proceedings claiming compensation for the breach of their Convention rights, an application which was duly successful. In the course of its lengthy decision, the Grand Chamber reviewed the law and practice of the old detention regime, and accepted that the Special Advocate procedure was consistent in principle with the government's Convention obligations. The Court held, however, that where the open material disclosed to the individual 'consisted purely of general assertions', and SIAC's decision was based 'solely or to a decisive degree on closed material' not disclosed, the procedural requirements of the Convention would not be met.[98] This decision applied with equal force to the control order regime as it did to the detention regime which it replaced, thereby tying the hands of the House of Lords in *AF (No 2)*, to the evident dismay of at least some members of the court, unhappy at being reduced to

---

[94] Ibid, para [74] (Baroness Hale).
[95] Ibid, para [54] (Lord Hoffmann).
[96] Ibid, para [72] (Baroness Hale). See also ibid, para [44] (Lord Bingham), para [84] (Lord Carswell), and para [92] (Lord Brown).
[97] [2009] ECHR 301.
[98] Ibid, para [220].

mere *amanuenses* for the Strasbourg Court, prepared to allow people to be banged up at 'home' indefinitely, without the chance to meet the full case against them.[99] Sitting again as a Bench of nine,[100] the House of Lords was thus forced to hold in this second application by AF that in reading down the Civil Procedure (Amendment) Rules 2005 (as the House of Lords had instructed in *Home Secretary v MB and AF*),[101] it was necessary to do so in a way that would ensure that the controlled person is 'given sufficient information about the allegations against him to give effective instructions to the Special Advocate'. That, said Lord Hope, 'is the bottom line, or the core irreducible minimum',[102] something it ought not to have required a Bench of nine Law Lords to confirm.

From Control Orders to Immigration Detention

In the cold light of the control order cases, the decisions in the *A* case looks like a curious kind of success. It has given way to a regime of de facto house arrest, with powers which apply not only to foreign nationals, but to British nationals

---

[99] Lord Hoffmann (para [70]) was to claim not only the decision of the Strasbourg court was 'wrong', but that 'it may well destroy the system of control orders which is a significant part of this country's defences against terrorism'. Such an outcome, however, seems implausible, having full regard to what the European Court of Human Rights said and the amount of material that it accepted could be withheld. This is what the Court said: 'The Court further considers that the Special Advocate could perform an important role in counterbalancing the lack of full disclosure and the lack of a full, open, adversarial hearing by testing the evidence and putting arguments on behalf of the detainee during the closed hearings. However, the Special Advocate could not perform this function in any useful way unless the detainee was provided with sufficient information about the allegations against him to enable him to give effective instructions to the Special Advocate. While this question must be decided on a case-by-case basis, the Court observes generally that, where the evidence was to a large extent disclosed and the open material played the predominant role in the determination, it could not be said that the applicant was denied an opportunity effectively to challenge the reasonableness of the Secretary of State's belief and suspicions about him. In other cases, even where all or most of the underlying evidence remained undisclosed, if the allegations contained in the open material were sufficiently specific, it should have been possible for the applicant to provide his representatives and the Special Advocate with information with which to refute them, if such information existed, without his having to know the detail or sources of the evidence which formed the basis of the allegations. An example would be the allegation made against several of the applicants that they had attended a terrorist training camp at a stated location between stated dates; given the precise nature of the allegation, it would have been possible for the applicant to provide the Special Advocate with exonerating evidence, for example of an alibi or of an alternative explanation for his presence there, sufficient to permit the advocate effectively to challenge the allegation. Where, however, the open material consisted purely of general assertions and SIAC's decision to uphold the certification and maintain the detention was based solely or to a decisive degree on closed material, the procedural requirements of Article 5 (4) would not be satisfied' ([2009] ECHR 301, para [220]).

[100] *Home Secretary v AF* [2009] UKHL 28.

[101] [2007] UKHL 46.

[102] *Home Secretary v AF* [2009] UKHL 28, para [81].

as well; to be exercised not only where they are suspected international terrorists, but on the ground only that there are 'reasonable grounds for suspecting that the individual is or has been involved in terrorism-related activity'. But not only that, several of those who were 'released' on control orders in March 2005 were subsequently rounded up on 11 August 2005 and detained under immigration law with a view to their extradition. They were now back to where they started, the government replacing one ground for their indefinite detention with another. Although deportation detention had previously been thought impossible after *Chahal* because of the risk of torture in the countries to which the individuals would be deported, the government was seeking to overcome this problem by securing diplomatic assurances from the dodgy regimes to guarantee that the individuals in question would not be ill-treated after their return. Following the arrests and detentions, some of the individuals in question were bailed by SIAC on conditions similar to control orders, but with restraints on their liberty that were said to be even more onerous. According to Tyndallwoods,

At least one is under 24 hour house arrest, one is allowed out for only 2 hours a day and one is allowed only into the garden. In effect, through immigration legislation ... the government has obtained indefinite internment for some—as there is no prospect of assurances being either reached or satisfactory, and derogating control orders for the others. (JCHR, 2006a: App 10)

This led the JCHR to question the legality of these detentions, which were thought to breach article 5 of the ECHR, on the ground that there was no realistic prospect of deportation within a reasonable time for those who had been detained while assurances were being sought—but had not been secured—from other countries. As was pointed out by Lord Carlile, 'it would have been far preferable for Memoranda of Understanding to have been reached before the deportation detentions took place' (Carlile, 2006a: paragraph 28).

Detention without Trial Again

Quite how long people would be kept in these conditions is far from clear. But they were now being detained indefinitely pending agreements with other States which were in various stages of negotiation. The issue about the length of the detention arose for consideration in the *Chahal* case, discussed above,[103] where the complainant disputed that he was being detained in accordance with a procedure 'prescribed by law' (as set out in article 5(1) of the Convention). This is because of the excessive delay in considering his application for refugee

---

[103] See pp 224–225.

status (16 August 1990 to 27 March 1991), followed by the legal proceedings to consider his asylum claim (9 August 1991 and 2 December 1991), and the time required to make a fresh decision refusing asylum (2 December 1991 to 1 June 1992). The European Commission of Human Rights (which in those days filtered cases before they got to the court) found that there was a breach of article 5 on the ground that the proceedings involving the applicant had not been pursued with the requisite speed, but before the Court the government claimed that they had been conducted as expeditiously as possible. In holding that there was no breach in this case, the Court accepted that where someone was detained under article 5(1)(f), the deportation proceedings must be 'in progress' and must be conducted with 'due diligence'. In this case, however, the duration of the deportation proceedings was not found to be 'excessive'.[104] This is despite the fact that the proceedings took three and a half years (taking into account the legal proceedings after the refusal of asylum in June 1992). But in the view of the Court, 'bearing in mind what was at stake for the applicant and the interest that he had in his claims being thoroughly examined by the courts, none of the periods complained of can be regarded as excessive, taken either individually or in combination'.[105] It is, however, another matter altogether to arrest and detain someone with a view to deportation when the individual in question cannot be lawfully deported, as is the case with many of the nine detained on 11 August 2005, with a view to their deportation to countries where there is a risk of torture or other mistreatment.

What then of the government's attempts to secure diplomatic assurances from other countries while a number of people were in custody awaiting deportation? In his first report under the 2005 Act, Lord Carlile pointed out that one such agreement had been reached with the Kingdom of Jordan 'whereby the person to be deported will be protected from any breach of equivalent rights to those guaranteed under European Convention on Human Rights Articles 2 and 3, the right to life and the prohibition of torture'. Lord Carlile also pointed out that the agreement had 'caused some protest, on the basis that despite assurances Jordan would not honour agreed guarantees of individual liberties' (Carlile, 2006a: paragraph 22). Although these were not matters for him as reviewer of the 2005 Act, Lord Carlile pointed out further that

the person concerned, having been convicted in Jordan in his absence of serious offences, is entitled to a fresh trial if returned there. A right to a fresh trial that would not be available in any UK jurisdiction without a successful appeal, following conviction in absence (ibid).

---

[104] *Chahal v United Kingdom*, above, p 465.
[105] Ibid, at p 466.

However, as Lord Carlile also pointed out, only one of the detainees was from Jordan and there was no memorandum in respect of any of the other eight people, even if civil servants were 'working hard to achieve such Memoranda', involving 'frequent and intensive contact with the government(s) concerned'. Although it was reported that a 'small single-purpose group has been set up to progress this issue, including a former Foreign Office Minister and a recently retired senior civil servant with specialist and profound knowledge of terrorism issues', nevertheless after several months of discussions the 'issues remain[ed] unresolved', and 'rendition cannot be achieved' (ibid: para 23), though the individuals remained in custody with a view to their deportation which under the ECHR is supposed to take place expeditiously. Ironically, although the Memorandum of Understanding (MOU) with Jordan was the first, its target (Abu Qatada) is still here.

Diplomatic Assurances

The government was thus criticised for detaining people under immigration powers before it had the authority to deport, and was also criticised for seeking diplomatic assurances from dodgy regimes as a cover for detention. By May 2006, however, Memoranda of Understanding had been agreed also with Lebanon and Libya, while negotiations with Algeria, Egypt, and Morocco were well advanced. Concern about these documents was expressed by the Joint Committee on Human Rights in yet another report, where it was said that:

The existing Memoranda specify that, if detained following deportation, the deported person will be 'afforded adequate accommodation, nourishment, and medical treatment, and will be treated in a humane and proper manner, in accordance with internationally accepted standards.' None of the Memoranda contain express references to torture. Each provides for prompt and regular private visits from representatives of an independent body nominated jointly by both states, though the minimum frequency of the visits is different in each Memorandum. Whilst the Libyan and Lebanese Memoranda provide for medical examinations to assess any ill treatment, the Jordanian memorandum does not. None of the Memoranda make clear that the medical personnel involved will be independent of the detaining authorities, or whether the medical examination will take place privately without representatives of the detaining authorities being present, or to whom if anyone it will report. (JCHR, 2006b: para 105)

Concern was also expressed about the monitoring mechanisms, leading the Committee more generally to question the propriety of relying on diplomatic assurances, as the House of Commons Foreign Affairs Committee had expressed concerns before it (FAC, 2006: paragraph 66). The JCHR had 'grave concerns that the Government's policy of reliance on diplomatic assurances could place deported individuals at real risk of torture or inhuman and degrading treatment, without any reliable means of redress' (JCHR, 2006b: paragraph 105). Perhaps more to the point, the Strasbourg Court had called into question the value of diplomatic assurances in countries where torture was systematic, the Court being taken by the JCHR to have held in *Chahal* that

notwithstanding the acknowledged good faith of the Indian government in providing an assurance that the applicant would not be ill-treated following return to India, there was insufficient state control of individual officers on the ground to ensure the applicant's safety (ibid: paragraph 114).

These assurances thus did little to overcome real concern about the practices of the countries from which the assurances were secured, and few were as sanguine as the minister who expressed the view in evidence to the JCHR that 'the system of diplomatic assurances depended on mutual good faith between Governments', and that it is 'inappropriate to look behind that good faith', stressing that 'such agreements should not be entered into on the presumption that they were unlikely to be complied with' (ibid: paragraph 112). The government could perhaps draw some support for this position from Lord Carlile's first report under the Prevention of Terrorism Act 2005. Although Lord Carlile had concerns about detention taking place before agreements were concluded, he nevertheless said that:

24. The general issue of rendition is all too easily over-simplified. Subject to an appropriate system of law and compliance with international obligations especially relating to human rights, every country has the right and indeed the duty to its citizens to protect national security, if appropriate by excluding foreign nationals who threaten that security.
25. In my own political life I have been involved in activity against torture and unjustified deprivation of liberty in countries behind the old Iron Curtain. Those countries are now bastions of democracy and freedom, and in every case without a civil war or bloody revolution. It really is a counsel of despair to suggest that no verifiable or satisfactory agreement can ever be reached with apparently recalcitrant countries. There are international organisations and mechanisms available and devisable to ensure an appropriate level of verification. The effort is certainly well worth making.
26. It follows that I reject as naïve and simplistic those over-deployed arguments to the effect that any country with a bad human rights record must be regarded as beyond the pale in perpetuity. The development of a better world in terms of rights and liberties inevitably will be founded on a subtle and variable blend of diplomacy, economics, sharing of natural resources, the environment and the hopefully ubiquitous desire for security and comity. (Carlile, 2006a)

The weight of opinion, however, seems to be the other way, with witness after witness before the JCHR not only highlighting the problem of torture in many of the countries with which assurances were sought, but also questioning the value of the assurances (JCHR, 2006b: paragraph 110). For its part, the JCHR agreed with the UN Special Rapporteur on Torture, the European Commissioner for Human Rights, and others that 'the Government's policy of reliance on diplomatic assurances against torture could well undermine well-established international obligations not to deport anybody if there is a serious risk of torture or ill-treatment in the receiving country'. It also considered that, if relied on in practice, the diplomatic assurances, 'such as those to be agreed under the Memoranda of Understanding with Jordan, Libya and Lebanon', leave the UK in breach of its obligations under Article 3 [of the UN Convention against Torture], as well as Article 3 ECHR' (ibid: paragraph 113). In the light of such trenchant criticisms, it is difficult to see how these deportations could lawfully go ahead, even if the assurances were granted.

Round Three: Legal Challenges to Rendition Powers

We were soon to find out, in what was to become Round Three in the battle between government and the courts, with these powers also to be the subject of various legal challenges, just as predictably as the powers of internment and control orders before them. The return of the unwanted individuals (still referred to by the courts as 'aliens') now goes under the soubriquet of 'rendition', like alien an unfortunate word with multiple meanings (simultaneously a performance, a surrender, and a purification by extraction). The challenges were brought before SIAC against proposed renditions to Algeria, Libya, and Jordan by a number of aliens who claimed variously that they would be tortured were they to be rendered to these countries, and that they would not receive a fair trial in breach of their rights under article 6.[106] By no means all of those caught up in this process had been detained previously under the 2001 Act (though some were, including Abu Qatada), and indeed because of the anonymity of the parties in litigation before SIAC and elsewhere it is now difficult to tell how many of them had been so detained. However, the procedure has been used against a number of individuals involved in high profile incidents or who themselves had acquired notoriety because of events in which they had been involved or allegedly involved. The latter include Y who was served with notice of deportation to Algeria, having been found not guilty in the so-called ricin

---

[106] See for example, *MT (Algeria) v Home Secretary* [2007] EWCA Civ 808; *AS and DD (Libya) v Home Secretary* [2008] EWCA Civ 289; *Othman (Jordan) v Home Secretary* [2008] EWCA Civ 290.

or poisons plot trial in which five people were tried at the Old Bailey in 2004–05 on charges of conspiracy to murder and conspiracy to cause a public nuisance, after having been arrested under the Terrorism Act 2000. Along with three other defendants, Y was found not guilty on all counts, though a fifth man was convicted of conspiracy to commit a public nuisance. Nevertheless, the Home Secretary made a deportation order against him on the ground that he was a risk to national security, being 'an Islamic extremist of long standing'.

Deportation to Algeria

Despite the concerns about the Memoranda of Understanding, SIAC has nevertheless been willing to dismiss appeals against deportation, notably in cases concerning deportations to Algeria which involved several suspected terrorists—including Y—on whom deportation notices were served.[107] Concerns about the use of torture in Algeria were raised in the proceedings before SIAC,[108] with Amnesty International reporting in 2006 that while there had been fewer arrests and fewer allegations of torture in recent years, nevertheless 'torture and other ill-treatment remain both systematic and widespread in cases of arrests linked to alleged terrorist activity'. SIAC made its own detailed assessment of the evolving political situation and concluded that for a number of reasons—the decline in terrorism in Algeria which had led to the mistreatment of prisoners; the emergence of democracy and the what might loosely be referred to as the rule of law; and the diplomatic interest of Algeria in complying with assurances given to the United Kingdom—'Y would face no risk of Article 3 ill-treatment.'[109] It is important to point out, however, that this assessment is heavily dependent on evidence supplied by the Foreign Office, which had a powerful voice in these proceedings. For although there was no question of 'constitutional deference [to the government] in relation to safety on return',[110] nevertheless,

it is perfectly clear that the FCO has an expertise in assessing why a foreign government adopts a particular stance in negotiations, how significant that is for the reality of the attitudes it presents, how weighty, reliable or trustworthy its assurances are, and what incentives it has to abide by or breach its assurances. It has expertise in assessing the political situation and the trends in the broadest sense in a given country. We include in that the political strength of parties, factions and

---

[107] There appears to be no MOU with Algeria, but a number if diplomatic assurances about the treatment of people deported there.

[108] *Y v Home Secretary*, SIAC Appeal No SC/36/2005.

[109] Ibid, para [404].   [110] Ibid, para [324].

individuals, civil–military relations, policy trends over areas such as human rights, prisons and judicial roles, as well as economic and social conditions. It has particular expertise in assessing the basis and strength of diplomatic and other relationships between the UK and other countries, and prospective developments in them.[111]

The government's detailed assessment in this case clearly impressed the Court of Appeal (in an appeal by Y conjoined with appeals from two other Algerians), which was convinced that SIAC had adequately addressed the concerns of Amnesty International and others, and had gone to 'a good deal of trouble to establish that in Algeria there is not now a consistent pattern of gross, flagrant or mass violations of human rights or of a systematic practice of torture, nor anything like it'.[112] Although Algeria had refused to accept any independent monitoring of the diplomatic assurances it gave, it was also noted that a number of people who had been deported there after having withdrawn their appeals had not been mistreated on their return. And while rejecting claims in other cases that the bar should not be set too low, in the Algerian cases the Court of Appeal also made clear that it was not to be set too high:

a mere possibility that the returnee might be subject to torture or inhuman or degrading treatment is not sufficient to justify a refusal to return. There must be more; there must be substantial grounds for believing that there is a real risk of such treatment.[113]

The Court of Appeal nevertheless upheld all three appeals: in the case of Y, because SIAC had unfairly concluded that Y would have been able to rely on various safeguards in Algerian law which would have protected him from the risk of torture; in the case of BB because the closed evidence told a different story from the open evidence about the risk to his article 3 or article 6 rights; and in the case of U because the closed evidence again led the Court of Appeal to question whether in deporting U the United Kingdom would be in breach of its Convention obligations. But although the appeals were upheld, the nightmare continued. The appellants were not released; success simply meant that their cases were remitted to SIAC for reconsideration. In all three cases SIAC decided the same way after a fresh hearing, leading to yet another appeal to the Court of Appeal,[114] which was stayed pending the outcome of an appeal to the House of Lords from the first Court of Appeal decision, in which the House of Lords has given the green light to Algerian renditions, subject no doubt to procedural problems being resolved.[115]

---

[111] Ibid, para [325].   [112] [2007] EWCA Civ 808, para [126].

[113] Ibid, para [163].

[114] *BB (and 6 others) (Algeria) v Home Secretary* [2008] EWCA Civ 844.

[115] *RB and OO v Home Secretary* [2009] UKHL 10.

Deportation to Jordan

It is not only in cases from Algeria where problems have arisen. The same is true in relation to Jordan, with which (as already pointed out) a Memorandum of Understanding was concluded in 2005 (shortly after the men were arrested with a view to deportation).[116] 'Relying on the effectiveness of the MOU',[117] in this case SIAC rejected Abu Qatada's complaint that he would be ill-treated if rendered to Jordan, though it appears to be the case that he had been tortured there in the past. In upholding this decision, the Court of Appeal rejected the argument for Abu Qatada that 'as a matter of principle a state could not rely on an MOU when returning a person to a country where they were prima facie threatened with ill-treatment'.[118] The Court of Appeal could thus not be drawn to accept that there was a distinction between Jordan and Algeria, where— according to SIAC—'gross violations of human rights no longer took place'.[119] The deportation was, however, challenged on the alternative ground that evidence obtained by torture would be used against Abu Qatada, thereby depriving him of his right to a fair trial under article 6 of the Convention, it being likely that he would be retried for a number of terrorist offences for which he had been tried and found guilty in his absence, and that fresh charges would be brought against him. But although these concerns were also dismissed by SIAC, they were upheld by the Court of Appeal which ruled that the former had 'erred by applying an insufficiently demanding test to determine the issue of whether article 6 rights would be breached'.[120] According to the Court of Appeal—in what is at times a damning judgment—SIAC 'treated the possible use of evidence obtained by torture pari passu with complaints about the independence of the court'; SIAC failed 'to recognise the high degree of assurance that is required in relation to proceedings in a foreign state before a person may lawfully be deported to face trial that may involve evidence obtained by torture';[121] and SIAC was led to 'undervalue the importance of the risk that the impugned evidence would in fact be used at the retrials'.[122]

But although Abu Qatada (known in the legal proceedings as Omar Othman) succeeded in the Court of Appeal, this was a truly pyrrhic victory. First, the case went back to SIAC to determine whether he should be released from custody pending the outcome of the government's appeal to the House of

---

[116] See pp 254–255, above.
[117] [2008] EWCA Civ 290, para [6]. [118] Ibid.
[119] Ibid, para [7]. [120] Ibid, para [46].
[121] Ibid, para [49].
[122] Ibid, para [53].

Lords. There was no question of him being released, and he was admitted to bail on conditions which SIAC said—not without understatement—were 'stringent'. According to SIAC in its own words:

There will be a 22-hour curfew and there will be a full package of restrictions upon his ability to communicate with the outer world and, in particular, upon those with whom he may meet and converse. We will entertain submissions as to whether or not the two hours of liberty permitted should be taken in one go or divided into two periods of one hour.[123]

Secondly, however, the House of Lords reversed the Court of Appeal and reinstated the decision of SIAC. In another quite remarkable decision in which Lord Hope was 'astonished at the amount of care, time and trouble that has been devoted to the question whether it will be safe for the aliens to be returned to their own countries',[124] Lord Phillips rejected the need for 'a high degree of assurance that evidence obtained by torture would not be used in the proceedings in Jordan before it would be lawful to deport Mr Othman to face those proceedings'.[125] The desire to 'stand firm' against torture 'does not require this state, the United Kingdom, to retain in this country to the detriment of national security a terrorist suspect unless it has a high degree of assurance that evidence obtained by torture will not be adduced against him in Jordan'.[126] What was relevant was 'the degree of risk that Mr Othman will suffer a flagrant denial of justice if he is deported',[127] Lord Phillips having observed in an earlier passage that:

If an alien is to avoid deportation because he faces unfair legal process in the receiving state he must show that there are substantial grounds for believing that there is a real risk not merely that he will suffer a flagrant breach of his article 6 rights, but that the consequence will be a serious violation of a substantive right or rights.[128]

Conclusion

The story of internment, control orders, and rendition provides a revealing insight into the limitations of the human rights culture which was introduced by the Human Rights Act 1998, and the inability of the Act to do much to address the corruption of that culture by a government determined in this case to overcome the obstacles presented by *Chahal*. It is hard to

---

[123] Ibid, para [12].   [124] *RB and OO v Home Secretary* [2009] UKHL 10, para [209].
[125] Ibid, para [153].   [126] Ibid.
[127] Ibid.   [128] Ibid, para [138].

imagine more serious violations of human rights than the indefinite detention of people without trial in what have been revealed to be extremely harsh
conditions. Although internment without trial has been replaced with a
form of house arrest, for many of those concerned the improvement in their
condition is at best marginal, and may still constitute inhuman and degrading treatment, even if not so regarded under the HRA. For others it simply
led to their detention under different legal powers as the government sought
to remove them from the jurisdiction by negotiating terms with regimes
with bad human rights records. This perhaps ought to be a sufficient answer
to the gullible who see the *A* case as having met the doubts of those sceptical about the capacity of the HRA to protect human rights. In a very real
sense, the whole affair reveals the conceit of human rights, human rights
law, and human rights litigation. 'Yes', great legal victories have been won;
and 'Yes', great courage has been shown by solicitors, barristers, and judges
in confronting an unpleasant government department, courage albeit not
nearly as great as that shown by the 'known associates of terrorist suspects'
who have been prepared to go on the record.[129] But for all that courage and
for all the cheers of the judges' many admirers, one question is always overlooked. Looking back, precisely what benefit did these legal 'victories' secure
for those interned in Belmarsh in 2001? The utility of human rights law (and
indeed the legal process generally) is to be judged not by what happens in
the court-room, but by what happens in the prison cell, or (in this instance)
what happens in the living room of a dingy one-bedroom flat liable to invasion by the State at any time, and under constant surveillance somewhere
in England.

But that is not even the half of it, with the contempt for human rights
which these developments reveal also reflecting as great a contempt for the
rule of law. That contempt began with indefinite detention of individuals,
(a) on the authority of the Home Secretary rather than a judge, (b) without
the individual being given notice of the case against him and without a hearing in advance, and (c) without having been found guilty of having committed any offence. It is continued with control orders, where again we have
detention without conviction, as well as concerns about the arbitrariness
that pervades the whole procedure, from Lord Brown's disarming comment
in *JJ* that it is all 'a matter of pure opinion', to the conditions under which the
controlled persons are subjected, and the arbitrary treatment they claim they
are forced to endure. Under the system of non-derogating control orders:

---

[129] See p 244 above.

- people are being deprived of their liberty (using these terms in Oldspeak rather than Newspeak) indefinitely;
- people are being deprived of their liberty without having been found guilty of any offence;
- people are being deprived of their liberty on the basis of reasonable suspicion rather than beyond reasonable doubt;
- people are being deprived of their liberty following secret 'trials', from which the individuals may be excluded;
- people are being deprived of their liberty without the right to full legal representation;
- people are being deprived of their liberty without seeing all the evidence against them;
- people are being deprived of their liberty without being given an opportunity to confront their accusers; and
- people are being subjected to a regime of arbitrary interference by unaccountable public officials and private companies.

Responsibility for these departures from the rule of law, of course, lies with Parliament in enacting the control order regime and the executive in operating it. Although some may argue that litigation has taken off some of the harsher edges of this regime (and continues to do so),[130] the House of Lords is not, however, free from culpability, the government taking the view (not without cause) that the courts have 'endorsed the principles of the control order regime'.[131]

And that is still not the half of it. Of just as great a cause for concern is the question of torture, an affront to the rule of law in this country (if not in those countries where it is permitted) and to human rights principles everywhere. The concern is twofold:

- the first is the soft approach of the courts as reflected in two decisions of the House of Lords discussed above, with one allowing evidence to be admitted unless it can be shown on a balance of probabilities that it was obtained by torture (an impossible burden), and with the other giving the green light to the rendering of people to states with poor human rights records to stand trial and face evidence that may have been obtained by the torture of third parties.[132] This is hardly the signal

---

[130] *Home Secretary v GG* [2009] EWCA Civ 786.

[131] *The Guardian*, 24 December 2007 (Letter by Tony McNulty MP, Minister of State for Security, Counter-terrorism, Crime and Policing).

[132] *A v Home Secretary (No 2)*, above (pp 228–229), and *RB and OO v Home Secretary*, above (pp 260–261).

of a country that condemns torture wherever it may take place, and is hardly likely to discourage its use in the future; and

- the second relates to the allegations being made with growing frequency and increasing credibility that British governments have been complicit in the torture of British citizens and residents, leading to calls in Parliament for a 'proper judicial inquiry into [these] allegations'.[133] It is alleged that British citizens and residents have been tortured by regimes as varied as Pakistan, Saudi Arabia, and the United States, with several British citizens and residents ending up in Guantanamo Bay by virtue of 'extraordinary rendition',[134] a process which shames civilised nations and the constitutional principles by which they are underpinned.[135]

After indefinite detention without trial, house arrest under control orders, and the rendition of British residents to unpleasant regimes, is the role of British officials in the torture and ill-treatment of third parties to be the depressing new frontier for legality and human rights? If so, who is within the boundary of complicity? Those who commit and connive at torture? What about those who condone passively by failing unequivocally to condemn it?

---

[133] HC Debs, 7 July 2009, col 943 (David Davies MP).

[134] On the failure of the British courts to assist British citizens and British residents in this legal black hole, see *R (Abbasi) v Foreign Secretary* [2002] EWCA Civ 1598, [2003] UKHRR 76, and *R(al Rawi) v Foreign Secretary* [2006] EWHC 972 (Admin).

[135] In the case of the last British resident to be released from Camp Delta, the High Court reported that 'It was rightly accepted on behalf of the Secretary of State for Foreign and Commonwealth Affairs (the Foreign Secretary) that BM had an arguable case that he had been subject to torture and cruel, inhuman and degrading treatment by or on behalf of the United States Authorities during his two year period of incommunicado detention': *R (Binyam Mohamed) v Foreign Secretary* [2009] EWHC 152 (Admin), para [2].

CHAPTER 8

Conclusion: Power not Rights

Introduction

IT is the fate of most books that only the introduction and the conclusion are ever read. So here are the edited highlights of the intervening six chapters. Under New Labour, the condition of liberty continues to give cause for concern, with liberty sustained by the spirit of the British people rather than the substance of their laws. We have seen a failure of constitutional principle on a massive scale in the sense that the rule of law is honoured in the breach, with State power of a different kind taken and exercised without legal authority;[1] with State authority being exercised excessively, arbitrarily, irrationally, disproportionately, and discriminatorily;[2] and with State power being exercised without proper channels of accountability, in the sense that rights can be violated without prior judicial authority over a wide range of issues, without due process and a fair trial, and without effective redress in the event of violation.[3] We have also seen a failure of rights, in the sense that the Human Rights Act is thus beginning to look more like a shroud than an elixir, and the strategy of rights rather than power to protect liberty is proving not to be wholly effective, if not wholly ineffective. It is one of several constitutional paradoxes of the New Labour era that the European Court of Human Rights has continued to be an indispensable institution for the protection of personal liberty, despite the enactment of the Human Rights Act. The impact of that Court continues to be felt on matters as diverse as the DNA database, and the role of secret evidence in cases involving terrorist suspects,[4] with its position on the treatment of demonstrators by the police at the anti-capitalism demonstration in 2001

---

[1] See pp 20–24, 55–56, 81–83.

[2] See pp 25–27, 28–30, 32–33, 60–68, 201–205.

[3] See pp 60–79, 91–93, 182–186, 198–200.

[4] *Marper v United Kingdom* [2008] ECHR 1581; *A v United Kingdom* [2009] ECHR 301.

being keenly awaited at the time of writing. The House of Lords failed on all of these matters, and on others as well.

What is to be done, in the words of one great political leader? Some lawyers and liberty activists disappointed by progress so far have nevertheless argued—apparently oblivious to irony—for more rights and more judicial review. They purred approvingly when the new Prime Minister announced in the summer of 2007 proposals for a new British Bill of Rights, and again when he spoke warmly of liberty in a speech peppered with references to all the great icons: John Locke, John Milton, John Stuart Mill, and George Orwell, as well as the greatest icon of them all, Magna Carta herself (Brown, 2007a). But these approving purrs soon turned to disapproving snarls when the Home Secretary subsequently announced her support for 42 day detention without charge for terrorist suspects,[5] an episode instructive for reasons other than exposing only an equivocal commitment to liberty on the part of yet another administration. The proposals were stopped dead in their tracks not by rights, but by the power of Parliament lined up in opposition. As such, the episode reinforces the blindingly obvious point already alluded to, that the solution to the problem of liberty lies not with rights, lawyers, or judges, but with power, procedures, and politicians. It is true of course that there is already power in the British constitution to constrain the ambitions of the executive, with every first year law student aware that our sovereign Parliament is free to make any law it likes (though sometimes if poorly taught these same students will go on erroneously to qualify this otherwise admirable statement of constitutional principle with something like, 'subject to obligations now arising under EU law'). But not only is Parliament free to pass any Bill presented to it by the executive, it is also free not to pass any such Bill, and to reject any proposals placed before it by the government. The challenge for modern liberty is not more rights and more litigation, but more political authority to enable Parliament to exercise its formal legal power of scrutiny and restraint more frequently and more effectively than has recently been the case. It was ever thus.

Civil Liberties and the Role of Parliament

In a parliamentary democracy, it is the job of Parliament first and foremost to protect the liberty of the individual from the ambitions of the government, though this is hardly the time to be celebrating the role or work of Parliament. The institution is in danger of being overwhelmed by the stench

---

[5] *BBC News*, 'Smith Plans 42-Day Terror Limit', 6 December 2007.

of the 'Manure Parliament' of 2005–2010 in which the political system was rocked by the crisis of MPs' expenses, with some elected representatives apparently claiming manure (and much else besides) on the taxpayer for their country estates. However, while it is rightly unfashionable to celebrate the current Parliament, it is nevertheless the case that Parliament is and will remain central to the British constitution, that the reputation of Parliament has been traduced in the past, and that Parliament as an institution will recover. It is thus highly likely that while historians will condemn the avarice of some of the Manure parliamentarians, so the same historians will continue to record the notable achievements of earlier Parliaments as *agents of change* in response to popular struggles for civil liberties. Parliament was primarily responsible for many of the core political rights which are now taken for granted: universal suffrage, the freedom of trade unions to form a political party, and the creation of fair rules for elections (with a reduction of the human rights of the wealthy in election campaigns). The wonder for historians will be how the people failed to turn these constitutional opportunities into political advantage, and why so many have been failed by a form of government established by revolution, in which the people and their Parliament are—at least nominally—politically and legally sovereign.[6] Coming back to the task at hand, however, it will be for the historian also to explain how despite being an important agent of change, Parliament has been a much less successful *agent of restraint*, particularly in the field of civil liberties, with a mixed legacy of failure and only limited success, at least in modern times.

The Historic Failure of Parliamentary Scrutiny

History thus records, that Parliament's record in standing up to executive demands for more power has at best been mixed. The alacrity with which Parliament enacted the Official Secrets Act 1911 on the eve of the First World War is well known. According to Professor DGT Williams, the Bill 'was introduced in the Commons on 17 August. On the following day it took less than an hour for [it] to pass through all its stages in the House of Commons under the guidance of Colonel Seely, the Under-Secretary of

---

[6] It ought not to be forgotten, in an era in which constitutional lawyers now celebrate the judge rather than the politician, and in which many would displace democracy with juristocracy, that many of the liberties that are now taken for granted were secured by Parliament in the face of a hostile common law. Classic examples are the right to freedom of association, and in particular (a) the freedom of workers to form and join trade unions, (b) the right to strike, as expressed in the Trade Disputes Act 1906 (organised labour's Magna Carta), and (c) protection from racial discrimination in the workplace and elsewhere.

State for War' (Williams, 1965: 26). Less well known is the story of the first of three Defence of the Realm Bills introduced in 1914 and 1915:

the Home Secretary (Reginald McKenna) was given leave to introduce the Bill which was read the first time, and ordered to be printed. It was then immediately read a second time, whereupon the House resolved into committee and the Bill 'reported without amendment, read the third time, and passed', the entire procedure consuming no more than two columns of Hansard' (Ewing and Gearty, 2000: 44).

In the 1920s, Parliament proved unwilling or unable to resist the government's demand for emergency powers to deal with anticipated industrial action and passed the Emergency Powers Act 1920, which allowed for a number of war-time restraints to be introduced in peacetime, while in the 1930s worries about communism and fascism led to the enactment of restraints of freedom of expression, assembly, and association in the Incitement to Disaffection Act 1934 and the Public Order Act 1936. It would be true to say that important parliamentary initiatives by Lords Robert Cecil and Parmoor respectively were decisive in protecting freedom of expression and restoring trial by jury during the First World War, while the Incitement to Disaffection Bill was watered down as a result of parliamentary resistance, by the requirement that any search for literature likely to incite disaffection should only be with the authority of a warrant issued by a High Court judge, in a debate that was to be replayed several times in relation to other government bills (ibid).

For the most part, however, the traffic was all one way, the government typically getting what it wanted, though sometimes having to make more concessions than it would have preferred. War saw the taking of fresh emergency powers in 1939, and although—with a few notable exceptions-matters were relatively quiet on the legislative front until 1979 (with the notable exception of the Prevention of Terrorism Act 1974), there was an explosion of legislation during the Thatcher years as liberties were swept aside like skittles on a bowling alley (Ewing and Gearty, 1990). With a wide range of restraints on liberty, privacy, freedom of expression, freedom of assembly, and freedom of association, this was the era in which many of the statutory foundations were laid for the edifice that has since been built by New Labour, especially in relation to executive justice. It was during this era that Parliament—with a poor memory of constitutional history—endorsed government proposals for phone tapping by the police and the security service with the authority of a Home Office warrant, endorsed government proposals for the bugging of private property by the security service again with the authority of a Home Office warrant, and endorsed the executive detention of terrorist suspects (in breach of the European Convention on Human Rights (ECHR)) yet again with the authority of ministerial approval. It was also an era in which new public order laws were introduced to give the police extended powers to ban or impose conditions on marches and processions, and to give the police for the first time in legislation the power to impose limits on conditions on the timing, location, and duration of public assemblies, a measure since extended by New Labour and used controversially at the G20 assembly on 1 April 2009. It was also the era in which Parliament sharpened up the official secrets legislation, replacing the unserviceable blunderbuss that was section 2 of the Official Secrets Act 1911, with the armalite that was to be the Official Secrets Act 1989, absent a crucial public interest defence. There is thus every reason to be scornful of Parliament's role under Conservative and Labour governments.

The Continuing Failure of Parliamentary Scrutiny

As should be by now abundantly clear, the Blair/Brown governments have built extensively on these foundations, despite the Human Rights Act passed while Mr Blair was Prime Minister and despite warm words about liberty expressed by his successor. But while the tide of restrictive legislation thus continues inexorably to rise, Parliament has not been wholly calm, with the flame of liberty being seen to burn from time to time in the Palace of Westminster. Despite their large majorities, governments seem no longer in control of Parliament in the way that they were in the past, with the House of Commons playing host to a number of independently minded backbenchers on the government side whose support can no longer be taken for granted (Cowley, 2002), while the House of Lords has claimed a new legitimacy (albeit of doubtful proportions) following the removal of the bulk of the hereditary peers, and is much more willing to test the considerable powers that it has always had (but has not always used) in recent times. Yet while it is true that a number of concessions have been wrung from governments, with a few exceptions (such as the rejections of 42 and 90 day detention without charge) these are modest compared to the scale of the substantive restrictions introduced. This is a Parliament willing to contemplate indefinite detention without trial, and control orders, and much else besides. It is also a Parliament that has been willing to sign off all power to the executive in times of emergency, for in addition to the spate of statutory restraints on liberty considered in the foregoing pages, reference may also be made to the Civil Contingencies Act 2004, a measure designed to deal with national and local emergencies of various kinds. This empowers the executive to make emergency regulations to do no fewer than 22 different things, including deployment of the armed forces by the Defence Council and the requisition and confiscation of property (with or without compensation).[7] Regulations may also prohibit freedom of assembly, freedom to travel, and freedom of movement, the last being read by the Home Office as including a power to impose control orders.[8] Other powers permit the government to prohibit 'other specified activities', a specified activity being one 'specified by, or to be specified in accordance with, the regulations'.[9]

This extraordinary measure effectively gives the government the power to write its own law, with another provision of the Act authorising regulations to disapply or modify an Act of Parliament, which means that the government can, by regulation, repeal or amend primary legislation.[10] The only restraint on this last power is that it cannot be used to amend either the Human Rights Act or parts of the Civil Contingencies Act itself,[11] though quite what value the Human Rights Act would be in an emergency remains to be seen. The government had originally proposed that emergency regulations should be designated as a primary legislation in order to protect them from being struck down under the Human Rights Act. This attracted a great deal of criticism, and although the government changed its mind, it does not expect the courts to be lining up to strike down regulations on the ground that they are inconsistent with Convention rights. The government explained that it had considered the courts' attitude to the exercise of emergency powers and concluded that 'in light of the range of tools available to the courts to ensure that the response to an emergency is not impeded inappropriately by legal challenges, and the likely approach that the courts would take to emergency powers', that 'no further provision is needed to protect procedurally emergency regulations from challenge in the courts' (Cabinet Office, 2004). This is hardly a ringing endorsement for judicial review, the government in effect saying that it trusts the courts to be on its side in an emergency. The emergency regulations may otherwise create new tribunals (though only after consultation) and may create new offences.[12] Although any new offences are to be tried in the magistrates' courts and not before the tribunals created by the regulations, these tribunals could nevertheless have jurisdiction to impose or review restraints on liberty in the manner of ASBOs or the equivalent of control orders. It is true that the emergency regulations must be approved by Parliament and that they must be renewed every 30 days. But it is also true that this approval is required only where the regulations last for more than seven days.[13]

---

[7] Civil Contingencies Act 2004, s 22.
[8] On which see pp 238 – 252 above. See also Campbell, 2009.
[9] Civil Contingencies Act 2004, s 22(4).
[10] Ibid, s 22(3)(j).   [11] Ibid, s 23(5).   [12] Ibid, s 22(3)(n).   [13] Ibid, s 27.

The Emergence of Enhanced Parliamentary Scrutiny

The record suggests that Parliament is unlikely to divert the government from its destination, though it may succeed in placing obstacles in the way that make the journey longer and more difficult. However, the role of Parliament need not be so limited, and recent initiatives suggest that there is potential for a much more intense, formalised method of human rights scrutiny. These initiatives include the provisions of the Human Rights Act itself requiring ministers to include a statement in all bills declaring either that they are compatible or incompatible with Convention rights.[14] Almost all government bills contain a statement of compatibility, with statements of incompatibility being extremely rare, one notable example being the Communications Bill 2003, the government unable to say that the television ban on party political (and other political) advertising was compatible with Convention rights (in this case, article 10).[15] The other major pre-legislative innovation is the Joint Committee on Human Rights, with one of its functions being to scrutinise bills to ensure that they are compatible with Convention rights.[16] In recent years, the Committee has been a valuable source of criticism of the government, even if the courts have tended to underestimate its significance by claiming that 'insofar as the Joint Committee expresses opinions on compatibility and other matters of law, such opinions are of persuasive value but they can have no greater weight than, for example, the views of distinguished academic writers'.[17] But before considering how the role of the Committee—or something like it—could be enhanced, it is necessary first to highlight some examples of its work, the focus here being on the scrutiny of the control order regime introduced by the Prevention of Terrorism Act 2005, where favourable comparisons may be made with the House of Lords decisions on the same subject, these discussed in Chapter 7.[18]

---

[14] Human Rights Act 1998, s 19.

[15] For an account of this episode, see JCHR, 2003a: para 40.

[16] See <http://www.parliament.uk/parliamentary_committees/joint_committee_on_human_rights.cfm>. See now *R (Animal Defenders International) v Secretary of State for Culture, Media and Sport* [2008] UKHL 18.

[17] See *R (Baiai) v Home Secretary* [2006] EWHC 823 (Admin), para [37]; and [2006] EWHC 1454 (Admin), para [37]. See also *A v The Scottish Ministers* 2002 SC (PC) 63, para [7].

[18] See *Home Secretary v JJ* [2007] UKHL 45; *MB and AF v Home Secretary* [2007] UKHL 46; *Home Secretary v E* [2007] UKHL 47; and *Home Secretary v AF* [2009] UKHL 28.

The JCHR and Prevention of Terrorism Bill 2005: First Report

Two examples of the Committee in operation relate to the terrorism legislation in 2005 and 2006. In the first of these examples, the Committee expressed concern about the Prevention of Terrorism Bill 2005, though it welcomed the provisions in the Bill repealing those aspects of the Anti-terrorism, Crime and Security Act 2001 providing for the indefinite detention of international terrorist suspects without trial. One concern of the Committee, however, was not so much with the content of the 2005 Bill as with the speed with which it was passed. Although the House of Lords decision in the *A* case had been reached on 16 December 2004 (ruling that the applicants were being detained in breach of Convention rights), it was not until 22 February 2005 that a Bill was introduced into the House of Commons (the detained people remaining in detention in the meantime). Yet despite thus having taken two months to get there, the Bill was pushed through with great speed, receiving the Royal Assent on 11 March 2005. Although the Joint Committee had little time to review the Bill—which bore a statement of compatibility on its face—it nevertheless raised a number of human rights concerns in a preliminary report published on 25 February 2005 and again in a more considered report published on 4 March 2005 (JCHR, 2005b; 2005c). It will be recalled (from the discussion in Chapter 7) that the Bill made provision for both 'derogating' and 'non-derogating' control orders, and in its preliminary report the Committee had serious reservations about both, taking the view that the former were unnecessary in light of the Home Secretary's announcement that:

> there is currently no need to derogate from Article 5, because there are no individuals in respect of whom deprivation of liberty could be said to be strictly required, there would seem to be no need for the Government to take in this legislation the power to make derogating control orders depriving individuals of their liberty by, for example, placing them under house arrest. (JCHR, 2005b: para 6)

Quite apart from whether there was a need for such powers, the Committee was excoriating about the contents of the Bill. A particular concern was that as originally drafted, derogating control orders were to be made by the Home Secretary, 'without any prior judicial involvement, and without any intention of bringing [the respondents] before a court on a criminal charge' (ibid: para 10). It is true that there would be an automatic consideration of such control orders after the event, but this was denounced as being inadequate 'in the decision to deprive of liberty', with prior judicial authorisation in such circumstances being regarded 'as an inherent feature of the rule of law, which requires safeguards against arbitrary detention' (ibid). The Home Secretary had argued that judicial authorisation would be to 'abdicate to the judiciary the executive's responsibility for national security, for which it is rightly accountable to Parliament'. This, however, was met with derision, as an 'eccentric interpretation of the constitutional doctrine of the separation of powers', it being:

a long established principle of the British constitution that, outside of the field of immigration, the executive has no power to detain individuals without prior judicial authorisation or in circumstances where it is intended to bring the individual before a court as soon as possible for further detention to be authorised.

In any event, the Committee continued by claiming that even:

if there were room for argument about the proper separation of powers in the British constitution, it is unlikely that the European Court of Human Rights would regard the exclusion of prior judicial involvement in deprivations of liberty to be Convention compatible (ibid: paragraphs 12–13).

Concern was also expressed about the use of the Special Advocate procedure in cases involving the deprivation of liberty, raising questions about whether the derogating control order procedure violated both articles 5 and 6 of the ECHR.

The JCHR and Prevention of Terrorism Bill 2005: Second Report

In the event, the government brought forward amendments to the derogating control order procedure which would require prior judicial authorisation, though in practice the procedure became redundant as the government's needs could be met by its generous reading and use of the non-derogating procedure. Here too, however, the Joint Committee had a number of concerns, despite operating under the apprehension that non-derogating orders would impose obligations falling short of deprivation of liberty. Although presuming that such orders would not engage article 5, they were nevertheless likely to interfere with other Convention rights, including the right to privacy, the right to freedom of expression, and the right to freedom of association. Here the concern was not with the lack of prior judicial authorisation but with the limited nature of the judicial scrutiny of the Home Secretary's decision to make a control order, contending that a 'supervisory jurisdiction over a decision based on "reasonable grounds for suspicion" is not a very strong measure of judicial control' (ibid: para 16), with the result that the procedure may fail to meet the requirements of article 6 which deals with the right to a fair trial. By the time of the Committee's second report, however, it was now fully understood that non-derogating control orders could involve a loss of liberty, and at this point the Committee's position toughened up, proposing that there should be prior judicial authorisation here as well. The Committee was equally dismissive of the government's claims in this context that 'if a non-derogating control order overstepped the mark and imposed obligations amounting in combination to deprivation of liberty the individual would have a remedy because the order would be found unlawful by the Court of Appeal'. But as the Committee pointed out, 'this does not meet the point' because 'by that time the individual's liberty will already have been taken away' (JCHR, 2005c: para 14).

This, however, was not the only area where there was concern about the lack of judicial protection in the context of non-derogating control orders. Returning to matters that had been addressed in the preliminary report, the Committee noted again that non-derogating control orders 'will be capable of imposing restrictions which fall short of deprivations of liberty but which nevertheless interfere with important rights in respect of which prior judicial authorisation is already required by law' (JCHR, 2005c: para 15). The Committee gave the example of a non-derogating control order imposing a 'requirement that the subject of the order agree to specified persons having virtually unlimited powers of entry, search and seizure over their home' (ibid). Such searches would constitute a prima facie breach of article 8 unless they could be justified, and any such search would normally require a warrant issued by a judge. As the Committee pointed out, however, 'this important safeguard will effectively be dispensed with in relation to those made subject to non-derogating control orders'. It was thus argued that these orders should be accompanied by better procedural safeguards 'such as access to an independent judicial determination of whether the underlying allegation was well-founded' (ibid). The clear message then was that there was inadequate judicial involvement in the process of control orders, reflecting the government's claim that it was 'proposing legislation of this exceptional kind because [it did] not want it to be possible for [it] to be accused of not doing more to protect the public in the event of a terrorist attack succeeding' (ibid: para 16). But although the Committee found this sentiment to be 'entirely understandable in elected representatives who are directly accountable to the public', the same sentiment was said to demonstrate 'precisely the reason why independent safeguards for individual liberty are essential'. This is because 'a person who is determined to avoid being accused of failing to do more to protect the public is extremely unlikely to be the best person to conduct a rigorous scrutiny of the strict necessity of a particular order' (ibid). Great stuff!

Unlocking the Power of Parliament

The emerging strategies for the parliamentary scrutiny of the executive on human rights grounds raises questions about how this work can be made more effective, and how the role of Parliament can be enhanced. Such strategies are an important acknowledgement of the point made above that the responsibility for dealing with human rights matters rests primarily with Parliament, which has the opportunity to prevent legislation being enacted in the first place, though this is not to deny an important role for the courts subsequently in supervising the way in which statutory (and other) powers are exercised in any given case. However, Parliament can only be as effective as it is powerful, and although there is a tendency to underestimate the power of Parliament in the Westminster system, it is clear that its reputation needs to be enhanced (for obvious reasons at the present time), along with its capacity in practice to use the considerable powers at its disposal. As already pointed out, it is true that in recent years the House of Commons has begun to find a voice on human rights issues, while the second chamber was identified by the Royal Commission on House of Lords Reform in 2000 as having a special role to play in this area. But in both cases the ability of Parliament is constrained politically in different ways by its faltering legitimacy. In the case of the House of Commons, it is constrained by continuing government control of the chamber, despite the fact that the government can claim a mandate from what appears to be an ever declining proportion of the population, with no modern government claiming a mandate from a majority of those voting, far less those eligible to vote. In the case of the House of Lords, the legitimacy crisis is more fundamental still, with a predominantly nominated body of unaccountable people having the power to subvert the wishes of the (albeit imperfectly) elected lower House, even if this is done for the noblest of reasons.

Civil Liberties and Constitutional Reform

A more representative Parliament would thus not only respond to concerns of principle about the declining popular legitimacy of our political institutions. It is highly likely also to respond to practical concerns about the outcomes of these political institutions, on human rights issues specifically, though in other areas as well. Two proposed constitutional reforms in particular currently in circulation would significantly strengthen the role of Parliament in the protection of human rights, and indeed would more generally transform the role of Parliament. The first is electoral reform, though much would depend on the method adopted. But the additional member system such as that now operating in Scotland (and elsewhere in Europe) would mean that no one party would have total control of the House of Commons if modern voting patterns were to continue. In an era of growing political party fragmentation, there would have to be either a coalition government, or a minority government would have to govern with the consent of other parties as issues arise. In the Parliament elected in 2005, it is unlikely on the additional member system that Labour with 36 per cent of the vote would have ended up with a majority of the seats, with the Liberal Democrats in particular gaining in numbers. The power of Parliament to address human rights questions in a manner which both allowed for the rigorous scrutiny of policy as well as its content would thus be greatly enhanced by a legislature that more fairly reflected electoral choice, thereby ensuring that all legislation would have to be the result of agreement and compromise between different political parties, whichever of these two options (that is to say coalition or minority government) was to prevail. Quite whether greater respect for human rights in legislation would be consistent with the wishes of the bulk of the electorate is, however, another matter altogether, though on recent evidence it is doubtful if the Labour government would have been able to push through identity cards if it had depended on Opposition support for its measures, while much of the anti-terrorism legislation would also have been compromised.

The other possible constitutional change with implications for parliamentary scrutiny on human rights grounds is House of Lords reform. The House of Lords as currently constituted represents no one. As already pointed out, however, the role of the House as a defender of human rights was most recently acknowledged by the Royal Commission on the Reform of the House of Lords which reported in 2000 that one of the most important functions of a reformed second chamber should be to act as a 'constitutional long-stop', ensuring that 'changes are not made to the constitution without full and open debate and an awareness of the consequences' (Wakeham, 2000: R 15). The Royal Commission also anticipated that the reformed House would have an enhanced role in relation to human rights (though not necessarily with any additional powers in this area), it being acknowledged also that there is 'a fine line between constitutional matters and human rights issues' (ibid: para 5.23). Since the publication of the Wakeham report, the House of Lords has been a most persistent and effective champion of human rights, on a wide range of issues. The unelected nature of the House (along with the arbitrary method of selection) is, however, a major and continuing challenge to its authority, notwithstanding the expertise of many of its members. Some members of the House of Lords claim that the House now has greater legitimacy after the reforms introduced in 1999 that saw the removal of the great bulk of hereditary peers. But a House nominated by the executive has barely any more democratic legitimacy than one based on inheritance. Nevertheless, the challenge to the legitimacy of the House could be met if proposals for a partially or wholly elected second chamber are accepted, unless reform on composition also leads to a significant reduction of powers. It would, however, be a curious outcome that saw the House of Lords agreeing to greater democratic legitimacy in return for fewer political powers, or to fewer political powers in return for greater democratic legitimacy.[19]

Civil Liberties, Parliamentary Reform, and Parliamentary Procedure

Within the context of a Parliament empowered by the enhanced legitimacy derived from its changed composition, it would be possible to contemplate procedural steps that could be taken to enhance the human rights scrutiny of legislation. At the present time the work is now done by the Joint Committee on Human Rights, which communicates with the relevant government department and reports to the House,[20] highlighting any human rights concerns that may arise.[21] However, in addition to the reform of the composition of Parliament, there is a compelling case for procedural reforms of two kinds to enhance the work of the JCHR or an equivalent body. The first and least radical would be to create an expectation that JCHR reports should be formally considered at some stage of the legislative process in both Houses, with MPs and peers being required directly to confront human rights issues as part of the enactment of legislation. It would be possible to contemplate a model whereby MPs and peers would not be bound by the advice of the Committee, whose views could be both contested and rejected: on this model there would be no question of a human rights veto. A second procedural reform would, however, be more radical and would go one step further and follow the example of Sweden, where historically there was the same antipathy on the social democratic left to the idea of judicial review of legislation (Holmstrom, 1994). Although the provisions of the European Convention on Human Rights were incorporated into the Swedish Instrument of Government (IG) in 1974, it was done in a way that relied on the Riksdag rather than the courts to act as the guardian of the constitution, principally through

---

[19] It is also difficult to see why an elected second chamber—currently with considerable power which it does not always use—would feel constrained by the Salisbury Convention, given that its own election would remove one of the principle reasons for the Convention. It is all the more difficult to see why an elected second chamber would feel constrained by the Salisbury Convention in the specific context of human rights, particularly if the second chamber were to be acknowledged as having a role to play in this area in particular.

[20] This contrasts with the position in the Scottish Parliament where there is no specialist Committee but human rights issues are integrated into the normal process of scrutiny of bills.

[21] For an account of its working practices, see JCHR, 2006c.

the medium of the Riksdag's powerful Constitutional Committee (which does not include any lawyers, an omission which is not thought to be a disadvantage),[22] working in conjunction with the Riksdag as a whole. Thus, under the IG, a bill which has been identified as violating a wide range of constitutional rights (such as freedom of expression, assembly, and association) may be 'held in abeyance' for at least 12 months at the request of 10 members of the House (which has 349 members in total).

In the Swedish system of 'negotiated constitutionalism' (which presumes the existence of countervailing sources of real political power), all bills are allocated to a Riksdag Committee for consideration. A bill may be referred to the Constitution Committee initially, or a matter may be referred to that Committee by another committee to which a Bill has been allocated. At this point the bill will already have been subject to a process of judicial pre-view by the Law Council (a judicial body composed of Supreme Court and Administrative Court judges which scrutinises bills for consistency with Constitution). The views of the Law Council will be made known to the government and Parliament, and while its views are binding on neither, they will be given great weight by both. The overwhelming majority of bills examined by the Constitution Committee (and by other committees) are found not to violate the constitution. However, where a breach is found and reported to the Riksdag, the bill can only be passed by a special majority (five-sixths) of the Riksdag itself (Ewing, 1996), failing which the bill will be referred back to the Constitution Committee or another committee where it had been previously considered. If this procedure is adopted, the bill is said to be 'resting' for the year, the resting period providing an opportunity for the government to consider amendments, and for the Committee itself to propose amendments which would make the bill compatible with the Constitution. The procedure is thought to operate as a restraint on government and its willingness to bring forward measures that may be unconstitutional, and as a result does not need to be used in a formal sense very often.[23] The power to delay a bill for a year and perhaps indefinitely would indeed be a salutary restraint on a government, particularly if as in Sweden it does not even have a simple majority in the single chamber Riksdag. We can only contemplate how much more of a restraint that would be in a bicameral legislature where electoral reform and an elected second chamber

---

[22] This is because non-lawyers are well able to make constitutional judgments if given the parameters in which decision must be taken, reflecting the reality that constitutional construction is a political rather than a legal matter.

[23] The committee has raised concerns about a range of matters, including legislation dealing with film censorship, immigration, the right of housing association tenants to buy rented property, the privatisation of commercial radio, and most recently surveillance.

were to deliver the government with a majority in neither House, though much would depend on the willingness of Committee members to follow the example of their Swedish counterparts, said to operate in a deliberative and independent way.[24]

The Role of the Courts

The strengthening of the role of Parliament in these ways would have implications for the role of the courts. In the first place, there continue to be serious concerns about the legitimacy of judicial scrutiny, especially of legislative power. The issue of legitimacy is well known, but no easier to overcome today than it was when raised as an objection to a judicially enforceable Bill of Rights in the 1980s and before. This is notable for example in Scotland where alone of British judges, the Court of Session has the power to strike down primary legislation on a number of grounds, including its non compliance with Convention rights. Yet the Scottish judges so far have seemed rather embarrassed about such a power and have come close to question its propriety, revealing 'a general reluctance on the part of the courts to interfere with legislation passed by the Scottish Parliament' (Tierney, 2001: 71). The point was made with some force in *Adams v The Scottish Ministers*,[25] the first of two challenges to the Protection of Wild Mammals (Scotland) Act 2002 which bans fox hunting with dogs, in this case on the ground that it violated articles 8 and 14 of the Convention. In dismissing the claim, Lord Nimmo Smith said that although the issue was one of 'considerable public controversy', issues of this kind were nevertheless 'recognised as being more appropriate for decision by a democratically elected representative legislature than by a court'. Moreover, this was not an area 'where the subject matter lies more readily within the actual or potential expertise of the courts: the making of a moral judgment is more suitable for a legislature rather than

---

[24] To be precise, the committee is thought to be constrained to some extent by party considerations, but is thought to operate in a more deliberative and independent way than other committees of the Riksdag. For completeness, it should be noted that a greater measure of *ex post facto* judicial review for breach of Convention rights has recently been introduced in Sweden. There is not thought, however, to be much evidence that the courts have become more assertive since the ECHR was formally incorporated into Swedish law, though in a hate speech case someone engaging in homophobic preaching was acquitted. Although possibly a breach of the Criminal Code, the court expressed concerns that it would breach Convention rights. It is said still to be the case that discussions in Sweden about giving the courts a greater role comes mainly from parties on the right, and opposed mainly by parties on the Left.

[25] 2004 SC 665.

for a court'. In *Whaley v The Scottish Ministers*[26] Lord Brodie was to be heard in a long, learned, and fascinating judgment to echo the remarks of Lord Nimmo Smith when he also said that:

where what is under consideration is a conscious decision by a democratically elected Parliament in a matter which came to turn on moral judgments, it is appropriate that a court, in exercise of its purely supervisory jurisdiction, should accord considerable deference to such judgments as the Parliament has made.

The Enduring Strength of Parliamentary Sovereignty

It is not only questions of political legitimacy that constrain judicial review. There is also the small matter of constitutional law. It is true that Lord Steyn famously expressed the view in *Jackson v Attorney General*[27] that the Human Rights Act 'created a new legal order', that the 'classic account given by Dicey of the doctrine of the supremacy of Parliament, pure and absolute as it was, can now be seen to be out of place in the modern United Kingdom', and that while 'the supremacy of Parliament is still the *general* principle of our constitution', it was simply a 'construct of the common law', which could be qualified by the courts. This led him to speculate whether there were certain 'constitutional fundamental[s]' which 'even a sovereign Parliament acting at the behest of a complaisant House of Commons cannot abolish'.[28] It is also true that similar remarks were made in the same case by Lord Hope and Baroness Hale, with the former expressing the view that 'the rule of law enforced by the courts is the controlling principle upon which our constitution is based', observing also that 'it is no longer right to say that [Parliament's] freedom to legislate admits of no qualification'.[29] According to Baroness Hale, the courts will 'treat with particular suspicion (and might even reject) any attempt to subvert the rule of law by removing governmental action affecting the right of the individual from all judicial powers'.[30] But although attracting some support (Jowell, 2006),[31] these eccentric views have not gone unchallenged, with one academic commentator claiming forcefully that they are 'unargued and unsound', 'historically false', and 'jurisprudentially absurd' (Ekins, 2007). In less 'acerbic' terms, but perhaps more significantly, the

---

[26] 2004 SLT 424 (Outer House); 2006 SC (Inner House); and subsequently [2007] UKHL 53.
[27] [2005] UKHL 56.
[28] Ibid, para [102].
[29] Ibid, para [105].
[30] Ibid, para [159].
[31] See also *A v H M Treasury* [2008] EWCA Civ 1187, para [129] (Sedley LJ).

then senior Law Lord was heard to say extra-judicially that he could not 'accept that [his] colleagues' observations are correct', in a strong defence of the principle of parliamentary sovereignty (Bingham, 2008). There is indeed much to contest in the remarks of the *Jackson Three*—not least the claim that the principle of parliamentary sovereignty is simply a judicial indulgence rather than something established by revolution.

Just as remarkable, however, is that the comments of the *Jackson Three* appear so conspicuously to contradict what has been happening under the Human Rights Act, where the prevailing strength of constitutional principle in the form of parliamentary sovereignty is abundantly clear. Despite his remarks in *Jackson*, in *ex parte Kebeline* Lord Hope was heard to express the view that the courts should 'defer, on democratic grounds, to the considered opinion of the elected body as to where the balance is to be struck between the rights of the individual and the needs of society'.[32] In an admittedly more qualified tone, Lord Bingham spoke in *Brown v Stott* of the need of the courts to give weight to 'the decisions of a representative legislature and a democratic government', albeit 'within the discretionary area of judgment accorded to those bodies'.[33] Both of these comments were to find an echo in the speech of Lord Nolan in the *Alconbury* case where referring to the planning system he said that 'Parliament has entrusted the requisite degree of control to the Secretary of State, and it is to Parliament which he must account for his exercise of it'. Moreover, 'to substitute for the Secretary of State an independent and impartial body with no central electoral accountability would not only be a recipe for chaos: it would be profoundly undemocratic'.[34] More recently, Lord Bingham was heard to express concern in the *Countryside Alliance* case about the danger that 'The democratic process is liable to be subverted if, on a question of moral and political judgment, opponents of [legislation] achieve through the courts what they could not achieve in Parliament.' On this occasion, however, the commitment to the 'respect to be shown to the considered judgment of a democratic assembly' was said to 'vary according to the subject matter and the circumstances', though that particular case was 'pre-eminently one in which respect should be shown to what the House of Commons decided'.[35] And more recently still, Baroness Hale appeared to contradict her *Jackson* remarks in the following exchange with the chairman of the JCHR:

---

[32] *R v DPP, ex parte Kebeline* [2000] 2 AC 326, p 381.

[33] [2003] 1 AC 681, p 703.

[34] *R (Alconbury Developments Ltd) v Environment Secretary* [2001] UKHL 23, para [60].

[35] *R (Countryside Alliance) v Attorney General* [2007] UKHL 52, para [45].

Q 192 Chairman: Perhaps we can start with you Lady Hale. Do you think the courts in our country would ever be comfortable with a power to strike down legislation passed by parliament?
Baroness Hale of Richmond: I think we would find it extremely novel, quite alarming and would hesitate to use it. That is about as far as I need to go.[36]

The Deception of Judicial Rhetoric

Apart from political legitimacy and deep constitutional roots, there is a third enduring truth which helps to explain the relative ineffectiveness of judicial review. Quite simply, this is the historically unresponsive nature of British judges to the challenge of liberty. It is true that recent cases have been heavily pregnant with big rhetoric.[37] In *Gillan*, Lord Bingham asserted that '[i]t is an old and cherished tradition of our country that everyone should be free to go about their business in the streets of the land, confident that they will not be stopped and searched by the police unless reasonably suspected of having committed a criminal offence'. Indeed, 'so jealously has this tradition been guarded that it has almost become a constitutional principle'.[38] On the question of privacy in the widest sense of that term, Lord Hoffmann spoke in *Campbell v Mirror Group Newspapers* about the need to 'identify private information as something worth protecting as an aspect of human autonomy and dignity', while in *Marper*, Baroness Hale adopted the words of the Canadian Privacy Commissioner to proclaim that 'unless we each retain the power to decide who should know our political allegiances, our sexual preferences, our confidences, our fears and aspirations, then the very basis of a civilised, free and democratic society could be undermined'.[39] The right to freedom of expression finds equally powerful expression in a number of leading cases which are peppered liberally with references to its importance. In *Campbell*, for example, Baroness Hale said that 'the free exchange of information and ideas on matters relevant to the organisation of the economic, social and political life of the country is crucial to any democracy'. 'Without this', she continued, 'it can scarcely be called a democracy at all', noting that the right to freedom of expression includes 'revealing information about public figures, especially those in elective office, which would

[36] Joint Committee on Human Rights, *A British Bill of Rights*, Minutes of Evidence, 3 March 2008, HC 150-v (2007–08).
[37] See *A v Home Secretary* [2004] UKHL 56, where extremely powerful rhetoric from Lords Scott and Hoffmann in particular drew a strong response from *The Times* and from Lord Carlile. See p 237 above. Some of the extrajudicial comments are also powerful: see for example, Steyn, 2004.
[38] *R (Gillan) v Metropolitan Police Commissioner* [2006] UKHL 12, para [1].
[39] See repectively *Campbell v MGN Ltd* [2004] UKHL 22, para [50], and *R (Marper) v South Yorkshire Chief Constable* [2004] UKHL 39, para [69].

otherwise be private but is relevant to their participation in public life'.[40] We have already seen (in Chapter 5) Lord Bingham's robust defence of freedom of expression in *Shayler*,[41] and there is an equally robust view in the *Animal Defenders International* case:

Freedom of thought and expression is an essential condition of an intellectually healthy society. The free communication of information, opinions and argument about the laws which a state should enact and the policies its government at all levels should pursue is an essential condition of truly democratic government. These are the values which article 10 exists to protect, and their importance gives it a central role in the Convention regime, protecting free speech in general and free political speech in particular.[42]

But it is not enough to look at what the judges say, without looking at what they do. And here we find the continuing influence of a long legacy of deference to the needs of the State[43] even if judges are better at expressing regret than they were in the past. So although the rhetoric is thus strong, there is a chasm that separates it from the reality. Some will contend that a Rubicon was crossed in the *A* case, where the House of Lords held that indefinite detention powers introduced since 9/11 were in breach of the ECHR.[44] But this seems an exaggerated reading of the decision, for as has been forcefully pointed out, it was reached with due deference to the judgment of the government that there is a public emergency threatening the life of the nation (Tomkins, 2005). In any event, while it is true that in the *A* case the judges demonstrated their capacity to protect liberty, much of this was undone by subsequent decisions which would appear de facto to allow the use of evidence obtained by torture and only shaved rather than removed the power of the executive to make control orders. As we have seen, it is also the case that many of the infringements of liberty that caused so much consternation in the 1980s have survived the human rights era largely unscathed, whether it be statutory constraints such as the Official Secrets Act 1989 or common law developments such as *Moss v McLachlan*,[45] itself the direct progeny of another bête noire of civil libertarians, namely *Duncan v Jones*.[46] The House of Lords has, moreover, upheld stop and search powers in the

[40] *Campbell v MGN Ltd* [2004] UKHL 22, para [148].
[41] *R v Shayler* [2002] UKHL 11, para [21].
[42] See note 16 above, para [27].
[43] See *R v Halliday* [1917] AC 260; *Duncan v Jones* [1936] 1 KB 218; *Liversidge v Anderson* [1942] AC 206; *R v Home Secretary, ex p Hosenball* [1977] 1 WLR 766; *R v Home Secretary, ex p Cheblak* [1991] 1 WLR 890; *Council of Civil Service Unions v Minister of State for Civil Service* [1985] AC 374.
[44] *A v Home Secretary*, note 37 above.
[45] [1985] IRLR 76.
[46] [1936] 1 KB 218.

Terrorism Act 2000, and indeed none of the provisions of that Act have been successfully challenged in the courts. Lower courts have upheld the new restrictions on freedom of assembly in the Serious Organised Crime and Police Act 2005, and the Human Rights Act has proved to be a weak tool in the field of freedom of assembly, with the most far-reaching injunctions ever known having been issued since the 1998 Act was introduced.[47] For completeness, it would be hard to find any examples of freedom of expression prevailing, with many of the existing restrictions being upheld, and new ones being created in the shape of a privacy law for the benefit of rich media celebrities, these remarkably being the principal beneficiaries of this extraordinary law so far.[48]

Conclusion

It is thus the supreme irony of the British constitution that liberty and legality would be better served by politics rather than by law; or by power rather than by rights. For those interested in human rights and civil liberties, a wrong call was made in 1998. Given the choice of the HRA or electoral reform, the liberals—led by the nose by the lawyers—plumped for the former when it is the latter that would have made a greater long-term impact (though not necessarily if the method of electoral reform chosen had followed the lines suggested by Lord Jenkins unless accompanied by meaningful reform of the House of Lords). The question of civil liberties' protection and erosion thus cannot be separated from wider questions of constitutional practice and constitutional reform. This chapter has made a case for radical parliamentary reform and (what would be in the British system) radical parliamentary scrutiny of legislation to comply with human rights instruments, which need not be confined to civil and political rights of the kind found in the ECHR. So, returning to Lord Bingham's definition of the rule of law encountered in Chapter 1, there is no reason why more powerful parliamentary scrutiny of the kind considered above should not include also social and economic rights found in International Labour Organisation (ILO) Conventions 87 and 98, and in the European Social Charter of 1961. One consequence of greater parliamentary scrutiny is that it ought to render redundant the existing powers of the courts in sections 3 and 4 of the Human Rights Act (at least to the extent that they apply to legislation passed after its enactment). There are, in any event, compelling objections on grounds of parliamentary

---

[47] See *Oxford University v Broughton* [2004] EWHC 2543 (QB).
[48] *Campbell v MGN*, above.

sovereignty to the courts having the power to issue declarations of incompatibility in relation to legislation passed after the Human Rights Act was introduced. In contrast, however, there can be no objection on grounds of parliamentary sovereignty to the courts having the power to issue declarations of incompatibility in relation to legislation passed before the Human Rights Act itself was introduced. The same role could be performed, however, by a systematic scrutiny of the statute book by the government and by a parliamentary committee, though the job could be done just as well by the standard doctrine of implied repeal which has been excluded from the Human Rights Act.

The evidence from the JCHR reports to date suggests that a great deal of legislation—relating not only to the question of terrorism—would be stopped by more intense parliamentary scrutiny than by the risk of ex post facto judicial scrutiny. It is here that we confront the paradox that general powers of restraint are better than specific powers of review. Although these are thus perhaps uncomfortable implications for the juristocracy (and its pom-pom waving cheerleaders in the law schools), it does not follow that—if the HRA were to be repealed in its entirety—there would cease to be a role for the judges. The right to complain to Strasbourg—which has by no means been made redundant by the HRA—would continue to be available as a longstop to challenge legislative action, with a right of individual petition which distinguishes the ECHR from other international treaties, such as the European Social Charter, though in the latter case there is an equivalent collective complaints process to which the United Kingdom does not—but should—subscribe.[49] The judges would also have a role to play in using Convention rights as an instrument in reviewing the exercise of executive or administrative action, and indeed the workload may well increase if it were to include the social and economic rights 'left behind' when the ECHR was 'brought home'. There can also be no objection to public bodies of a wide and varied nature being required to comply with a wide and varied range of human rights obligations of the State when exercising discretion under statutory, prerogative, or other powers. This is not to make claims about the efficiency of rights protection in this more limited field, though there can be no further objection of principle if Parliament instructs the courts that they must ensure that the executive complies with human rights obligations. Recent evidence about the meaning of public authority in the Human Rights Act suggests, however, that the courts would continue to

---

[49] There is, nevertheless, external scrutiny by a process of regular reporting and supervision to check compliance with the relevant standards, which is how we know that the United Kingdom is in breach on multiple grounds (Ewing and Hendy, 2004).

need advice and encouragement from Parliament to make better use of the more limited powers that would be available to them, if they are to apply human rights in the manner Parliament intends.[50] Such is the extraordinary nature of human rights law in the United Kingdom.

[50] In the *Southern Cross Nursing Homes* case (*YL v Birmingham City Council* [2007] UKHL 27), the House of Lords refused to apply the Act to a private company running a public service on behalf of a local authority, the JCHR having previously criticised Court of Appeal decisions to the same effect as being 'unsatisfactory' case law, whereby 'a serious gap has opened in the protection which the Human Rights Act was intended to offer, and a more vigorous approach to re-establishing the proper ambit of the Act needs to be pursued' (JCHR, 2004a: para 41). It is highly unusual for a parliamentary body to complain that the courts are not making enough use of their powers, and very embarrassing for such bodies to be giving the judges a lesson in human rights. But it was not the last time. See *MB and AF v Home Secretary* [2007] UKHL 46; and subsequently JCHR, 2008: para 47.

Bibliography

Allan, 2003: T R S Allan, *Constitutional Justice: A Liberal Theory of the Rule of Law* (Oxford, 2003).

Allan, 2006: J Allan, 'Portia, Bassanio, or Dick the Butcher? Constraining Judges in the Twenty-First Century' (2006) 17 *King's College Law Journal* 1.

Allan and Huscroft, 2006: J Allan and G Huscroft, 'Constitutional Rights Coming Home to Roost? Rights Internationalism in American Courts' (2006) 43 *San Diego Law Review* 1–59.

Allan and Huscroft, 2007: J Allan and G Huscroft, 'The Citation of Overseas Authority in Rights Litigation in New Zealand: How Much Bark? How Much Bite?' (2007) 11 *Otago Law Review* 433.

Arbib, 2009: A Arbib, Memorandum submitted to Joint Committee on Human Rights, *Demonstrating Respect for Rights? A Human Rights Approach to Policing Protest*, HL 47-II/HC 360-II, 2008–09.

Bingham, 1993: T H Bingham, 'The European Convention on Human Rights: Time to Incorporate' (1993) 109 *Law Quarterly Review* 390.

Bingham, 1993a: Sir Thomas Bingham, Interception of Communications Act 1985, chapter 56 report of the Commissioner for 1992 Cm 2173, 1993.

Bingham, 2007: Lord Bingham, 'The Rule of Law' (2007) 66 *Cambridge Law Journal* 67.

Bingham, 2008: Lord Bingham, 'The Rule of Law and the Sovereignty of Parliament' (2008) 19 *King's College Law Journal* 223.

BIS, 2009: Department for Business, Innovation and Skills, *The Blacklisting of Trade Unionists: Consultation on Revised Draft Regulations* (2009).

Bogdanor, 2009: V Bogdanor, *The New British Constitution* (Oxford, 2009).

Bonner, 2009: D Bonner, 'The Myth of Liberty's Golden Age', *The Guardian*, 9 April 2009.

Bradley, 1987: A W Bradley, 'Why National Registration Had to Go: The Judges' Contribution' (1987) 65 *Public Administration* 209.

Bradley and Ewing, 2007: A W Bradley and K D Ewing, *Constitutional and Administrative Law* (14th edition, Harlow, 2007).

Brown, 2007: Lord Brown of Eaton-under-Heywood, *Report of the Intelligence Services Commissioner for 2005–2006*, HC 314 (2007); SG 2007/18.

Brown, 2007a: G Brown, 'Speech on Liberty', 25 October 2007: <http://www.number10.gov.uk/Page13630>.

Browne-Wilkinson, 1992: Lord Browne-Wilkinson, 'The Infiltration of a Bill of Rights' [1992] *Public Law* 397.

CAAB, 2009: Campaign for the Accountability of American Bases, Memorandum submitted to Joint Committee on Human Rights, *Demonstrating Respect for Rights? A Human Rights Approach to Policing Protest*, HL 47-II/HC 360-II, 2008–09.

CAAT, 2009: Campaign Against Arms Trade, Memorandum submitted to Joint Committee on Human Rights, *Demonstrating Respect for Rights? A Human Rights Approach to Policing Protest*, HL 47-II/HC 360-II, 2008–09.

Cabinet Office, 2004: Cabinet Office, *The Government's Response to the Report of the JCHR on the Draft Civil Contingencies Bill* (Cabinet Office, 2004).

Campbell, 2009: D Campbell, 'The Threat of Terrorism and the Plausibility of Positivism' [2009] *Public Law* 501.

Carlile, 2006: Lord Carlile, *Report on the Operation in 2005 of the Terrorism Act 2000* (Home Office, 2006).

Carlile, 2006a: Lord Carlile, *First Report of the Independent Reviewer Pursuant to Section 14(3) of the Prevention of Terrorism Act 2005* (Home Office, 2006).

Carlile, 2008: Lord Carlile, *Report on the Operation in 2007 of the Terrorism Act 2000 and of Part 1 of the Terrorism Act 2006* (Home Office, 2008).

Carlile, 2008a: Lord Carlile, *Third Report of the Independent Reviewer Pursuant to Section 14(3) of the Prevention of Terrorism Act 2005* (Home Office, 2008).

Carlile, 2009: Lord Carlile, *Report on the Operation in 2008 of the Terrorism Act 2000 and of Part 1 of the Terrorism Act 2006* (Home Office, 2009).

Carlile, 2009a: Lord Carlile, *Fourth Report of the Independent Reviewer Pursuant to Section 14(3) of the Prevention of Terrorism Act 2005* (Home Office, 2009).

Chilcot, 2008: Sir John Chilcot (chair), *Privy Council Review of Intercept as Evidence: Report to the Prime Minister and the Home Secretary*, Cm 7324, 2008.

Choo and Nash 1999: A Choo and S Nash, 'What's the Matter with Section 78?' [1999] *Criminal Law Review* 929.

Cohen, 2008: N Cohen, 'Meet Sally. Her Case Should Scare us All', *The Observer*, 21 September 2008.

Cowley, 2002: P Cowley, *Revolts and Rebellions: Parliamentary Voting Under Blair* (London, 2002).

Craig, 2005: P Craig, 'The Rule of Law', House of Lords Constitution Committee, Relations between the Executive, the Judiciary and Parliament, Report, HL 151, 2006–07, App 5.

Crawford and Lister, 2007: A Crawford and S Lister, *The Use and Impact of Dispersal Orders: Sticking Plasters and Wake-up Calls* (Bristol, 2007).

Defend Peaceful Protest, 2009: Defend Peaceful Protest, Memorandum Submitted to Home Affairs Committee, HC 418, 2008–09.

Denning, 1982: Lord Denning, *What Next in the Law?* (London, 1982).

Dicey, 1959: A V Dicey, *An Introduction to the Study of the Law of the Constitution* (10th edition by E C S Wade, London, 1959).

Ekins, 2007: R Ekins, 'Acts of Parliament and the Parliament Acts' (2007) 123 *Law Quarterly Review* 91.

Ewing, 1996: K D Ewing, 'Human Rights, Social Democracy and Constitutional Reform', in C A Gearty and A Tomkins (eds), *Understanding Human Rights* (London, 2006).

Ewing, 1999: K D Ewing, 'The Human Rights Act and Parliamentary Democracy' (1999) 62 *Modern Law Review* 79.

Ewing, 2004: K D Ewing, 'The Futility of the Human Rights Act' [2004] *Public Law* 829.

Ewing, 2007: K D Ewing, 'The Parliamentary Protection of Human Rights', in K S Ziegler, D Baranger, and A W Bradley (eds), *Constitutionalism and the Role of Parliaments* (Oxford, 2007).

Ewing, 2009: *Ruined Lives: Blacklisting in the UK Construction Industry* (UCATT, 2009).

Ewing and Gearty, 1990: K D Ewing and C A Gearty, *Freedom under Thatcher: Civil Liberties and the Rule of Law in Modern Britain* (Oxford, 1990).

Ewing and Gearty, 2000: K D Ewing and C A Gearty, *The Struggle for Civil Liberties: Political Freedom and the Rule of Law in Britain, 1914–1945* (Oxford, 2000).

Ewing and Hendy, 2004: K D Ewing and J Hendy, Memorandum submitted to Joint Committee on Human Rights, *The International Covenant on Economic, Social and Cultural Rights,* HL 183-II/HC 1188-II, 2004–05.

Ewing and Tham, 2008: K D Ewing and J-C Tham, 'The Continuing Futility of the Human Rights Act' [2008] *Public Law* 668.

FAC, 2003: Foreign Affairs Committee, *The Decision to go to War in Iraq*, HC 813, 2002–03.

FAC, 2003a: Foreign Affairs Committee, *Evidence from Mr Andrew Gilligan to the Committee's Inquiry into the Decision to go to War in Iraq*, HC 1044, 2002–03.

FAC, 2006: Foreign Affairs Committee, *Human Rights Annual Report 2005*, HC 522, 2005–06.

Flanagan, 2008: Sir Ronnie Flanagan, *Independent Review of Policing—Final Report* (Home Office, 2008).

Franks, 1972: Lord Franks, *Report of Departmental Committee on Section 2 of the Official Secrets Act 1911*, Cmnd 5104, 1972.

Gearty, 2007: C Gearty, *Civil Liberties* (Oxford, 2007).

Gearty, 2009: C Gearty, 'A Convention of Cant', *New Statesman*, 19 March 2009.

Geddis, 2004: A Geddis, 'Free Speech Martyrs or Unreasonable Threats to Social Peace? "Insulting" Expression and s.5 of the Public Order Act 1986' [2004] *Public Law* 853.

Gibson, 2008: Sir Peter Gibson, *Report of the Intelligence Services Commissioner for 2007*, HC 948 (2008); SG 2008/128.

Goldsworthy, 2001: J Goldsworthy, 'Legislative Sovereignty and the Rule of Law', in T Campbell, K D Ewing, and A Tomkins (eds), *Sceptical Essays on Human Rights* (Oxford, 2001).

Goodhart, 1936: A L Goodhart, 'Thomas *v* Sawkins: *A Constitutional Innovation*' [1936] 6 CLJ 22.

Groves and Campbell, 2007: M Groves and E Campbell, 'Parliamentary Privilege and the Courts', (2007) 7 *Oxford University Commonwealth Law Journal* 175.

HAC, 2005: Home Affairs Committee, *Anti-Social Behaviour*, HC 80, 2004–05.

HAC, 2007: Home Affairs Committee, *Young Black People and the Criminal Justice System*, HC 181, 2006–07.

HAC, 2008: Home Affairs Committee, *A Surveillance Society?*, HC 58, 2007–08.

HAC, 2009: Home Affairs Committee, *Policing Process of Home Office Leaks Inquiry*, HC 157, 2008–09.

HAC, 2009a: Home Affairs Committee, *Policing the G20 Protests*, HC 418, 2008–09.

HAC, 2009b; Home Affairs Committee, *The Macpherson Report—10 Years On*, HC 247, 2008–09.

Harbour, 2009: P Harbour, Memorandum submitted to Joint Committee on Human Rights, *Demonstrating Respect for Rights? A Human Rights Approach to Policing Protest*, HL 47-II/HC 360-II, 2008–09.

Hayes, 2008: B Hayes, 'Britain's Financial Guantanamo', *Statewatch*, 22 April 2008; <http://www.tni.org/detail_page.phtml?act_id=18205&menu=11e>.

HC, 2003: House of Commons Procedure Committee, *Sessional Orders and Resolutions*, HC 855, 2002–03.

HC, 2005: House of Commons Constitutional Affairs Committee, *The Operation of the Special Immigration Appeals Commission (SIAC) and the Use of Special Advocates*, HC 323-I, 2004–05.

HC, 2005a: House of Commons Constitutional Affairs Committee, *The Operation of the Special Immigration Appeals Commission (SIAC) and the Use of Special Advocates, Evidence Submitted by a Number of Special Advocates*, HC 323-II, 2004–05.

Hewart, 1929: Lord Hewart of Bury, *The New Despotism* (London, 1929).

Hiebert, 2005: J Hiebert, 'Parliamentary Review of Terrorism Measures' (2005) 68 *Modern Law Review* 676.

HL, 1998: House of Lords, Select Committee on Science and Technology, *Digital Images as Evidence*, HL 64, 1997–98.

HL, 2009: House of Lords, Select Committee on the Constitution, *Surveillance: Citizens and the State*, HL 18-I, 2008–09.

HMIC, 2009: Her Majesty's Inspectorate of Constabulary, *Adapting to Protest* (Home Office, 2009).

Holmstrom, 1994: B Holmstrom, 'The Judicialisation of Politics in Sweden' (1994) 15 *International Political Science Review* 153.

Holt and Hartley, 2009: ACC A Holt and Superintendent D Hartley, *Strategic Review—Operation Oasis—Kingsnorth Power Station. Kent, Final Report* (2009), <http://www.kent.police.uk/Climate%20Camp/Climate%20Camp/Op%20 Oasis%20-%20FINAL%20REPORT1.pdf>.

Home Office, 1988: Home Office, *Reform of Section 2 of the Official Secrets Act 1911*, Cm 408, 1988.

Home Office, 2004: Home Office, *Policing: Modernising Police Powers to Meet Community Needs* (Home Office, 2004).

Home Office, 2005: Home Office, *Policing: Modernising Police Powers to Meet Community Needs—Summary of Responses* (Home Office, 2005).

Hutton, 2004: Lord Hutton, Investigation into the Circumstances Surrounding the Death of Dr David Kelly (London, 2004), <http://www.the-hutton-inquiry. org.uk>.

Hutton, 2006, Lord Hutton, 'The Media Reaction to the Hutton Report' [2006] *Public Law* 807.

Information Commissioner, 2008: Information Commissioner's Office, *CCTV Code of Practice* (Revised Edition, 2008).

IPCC, 2007: Independent Police Complaints Commission, *Independent Investigations into Complaints made Following the Forest Gate Counter-Terrorist Operation on 2 June 2006* (IPCC, 2007), <http://www.ipcc.gov.uk/forest_gate_2_3report.pdf>.

JCHR, 2003: Joint Committee on Human Rights, *Anti-social Behaviour Bill*, HL 120/HC 766, 2002–03.

JCHR, 2003a: Joint Committee on Human Rights, *Scrutiny of Bills: Further Progress Report*, HL 50/HC 397, 2002–03.

JCHR, 2004: Joint Committee on Human Rights, *Anti-terrorism, Crime and Security Act 2001: Statutory Review and Continuance of Part 4*, HL 38/HC 381, 2003–04.

JCHR, 2004a: Joint Committee on Human Rights, *The Meaning of Public Authority under the Human Rights Act*, HL 39/HC427.

JCHR, 2005: Joint Committee on Human Rights, *Scrutiny: First Progress Report*, HL26/HC 224, 2004–05.

JCHR, 2005a: Joint Committee on Human Rights, *Counter-Terrorism Policy and Human Rights: Terrorism Bill and Related Matters*, HL 75/HC 561, 2005–06.

JCHR, 2005b: Joint Committee on Human Rights, *Prevention of Terrorism Bill: Preliminary Report*, HL 61/HC 389, 2004–05.

JCHR, 2005c: Joint Committee on Human Rights, *Prevention of Terrorism Bill*, HL 68/HC 334, 2004–05.

JCHR, 2006: Joint Committee on Human Rights, *Government Response to the Committee's Third Report of this Session: Counter-Terrorism Policy and Human Rights: Terrorism Bill and Related Matters*, HL 114/HC 888, 2005–06.

JCHR, 2006a: Joint Committee on Human Rights, *Counter-Terrorism Policy and Human Rights: Draft Prevention of Terrorism Act 2005 (Continuance in force of sections 1 to 9) Order 2006*, HL 122/HC 915, 2005–06.

JCHR, 2006b: Joint Committee on Human Rights, *The UN Convention Against Torture (UNCAT)*, HL 185/HC 701, 2005–06.

JCHR, 2006c: Joint Committee on Human Rights, *The Committee's Future Working Practices*, HL 239/HC 1575, 2005–06.

JCHR, 2008: Joint Committee on Human Rights, *Counter-Terrorism Policy and Human Rights (Eighth Report): Counter-Terrorism Bill*, HL 50/HC 199, 2007–08.

JCHR, 2009: Joint Committee on Human Rights, *Demonstrating Respect for Rights? A Human Rights Approach to Policing Protest*, HL 47/HC 360, 2008–09.

JCHR, 2009a: Joint Committee on Human Rights, *Counter-Terrorism Policy and Human Rights (Fifteenth Report): Annual Renewal of 28 Days 2009*, HL 119/HC 726, 2008–09.

Jowell, 2004: J Jowell, 'The Rule of Law Today', in J Jowell and D Oliver (eds), *The Changing Constitution* (5th edn, Oxford, 2004).

Jowell, 2006: J Jowell, 'Parliamentary Sovereignty under the New Constitutional Hypothesis' [2006] *Public Law* 562.

Kennedy, 2008: Sir Paul Kennedy, *Report of the Interception of Communications Commissioner for 2006*, HC 252 (2008); SG/2008/9.

Kennedy, 2008a: Sir Paul Kennedy, *Report of the Interception of Communications Commissioner for 2007*, HC 947; SG 147/2008.

Labour Party, 2005: Labour Party, *Britain Forward Not Back* (Labour Party, 2005).

Laws, 1995: Sir John Laws, 'Law and Democracy' [1995] *Public Law* 72.

Liberty, 2003: Liberty, *Casualty of War—8 Weeks of Counter-terrorism in Rural England* (London, 2003).

Liberty, 2007: *Memorandum Submitted by Liberty*, HC 58-II, 2007–08.

Liberty, 2009: Liberty, *Response to the Joint Committee on Human Rights, Demonstrating Respect for Rights? A Human Rights Approach to Policing Protest*, HL 47-II/HC 360-II, 2008–09.

Lloyd, 1996: Lord Lloyd of Berwick, *Legislation Against Terrorism: A Consultation Paper*, Cm 3420, 1996.

Lustgarten, 2002: L Lustgarten, 'The Future of Stop and Search' [2002] *Criminal Law Review* 603.

MacCormick, 1970: D N MacCormick, 'Delegated Legislation and Civil Liberty' (1970) 86 *Law Quarterly Review* 171.

Macpherson, 1999: Sir William Macpherson, *The Stephen Lawrence Inquiry, Report of an Inquiry by Sir William Macpherson of Cluny*, Cm 4262-I, 1999.

McCluskey, 1987: Lord McCluskey, *Law, Justice and Democracy* (London, 1987).

McCluskey, 2007: Lord McCluskey, 'The Time has Come to 'Clean Up' Our Human Rights Act', *The Scotsman*, 29 October, 2007.

Ministry of Justice, 2009: Ministry of Justice, *Rights and Responsibilities: Developing our Constitutional Framework*, Cm 7577, 2009.

Morrison, 2008: 'D Morrison, 'Victory for the Raytheon 9', *Labour and Trade Union Review*, October 2008.

National Council of Bioethics, 2007: Nuffield Council of Bioethics, *The Forensic Use of Bio-information—Ethical Issues* (2007).

NAPO, 2005: NAPO, *Anti-social Behaviour Orders—Analysis of the First Six Years*, HC 80-III, 2004–05.

NDNAD, 2006: The National DNA Database, *Annual Report 2005–2006* (Home Office, 2006).

Newton, 2003: Privy Counsellor Review, *Anti-terrorism, Crime and Security Act 2001 Review: Report*, HC 100, 2003–04.

NUJ, 2009: National Union of Journalists, Memorandum submitted to Joint Committee on Human Rights, *Demonstrating Respect for Rights? A Human Rights Approach to Policing Protest*, HL 47-II/HC 360-II, 2008–09.

Ormerod, 2002: D Ormerod, 'Public Order' [2002] *Criminal Law Review* 835.

OSC, 2007: Office of Surveillance Commissioners, *Annual Report of the Chief Surveillance Commissioner to the Prime Minister and to Scottish Ministers for 2006–2007*, HC 713, 2008; SG/2007/126.

OSC, 2008: Office of Surveillance Commissioners, *Annual Report of the Chief Surveillance Commissioner to the Prime Minister and to Scottish Ministers for 2007–2008*, HC 649, 2008; SG/2008/86.

Pollard, 2004: S Pollard, *David Blunkett* (London, 2004).

Prime Minister's Office, 2002: Prime Minister's Office, *Iraq's Weapons of Mass Destruction* (2002).

Prime Minister's Office, 2003: Prime Minister's Office, *Iraq: Its Infrastructure of Concealment, Deception and Intimidation* (2003).

Raz, 1977: J Raz, 'The Rule of Law and its Virtue' (1977) 93 *Law Quarterly Review* 195.

Scarman, 1981: Lord Scarman, *The Brixton Disorders, 10–12 April 1981*: Report of an Inquiry by the Rt Hon Lord Scarman, Cmnd 8427, 1981.

Simpson, 1992: A W B Simpson, *In the Highest Degree Odious: Detention Without Trial in Wartime Britain* (Oxford, 1994 ed).

Special Advocates' Support Office, 2006: Special Advocates' Support Office, *A Guide to the Role of Special Advocates and the Special Advocates Support Office (SASO)* (Attorney General's Office, 2006).

Steyn, 2004: J Steyn 'Guantanamo Bay: The Legal Black Hole' (2004) 53 *International and Comparative Law Quarterly* 1.

Tham and Ewing, 2007: J-C Tham and K D Ewing, 'Limitations of a Charter of Rights in the Age of Counter-terrorism' (2007) 31 *Melbourne University Law Review* 462.

Thomas, 2007: Sir Swinton Thomas, Report of the Interception of Communications Commissioner for 2005–2006, HC 315 (2006–07).

Tierney, 2001: S Tierney, 'Constitutionalising the Role of the Judge: Scotland and the New Legal Order' (2001) 5 *Edinburgh Law Review* 49.

Tomkins, 2003: A Tomkins, 'The Rule of Law in Blair's Britain' (2003) 26 *University of Queensland Law Journal* 255.

Tomkins, 2005: A Tomkins, 'Readings of *A v Secretary of State for the Home Department*' [2005] *Public Law* 259.

Vallee, 2009: M Vallee, Memorandum submitted to Joint Committee on Human Rights, *Demonstrating Respect for Rights? A Human Rights Approach to Policing Protest*, HL 47-II/HC 360-II, 2008–09.

Voices in the Wilderness, 2009: Voice in the Wilderness, Memorandum submitted to Joint Committee on Human Rights, *Demonstrating Respect for Rights? A Human Rights Approach to Policing Protest*, HL 47-II/HC 360-II, 2008–09.

Wakeham, 2000: *A House for the Future. Royal Commission on the Reform of the House of Lords*, Chairman: The Rt Hon Lord Wakeham, Cm 4534, 2000.

Wallington, 1972: P Wallington, 'The Case of the Longannet Miners and the Criminal Liability of Pickets' (1972) 1 *Industrial Law Journal* 219.

Weir, 2007: S Weir, 'Democracy's Last Resort', *Red Pepper*, 1 July 2007.

Williams, 1965: D G T Williams, *Not in the Public Interest: The Problem of Security in Democracy* (London, 1965).

Woolf, 2004: Lord Woolf, 'The Rule of Law and a Change in the Constitution' (2004) 63 *Cambridge Law Journal* 317.

Yezza, 2008: H Yezza, 'Britain's Terror Laws Have Left Me and My Family Shattered', *The Guardian*, 18 August 2008.

Zander, 2001: M Zander, 'The Anti-Terrorism Bill—What Happened?', *New Law Journal*, 21 December 2001.

Index

Abdulla, Bilal, terrorism conviction   180
Abu Qatada, deportation case   258–259
Afghanistan
    Brian Haw protest   116–120
    funding of orphanages in   228
    terrorist activity in   10, 210, 212
Agee, Philip, deportation case   221
air bases, protests at   111–115 *see also*
    Fairford RAF base
airship used for police surveillance   135
al-Jazeera Memorandum case   153–161
al-Qaeda
    banning   183
    dilemma in banning   184
    training manual downloading
        case   212–214
    use of detention against
        suspects   234–236
Algeria, deportation to   256–258
animal rights protests, injunctions
    restraining   120–125
anti-social behaviour orders (ASBOs)
    children, and   15–17
    concerns over abuse of   28–30
    examples of abuse of   29–30
    human rights issues   30–31
    incidence of   28–30
    judicial approval of   30–31
    operation of   27–28
    use of   18, 28–30
anti-terrorism *see* terrorism
anti-war/weapons protests, pre-emptive
    tactics by police   105–106

Apple, Emily, police treatment of   9,
    127–128
arms trade, protests against   125–127
arrests
    anti-terrorism measures   11
    anti-war/weapons protestors,
        of   105–106
    breach of the peace   98–100
    complaints   36, 219
    conformity of powers with ECHR   38
    constitutional principle as to   19–20
    debate over new powers   36–37
    discrimination in use of powers   25–27
    environmental protestors, of   105–106
    extension of other powers related to   39
    JCHR concerns over powers   35
    MPs' freedom from   165–166
    new powers of   35–39
    obstructing a police officer   98–100
    operation of powers   37–39
    police powers   110–115
    pre-empt protests, to   105–115
    trespassory assembly   103–104
    without warrant   39–41
Asian communities, likelihood of
    arrest   26–27
'assembly', meaning of (Public Order
    Act)   101
Australia, *Spycatcher* case   141–143

bail
    conditional bail, release on   236
    conditions of   110–111, 112, 251

banning *see* political organisations,
    banning of
BBC
    effect of David Kelly inquiry   147–148
    surveillance powers   64
behaviour, threatening, insulting or abusive
    Lindis Percy case   111–113
    offence of   110
Bellmarsh prison, detainees kept in   227
Bill of Rights, proposals for new   16, 264
black communities
    approach to policing of   26
    likelihood of arrest   26–27
Bradlaugh, Charles, ejection from
    Commons   170
breach of the peace
    arrests   98–100
    custody as punishment   111
    JCHR concerns over abuse of
        powers   115–116
British Transport Police, 'stop and search',
    use of   203
British Union of Fascists, public order
    threat from   98
Broadmoor prison, detainees kept in
    227, 236
bugging devices
    authorisation of police usage   69
    non-police use of   54

Cambridge City Council Code of Practice
    on CCTV cameras   56, 59–60
Campaign Against the Arms Trade
    (CAAT)
    complaints about excessive police
        presence   125
    protests   125–127
    Wood case   126–127
Campaign for Accountability of American
    Bases (CAAB)
    complaints about excessive police
        presence   125
    protests   111–113
Campbell, Duncan, secrets case   10
Canada, constitutional protection
    of rights   13
Carltona principle as to surveillance   70
CCTV cameras
    absence of systemic law of   55

authority for use in public places   57–58
    compliance with DPA and Information
        Commissioner's Code   58–60
    growth of   55
    Liberty's comments   57
    local authorities' usage   55–56
    random surveillance by   55–60
    regulatory framework   55–58
    rule of law, and   58–60
    significance of   54
    surveillance use of   8
celebrities, protection of privacy   94
centralised power as core problem
    of government   2
Chahal deportation case   222, 223–224,
        251, 251–252
Cheblak, Abbas, deportation case   221
children
    ASBOs and   15–17
    curfew   34
    detention, and   242–244
    removal of DNA database samples
        from   87–88
    search of   202
    surveillance, and   65–67
Church of Scientology protest, police
    action   115
civil disobedience
    extent of HRA protection   130
    place in history   135–136
    relation to protest   130–134
civil liberties *see also* human rights
    anti-terrorism powers, effect of   219–220
    constitutional reform, and   273–275
    courts' role in protecting   276–281
    New Labour's policy   7–11
    Parliament, role of   264–268
    reform of Parliamentary procedures,
        and   275–276
    rule of law implications   6
Civil Procedure Rules, JCHR
    recommendations on
        amendment   125
Climate Camp protest, dispersal
    of   128–130
climate change protests *see* G20 protest
Communist Party
    effective outlawing of   181
    public order threat from   98

community support officers (CSOs),
　　dispersal powers　32
confiscation orders, conditions for
　　issue　195–196
Connor, Neil, surveillance case　61
constitutional principle
　　anti-terrorism powers,
　　　effect of　219–220
　　civil liberties, and　2–7
　　failure of　263
　　police powers, as to
　　　effectiveness of　50–52
　　　significance of　19–20
constitutional reform
　　civil liberties, and　273–275
　　New Labour measures　2
contempt of court
　　journalists' defence　140
　　protection for journalists' sources　149
　　relation to Official Secrets
　　　Acts　139–141
　　reporting restrictions in *al-Jazeera*
　　　Memorandum case　157–161
　　Shayler case　174
control orders
　　curfew, use of　241, 246, 247–8, 249, 259
　　definition　237
　　derogable orders　237
　　ECHR as to　246–248
　　family life, and　243–244
　　impact　241–245, 261
　　JCHR concerns　242–244
　　judicial proceedings under　240
　　kinds　237
　　legal challenges to　245–255
　　non-derogable orders　237
　　personal liberty, and　241–243
　　powers to impose　10
　　privacy, and　243–245
　　procedures　239–240
　　refugees, impact on　243
　　released detainees, on　236–240
　　responsibility for enacting　261
　　restrictions under　237–238
　　right to fair trial, and　248–250
　　right to liberty, and　246–248
　　scope　237–239
　　tagging, use of　243–244
　　usage level　241

Convention on Modern Liberty
　　Parliamentary response to　15
　　purpose　1
　　reasons for　8
Convention rights *see* European
　　Convention on Human Rights
　　(ECHR)
Conwy Council, surveillance by　66–67
coroners
　　role in de Menezes case　46–50
　　withholding of judgment of unlawful
　　　killing　47–50
corrosion of liberty, existence of　15
Council of Europe, views on
　　derogation　232–233
courts *see also* contempt of court; European
　　Court of Human Rights (ECtHR)
　　permissive approach to surveillance
　　　society　94–95
　　power to review legislative
　　　procedure　3
　　power to review political questions
　　　see also contempt of court
　　reluctance to review national security
　　　decisions　222
　　role in protecting civil
　　　liberties　276–281
covert human intelligence sources (CHIS)
　　agencies empowered to use　63–64
　　informers *see* informers
　　local authorities' use of
　　　management　65
　　　Surveillance Commissioners'
　　　　concerns　68
　　security services usage　71
　　usage level　64
　　use of　62
covert surveillance
　　authorisation required　62
　　local authorities, by　65–68
　　types　61–62
　　use of　60–65
Cullen, James, denial of access to
　　solicitor　45–46
curfew
　　children　34
　　control orders　241, 246,
　　　247–8
custody, overnight, as punishment　111

damages
  denial of   45–46
  surveillance, resulting from   60–61
Danish Embassy protest   215–216
Data Protection Act 1998 (DPA)
  CCTV cameras, as to   57–60
  DNA database, as to   79, 82
data storage *see* information storage
de Menezes, Jean Charles
  coroners' role   46–50
  death of   179–180
  implications of death of   17–19
defamation of government and freedom
  of expression   151–152
demonstrations *see* protests
deportation *see also* rendition
  Algeria, to   256–258
  detention as alternative   224–225
  detention prior to   214
  ECHR as to   222
  independent advisory panel   221–222
  Jordan, to   258–259
  national security grounds, on   11, 221
  obstacles to judicial review   222
  procedural fairness   222
  response to *Chahal* judgment   223–224,
    251–252
  torture of deported persons, danger
    of   226–231
derogation
  Council of Europe's views   232–233
  ECHR, from *see* European Convention
    on Human Rights (ECHR)
  ICCPR Principles   232
detention
  42-day detention proposals   264
  alternative to deportation, as   224–225
  Bellmarsh prison, in   227
  Broadmoor prison   227, 236
  children, effect on   242–244
  conditional bail, release on   236
  control orders upon release   236–240
  deportation, for   214
  derogation from ECHR   225–226
  discriminatory use   234–236
  disproportionate use   234–236
  ECHR as to   225, 231–232
  immigration, for *see* immigration
    detention

legal challenges to   231–245
new powers of   39
operation of powers   226–227
procedural fairness   227–229
release of detainees   236–237
secret evidence, use of   226–231
SIAC proceedings   231
Special Advocate's role   229–231
torture, potential danger to
  detainees   226–231
without trial   223–226
devolution, constitutional reform
  measures   2
diplomatic assurances *see* memorandum
  of understanding
directed surveillance
  agencies empowered to use   63–64
  number of authorisations   64
  security services, by   71
  technique   61
discrimination
  detention, in use of   234–236
  DNA database   82–83
  police   25–27
dispersal of protestors   128–130
dispersal orders
  examples of abuse of   33
  'function creep' in use of   34
  human rights issues   34–35
  Joseph Rowntree Trust study   32–33
  judicial review of use of   33–35
  use of   32–33
dispersal zones, designation of   32
DNA database
  claims for success   79
  conformity with ECHR   84–88
  conformity with European provisions
    on   84, 86–87
  court oversight   80–81
  discrimination issues   82–83
  DPA as to   79, 82
  ECtHR rulings   83–88
  European countries' provisions
    84, 86–87
  expansion of, plans for   87–88
  growth of   8, 54
  legal basis   79
  Marper case   84–88, 94
  privacy issues   84–86

proposal for mandatory database 83, 95
removal of children's samples 87–88
removal of information 80–88
rule of law and 81–83
size 79
Strategy Board 79–80
DNA samples
    identification from 81
    information storage 80–81
    retention of 80
    right to take 80
    Scottish law on retaining 80
    taking of 37, 43–44, 79–80, 82, 219
    use as evidence 43–45
dogs *see* police dogs
Duncan v Jones and freedom of
    assembly 98–99

electoral reform, protection of
    liberty by 282
email interception
    growth of 54
    Interception Commissioner's
        oversight 77–79
    powers 74
    rule of law and 75–77
email storage by ISPs 54
entry, new powers of 39
Environment Agency, surveillance
    powers 63
environmental protests
    injunctions against 123–125
    pre-emptive tactics by police 105–106
European Convention on Human Rights
    (ECHR) *see also* Human Rights Act
    1998
    admissibility of evidence under 43–45
    confiscation of political literature,
        as to 192–193
    conformity of arrest powers with 38
    control orders, as to 237, 246–248
    deportation procedures, as to 222
    derogation from
        power of 225–226
        public emergency grounds 232–234
    detention, as to 225, 231–232
    DNA database, as to 80–81, 84–88
    effectiveness as to arrest and
        search 50–52

free speech, as to 137–138
freedom of assembly, as to 101–105
freedom of expression, as to 112–113
freezing of assets, as to 196–197
glorifying terrorism offence, as to
    216, 218
immigration detention, as to 251,
    252–253
incorporation into UK law 12–15
judicial support for 11–13
liberty, right to 225
memoranda of understanding,
    as to 255
misconduct in public office offence,
    as to 164
protection against discrimination 27
retention of photographs, as to 127
right to fair trial, as to 248–250
right to liberty, as to 105–110
right to life violations 47–50
rule of law, as to 3
'stop and search', as to 205–209
surveillance violations 61, 69
violation of rights generally 45–46
European Court of Human Rights
    (ECtHR)
    approach to surveillance 61
    case law on public emergencies 232
    continuing role in protecting
        liberty 263–264
    memoranda of understanding, ruling
        as to 254
    protection for journalists' sources,
        judgment as to 149
    rulings on DNA database 83–88
    rulings on telephone tapping 74
    Spycatcher cases judgments 142–143
evidence *see also* Police and Criminal
    Evidence Act 1984 (PACE)
    admissibility under ECHR 43–45
    admission of illegally obtained
        43–45, 59
    David Kelly inquiry 145–147
    DNA samples 43–45
    secret evidence
        control orders 248, 250
        detention cases 226–231
executive dominance as core problem
    of government 2

Exeter City Council Code of Practice on
    CCTV cameras   56, 60

fair trial, right to, control orders
    and   248–250
Fairford RAF base
    bail conditions on protestors   111
    Fairford Five case   130–134, 135–136
    Liberty's comments   111, 125, 201
    police presence   125
    protests at   106–108
    'stop and search', use of   201–202
family life
    impact of control orders   243–244
    threat to right of   237
Faslane base, custody as punishment
    of protestors   111
fishermen, surveillance of   65–66
Fit Watch, anti-FIT activities by   127–128
Food Standards Agency, surveillance
    powers   63
Foreign Affairs Committee (House
    of Commons), David Kelly
    inquiry   143–147
Forest Gate terrorism arrests   219
Forward Intelligence Teams (FITs)
    Fit Watch activities against   127–128
    storage of information from   126–127
    use of   126
Frankel, Maurice, critique of new Official
    Secrets Act   164–165
free speech see also freedom of expression
    common law as to   137
    effect of dispersal orders on   34
    effectiveness of HRA
        protection   172–176
    glorifying terrorism offence,
        and   214–218
    MPs   165–172
    national security restrictions   172–178
    New Labour and Thatcher government
        compared   138–143
    powers to restrain   10–11
    restrictions on speech   137
    unlawful forms of speech   137
freedom from arrest, MPs'   165–166
freedom of assembly see also trespassory
    assembly
    common law principle   97–98

Duncan v Jones, effect of   98–99
    ECHR as to   101–105
    effect of banning of political
        organisations   184–185
    HRA as to   101–105
    meaning of 'assembly' (Public Order
        Act)   101
    miners' strike 1984 and   99–100
    new restrictions   115–120
    police powers   96–136
    pre-HRA   97–101
    threat to   220, 237
freedom of association
    banning of political
        organisations   181–190
    threat to   220, 237
freedom of expression see also free speech
    al-Jazeera Memorandum case   153–161
    defamation of government,
        and   151–152
    effect of banning of political
        organisations   184–185
    national security restrictions   172–178
    protection for journalists'
        sources   148–151
    reporting restrictions in al-Jazeera
        Memorandum case   157–161
    restriction of   111–113
    terrorism, and   209–214
    threat to   220, 237
freedom of movement, threat to   237
freezing of assets see terrorist finance and
        property, confiscation of
freezing orders
    conditions for issue   195–196
    Landsbanki case   196
'function creep'
    dispersal orders, as to   34
    Protection against Harassment Act 1997
        as case of   124

G8 protest
    police presence   135
    'stop and search', use of   202
G20 protest
    dispersal of protestors   128–130
    significance of Ian Tomlinson's death   8
Galley, Christopher, role in Damien Green
        arrest   162

GCHQ
  issue of warrants for surveillance to 70
  Sarah Tisdall case 10, 139–140
Gifford, Martha, attempted bribery of 9
Gilligan, Andrew
  evidence to Foreign Affairs Committee
    inquiry 145
  meeting with David Kelly 144
  refusal to name source 148–151
Glasgow airport terrorist attack 180
Gloucestershire Weapons Inspectors,
    arrest of 106–108
'golden age of liberty', existence of 15
Green, Damien, arrest of 38–39, 162–172
Gun, Kathryn, prosecution of 10, 153, 178

Harbour, Dr Peter Harbour, injunction
    against 123–125
Haw, Brian, use of SOCPA
    against 116–120
Health and Safety Executive, surveillance
    powers 63
Healthcare Commission, surveillance
    powers 64
helicopters used for police
    surveillance 135
Hewitt, Gavin, role in David Kelly
    investigation 144, 146–147
HM Revenue and Customs, surveillance
    powers 63
Homage to Catalonia, definition of
    terrorism 216
Home Office
  growth of Surveillance Society, and 8
  warrants see warrants
Hosenball, Mark, deportation case 221
House of Commons
  Charles Bradlaugh affair 170
  parliamentary privilege and Damien
    Green's arrest 162–172
  safe haven from injunctions, as 170
  'Zircon' affair 170
House of Lords, reform of 2
human rights see also civil liberties;
    European Convention on Human
    Rights (ECHR); Human Rights Act
    1998 (HRA)
  ASBOs, issues as to 30–31
  contradictions in New Labour policy 5

denial of 45–46
dispersal orders, issues as to 34–35
effectiveness as defence 11–15
freezing of terrorists assets,
    and 194–199
greater protection of liberty by power
    rather than 282–284
international instruments 6
Joint Committee see Joint Committee on
    Human Rights (JCHR)
official contempt for 260–261
rule of law commitment to 5
terrorism, and 180
whether beneficial 260
Human Rights Act 1998 (HRA) see also
    European Convention on Human
    Rights (ECHR)
  civil disobedience, and 130
  debate on Bill 12–13
  effectiveness
    anti-terrorism measures 220
    detention, control orders and
      rendition 260–262
    free speech, protection of 172–176
    generally 16
    policing of protests, as to 105–115,
      134–136
  failure of 263
  freedom of assembly, as to 101–105
  growth of surveillance society, and 54
  judicial powers under 13–15
  purpose 12
  'stop and search', as to 207–209
Huntingdon Life Sciences, injunctions
    restraining protests against 120–125

Icelandic banking case 196
identity cards see also National Identity
    Register
  concerns over 9
  potential police use of 54
immigration
  Appeals Commission see Special
    Immigration Appeals Commission
    (SIAC)
  refugees, by 221
immigration detention
  alternative to deportation detention,
    as 250–251

immigration detention (*cont.*)
  bail conditions following 251
  detention without trial, as 251–253
  diplomatic assurances *see* memorandum
    of understanding
  duration of proceedings 251–252
  JCHR concerns 251, 253–255
  memoranda of understanding *see*
    memorandum of understanding
  response to *Chahal* judgment, as 251
independent advisory panel for deportation
    cases 221–222
inequality, increase under New Labour 16
infiltration
  oversight of 63–65
  regulatory framework 61–63
  use of 60–61
Information Commissioner
  Code of Practice on CCTV
    cameras 57–60
  surveillance powers 64
information leaks
  al-Jazeera Memorandum case 153–161
  Clive Ponting case 10, 140–141
  David Kelly inquiry *see* Kelly, David,
    investigation of
  David Shayler case 172–178
  Duncan Sandys case 166
  Kathryn Gun case 10, 153, 178
  Sarah Tisdall case 10, 139–140
  Spycatcher case 141–143, 161
information storage
  emails 54
  European countries' provisions for DNA
    samples 84
  information from FITs 126–127
  samples 80–81
informers
  oversight of 63–65
  regulatory framework 61–63
  use of 60–61
injunctions
  abuse of 123–125
  David Shayler case 173–174
  House of Commons as safe haven 170
  NECTU website, on 121, 123, 124
  restrain protests, to 120–125
  Spycatcher case applications 141–143
  'Zircon' affair 168–169

intelligence services *see also* security services
  issue of warrants for surveillance to 70
  surveillance powers 63
Intelligence Services Commissioner,
    oversight of surveillance 72–74
Interception Commissioner
  oversight by 77–79
  postholders 75–76
  report 75–77
  workload 76–77
Interception Modernisation Programme,
    launch of 54
interception of communications
  greater regulation of 8
  telephone tapping *see* telephone tapping
International Covenant on Civil and
    Political Rights (ICCPR), derogation
    principles 232
internet service providers (ISPs), email
    storage 54
internment *see* detention
intrusive surveillance
  authorisation required 62
  security services, by 71
  technique 62
  use of 63
Investigatory Powers Tribunal, right
    of complaint to 63, 71
Iraq War
  al-Jazeera Memorandum case 153–161
  Brian Haw protest 116–120
  Foreign Affairs Committee
    inquiry 143–147
  London march against
    police response to 96–97
    significance of 96–97
  Official Secrets Act as to 153
  weapons dossier *see* Kelly, David,
    investigation of
Irish organisations, banning of 181–183
Islamic organisations
  banning 183
  challenges to banning 184
Islamic protests 215–216

Joint Committee on Human Rights
    (JCHR), comments by
  abuse of breach of the peace
    powers 115–116

ASBOs 30
control orders 242–244
freezing of assets 197, 198
glorifying terrorism offence 215–218
immigration detention 251
memoranda of understanding 253–255
new arrest powers 35
new laws on search warrants 40–41
Prevention of Terrorism Bill 2005,
    reports on 270–272
protest law reform 124
Jordan
deportation to 258–259
memorandum of understanding
    with 252–253
Joseph Rowntree Trust, study on dispersal
    orders 32–33
journalists
Contempt of Court Act 1981
    defence 140
David Kelly inquiry *see* Kelly, David,
    investigation of
David Shayler case 172–178
national security restrictions 172–178
Official Secrets Act restrictions 139
protection for sources 148–151
reporting restrictions in *al-Jazeera*
    Memorandum case 157–161
Sally Murrer case 164
Spycatcher injunctions against *Guardian*
    and *Times* 142–143
judicial commissioner, oversight of issue
    of warrants 8
juries
challenge to verdicts of 49–50
support for protestors 136

Kelly, David, investigation of
background 10, 143
decision to reveal identity 146
defamation of government,
    issue of 151–152
effect on BBC 146
evidence to Foreign Affairs Committee
    inquiry 145–147
identification as Andrew Gilligan's
    source 144–147
protection for journalists' sources,
    issue of 148–151

Keogh, David, prosecution of 10, 153–161
kettling
G20 protest 128–130
legality of 9–10
use of 108–110
Khan, Mohammed Sidique, widow's arrest
    and release 179
King's College London students, stop and
    search of 200, 201
Kratos, Operation, 'shoot to kill'
    policy 17–18
Kurdish independence groups
banning 183
challenges to banning 184

Landsbanki, freezing of assets 196
Laporte case 107–108
Lawrence, Stephen, Macpherson Report
    on death of 21, 26
legal process as means of protest 136
lethal force in *de Menezes*, coroners'
    role 46–50
liberty
breach of protestors' 105–110
constitutional irony 282
control orders, and 241–243, 246–248
Convention right to 225
corrosion of 15
corrosion under New Labour 15
deprivation of 246–248
ECtHR's continuing role in
    protecting 263–264
existence of 'golden age' 15
'golden age', whether 15
national spirit as sustainer of 263
protection by electoral reform 282
protection by Parliament 263–284
protection by power rather than
    rights 282–284
protection for journalists' sources 282
threat to right of 237
Liberty (organisation), comments by
CCTV cameras 57
Church of Scientology protest 115
Fairford RAF base protest 111, 125, 201
POAC 190
relative institutional competence 233
limitation, Siracusa Principles
    (ICCPR) 232

local authorities *see also* public officials
    CCTV cameras usage   55–56
    CHIS usage *see* covert human
        intelligence sources (CHIS)
    covert surveillance by   65–68
    Press Association survey on surveillance
        usage   66–67
    surveillance by   8, 55–56, 65–68
    Surveillance Commissioners'
        concerns   65–68
Lockerbie death toll   179
London terrorist attacks *see* terrorism

Macpherson, Sir William
    concerns over police
        discrimination   26–27
    recommendations on 'stop and
        account'   21
    report on death of Stephen
        Lawrence   21, 26
magistrates, issue of search warrants   42
Mail on Sunday and *Shayler* case   173,
    175, 176
Malik, Samina, possession of terrorist
    literature   210, 212
Mandela, Nelson, justification for
    terrorism   216
Marper, Michael, DNA database
    case   80–88, 94
medical examinations under memoranda
    of understanding   253
Members of Parliament (MPs), arrest
    of   38–39, 162–172
memorandum of understanding
    ECtHR ruling   254
    JCHR concerns   253–255
    Jordan   252–253
    medical examinations under   253
Menwith Hill RAF base, protests at
    114–115
MI5 *see* security services
MI6 *see* intelligence services
miners' strike 1984 and freedom
    of assembly   99–100
misconduct in public office, offence of
    163–164
Mosley, Oswald, public order threat from   98
Mujaheddin e Khalq (PMOI) *see* PMOI
Murrer, Sally, collapse of trial   164

National Assembly for Wales, surveillance
    powers   64
National Association of Probation Officers
    (NAPO), concerns over abuse of
    ASBOs
    concerns over abuse of ASBOs   28–30
National Extremism Tactical Coordination
    Unit (NECTU), injunctions posted
    on website   121, 123, 124
National Health Service
    patient database   54
    surveillance powers   63
National Identity Register *see also* identity
    cards
    advent of   54
    categories of registered persons   90–91
    Commissioner   92
    comparison with wartime measures   89
    concerns over   9
    enforcement powers   92–93
    registration a duty or a right?   90–91
    rule of law and   91–93
    significance of   88–89
    statutory framework   89–91
National Identity Scheme Commissioner,
    office of   92
national security
    accountability mechanisms   220
    courts' reluctance to review
        decisions   222
    deportation on grounds of
        justifying   222
    powers   221
    Government's obsession with   178
    linkage to public emergency   226
    restrictions on journalists   172–178
New Labour
    commitment to HRA   16
    constitutional reform measures   2
    contradictions in human rights policy   1
    corrosion of liberty under   15–16
    free speech approach compared
        with Thatcher government
        138–143
    increase in inequality under   16
    policy on civil liberties   7–11
newspapers *see* journalists
Nineteen Eighty-Four, prediction of
    surveillance society, as   53, 93

Northern Ireland
  banning of political
    organisations   181–183
  devolution measures   2
number plate recognition, police
  use of   135

obstructing a police officer,
  arrests   98–100
obstruction of the highway
  Lindis Percy case   113–115
  offence of   110
O'Connor, Leo, prosecution of   10,
  153–161
O'Driscoll, Rory, *Vatan* confiscation
  case   191–194
OFCOM, surveillance powers   64
Official Secrets Acts
  1989 reform   143, 164–165
  critique of 1989 Act   164–165
  Duncan Sandys case   166
  Iraq War, as to   153
  offences   138–139
  prosecutions under   10, 153–161
  public interest defence, need
    for   175–178
  relation to contempt of court   139–141
  safeguards   139
  Spycatcher case   141–143, 161
  Thatcher government's use   139–141
  trespass as to   130
  use of   10
Orwell, George, defining terrorism   216
overnight custody as punishment   111

Parliament
  enhanced scrutiny   269–272, 282–284
  protection of liberty   264–268
  reform of procedures   275–276
Parliament Square protest (Brian Haw), use
  of SOCPA against   116–120
parliamentary privilege and Damien
  Green's arrest   162–172
parliamentary sovereignty, power
  of   278–280
Percy, Lindis, arrest of   111–115
personal freedom, link with rule of law   3, 7
phone tapping *see* telephone tapping
photographing of protestors   126–127

picketing
  effect of dispersal orders on   34–35
  miners' strike 1984   99–100
Plane Stupid, attempted infiltration of   9
PMOI
  activities   187
  challenge to banning   184–190
  Wednesbury test applied to banning
    appeal   188–189
police *see also* British Transport Police;
    police dogs
  accountability   36, 42–50
  anti-terrorism powers   200–209
  arrest powers *see* arrests
  complaints
    anti-terrorism operations   219
    arrests   36, 219
    dispersal of protestors   128
    entering of detainees' homes   243
    interference with property   71–72
    search of detainees' families   227
    search of protestors' children   202
    surveillance   61
  costs of operations   135
  CSOs, dispersal powers   32
  Damien Green arrest   163–166
  declining accountability of   19
  discrimination by   25–27
  effect of HRA on conduct   105–115
  effect of powers as to constitutional
    principle   19–20, 50–52
  exercise of power   125–130
  extension of powers   7, 17–52
  firearms usage
    anti-terrorism operations   219
    de Menezes case   17
    Stanley case   47
  Forward Intelligence Teams   126–127
  implications of de Menezes death   17–18
  increased statutory regulation of   7
  informal powers   42–43
  interference with property, authorisation
    for   62
  kettling *see* kettling
  legality of powers   19–27
  lethal force, use of   46–50
  militarisation of   7–8
  obstructing *see* obstructing a police
    officer

police *see also* British Transport Police (*cont.*)
  powers as to protests *see* freedom
    of assembly; protests
  pre-emptive tactics, use of   105–115
  surveillance powers   63
  tolerance of unlawful conduct of   43,
    51–52
  violation of rights by   45–46
Police and Criminal Evidence Act 1984
  (PACE)
  confiscation of political literature   192
  Damien Green arrest, and   169–170
  search powers   39, 110
  warrants provisions   168–169
police dogs, use of   8, 106, 107
political activism *see* protests
political freedom, link with rule of law   3, 7
political organisations, banning of
  appeal body *see* Proscribed Organisations
    Appeal Commission (POAC)
  Communist Party   181
  glorifying terrorism, for   183
  history   181
  Irish organisations   181–183
  statutory powers   182–183
political questions, courts' power to
  review   233–234
Ponting, Clive, prosecution of   10, 140–141
Poole Borough Council, use of
  surveillance   65–66
Post Office, surveillance powers   63
power, protection of liberty by   282–284
power stations, protests at   106
Press Association, survey on surveillance
  usage   66–67
Preston City Council Code of Practice on
  CCTV cameras   59
Prevention of Terrorism Bill 2005, JCHR
  reports   270–272
privacy
  CCTV cameras and   59–60
  control orders, impact of   243–245
  DNA database and   84–86
  protection for celebrities   94
  role in *Nineteen Eighty-Four*   53–54
  tagging, impact of   243–244
  threat to right of   237
procedural fairness
  deportation, as to   222

detention, as to   227–229
property, interference with
  complaint to Investigatory Powers
    Tribunal   71–72
  police authority for   62
  warrants for   70
property owners, rights balanced with right
  to protest   102–105
property related to terrorism, possession
  of   209–210
Proscribed Organisations Appeal
  Commission (POAC)
  appeal to   185
  Liberty's comments   190
proscription *see* political organisations,
  banning of
Protection against Harassment Act 1997
  'function creep'   124
  protests, as to   121–123
protestors
  dispersal of   128–130
  juries' support   136
  measures against   9–10
  'stop and search' of   201–202
  surveillance of   126–127
protests *see also* civil disobedience
  children, search of   202
  common law restraints   98–100
  custody as punishment   111
  effect of dispersal orders on   34
  House of Lords decisions   9–10
  HRA as to   105–115, 134–136
  injunctions to restrain   120–125
  kettling *see* kettling
  legal process, through   136
  obstruction of the highway, arrest
    for   113–115
  police powers   96–136
  police presence   125
  police treatment of protestors   9
  pre-emptive tactics by police   105–115
  preventing attendance at   106–108
  preventing participation in   108–110
    see also kettling
  Protection against Harassment Act 1997
    as to   121–123
  Public Order Acts restrictions
    100–101, 111–113
  relation to civil disobedience   130–134

right balanced with property owners'
   rights 102–105
right on public highway 102–104
soliciting to murder, convictions
   for 215–216
sources of protest 1930's-80's 98
statutory restraints 100–101
threatening, insulting or abusive
   behaviour, arrest for 111–113
public emergency
   derogation from ECHR, grounds
    for 232–234
   ECtHR case law 232
   linkage to national security 226
public highway, right to protest on 102–104
public interest defence to Official Secrets
   Act 175–178
public officials *see also* local authorities;
   State officials
   operation of surveillance powers 93–94
   prosecution for public interest disclosure
    of secret information 10
   rule of law restrictions on 6–7
Public Order Acts as to protests 100–101,
   102–105, 111–113, 128, 215–216
public places, authority for use of CCTV
   cameras in 57–58
Punch magazine and *Shayler* case 173–177

Queen's peace *see* breach of the peace

Redknapp, Harry, search of premises of 42
Reed Elsevier AGM, police presence at 125
refugees, immigration by 221
refugees, impact of control orders on 243
Regulation of Investigatory Powers Act
   2000 (RIPA)
   Nineteen Eighty-Four as
    foreshadowing 53–54
   operation of powers 63–79
   regulatory framework within 61–63
Rehman deportation case 223
relative institutional competence,
   demarcation of 233
rendition, legal challenges to 255–259
Robertson, Margaret, surveillance
   case 60–61
Royal Pharmaceutical Society, surveillance
   powers 64

rule by law, distinction from rule of law 3–4
rule of law
   CCTV cameras, and 58–60
   commitment to human rights 5
   defining 3–6
   distinction from rule by law 3–4
   DNA database, and 81–83
   email interception and 75–77
   foundational constitutional
    principle, as 2–3
   honouring of 263
   implications for civil liberties 6
   link with personal and political
    freedom 3, 7
   minimum requirements 4
   National Identity Register, and 91–93
   principle of 4–5
   requirement of compliance with
    international treaties 5
   restrictions on State and public
    officials 6–7
   role of 4
   security service surveillance, and 70–71
   sub-rules 5
   telephone tapping and 75–77

Sabir, Rizwan, arrest and
   detention 212–214
Salisbury District Council, Stonehenge
   exclusion order 102
samples *see* DNA samples
Sandys, Duncan, threatened prosecution
   of 166
Scarman Report, call for new approach to
   policing black communities 26
school admissions applications, surveillance
   of suspected fraud 65–66
scope of book 1–2
Scotland
   devolution measures 2
   dispersal zones 32
   Faslane base protest 180
   Glasgow airport terrorist attack 180
   overnight custody of Faslane
    protestors 111
   retention of samples, law on 80
   seizure of terrorist cash 195
   'stop and search', use of 202–203
   surveillance 61

search
  after arrest   110
  children, of   202
  JCHR concerns over powers   40
  new powers of   35–36, 39–41
security services *see also* intelligence services
  CHIS usage   71
  directed surveillance   71
  intrusive surveillance   71
  issue of warrants for surveillance to   70
  rule of law as to surveillance by   70–71
  surveillance by   69–73
  surveillance powers   63
  Sedley, Lord Justice Stephen, proposal
    for mandatory DNA database
    83, 95
Serious Organised Crime and Public Order
  Act 2005 (SOCPA)
  Brian Haw case   116–120
  operation of powers   118–120
Serjeant at Arms, role in Damien Green
  arrest   167–168
Shayler, David, prosecution of   172–178
'shoot to kill' policy, existence of   17–18
sickness absence, surveillance of working
  during   67
Siracusa Principles (ICCPR) on derogation
  and limitation   232
soliciting to murder, offence of
  215–216
solicitor, denial of access to   45–46
Speaker of the House of Commons, role in
  Damien Green arrest   167–172
Special Advocate's role
  control orders   248
  detention cases   229–231
Special Immigration Appeals Commission
  (SIAC)
  appeal to   224–225
  assessment of Algerian political
    situation   256–257
  bail conditions imposed by   251
  creation   222
  membership   22–23
  powers   227–228
  proceedings   231
  status   222
speech *see* free speech
Spycatcher case   141–143, 161

Stanley, Harry, death of   47
state authority, exercise of   263
State officials *see also* public officials
  increased statutory regulation of   7
  police *see* police
  rule of law restrictions on   6–7
Stonehenge, protests at   102–105
'stop and account'
  discrimination in use of   25–27
  form filling   23
  incidence of   21
  Macpherson Report
    recommendations   21, 22
  police time spent on   22
  practice of   20–22
  procedures   22–23
  safeguards   22–23
  use of   18
'stop and question', legality of   19
'stop and search'
  anti-terrorism   200–209
  Code of Practice   21–23, 24
  debate over need for powers   202–204
  discrimination in use of   25–27
  disproportionate use against
    Asians   209
  exercise of   200–202
  extension of powers   24
  judgments on of use of   205–209
  legality   19, 24, 205–207
  safeguards   24, 206
  Scotland, use in   202–203
  usage level   209
  use of   24–25
Stop Huntingdon Animal Cruelty
  (SHAC), injunctions
  restraining   120–125
Straw, Jack, 'golden age of liberty', on   15
students
  possession of terrorist literature by
    student radicals   210–212
  'stop and search' of   200, 201
summary of book   263–264
surveillance
  Carltona principle   70
  children, and   65–67
  CHIS, use of *see* covert human
    intelligence sources (CHIS)
  Commissioners   63

complaints 61
courts' permissive approach 61
covert surveillance *see* covert surveillance
directed surveillance *see* directed
surveillance
ECtHR's approach 61
Intelligence Services Commissioner's
oversight 72–74
intrusive surveillance *see* intrusive
surveillance
issue of warrants 70
oversight of powers 69–70
protestors of 126–127
random surveillance by CCTV
cameras 55–60
right of complaint 63
security services, by 69–73
targeted surveillance 60
Surveillance Commissioners
concerns over covert surveillance by local
authorities 65–68
exercise of authority 63–65
report 64
surveillance society
concerns at growth of 8, 53–54
courts' permissive approach 94–95
Nineteen Eighty-Four as prediction of 53
operation of powers 93–94
Swain, Val, police treatment of 9, 127–128

tagging, use of 243–244
telephone tapping
authority for 82
ECtHR rulings 74
growth of 54
increase in 8
Interception Commissioner's
oversight 77–79
issue of warrants 76–77
legality 3
MPs' freedom from 171
powers 74
rule of law and 75–77
Wilson doctrine 171
terrorism
arrests 11
banning of political
organisations 181–190
banning reversal procedures 184–185

conviction rate 219
definition
George Orwell, by 216
statutory 10
freedom of expression, and 209–214
Glasgow airport attack 180
glorifying
banning of political organisations
for 183
debate over new offence of 214–218
human rights, and 180
justification by Nelson Mandela 216
legislation 10–11
literature
offence of possession 210
possession by student
radicals 210–212
possession for academic
study 212–214
Lockerbie death toll 179
London attacks
21 July 2005 179–180
29 June 2007 180
7 July 2005 179–180
police powers 200–209
possession related to 209–210
renunciation of 188
'stop and search' 200–209
use of powers 218–220
terrorist finance and property,
confiscation of
characteristics of terrorist finance 190
confiscation orders, conditions for
issue 195–196
definition of 'property' 190
freezing of assets
Orders in Council, under 197–199
powers in domestic
legislation 194–197
powers originating in UN
measures 197–199
safeguards 195–196
measures for 190–191
political literature 191–194
Thatcher government
free speech approach compared with
New Labour 138–143
Official Secrets Acts usage 139–141
security measures 16

Tisdall, Sarah, prosecution of   10, 139–140
Tomlinson, Ian, significance of death   8
torture of deported persons
    British citizens   262
    danger of   226–231
    diplomatic assurances *see* memorandum
        of understanding
    official complicity with   261–262
trade union rights, effect of dispersal
    orders on   34–35
traffic cameras, police surveillance
    usage   135
treaties, rule of law requirement to comply
    with   5
trespass
    civil disobedience, as   130
    offences of   110
trespassory assembly
    arrests   103–104
    meaning   103

United Nations (UN), measures for
        freezing of terrorists assets   197–199
United States
    air bases in UK, protests at   111–115
    al-Jazeera Memorandum case   153–161
    constitutional protection of rights   13
    DNA database size   79
    flag burning as freedom of
        expression   113
    freedom of expression as to political
        debate   152
unlawful killing, withholding of
    judgment   47–50

Vatan confiscation case   191–194

Wales
    devolution measures   2
    surveillance powers   64
'war on terror' *see* terrorism
warrants
    anti-terrorism operations   219
    arrests without   39–41
    effectiveness of safeguards   41–42
    greater regulation of issuing   8
    PACE provisions   168–169
    parliamentary privilege and   168–172
    surveillance, for   70, 72
    telephone tapping   76–77
watching of people
    oversight of   63–65
    regulatory framework   61–63
    use of   60–61
Wednesbury test applied to PMOI banning
    appeal   188–189
Wilson doctrine   171
wireless telegraphy, warrants for
    interference with   70
witnesses, failure to call   48–50
Wolfgang, Walter, stop and
    search of   201
'Wombles, The', arrest of   106–108
Wood, Andrew, retention of photographs
    of   126–127
working while off sick, surveillance
    of   66–67
Wright, Peter *see Spycatcher* case

Yezza, Hicham, arrest and
    detention   212–214

'Zircon' affair   170